NOTABLE MEN OF TENNESSEE

FROM 1833 TO 1875

Their Times and Their Contemporaries

By

Oliver P. Temple

Compiled and Arranged
by His Daughter

Mary B. Temple

HERITAGE BOOKS
2019

HERITAGE BOOKS
AN IMPRINT OF HERITAGE BOOKS, INC.

Books, CDs, and more—Worldwide

For our listing of thousands of titles see our website
at
www.HeritageBooks.com

A Facsimile Reprint
Published 2019 by
HERITAGE BOOKS, INC.
Publishing Division
5810 Ruatan Street
Berwyn Heights, Md. 20740

Copyright © 1912 Mary B. Temple

Originally published New York:
The Cosmopolitan Press
1912

— Publisher's Notice —
In reprints such as this, it is often not possible to remove blemishes from the original. We feel the contents of this book warrant its reissue despite these blemishes and hope you will agree and read it with pleasure.

International Standard Book Numbers
Paperbound: 978-0-7884-4703-7
Clothbound: 978-0-7884-6835-3

OLIVER PERRY TEMPLE

TABLE OF CONTENTS

	PAGE
NOTABLE MEN OF TENNESSEE FROM 1833 TO 1875—THEIR TIMES AND THEIR CONTEMPORARIES	31

Three Remarkable Facts—November, 1860, to February Election, 1861—South Carolina Secedes, December 26, 1860—Grave Questions in Border States—Bewildering Uncertainty as to Interest and Duty—Ambitious Leaders in Cotton States—Vague Fear of the Abolitionists—Widespread Secession Movement—Attitude Toward Slavery—First Union Speech—Knoxville Streets Full of Secessionists—November 26, Public Meetings Adjourned Without Decisive Vote—December 8, Secession Resolutions Defeated, Victory for Union Overwhelming—Meetings in Other Counties—Author Reluctantly Assumed Leadership—Brownlow's Paper Plays an Important Part—Johnson's Part — Local Leaders — Third Crisis — Emancipation — Brownlow's Quarrel with Johnson—Alexander Stephens at Milledgeville—Firing on Sumter—Lincoln's Inaugural.

THOMAS D. ARNOLD 56

Born Two Years After Tennessee Became a State—Served Under Jackson—Admitted to Bar, 1822—Defeated for Congress, 1827 and 1829—Elected, 1831, Though Anti-Jackson — Moved to Greeneville — Defeated by Blair, 1835—Elector, 1840—Encounter with Felix Grundy at Greeneville — At Rogersville Next Day — In Congress Again, 1841-43—Second Time, District Changed to Defeat Him—Attitude in 1861—Success in Jury Causes—Peculiarly Emotional Nature.

JUDGE JOHN BAXTER 66

Rose Rapidly in Profession in North Carolina—Clay Elector in 1844—In Legislature, Speaker of Lower House—Removed to Knoxville, 1857—Rank and Characteristics as a Lawyer—Believed Union Could be Preserved — Bitter Speeches — Favored Moderate Measures at Greeneville Convention—Followed Nelson to Richmond—Influence of Zebulon Vance—Defeated for Confederate Congress by William G. Swan—Co-operates with Secessionists—Arrested at Memphis—Drifts Back Into Union Ranks—1864, Joins McClellan Movement—Attacks Brownlow—1870, Elected to Constitutional Convention—1872, Call to Organize New Political Party—Supports Hayes, 1876—Appointed U. S. Circuit Judge—Summary.

REESE B. BRABSON 75

Member of Congress—Lawyer—Whig Elector—Vehement Speaker—Spotless Integrity.

R. R. BUTLER 77

Member of Legislature Eleven Terms—Lieutenant-Colonel—Circuit Judge—Member of Congress Five Terms.

ROBERT K. BYRD 79

Bold Leader—Slaveholder—Born in Roane County—Farmer—Entered Into Agreement at Greeneville Convention to Raise Troops—The First Tennessee, Colonel Byrd.

DANIEL A. CARPENTER 81

Born in Kentucky—One of First Volunteer Soldiers—After Number of Engagements, Destroyed Mill at Cumberland Gap—Captured Near Rogersville, Taken to Libby Prison and Charleston—Sheriff of Anderson County—Mayor of Knoxville—Pension Agent—Receiver Southern Building and Loan Association—Natural Leader.

ALFRED M. CATE 85

In Army—Personally Popular—Actor in Bridge Burning—Escaped to Kentucky—Member of Legislature.

TABLE OF CONTENTS.

WILLIAM BLOUNT CARTER 88
Great-grandson of John Carter—Washington College and Princeton—Church at Rogersville—Whig—Interview with Lincoln, Seward, McClellan—Bridge Burning—Member of 3d Knoxville-Greeneville Convention—Pocahontas Blood.

COLONEL WILLIAM CLIFT 94
Born 1795—A Whig, but Became a Democrat in 1855—Violent Unionist—Defiant of Confederate Government—Wooden Cannon—Agreement with James W. Gillespie—Courier Line Between Knoxville and Chattanooga—In Prison—Atlanta—Escape—Died in Ninety-first Year.

GENERAL JOSEPH A. COOPER 101
Father from Maryland—Mexican War—Greeneville Convention—Drilled Men on the Farms—Second Refugee—At Cumberland Gap, Chickamauga, Nashville—Internal Revenue Collector at Knoxville—Greatest Union Soldier.

WILLIAM CRUTCHFIELD 109
Early Settler of Chattanooga—Replied to Jefferson Davis—Sought Safety in Union Army.

PEREZ DICKENSON AND JOHN WILLIAMS 114
Dickenson a Native of Massachusetts—Accumulated Fortune—Ardent Whig—Decided in Stand for Union—Arrested and Discharged—Williams' Family Old and Distinguished—Battle of the Horseshoe—Opposition to John Williams' Father to Jackson—John Williams in Legislature—Fearless Union Man.

JOHN M. FLEMING 118
Born in Hawkins County—Educated at Emory and Henry College—Takes Charge of Whig *Register* in 1855—Supports John Bell—One of Three or Four to Oppose Secession—Elected to Legislature in 1861—Humorous Letter on Fall of Nashville—Secretary of Knoxville-Greeneville Convention—Supports General McClellan—Opposes Reconstruction Measures—Superintendent Public Instruction—Editorial Work—Encounter with John Mitchell—Controversy with Phelan.

ANDREW J. FLETCHER 123
Attended Washington College—Practiced Law in Newport—State Senator—Difficulty with Mason—A Refugee—Secretary of State—Candidate for U. S. Senate—Speech in Defense of State Administration—Origin of Term "Carpet Bag."

LEONIDAS C. HOUK 128
Born in Sevier County—Appearance Before Judge Alexander—Read Law at Night—Encounter with Foote in 1861—Contradictory Qualities—Member of Johnson Convention—Career in Congress.

HORACE MAYNARD 137
Born in Massachusetts—Graduate of Amherst—Professor in East Tennessee University—Defeated for Congress by Churchwell in 1853—Elector for State at Large in 1856—Elected to Congress in 1857, 1859, and 1861—At Disadvantage Among Southerners—Went Into Kentucky After August Election, 1861—Attorney General of the State—Twice Elected to Congress in the '60's—In 1865 Defeated for U. S. Senate—In 1872 Elected to Congress from State at Large—In 1874 Defeated for Governor by James D. Porter—In 1877 Appointed Minister to Turkey—Postmaster General Under Hayes—Defeated for U. S. Senate by Howell E. Jackson in 1881—Ability—Oratory—Personal Characteristics—Rank as a Lawyer—Early Political Experiences—Last Days.

JOHN McGAUGHEY 150
Exponent of Justice and Goodness—Arrested Near Athens—Provost Marshall—Raised Union Regiment.

TABLE OF CONTENTS.

	PAGE
SAM MILLIGAN	152

College Career—Physique—Influence with Pupils—Elected to Legislature in 1841—Re-elected in 1845—Read Law in Interval—Quartermaster in Mexican War in 1846—Greeneville *Spy*—In 1857 Defeated for Congress—In 1861 Aggressive for Union—In 1865 Appointed to Supreme Court of Tennessee—Appointed to Court of Claims in 1868—Influence Over Andrew Johnson—Personality.

JOHN NETHERLAND 159

Born in Virginia—Educated at Tusculum Under Doak—Two Years in Franklin, Tenn.—State Senator in 1833—Elector for State at Large in 1848—Defeated by Harris in 1859—Constantly in Politics—Jury Lawyer—Personal Characteristics.

THOMAS A. R. NELSON 166

His Phenomenal Rise at the Bar—An Old-line Whig—Nelson and Haynes Canvass of 1858—First Speech in Congress, December, 1859—Nelson and Johnson in Tennessee, Spring of 1861—Re-elected to U. S. Congress—Captured and Taken to Richmond—Letter Published on Return to His Home—Attitude Toward Lincoln's Proclamation of Emancipation—Attitude in 1872.

DeWITT C. SENTER 182

Active in Influence for Undivided Country—Father Prominent—Speaker of Senate and Governor—Later Years Passed in Retirement.

GENERAL JAMES G. SPEARS 186

Early Struggles—Clerk of Circuit Court—Happy Marriage—A Democrat—Delegate to Knoxville Convention—Daring Operation—Led His Regiment at Fishing Creek—In Battle at Murfreesboro—Hot-headed—A. L. Spears, His Son, a Brave Officer in Union Army—A Lawyer.

BENJAMIN TOLLIVER STAPLES 191

Family Among Settlers of Jamestown—Taught by Parents—Leader in Cumberland Plateau—Defeated Twice for Legislature—Activity in Behalf of Union—Raised a Regiment—Wounded and Taken Prisoner—Tortured and Shot—The Mountain Man—"Tinker Dave."

DR. JOSEPH C. STRONG 195

Earnest Friend of Union—His Father in U. S. Navy—Family Prominent in Social and Business Affairs—Aided Union Guides—Strong Family Dates in United States from 1630.

NATHANIEL G. TAYLOR 198

Grandfather Owned Immense Estates—Graduated at Washington College and Princeton—Became a Minister—Distinguished Appearance—Rare Gifts—Raised Funds for Relief of Destitute People of East Tennessee—Aided by Rev. Dr. T. W. Humes—Elector, 1860.

MONTGOMERY THORNBURGH 203

Studied Law—State Senate Three Terms—Attorney General—Active in Conciliation—Confined at Tuscaloosa.

DANIEL C. TREWHITT 206

Lawyer—Chancellor—Circuit Judge—Mind Clear and Quick.

JUDGE CONNALLY F. TRIGG 208

Born in Abingdon—Defeated for Congress in 1853—In 1855 in Partnership with Author—Delegate to State Convention in 1861—Favorite with Union People—Left Tennessee in 1861—Took Part in Gubernatorial Canvass in Ohio in 1863—Appointed U. S. Judge in 1864—Crowded Docket—Sympathizes with Those Lately Opposed—U. S. vs. Moses Gamble—Never Severe.

TABLE OF CONTENTS.

DAVID K. YOUNG 213
  Born and Lived in Anderson County—Circuit Judge—Exceptional Land Lawyer—Arrested—Captain of Tennessee Artillery—Good Financier.

JOHNSON AND TEMPLE RACE FOR CONGRESS IN 1847 .. 216
  Attracted Great Interest—Democratic District—Temple Young, Unknown, Inexperienced—Johnson's Position Impregnable, but Record Vulnerable—First Debate, July 11—Lively Contentions—Disaffection Toward Johnson—Temple's Letter to W. G. Brownlow—Temple Had Good Voice—Ardor, Enthusiasm—Johnson Approaches Competitor to Withdraw—Fifteen Appointments—Less Than Three Weeks' Campaign—No Personalities—Notice in Brownlow's Paper—Enthusiasm Over Temple at Washington College Among His Fellow-Students—Political Conditions—Temple Fought Johnson with His Own Weapons—Whig Leaders Stood Aloof from Temple—Time Too Short to Overcome Inertia of the Whigs—They Were Too Indifferent to Go to Polls—Johnson's Majority 314—In the County Canvassed Thoroughly by Temple His Vote Largest Ever Given a Whig—Temple Changed Residence to Avoid Politics.

MEREDITH POINDEXTER GENTRY 233
  Born in North Carolina in 1809—Removes to Tennessee in 1813—Early Education—Extensive Reader—Studied Law—Elected to Legislature, 1835—In Congress, 1839—Powerful Debater—Opinions as to His Ability as an Orator—Runs Against Johnson for Governorship in 1855—Contrast of Their Characters—Defeated by Johnson—In Retirement on His Farm—A Union Man Until Sumter—Then a Secessionist—Elected to Confederate Congress—Loses All His Property Through Failure of Confederacy—Died in 1866.

THE RACES OF JONES AND POLK IN 1841 AND 1843 ... 246
  Jones' Limited Education—In Legislature, 1839—Nominated for Governor by Whigs in 1841 at Age of Thirty-two—His Personality—His Opponent, Polk, Highly Educated and an Experienced Politician—Polk Not a Great Orator—Jones Not a Buffoon—His Debates with Polk—Polk's Personality—Polk's Secret Trip to East Tennessee—Discovered by Jones—Jones' Stinging Reproaches—Jones' Election—Jones in United States Senate, 1851—Votes to Repeal Missouri Compromise—Becomes a Democrat—Polk's Nomination for Presidency—A Strict Party Man—His Election.

DISTINGUISHED PERSONAGES OF LAST GENERATION WHOM I MET OR KNEW 262
  Andrew Jackson—General Winfield Scott—James K. Polk—Bailie Peyton—Felix Grundy—John J. Crittenden—William C. Preston—John C. Calhoun—President Taylor—Henry Clay—General Brooks—Joseph E. Johnston—General Hardee—General Garland—Albert Sidney Johnston—General Harney—General Sam Houston.

WILLIAM GANNAWAY BROWNLOW.

CHAPTER I 271
  Brownlow a Native of Virginia—A Mechanic—Methodist Preacher—Established *Tennessee Whig* at Elizabethton, 1838—In 1839 Removed to Jonesboro, Paper Taking Name Jonesboro *Whig and Independent*—Editorial Contest Between Haynes and Brownlow—1849, Removed Family and Paper to Knoxville—Bitter Quarrel with Knoxville *Register*—Controversy with John H. Crozier, William and James Williams, and William G. Swan—In 1860 Circulation of *Whig* 14,000—Personal Characteristics—Public Spirit—As a Speaker—Influence in 1861.

CHAPTER II 287
  Fidelity to Friends—Newspaper Warfare with George D. Prentice—Attitude Toward Slavery—*Whig* of April 20, 1861—After Battle of Bull Run—Belief in Long Continuance of War—North Had No Conception of Spirit of War in South—North and South Not Alien

6

TABLE OF CONTENTS.

WILLIAM GANNAWAY BROWNLOW—*Continued.*

Races—The Covenanter—The Merrimac—The Dutch, Irish, and German Contingent—Not Surprising Southern Soldiers Won First Victories—The Puritan—Small Farmer.

CHAPTER III 303
Discontinued Publication of Paper, October 24, 1861—Flight of Union Men to Kentucky—Thornburg and Perez Dickinson Arrested—Brownlow Refuses to Take Oath—Abortive Attempt to Escape Into Kentucky—Bridge-burning, November 8, 1861—Brownlow Escapes to Mountain—Crittenden Offers Passport After Letter from Benjamin—Brownlow Arrested—March 3, 1862, Permitted to Start for Nashville—Flag of Truce—Brownlow Meets Johnson at Capitol.

CHAPTER IV 317
In the North—Published Book, May, 1862—Mrs. Brownlow and Mrs. Maynard Sent Beyond the Lines—Brownlow and Family Return to Knoxville, October, 1863—January 9, 1865, Meeting in Nashville—State Constitution Amended—Elected Governor—Ku-Klux—Bond Issues—Reconstructive Measures—Review of Secession Movement.

CHAPTER V 334
Brownlow Re-elected, 1867—Emerson Etheridge—Isham G. Harris—Brownlow Elected to United States Senate, October, 1867—Johnson Arraigns Brownlow—The Reply—Author's Personal Relations with Brownlow.

CHAPTER VI 349
Brownlow's Popularity—An Editor Rather Than a Party Politician—Remarkable Individuality—Compliment from Knoxville *Register*—Press Tributes to Governor Brownlow—Memory—Place in History.

ANDREW JOHNSON.

CHAPTER I 357
Early Youth—Apprenticeship in Greeneville, S. C.—Removal to Greeneville, Tenn., Where Tailor Shop Still Stands—Elected to Legislature, 1835—Defeated, 1837—Again Elected, 1839.

CHAPTER II 369
Democracy of Greene County—Johnson Elector for State at Large on Van Buren Ticket, 1840—Elected State Senator, 1841—Elected to Congress, 1843—Represented First District for Ten Years—Introduced Homestead Bill During Second Term—Elected Governor of Tennessee, 1853.

CHAPTER III 383
Succeeded Himself as Governor, 1855—Campaign with Gentry—Arraignment of "Know-Nothing Party."

CHAPTER IV 391
Elected to United States Senate, 1857—In 1860 the Democratic Delegates from Tennessee to Charleston Instructed to Vote for Johnson for President—December 18, 19, Speech in United States Senate in Opposition to Secession—Spring of 1861, Canvass with Nelson to Save the State—Hindman's Proposition to Arrest Johnson at Rogersville Thwarted by John R. Branner, President of Railroad—Made Brigadier General by Mr. Lincoln and Appointed Military Governor of Tennessee on Fall of Fort Donelson, February, 1862.

CHAPTER V 406
Policy as Military Governor—April 12, 1864, Knoxville-Greeneville Convention Convened for Third Time—Majority Report Aimed at Johnson—"Convention" at Nashville, January, 1865—Noted Oath for Regulation of Election of Electors—McClellan Electors Ask Lincoln to Revoke the Oath—Lincoln Declined—Johnson Takes Oath as Vice-

TABLE OF CONTENTS.

ANDREW JOHNSON—*Concluded.*

President March 4, 1865—Remarkable Utterances—Johnson's Change of Views After Lincoln's Death—Mr. Blaine's Views of President Johnson's Reconstruction Measures—Mr. Seward's Relations with the President.

CHAPTER VI 423

Bitter Quarrel Between President and Congress—Impeachment of Johnson—Failure of Southern States to Ratify "Fourteenth Amendment"—Contest Between Mr. Johnson and Republican Party—Attitude of Prominent Republicans Toward Negro Suffrage—Reconstruction—Negro Rule—Fifteenth Amendment—Civil Rights Bill—Johnson's Opposition to Fourteenth Amendment.

CHAPTER VII 439

Johnson Defeated for United States Senate by Henry Cooper, 1869—Defeated for Lower House of Congress by James White, 1870—Defeated for Congress from State at Large by Horace Maynard, 1872—January, 1875, elected to United States Senate—Assails President Grant in the Extraordinary Session Convened March 4—Johnson's Views as to Payment of National Bonds—Bonds Issued by Tennessee.

CHAPTER VIII 451

My Early Impressions of Andrew Johnson—Compared with Other Public Men of His Time—Some of His Peculiar Traits and Characteristics—Intimate Friends and Their Influence—Mr. Johnson in the Senate, 1860—Personal Character and Habits—Critical Attitude of Contemporaries—Celebrated Speech in Knoxville April, 1861.

INTRODUCTION.

By Mary B. Temple.

Oliver Perry Temple was born January 27, 1820, in Greene county, Tennessee, within a mile of Greeneville College. His father, James Temple, well educated, of a quiet disposition and noted for his integrity, was greatly respected for his many virtues. He was a farmer, owning a large farm and a number of slaves. He was also a surveyor, but this was an accomplishment rather than a profession, and no mean one a hundred years ago. He married at the age of forty, and died in 1822, when he was fifty years old.

The mother of Oliver Perry Temple was Mary Craig, eldest child of Samuel Craig and Jane Innis Burns. Samuel Craig was born in York, Pennsylvania. Enlisting at fifteen in the Continental Line from Pennsylvania, he served for six years as captain in the Revolutionary War. At one time he commanded the personal guard of General Washington. He was a man of commanding presence and of great gallantry. At the battle of Paola, September 19, 1777, he received a bayonet wound in the face. He belonged to the large Craig family that came over from Ireland before the Revolution, settled at Easton, Pennsylvania, and founded that town. The family was prominent; many of the Craigs have held high positions, especially in Army and Navy circles. Seven brothers, including Captain Craig, all unusual men, were in the Revolutionary War; one was a colonel, one was a major, and four others were captains. Samuel Craig removed to South Carolina at the close of the war. He married Jane Innis Burns, who was born in Maryland. Her parents, John Burns and Mary McCoy, natives of Ireland, immigrated to South Carolina before the war of independence. John Burns became a patriot soldier, and served under Sumter, or Marion. The parents of Mary, Samuel McCoy and Jane Innis, both belonged to wealthy families of Edinborough. In 1790, soon after his marriage, Captain Craig removed to Greene county, Tennessee, where he selected a fine farm on the waters of Richland creek, near Greeneville. This farm remained in the family until a few years ago.

Oliver Perry Temple's mother, Mary Craig, was a woman of fine judgment, superior business ability and strong will. She was unusually gentle and amiable. When left a widow, in 1822, with seven minor children, she managed her estate so well that it nearly doubled in value by the time the youngest child became of age. During this time she gave to her children the opportunity to become educated. She and James Temple were married in 1810 by the Rev. Charles Coffin, D.D., the celebrated president of Greeneville College, who was their neighbor and warm friend. They were both Presbyterians. On the maternal side all the ancestors of Oliver Perry Temple were of Scotch origin. Craig, Burns, McCoy and Innis are well-known and prominent Scotch names. On his father's side he was English. Thomas Temple of Heytesbury, Wiltshire, England, was the remote paternal ancestor of the subject of this sketch. His will was proved May 15, 1594. He left ten children. Among his grandsons were William Temple of Coombs Lane, Parish of Atworth, or Bradford-on-Avon, who was the ancestor of the Temples of Chester county, Pennsylvania, and William Temple of Tithing Wick, who was the ancestor of the Virginia Temples. The Wiltshire Temples have been prominent since 1600. There is little doubt that all the Temples have a common origin. It is an old and distinguished English family, dating back to the days of William the Conqueror. An estate named "Temple Hall" was granted to the first Temple, and it is likely that he received his name from the estate. This first Temple is said to have been a descendant of Leofric, Earl of Mercia, whose consort was Lady Godiva of Coventry. Neither in England nor in America has the family been numerous. However, the name is one that the bearer may justly be proud of. Sir Peter Temple and James Temple were two of the judges that condemned to death Charles I. They paid the penalty under Charles II with life imprisonment and with the confiscation of "Temple Hall." Sir William Temple was a privy councilor of Ireland. The Rev. Frederick Temple, Archbishop of Canterbury, is another person that honored the name.

William Temple of Coombs Lane married Susannah Carrington, and their third child was Thomas Temple, who was born in England in 1694. He was living in Goshen, Pennsylvania, in

1721. He married Jane Chandler Jefferis, and died in 1775. Major Temple, their third son, the grandfather of the subject of this sketch, was born in Chester county, Pennsylvania, in 1736, and he moved to Mecklenburg county, North Carolina, in 1766. His wife was Mary Kennedy of Pennsylvania, a relative of Gen. Daniel Kennedy, well known in the early history of East Tennessee, and the aunt of Gen. Thomas Kennedy, who was a man of wealth and who became distinguished in the early history of Kentucky. The Kennedy family was a prominent one in Scotland. In 1780 Major Temple was with the North Carolina forces in the celebrated battle of King's Mountain.* In 1786 he removed to Greene county, Tennessee, and selected a farm on Richland creek, adjoining the farm of the Rev. Hezekiah Balch, the founder of Greeneville College. On the Rev. Hezekiah Balch's farm the college was established. These two persons probably came together from North Carolina, as their farms were entered the same day, and each called for the line of the other. Both were Presbyterians. The Rev. Hezekiah Balch was a cousin of the celebrated Hezekiah J. Balch, who was said to have drafted the Mecklenburg declaration of independence. The Temple farm, like the Craig farm, two and a half miles distant, remained in the family until a few years ago, when it was sold and divided among the heirs. Major Temple had five sons and one daughter.†

The family became influential in Greene county, not only because of the property owned by its members, which was considerable for that day, but also because of their virtues. In fact, the Temple family has been prominent as far back as it can be traced, and its standing has been kept up. It has been said that Major Temple in 1884 had among his descendants twenty-five Presbyterian ministers and two hundred elders and deacons.

Oliver Perry Temple was reared on the Temple farm. Like the boys of his day, he worked during the summer and went to old field schools during the winter. He always rejoiced in the fact that he had had this early experience in the hardships and

---

*The musket that he carried, upon the handle of which he carved his initials "M. T." before the battle, long remained in the family, and was called "Old King's Mountain."

†He was an elder in the Presbyterian Church. In 1797 he was appointed by the Legislature a commissioner to lay out and govern the town of Greeneville, Tennessee. His son John was also appointed a commissioner.

toil of farm life, as it taught him to sympathize with the laboring classes. At sixteen he attended Greeneville College, but did not assiduously apply himself to his studies. At eighteen, when a call was made, May, 1838, by the Governor for volunteers to go to the Cherokee Nation to suppress a possible outbreak, young Temple promptly volunteered, but the number offering to go was greater than was required, and lots were drawn. Temple drew a blank, but at once purchased another man's lot in order to go along with his friends. Temple was made a non-commissioned officer. The service lasted only about three months, but, brief as was this army experience, it served a good purpose. It made Temple determine to go back to college, to apply himself in earnest to his studies, and to become a lawyer. From earliest boyhood he had been fond of debating, and when but fourteen years old he would walk five miles to take part in the debating societies held in the country schools. The neighbors came to hear the boys debate. In this early choice of a profession he was influenced by his success in these debates, by the reputation of Robert J. McKinney, then at his zenith, and by the phenomenal rise of T. A. R. Nelson, who sprang at once into a foremost place at the bar, and whose success captivated Temple's imagination. At nineteen, the venerable Greeneville College having gone down, he entered Tusculum Academy, in Greene county, then under the control of the Rev. Samuel W. Doak, a celebrated teacher in his day. Here he applied himself diligently. In the fall of 1841 he went to Washington College, then just resuscitated under the presidency of that brilliant young scholar, the Rev. Alexander A. Doak.

Washington College was founded in 1780, in the wilderness of Washington county, by the justly celebrated Rev. Samuel Doak. Washington College was the first classical institution west of the Alleghanies, and for a great many years it was the leading one.* It was originally chartered by the legislature of North Carolina as Martin Academy in 1783. In 1795 the territorial legislature of Tennessee chartered it, on the motion of John Sevier, under the name of Washington College, "in honor of the illustrious President of the United States." It was the first institution to bear his name. The elder Doak was a remarkable man. He was celebrated for intellect, learning and

---

*"Winning of the West," by Theodore Roosevelt.

wonderful will power. His grandson, Alexander A. Doak, was a worthy representative of his distinguished ancestor. In general culture the younger Doak, perhaps, has never had an equal in the State. Fresh from the halls of Princeton at the time of young Temple's college days, the youthful president brought all the spirit of his *alma mater* to Washington College. He threw around his pupils the atmosphere of intellectuality of the former, and breathed into them a love of culture in the broadest sense. He unconsciously transmitted to them his own elegance of manner and speech. The refined, high-strung nature of Temple bore through life the impress of the subtle influence of the beloved president, between whom and himself there grew a close and intimate friendship. At Washington College in the '40's a splendid set of young men from the best families of Tennessee, North Carolina, South Carolina, Georgia, Illinois and other States gathered. The father of Zebulon B. Vance met Temple while the latter was a student at this famous institution. Mr. Vance was so favorably impressed with the young man that he sent his son Zebulon to Washington College with the understanding that Temple would take him in charge. Thus Washington College claims as an alumnus Zebulon Vance, the late noted governor and senator from North Carolina.

In his college days Temple was the leader in organizing a literary society at Washington College in 1841, which society continues to the present time. In 1839, at Tusculum College, he also aided in starting a debating society. Thus early was showed the active mind that throughout life made him a suggester of useful innovations.

At Washington College young Temple pursued his studies with great assiduity, and he graduated in 1844. He was immediately tendered a professorship in the college, which he declined. On leaving college he at once entered the field of politics. He made speeches for Mr. Clay in Carter, Washington, Greene, Cocke, Jefferson and Sullivan counties, traveling and speaking with the late Hon. William G. Brownlow. A few months later he read law under the direction of the late Judge Robert J. McKinney. In the same class were F. W. Compton, afterwards one of the judges of the Supreme Court of the State of Arkansas; Robert H. Armstrong of Knoxville; John K. Howard, afterwards a well-known politician, and John A. McKinney, recently judge of the first judicial district. In 1846 these young men were admitted to the bar. Compton and Temple formed a partnership and located at Greeneville. Compton, Howard and Temple made their début as lawyers in the same case, before Judge Alexander, and were all publicly complimented by him from the bench for their efforts. In July, 1847, ten months after obtaining his law license, at the age of twenty-seven, Temple became the Whig candidate for Congress against Andrew Johnson, then a candidate for re-election for his third term. After a heated canvass of three weeks, the usual majority of Mr. Johnson in the district was reduced from about 1500 to 313 votes. With dismay Johnson saw fresh laurels won daily by his aggressive young adversary. The result of the election was a surprise to nearly every man in the district except the candidates themselves. "Temple, defeated as he was, felt that he was half conqueror, and Johnson, though elected, was deeply mortified and humiliated. This was one of the remarkable political contests of that day. . . . That a young man, without money or political experience, had entered that struggle in the face of a large Democratic majority, and had so reduced it after a joint canvass with Johnson, then in his prime, made it a wonderful and memorable campaign. Johnson was considered invincible on the stump, yet Temple made a reputation possessed by few men in the whole country.*

"It is useless to speculate on the effect the defeat of Johnson in that race might have had on his future political fortunes. He was a man of such ambition, such strong and recuperative powers, and of such infinite resources, that ordinary rules of calculation would fail to give a satisfactory conclusion. But it is almost certain that by a defeat he would have been thrown out of the line of success which he afterwards followed up to the very highest positions of honor. It is almost certain that Landon C. Haynes would have been the regular Democratic candidate for Congress at the next election, with Johnson probably as an independent candidate. Whether defeated or elected, he would have been somewhat out of line with his party, and the governorship and the senatorship would have been postponed or never attained. That he would have again appeared in politics, and with some success, none will doubt who knew his great powers and intense ambition. But the probabilities are that his sub-

---

*"Prominent Tennesseeans," by Hon. William S. Speer.

sequent career would have been greatly modified and changed by a defeat."*

Another writer says of this race: "Suppose Temple had defeated Johnson in 1847? Could Johnson have recovered his lost ground afterwards and been governor in 1853 and 1855 and United States senator in 1857? And without the prestige of his unbroken series of brilliant victories and the great influence coming to him by virtue of the high positions he held, could he have been such a tower of strength to the union cause in 1861? And had he not been able to line up his Democratic followers in East Tennessee on the side of the union in 1861, what would have been the effect on the Bell and Everett men? Left standing alone by their Democratic neighbors, would they have still stood by the union? And had East Tennessee not been for the union and not sent thousands of her sons into the federal army, what effect would that have had on the final result? These questions, so easily asked, are difficult to answer. But a careful study of the history of those stirring times will show that there was more involved in that race between Johnson and Temple away back in 1847 than merely a seat in congress and the privilege of sitting in that historic old hall of representatives, redolent with the memories of John Sevier, of Clay, of Bell and of Sam Houston; by the side of the venerable ex-President John Quincy Adams, and of Abraham Lincoln, the one lone Whig from Illinois."

As to the outcome of the civil war, had not the people of East Tennessee and nearby States sent thousands into the federal army, Mr. Thomas Nelson Page says: "These sterling people from the Appalachian region . . . a half century ago rendered to this country an invaluable service. . . . Without them this union would have been divided. . . . They espoused by a great majority the cause of the union. But, more than this, they furnished to the union cause a great friendly territory staunch for the union through its breadth and length, extending for hundreds of miles down through the south and cutting the Confederate south in two. But for them Maryland and Kentucky would have gone out of the union with a rush, and Tennessee and Virginia would have been solid from east to west. . . . But for them the cause of secession would have inevitably succeeded."

---

*"Prominent Tennesseeans," by Hon. William S. Speer.

The Johnson-Temple campaign for congress became the turning point in the life of Mr. Temple. A few months after this, in 1848, he removed to Knoxville, where he became the partner of the Hon. William H. Sneed, one of the ablest lawyers of his day. His principal reason for making this change was to get out of the first district and out of politics. Ever after, though active in nearly every political contest, except while on the bench, he constantly resisted the repeated efforts made to induce him to run for congress. Several times a nomination and an election were within easy reach. Before the civil war he was also prominently spoken of by leading Whig papers for governor.

In 1850, on the recommendation of his friend, the Hon. John Bell, then senator from Tennessee, Mr. Temple was appointed by President Fillmore a commissioner, jointly with Col. Charles S. Todd of Kentucky, late minister to Russia, and Gen. Robert B. Campbell, for years a prominent member of congress from South Carolina, to negotiate with the Indian tribes in Texas, Arizona and New Mexico, the territories then recently acquired from Mexico. This was done under a special act of congress. The appointment of Mr. Temple as the associate of two such widely experienced and noted men as Colonel Todd and General Campbell, and on so responsible a mission, was at the time justly considered a marked compliment. The appointment proved to be full of valuable and delightful experiences. The meeting with such men as Reverdy Johnson of Maryland, General Rush and others, who later became famous, and a taste of the social life at the military post at San Antonio, all gave interest to the trip. In Washington Mr. Temple had the privilege of seeing and knowing many of the striking men of that dazzling day—Clay, Webster, Benton and others.

In September, 1851, soon after returning home, Mr. Temple was married to Miss Scotia Caledonia Humes. Her father, David Humes, a remarkable man, both mentally and physically, was of the celebrated Scotch family of that name. His wife, Eliza Saunderson, also of Scotch birth, and related to many of the best Scotch families, was a woman of conspicuous worth, intelligence and strength of character. The wife of Mr. Temple was the youngest of four sisters. Mrs. Temple had rare personal charms: her striking presence, her winning manner, her ever-present sunshine of disposition, her kindliness of spirit, united in making her a favorite. While a leader socially, she was eminently a home-maker and devoted to her family and to her domestic duties. She was justly celebrated for the splendor of her hospitality.

Mr. Temple and Mrs. Temple had but one child, a daughter, Mary Boyce Temple, to whom they were devotedly attached, and who in affectionate remembrance of her father publishes this book.

After the return of Mr. Temple from Texas he again became the law partner of William H. Sneed. This partnership lasted until the latter was elected to congress in August, 1855. Mr. Temple then formed a partnership with the Hon. Connally F. Trigg, late United States district judge of Tennessee, and this partnership continued until 1859.

In 1856 the Southern Commercial Convention met in Knoxville. It was composed of notable men from all the Southern States, such as Benjamin Yancey of Georgia, a brother of William L. Yancey; L. W. Spratt; the Hon. William W. Boyce, member of congress from South Carolina; Gen. Roger A. Pryor of Virginia, now judge of the supreme court of New York, and others. Mr. Temple took an active part in the often heated discussions of this convention, and, with his usual sense of moderation, introduced resolutions against the reintroduction of the African slave trade, which had been boldly advocated.

In 1860 Mr. Temple was a delegate to the National Union Convention at Baltimore, and helped to nominate Bell and Everett for President and Vice-President. On his return to Tennessee, despite his remonstrance, he was chosen as the Bell elector for the second district. The joint canvass with the Breckinridge elector, James D. Thomas, lasted thirty days. It was heated from start to finish. After it was ended, Mr. Temple canvassed several of the adjoining counties, speaking until the day of the election. "More unequivocally and positively than any public speaker in the State, in that canvass Mr. Temple laid before the people and emphasized the question of union or disunion. He felt deeply and sorrowfully the danger of civil war. He foretold, almost with the spirit of prophecy, that disunion or secession, and then a conflict of arms, would follow the election of Mr. Lincoln. He charged distinctly that in that event there was a deliberate purpose on the part of the southern leaders to break up the union. He denounced the contemplated purpose in the most vigorous words, and appealed to the people to rebuke the scheme. He discussed this question, and this only. . . . In that campaign and in the discussions that followed he did as much as any one man to mould the union sentiment which was so conspicuously displayed by East Tennesseeans during the whole war, and which has guided their political action since. This union sentiment existed in the minds of the people by intuition and education, but it required such courageous men as Mr. Temple to cause it to crystallize and lead it to the accomplishment of results."*

In November, 1860, Mr. Temple made the first union speech delivered in Tennessee after the election of Mr. Lincoln. Among his papers is found this note: "I do not hesitate to affirm as a part of the truth of history, unknown to others, that the course taken by the union men in the two meetings of November and December, 1860, in Knoxville, was planned and arranged solely by Mr. Fleming and myself at my suggestion." In February, 1861, he was unanimously nominated by the union men to represent Knox and Sevier counties in the proposed State convention. The union candidates were overwhelmingly elected against strong opposition, while the convention was voted down. Mr. Temple received in Sevier county thirteen hundred votes out of a total of thirteen hundred and one.

Again, in the spring, when the question of secession was a second time brought before the people, he took the stump to oppose it, and spoke until the day of the election on June 8.† His last speech was at Concord, in a slaveholding community, where he told the slaveholders that by his course he was a truer friend of slavery than they; "that they were probably destroying this species of property; that if they went out of the union

---

*Speer.

†When Judge Temple spoke at Blaine's Cross Roads, among his audience was Robert Barnwell Rhett of South Carolina, and the ladies of his family, who were spending the summer nearby. So indignant did they become at the bold tenor of the speech that they soon left. Interesting, is it not, to note that this conspicuous and extreme advocate of slavery was the first cousin of John Quincy Adams? A brother of Abigail Smith Adams, the wife of John Adams, removed to South Carolina and married a girl that objected to the name Smith; consequently she induced him to take her family name, Rhett. The strong intellect of John Quincy Adams came from his mother, and this same intellect appears in Robert Barnwell Rhett, who was the successor to Calhoun in the United States Senate, presided over the Charleston Convention which voted to take the State out of the Union, and was a candidate for the presidency of the Southern Confederacy.

they would be whipped back into it again; that the government was powerful enough to accomplish this, and would do it."* He often declared during this canvass that if forced to make a choice between slavery and the union, he would say: "Live the union; perish slavery." In the celebrated Greeneville Convention of June, 1861, he was the author of the pacific substitute resolution, which saved East Tennessee from the most awful consequences.

In 1864 Mr. Temple resumed the practice of his profession, and took into partnership Samuel A. Rodgers, later a circuit judge. In January, 1866, George Andrews, afterwards a judge of the supreme court of the State, was admitted to the firm. The business of the firm was enormous, and later James W. Deaderick, afterwards a chief justice of the supreme court, was associated with them. Each of Mr. Temple's seven partners afterwards became a judge, excepting William H. Sneed, and he became a member of congress. In July, 1866, Mr. Temple was appointed chancellor. The appointment was unsolicited and was unknown to him until he received his commission. He kept the question of the acceptance under advisement for three weeks, and finally, through the influence of lawyers rather than by the approval of his own judgment, he accepted. He felt that he was perhaps committing an error, and later he looked back upon the acceptance of this appointment as the great mistake of his career. He was in the prime of life. After once going on the bench, though he constantly thought of resigning, like nearly all judges he could never quite bring himself to do so. He continued on the bench until September, 1878, a little over twelve years. By this time the harvest of business caused by the war had been gathered and new lawyers had come to the fore.

At the first judicial election after the war Judge Temple was re-elected chancellor without opposition. At the next election, after the amended constitution went into effect, he was a second time victorious. Although he was opposed by a very superior lawyer and a former judge his majority was about three thousand six hundred. He retired from the bench voluntarily, having the assurance of a re-election. He returned to the practice of law with all the vim of his younger days, and remained at the bar until November, 1881. During this time he was the attor-

---

*Speer.

ney of the Rugby Colony Company, Rugby, Tennessee, and was closely associated with Russell Sturgis of Boston and Thomas Hughes, author of "Tom Brown at Rugby," and other prominent Englishmen.

In 1867, on the resignation of Judge Milligan as one of the judges of the supreme court of the State, Governor Brownlow immediately tendered the vacant position to Chancellor Temple, who declined it, as he preferred the chancellorship.†

In 1874 Judge Temple was appointed by President Grant one of the board of visitors to the Military Academy at West Point, where he was associated with Senators Hoar, Howe and Don Cameron, Prof. Francis B. Wayland of Yale, and others. At this time he met and formed a strong friendship for the widow of Admiral Farragut. He also met and knew James G. Blaine.

Judge Temple always took a deep interest in the agricultural development of Tennessee. Some years before the war he was a member of the State Board of Agriculture. In 1885 he purchased a small farm in the suburbs of Knoxville, where, while on the bench, he found recreation. He delighted in everything that grew. Everything flourished under his cultivation. His flowers were the most luxuriant, his trees the most perfect, his fruits the most luscious, his grass the most velvety. He introduced every new and improved variety of fruit, and every new rose was soon lending its fragrance to his rose garden. From all over the world he gathered the rarest trees and shrubs, and "Melrose," as his home was named, in memory of the home in Scotland of Mrs. Temple's mother, was as beautiful as any place in the State, with its artistic winding driveways and gently sloping lawns. In this park to-day are the handsomest homes of Knoxville. Judge Temple here introduced the first Jersey cattle into East Tennessee.

In 1871 he was elected president of the Eastern Division Fair at Knoxville. By his efforts, with the aid of his efficient secretary, Mr. C. W. Charlton, the fair was made a magnificent success. Out of this success grew the idea in Judge Temple's mind of having the farmers come together for their own mutual

---

†One of the ablest, if not the ablest, jurist who ever sat on the supreme bench of Tennessee, William B. Turley of Memphis, uncle of the late United States Senator Thomas B. Turley, resigned from the supreme bench to accept the chancellorship at Memphis. Thus Judge Temple had a distinguished precedent for preferring the chancellorship to the supreme bench.

benefit. In 1872 Judge Temple and Mr. Charlton originated and organized the East Tennessee Farmers' Convention. As president of the East Tennessee Agricultural Society Judge Temple called the convention of farmers to meet on the 16th of May. In response to this call, about two hundred farmers assembled. Judge Temple welcomed them to the "first convention of farmers in our history," saying: "I have seen conventions of all other callings and classes. For the first time in our history have the farmers—the most numerous, the most important of all our classes—assembled in convention as a body to deliberate on their own great interests. *This fact is astonishing.* Let us indulge the pleasing hope, let us *resolve*, that this meeting shall not be the *last*, but merely the beginning of a long series of annual meetings, full of instruction, continuing indefinitely through the future." And so they have continued growing each year larger, stronger, more helpful. From 2000 to 2500 farmers come together each year in May. Judge Temple was made the first president, then vice-president, and later honorary vice-president for life. He never ceased to take profound interest in the advancement of the farmers. Every honor, both during his life and since his death, that could be shown their founder has been extended by the Farmers' Convention. In the four meetings held since he passed away the convention has never failed to pay some tribute to his beloved memory. In 1910 his daughter, Mary Boyce Temple, founded a "Short Course in Agriculture" to be held for one week, beginning December 26 of each year, in the respective counties of Eastern Tennessee, to be known as the "Oliver Perry Temple Short Course in Agriculture." By means of this course many farmers and their sons, who are not able to obtain the advantages of a college course in agriculture in the State University, are greatly helped.

On May 18, 1911, the largest Farmers' Convention that ever assembled in Tennessee met in Knoxville. This convention resolved to build an assembly hall on the State agricultural farm at Knoxville and to name it "The Oliver Perry Temple Hall."

The East Tennessee Farmers' Convention, called thirty-nine years ago, May 16 and 17, 1872, has become justly celebrated, and is probably the oldest body of its kind in the United States. Its power for good has been tremendous and inestimable. At the organization the leading paper was delivered by Judge Temple. Its subject was "Stock Raising," a subject in which he took the liveliest interest. Judge Temple was interested not only in the farmers, but in everything that helped his fellowman, in everything that led to the advancement of the people of his State. He was patriotic in the highest sense, and constantly aimed to develop both the people and the industries about him. For fifty-three years he was an active trustee of the East Tennessee University, later the State University of Tennessee. He worked earnestly for its progress. He wrote personal letters to enlist support for its advancement, he published communications in its behalf through the press to reach a larger public, and he was unceasing in his efforts to secure for it appropriations from the legislature. He worked also for years to obtain aid from the national government, and succeeded in getting an experiment station, a military department, an agricultural bureau and certain funds or land grants that went with them. In his outlook for the university's future he was progressive and ahead of his time. At a critical period in the university's career, 1886-1887, he was himself, as chairman of the board of trustees, its acting president, and was offered the presidency. In the face of strong opposition he effected a radical change in the university's organization, and influenced Dr. Charles W. Dabney to accept the presidency, with an entire change of faculty. He was Dr. Dabney's chief counsellor in all the improvements that followed. Later, in 1901, strongly advocating its prospective benefits when it was opposed by others, he took a vital interest in the founding of the Summer School of the South in connection with the university. Dr. P. P. Claxton was then at its head. On June 28, 1911, Dr. Claxton was appointed commissioner of education by President Taft. In no public work during his entire life of varied and great public service did Judge Temple labor so persistently, so zealously and so faithfully as in his untiring efforts for the upbuilding of the University of Tennessee.

Judge Temple was chairman of the agricultural committee until 1900. During this time the agricultural farm and the experiment station were particularly his province, and his direction of them was truly a labor of love. He hoped to interest and inspire the young farmers by the practical lessons scientifically given on the experiment farm. He held that the proper policy of the university was to emphasize the work of the agricultural department, both in order to carry out the laws of congress as

well as to fulfil the trust to the State. "His services to the university and to the cause of education of the State deserve to be remembered with gratitude by the people of the entire State. It is safe to say that he did more to build up the university, and especially the agricultural department, than any other man."[*]
He accomplished the scattering of the trustees over the State, though when, on February 25, 1884, he first offered a resolution bearing on that point, in order to make the university in reality as in name a State institution, it was discussed, opposed, and not even seconded.

He never ceased to have an abounding pride in his own *alma mater*, Washington College. He always aided it with advice and in more substantial ways. Through his help several of his nephews and great-nephews were enabled to take the college course. He never turned a deaf ear to an ambitious boy nor to a needy working man or woman. His benefactions were numerous and as generous as his means permitted.

Judge Temple at all times manifested a deep concern in all public enterprises calculated to improve his State and his adopted city. His mind was always busy to effect some improvement. He took a particularly active part in fostering the building of railroads. He was one of the originators of the Knoxville and Ohio Railroad in 1854, now a part of the Southern system. He was an original stockholder, one of the first directors and the first secretary of the board. He was also a director, for two or three years soon after the war, of the East Tennessee and Georgia Railroad, now the Southern, of which his brother, Major Temple, was the first civil engineer. He memorialized the legislature on good roads, and he himself built, giving largely both time and money, the first macadamized road in East Tennessee, the Kingston pike, and as president he personally superintended its construction.

He was a trustee in the Deaf and Dumb School before the war. He aided in the starting of a public library, and later was a trustee and president of the Lawson McGee Library. He was a trustee in the Second Presbyterian Church, in the tower of which to-day one of the memorial chimes rings forth in his memory.

He was a very active member of the Knoxville Industrial Association. An address that he delivered in 1869 before this

---

[*]Resolutions of the Knoxville Bar, in 1907, on the death of Judge Temple.

body on the resources and possibilities of his section was published and widely circulated. He was a member of the Board of Trade and of the Chamber of Commerce. He was a State commissioner to the World's Fair in Chicago. He was colonel on the staff of Governor Neill S. Brown in 1847. In 1899 Judge Temple was honored by the Scotch-Irish Society of America by being made its president to succeed the late Robert Bonner of the *New York Ledger*.

In politics Judge Temple was a Whig before the war, a union man during the war, and later an unswerving Republican. While on the bench he declined to make political speeches or to take any part in political conventions. No judge ever kept clearer of politics. In 1865 he worked to defeat the plan of Governor Johnson for reorganizing the State government, believing that a constitutional convention, made up of delegates duly elected, should have been called. He felt that a great deal of the discontent that followed in the State might have been prevented had a wisely selected constitutional convention been assembled.

Judge Temple gave his last days to authorship and to the conduct of his private business affairs. It is a remarkable fact that all his literary work was undertaken after he was seventy-five years old, when for a second time he had acquired a competency. He had lost his fortune in the panic of 1873.

Judge Temple was a scholar. He was exceedingly fond of books and literature, and his eager, active mind was stored with information. He was a close and careful observer; his judgment was discriminating; his spirit broad; his wisdom ripe. He was a profound thinker; his mind was clear, incisive and accurate. Because of his fine spirit and kindly temper, his study of events was dispassionate and calmly philosophical. His training as a lawyer and as a judge gave a judicial value to his conclusions. He calmly weighed in the balance the evidence on each side. He wielded a facile pen. He thus possessed in an unusual degree the qualities that make an accurate and successful historian, and he was regarded as an authority on the history of Tennessee. He was the author of "The Covenanter, the Cavalier and the Puritan," 1897, and of "East Tennessee and the Civil War," 1899, both masterly contributions to history. In the latter he showed himself free from all partisan bitterness—a generous, unbiased critic of the events in which he himself had taken a leading part. A lecture on the "Scotch-Irish of Tennessee" and many other lectures he delivered frequently. A sketch of "John Sevier," written for the dedication of the Sevier monument, in the building of which he was one of the foremost spirits, was published in 1910 by his daughter. It is said to be the best article ever written about Tennessee's first governor. Judge Temple was indefatigable in his literary labors, painstaking, industrious, persevering. He enjoyed the mental stimulus and exhilaration. He took great pleasure in the work, and even after an accident rendered him a great sufferer, his writing, though interrupted, was not entirely laid aside.

In the early and middle portion of his life Judge Temple was rather a delicate man, and he was constantly handicapped by eyes that were not strong. He was always extremely careful and abstemious, and after his seventieth year he gradually grew into perfect health; at seventy-five he was alert, active and as straight as an arrow in his stately and dignified carriage. He was apparently in his prime, and he had his hands full of both private and public business. These latter years of Judge Temple's life were rich in unexpected tokens of regard. His birthdays were occasions for felicitations on the part of friends at home and throughout the land—letters, telegrams, visits and remembrances bore to him the love and good wishes of the many admirers that he had in every station of life. The papers wrote of him as "The Grand Old Man of Tennessee," and in vigor of body and mind he bore a striking resemblance to Mr. Gladstone, the "Grand Old Man" of England. Until 1904 his perfect physical condition and his wonderful vigor of mind made him a marvel—the perfect fruition of a life generously spent; unselfish motives, honesty and high principles had been its mainspring. He was pure in heart. In July, 1904, he became seriously ill, and he lingered between life and death for weeks. Though he recovered, he was never quite strong again. The following June he had a fall, which left him with a fractured hip. For nearly three and a half years from the time of his first breakdown until his passing away his patience and his endurance were heroic. He was bright and hopeful, despite almost insupportable suffering, seeing his friends, recounting bits of history, or even giving expressions to an outburst of humor, which was always one of his greatest joys. Occasionally he wrote letters, or even at times worked on his "Union Leaders," his unfinished book, which he was eager to finish and publish. His spirit rose superior to physical pain; whenever possible, on his sick couch, he labored to complete his manuscript, his mind clear, alert, incisive and his memory perfect—a brave fight worthy the emulation of younger persons. It is the men that have accomplished at so advanced an age such feats as did Judge Temple that stand out as luminous landmarks.

Whatever harsh traits Judge Temple may have had were softened in his later years. While the virility, manliness and forcefulness that he was so splendidly endowed with were strengthened by the passing years, yet they were mellowed and enriched by time. His Christian faith was strong, and frequently he said, "I am ready, I am waiting." Judge Temple had always a high reverence for religion and for the Presbyterian church. He, his wife and his daughter belonged to that denomination, as his ancestors for generations before him had done. Reverence was one of his strongest traits. His temperament was deeply poetic, imaginative and artistic, yet in contrast was extremely practical and somewhat austere in its exactions upon himself and upon others. He loved perfection in all things, whether of one of nature's marvelous scenes or of art's most exquisite fashioning of fabric or color. His own dress was not only immaculate, but always elegant. He was always noticeable in appearance, his walk brisk, his head high and his carriage graceful, while his cordiality, his repose of manner, his fine poise made him the type of the old-time southern gentlemen.

The hospitality of Judge Temple and Mrs. Temple was far-famed, and later his daughter kept up the reputation of the Temple home as a social center. Judge Temple delighted to have his friends about him and to welcome them to his historic old home.*

---

*The first Union general to enter Knoxville in the sixties was Gen. John W. Foster, secretary of state under President Harrison, and the greatest diplomat and international lawyer of our country to-day. Upon his arrival in Knoxville, General Foster sent for Judge Temple to ask his advice. This friendship was continued with mutual high regard. One of the most pleasant incidents of Judge Temple's long illness was a visit, in March, 1906, from General Foster and Mrs. Foster, who were en route to Nashville, in a private car, in company with Sir Mortimer Durand, the British ambassador to the United States, Miss Durand, and Commissioner McFarland of the District of Columbia. They all stopped to see Judge Temple. He found great pleasure in welcoming them to his sick room, and in knowing that they were gathered around his hospitable table with a brilliant company to meet them.

"Among Judge Temple's many distinguished traits of character which marked him as a man of force was his keen perception of moral truth and an exemplification of it in every sphere of life. His personal honesty was proverbial. His industry and energy were of the highest order and were only equaled by his fidelity to friends and devotion to principle. The same rule of conduct marked his connection with public trusts, which was ascribed to his personal character. He was possessed of a large amount of what men call 'soul.' He was sympathetic and kind. He was always popular, as was shown by his success with Andrew Johnson in 1847. His popularity begun, grew into magnificent proportions on account of this giant-like battle up to the war."*

His great hold on the people from the highest to the lowest came from the fact that they had absolute confidence in him; they knew that they could rely upon what he said as true and upon what he did as honest.

With a Puritan's scrupulousness, truthfulness and honor, inherited from his English ancestors, Judge Temple united a quiet Scotch humor and love of a joke that made him a genial companion. He intimately knew the spirit that ruled the masses as well as the reasons that prompted their actions in critical times. "In the first two years of the civil war, when Johnson and Maynard were fugitives and Nelson in a Richmond prison, Temple's good temper and diplomatic skill enabled him to remain at home and sometimes to soften the rigors of Confederate rule over his fellow-citizens. When in 1863 Knoxville was occupied by the federal army, his influence with the authorities at Washington was again active, and he had a part in everything that concerned his region."†

Judge Temple as a boy was shrinking and timid. Later when he took the lead and assumed an aggressive attitude, it was because he felt the supreme need of carrying forward some vital principle. He was one of the best and most popular speakers in the State before he was thirty-five, his manner pleasing, his voice exceptionally good and his gesticulation dramatic. His facts were clear, his reasoning was logical; his arguments were simple, yet they were combined with power of imagination. He was

---
*Speer.
†Speer.

not only an orator, but also a debater. He never failed to impress his hearers, and generally won his cause. When it was known that he would speak, people would travel miles to hear him. "Long before the sixties he was among the foremost lawyers at the Knoxville bar, which was always strong, but never stronger than during that period. He was particularly effective before a jury, and rarely lost a criminal case. Subsequent to the war his judicial career was noted."*

Judge William A. Henderson writes of Judge Temple: "His universal kindness, aid, protection and instruction to the younger members of the bar who practiced before him, or whom he met socially, were remarkable. He would protect a sparrow hawk against the unjust attack of an eagle. Most of the members of the bar were young men when he was on the bench, and they all revere his memory."

Chief Justice Beard of the supreme court of Tennessee—one of his closest friends—in a letter on Judge Temple's eighty-second birthday, wrote: "Few attain your number of years and retain your wonderful interest in the general affairs of life. I wish that you may be spared many years of useful citizenship, and may continue to be a guide to your friends in all that you consider noble and uplifting."

The late Senator Bate, July 21, 1903, wrote: "I look back with pleasure to my two visits to your hospitable and historic home. It is so rare that one of your age is left with strength and health and retention of faculties that a casual visit to you in itself is of interest, even were it not associated with the lawyer, the chancellor and the author. Your green old age demonstrates the goodness of nature to those whose habits and taste in life have been those of the Christian philosopher, and . . . when I left you I felt like quoting the Prince of Denmark: 'I shall not look upon his like again.' "

Judge Temple was a man to be remembered with reverence and gratitude by his inmost circle of friends, as well as by those in the humbler walks of life that knew him.

Mr. W. B. Lenoir, of the opposite political party from Judge Temple, wrote: "I admired Judge Temple when I was a boy, I think, because he was an aristocrat. I did not attempt to define the word to myself at the time, but give a definition now in its

---

*Speer.

true sense as being one who is too intelligent and honest and too proud of himself, of his family and of his country ever to do a mean or unworthy thing. . . . I am as proud, perhaps more so, of O. P. Temple for what he did *not* do as for what he did do. He did not use his great influence to persecute those of opposite political sentiments after the civil war, but to protect them; he did not drag the ermine in the mire of partisan politics or let political prejudice weigh the balance, but dealt out even-handed justice. He was the just judge, the upright citizen, the graceful speaker, the polished southern gentleman."

A life-long admirer says: "He was the very ideal of a high-minded and courteous gentleman, the soul of honor as a man, and as a jurist an ornament to that noble profession of which he was an acknowledged leader. He left to his daughter a precious legacy in the memory of his home life, of his devotion to her mother and to herself, and in his long life and splendid record in the community as a lawyer, an author, a public servant and a Christian gentleman." Of his character it can well be said that he was a zealous and devoted patriot, pure and noble in his ideals, honest in all his dealings, truthful and sincere in all his utterances, and a worker who never stayed his hand, though he was over eighty-seven years old, until death commanded him to cease. He had set an example that even the worthiest would be honored by following.

Judge Temple died at his home in Knoxville, Tennessee, November 2, 1907, in the eighty-eighth year of his age, mourned by his community and by his State. He was the last of the great union leaders, his contemporaries having all gone before. His well-rounded old age was a crown of glory.

M. B. T.

Knoxville, Tenn.,
March 12, 1912.

NOTABLE MEN OF TENNESSEE
FROM 1833 TO 1875
THEIR TIMES AND THEIR CONTEMPORARIES

Three Remarkable Facts—November, 1860, to February Election, 1861—South Carolina Secedes, December 26, 1860—Grave Questions in Border States—Bewildering Uncertainty as to Interest and Duty—Ambitious Leaders in Cotton States — Vague Fear of the Abolitionists — Widespread Secession Movement—Attitude Toward Slavery—First Union Speech—Knoxville Streets Full of Secessionists—November 26, Public Meetings Adjourned Without Decisive Vote—December 8, Secession Resolutions Defeated, Victory for Union Overwhelming—Meetings in Other Counties—Author Reluctantly Assumed Leadership—Brownlow's Paper Plays an Important Part—Johnson's Part—Local Leaders—Third Crisis—Emancipation—Brownlow's Quarrel with Johnson—Alexander Stephens at Milledgeville — Firing on Sumter — Lincoln's Inaugural.

THREE remarkable facts mark the history and give interest to the people of East Tennessee. The first was the formation by them of the "Watauga Association" in 1774, composed of the infant settlements of the Watauga, the Holston, the Nolichucky, and the one in Carter's Valley. The articles of "association" united these settlements and the people thereof into a government, with a written constitution, republican in form and spirit, under which they lived and governed themselves for years. This was the first written constitution adopted west of the Alleghanies, as well as the first free and independent government established by men of American birth on the continent.*
Remote from the older settlements of North Carolina, neglected and apparently forgotten, without the protection of laws or courts, these brave and intelligent men, guided by the instinct of self-preservation and a natural genius for government, voluntarily came together, organized themselves into a little confederacy, adopted laws, selected agents to administer the laws, and bound themselves to obey the legal and executive authorities, and thus established in the wilderness their little self-constituted

---

*Ramsey's "Annals of Tennessee," p. 107. Roosevelt's "Winning of the West," Vol. I, pp. 163, 164, and notes on pages 162, 163.

government, and sent it forward upon its peaceful career of order and prosperity.

The second striking fact in the early history of these people was the formation, in 1784, of the State of Franklin, and its secession from the parent State of North Carolina. This secession was not an act of rebellion nor hostile revolution. By the Cession Act North Carolina transferred all of her territory west of the mountains, now forming the State of Tennessee, to the Congress of the Confederation, leaving the people of that territory a second time without the protection of laws or courts, or any means of defense against hostile Indians except their own stout arms. In this dilemma the people came together, through delegates duly chosen, as the settlements had done in 1772, and declared their independence, formed a government, and launched the State of Franklin on its stormy but short and ill-fated career. In both of these cases it was the impulse of freedom and the instinct of self-preservation that inspired these brave men to establish governments. This was not lawlessness. On the contrary, the people were animated by the purest love of law, order, security, and liberty.* It is a remarkable fact that these people were self-governed during nearly the entire period from the first settlement on the Watauga, in 1769 or 1770, until the organization of the "Territory South of the Ohio River," in 1790.

The third striking fact in reference to the people of East Tennessee is that in February, 1861, when the other grand divisions of the State, by a majority of nearly ninety thousand, voted to secede from the Union, they decided to adhere to the government of their fathers by a vote of about two and one-half to one. And this was done, too, amid the storm and tempest of war, when almost the whole South was shaking and rocking in the violent convulsion of revolutionary secession. In the midst of all this uproar and upheaval these people determinedly, heroically, stood by their convictions and their country.

After this brief reference to early history I shall attempt to point out and sketch the leaders of this people in the last and the supreme crisis of our government, in the dark and stormy days of 1861.

The period from November, 1860, to the February election,

---

*It is singular that the above should be written on December 31, 1900—the last day of the year and the last day of the nineteenth century.

1861, was by far the most critical in the history of the Union cause. It was the formative period—the time when public sentiment was crystallizing around new theories; the period of doubt, alarm, change. New conditions had come into being; new questions had arisen; old political elements were dissolving; old party organizations were melting away. A new and powerful sectional party—the Republicans and Abolitionists—had come into power and controlled Congress. The peculiar institutions of the South were supposed to be in danger, and great and perilous events were impending.

The announcement of the election of Mr. Lincoln was received nearly everywhere in the South with gloomy forebodings. South Carolina immediately commenced making preparations for withdrawal from the Union. On the 26th of December, with solemn pomp and ceremony, the ancient bonds of the Union, cemented by the blood of the Revolution, were broken, and that proud old State, so full of glorious deeds and memories, declared her independence, and assumed her position as a sovereign power. Other States were ready to follow her example. Already the sound of martial music and the mustering of troops were heard. Universal alarm and uncertainty prevailed. Men began to ask themselves: What will the end be?

In the Southern States, and especially in Tennessee, Virginia, Maryland, Kentucky and Missouri, other questions of grave import arose in the minds of men. What will my State do? Will it join in the movement to break up the Union? Is the institution of slavery in serious danger? Will the North respect or trample upon the constitutional rights of the slave States? Where shall I go; with the Abolitionists of the North to maintain the Union, or the Secessionists of the South, to dissolve it?

Thus, in the early stages of the development of the gigantic scheme to establish a Confederacy of the Southern States, the minds of perhaps a majority of people in these States were in a state of bewildering uncertainty as to their interest and duty.

With the exception of the ambitious leaders in the cotton States and with the exception of those who had imbibed the virus of secession from rabid leaders, a majority of the people—in spite of a greater or less degree of prejudice against the people of the North—still loved the Union. It was difficult for them to entertain the idea of severing the connection. Fifty years of peace had made them dread war, especially a civil war, a war among their own countrymen. Nor was anyone sufficiently gifted with prescience to be able to predict the results of either war or peace.

The best friends of the Union in the South had a vague fear of the Abolitionists, as the dominant party in the North was popularly called. These had been depicted in such dark colors, their purposes had been denounced as so infamous, so diabolical, by the friends of disunion, that in the course of time they came to be regarded as something to be feared, as well as hated and loathed, by nearly every Southern man and woman. It is true that intelligent men, who were free from the dominant prejudice, knew the difference between the Abolitionists proper and the Free Soilers—the infinitely larger party who constituted the real strength of the triumphant party which had elected Mr. Lincoln—but with perhaps an overwhelming majority of the people this difference was unknown, and both were regarded as Abolitionists and as enemies of the South.

Notwithstanding that the Whigs had been taught from infancy to revere the Union, the events following the Presidential election of 1860 were so sudden and startling, and succeeded each other with such rapidity, the movement in favor of secession became so widespread and alarming that many of them, if not a majority, became confused as to their duty. When they heard an almost universal outcry in the South against the election of Mr. Lincoln and the ascendency of the Abolition party, and beheld State after State preparing to secede from the Union; when it was daily proclaimed from the stump and through the press that the direst calamity would befall the Southern people unless they declared their independence and forever separated from their enemies in the North; when the evil purposes of the Abolitionists were everywhere proclaimed in the darkest colors, the people naturally came to a pause. They began to consider whether there might not be some good reason for the course of the advocates of disunion. These suggestions arose in the minds of patriotic men in view of the new and alarming conditions that surrounded them.

The overpowering influence of slavery, the fear of falling under the condemnation of the mighty oligarchy of slaveholders, to some extent had paralyzed the minds of men. Not a man in the South dared openly to question the morality of slavery. No one dared any longer to suggest either its removal or its amelioration. All, whether slaveholders or non-slaveholders, felt the crushing power and the omnipotence of this despotism of public opinion. The least suspicion of disloyalty to slavery, the least hint of anti-slavery sentiments on the part of anyone, brought upon such person infamy and the curse of social outlawry. He was to be shunned as a loathsome leper. Never was this feeling so strong, so bitter, so pervasive, as during the first few months after the election of Mr. Lincoln. Combined with this was another feeling nearly as potent; that is, that Southern men should go with the South, with their section, their State, their neighbors and their friends. With all this there was constantly presented by the press, by public speakers, and often by the pulpit, the dark picture of the horrible desolation to be wrought in the South by Abolition rule. And amid all these things, and sounding far above them, was the noise of the preparation for war.

With such scenes in their midst,—new and wonderful,—it is little surprising that many, indeed most, of the best Union men were at first bewildered. Most of those whom I met were at this time cautious and hesitating. They were for the Union, but a vague dread of "something they knew not of" fettered their minds. In a few weeks this feeling passed away, notably after the great meeting in Knoxville on December 8, and after Mr. Johnson's bold speech in the Senate, December 19 and 20. It needed only brave leaders and brave words to reassure the timid and the hesitating.

Two weeks after the Presidential election I was in attendance upon the Circuit Court in Sevierville. I found the people in a fearful state of doubt and perplexity. South Carolina was then on the point of withdrawing from the Union. By request I addressed the people on the condition of the country. I pointed out that secession was the causeless and ambitious project of a few Southern leaders, and explained at length that the triumph and ascendency of the Republican party did not menace the liberties of the people nor endanger the safety of the institution of slavery. This was the first Union speech made in Tennessee, or perhaps in the South, after the Presidential election.

On my return home a few days later I found a still more threatening aspect in the condition of public affairs in Knoxville. The streets were full of secessionists—noisy, aggressive, and domineering. Federal Court was in session, and jurors were wearing in the jury box secession badges, in a United States Court, presided over by West H. Humphreys, a United States Judge. Judge, clerk, marshal, jurors, and many witnesses and spectators were open and defiant in opposition to the government. A call had appeared in the newspapers for a public meeting to be held on the evening of the succeeding day, the 26th of November, to take into consideration the condition of public affairs. The object of this call was obvious. It was intended to get the citizens together, and in the confusion and doubt which prevailed in their minds, to pass resolutions favorable to the secession of Tennessee. On consultation with John M. Fleming I decided to attend the proposed meeting and take part in it, and, if possible, to defeat its object. When the meeting assembled the friends of secession were present in force; they were noisy and demonstrative. So great was the alarm and uncertainty among the Union men, and so timid were they, that it was difficult to get them to go to the meeting. As was anticipated, resolutions advocating the convening of the Legislature in extra session, a call for a State Constitutional Convention, and the endorsement of a conference of delegates from the Southern States were introduced by a committee and advocated with great earnestness by the leading secessionists. John Baxter and John J. Reese, both of whom were Union men, advocated that policy. The fight in opposition to these resolutions and measures was made by John M. Fleming, then a young man, and myself. Finally, after a long struggle and without a decisive vote, the meeting adjourned to meet nearly two weeks later, on the 8th of December, in the daytime. If the vote had been taken that night on the resolutions, it was clear to those in the opposition that they would have been triumphantly carried. Why the leaders in that movement allowed the meeting to adjourn without a vote, and to reassemble in the daytime, has always been a mystery. The result of a favorable vote that night on the propositions before the meeting would have given an impetus to the cause of secession that could have been counteracted only with great difficulty.

After the adjournment of this meeting those who had been active in opposition to its purpose took immediate steps to arouse the people of the country to the necessity of attending the public meeting on the 8th of December. When the day arrived the town was full of excited men from the country. They were present from every part of the county, and in some instances from adjoining counties. It was a day of anxious solicitude to those on the Union side who were to take part in the meeting, and one never to be forgotten. At an early hour the courthouse was filled and packed with people, with many on the outside. The same resolutions which had been presented at the previous meeting were again brought forward. They were advocated by John H. Crozier, John Baxter, William B. Reese, James W. Humes and Wayne W. Wallace, and by William H. Sneed. The fact was not disguised in the discussion that the object of the resolutions was to bring this meeting and the State of Tennessee into line with the Southern States. Secession was not openly advocated, but it was constantly insisted that common cause should be made with our brethren of the South. On the other side, the speakers who opposed this movement were Samuel R. Rogers and myself. Mr. Rogers spoke very briefly, but pointedly. Mr. William G. Brownlow was present, taking notes for his paper, but took no part in the proceedings until just before the close, when he made a few stirring and characteristic remarks against secession. The discussion lasted four hours. It was animated and spirited, but at no time acrimonious. The solemnity of the occasion, the momentous issues involved, the tremendous crisis that was impending, the uncertainty in the minds of all present as to the opinions and feelings of the people in reference to the new questions which had arisen, seemed to moderate the tone of the speakers as well as the temper of the crowd. At last, toward four o'clock in the afternoon, the resolutions offered by the committee were put to a vote and defeated by a large majority. Then John M. Fleming arose and offered some ringing resolutions, condemning secession as a heresy, and endorsing the Union, which were received with the wildest enthusiasm. The resolutions were put upon their passage and adopted by three or four to one. A loud shout of triumph went up. The pent-up feelings of the crowd, hitherto restrained by a sense of the awful solemnity of the questions at issue, at last burst forth in unrestrained demonstrations of joy. At this moment John J. Reese, who, as we have seen, started out a friend of the defeated resolutions, jumped upon the platform and proposed three cheers for the Union. The sound which followed in response was like the thunder of a cataract. The Union victory was complete and overwhelming.

No such public meeting as this perhaps was ever held in the

country. For nearly four hours a packed house had listened to speeches both for and against the dissolution of the Union. The people had patiently and quietly listened to all that could be said on either side, and had then pronounced their verdict. So calm and dispassionate a discussion of the great question involved was never before and never afterward heard. Its effect upon the public mind and the Union cause in East Tennessee was of transcendent importance. The news of it was carried abroad by those present, and proclaimed in exultant tones by Mr. Brownlow through his paper, until it became known to every intelligent man throughout East Tennessee. Soon public meetings were held in other counties, one after another, until nearly every county had declared for the Union.

It will be observed that neither Mr. Maynard nor Mr. Trigg was present at this meeting, and that Mr. Baxter, though a decided Union man, had a favorite remedy of his own. Mr. Trigg was absent from home, probably attending one of his courts. Up to this time, however, he had taken no part in politics since his removal from Virginia in 1855. Mr. Maynard was absent in Washington as a member of Congress.

The part of leadership thrust upon me in these meetings was reluctantly taken by me. I shrank from the responsibility of this position, but I saw no alternative unless willing to see an irretrievable injury inflicted on the Union cause. Mr. Baxter was not in favor of secession, but was the author of the plan supported by the secessionists. Mr. Maynard had declined to attend the meeting. Mr. Rogers was not a public speaker, and Mr. Fleming was a very young man. These were the only Union leaders who resided at Knoxville. It was therefore apparent to me that unless I took the lead in opposition to the movements of the secessionists, no one would do so. In the late Presidential canvass leadership had devolved upon me against my will by my party selecting me as elector for my district. It was therefore most natural that I should be forced to assume this position for this occasion, however reluctant I was to do so.

So far as the question of the Union was concerned, in 1861, when the greatest question that ever agitated this country arose, it was most fortunate that there were so many brave and able men in East Tennessee, capable of counseling the people and of assisting Mr. Johnson. Happily, there were available the very men for such a crisis—men endowed with qualities

NOTABLE MEN OF TENNESSEE 39

precisely adapted to stormy times. These possessed a power to control and guide the warring elements around them that was indeed sublime. No dangers could intimidate, no terrors silence them. Their courage rose with the magnitude of the peril. Nor were they distinguished for daring only. Some of them possessed talents such as are bestowed only on a gifted few, admirably fitting them either to resist or lead a revolution. There were no other men of like number in the State who, as a whole, were their equals.

The men to whom I refer as especially noted for the qualities that make leaders were Andrew Johnson, William G. Brownlow, Thomas A. R. Nelson and John Baxter. Of these four, Mr. Johnson was the best known, and possibly the most gifted. Mr. Brownlow was a man of great natural power. He had a dauntless spirit that knew no fear, and possessed a magnetism that attracted men with a force rarely witnessed. Mr. Nelson also had some of the highest qualities of a successful leader—eloquence, honesty and rare courage. Mr. Baxter was an extraordinary man. His courage and determination were of the highest order; in intellect he was equal perhaps, if not superior, to Johnson.

With his own political friends, no man had so much influence as Andrew Johnson. He had, however, bitter enemies in both parties. By his course in opposing secession he had separated from a large contingent of his old party friends. But he held a large number of Democrats who were by association and party affiliation inclined to go off into secession. He held others firm in the hour of temptation who could have been kept steady by no other man. But he was influential only with his own party. The Democratic party was in a minority in each of the three Congressional Districts in East Tennessee. The Whigs, who constituted the majority, were not accustomed to follow him. With them he had neither personal nor political influence. As a general rule they were for the Union anyway. They had been unmistakably so in the canvass of 1860, while Johnson was advocating the election of Breckinridge. They hated Johnson as they hated no other man, and had looked with cold distrust on his sudden change in December, 1860. He had been so bitter and brutal in his assaults on them in the past, his conduct as a politician had been so narrow and selfish that he was regarded by them as being outside of the circle of honorable statesmen. In fact, he never gained the full confidence of the Whig element. In Greene County, his home, the Whigs, who had long known him, seem to have gone into secession as they did in no other county. Why was this, unless from fear and distrust of him?

After his arrival at home from Washington, in the spring of 1861, Andrew Johnson entered the canvass for the Union with vigor and determination. This, it should be remembered, was the second canvass in the State. Previous to the election in the preceding February East Tennessee had been thoroughly canvassed by local speakers. Mr. Johnson did not make a speech to the people until after his return. His position on the question of secession was, however, already known to all intelligent people by his speech in the Senate, to which reference will be made. But this speech had infinitely more influence in the North than it had in East Tennessee, except with his own party friends. With them it produced a revolution.

Horace Maynard did not at that time possess the popularity with the mass of the people which he acquired at a later day in his brilliant canvass in the State for Congress at large in 1872 against Johnson and General Cheatham. After the election in November he did not make a speech in East Tennessee until after his return in March or April, 1861. In the meantime, as in the case of both Johnson and Nelson, the overwhelming Union victory of February had been won by other men. Maynard came home soon after the adjournment of Congress, but was not so prompt as Nelson in taking the stump. He did good service, however, in the canvass preceding the June election. He was a good speaker, but his calm, dispassionate manner was not what the hour demanded.

So far as Mr. Nelson is concerned, he stands on a little different ground. No man has lived in East Tennessee who has more largely commanded the confidence of the people. No man has lived in the State, except possibly Gentry and W. B. Campbell, in whose honesty there was more universal confidence. His influence was therefore marked. All parties, even in times of the highest excitement, admired him. On the stump he was nearly the equal of Johnson, and in fiery eloquence his superior. Nelson came home immediately after the adjournment of Congress, and without delay took the stump in defense of the Union. He entered the field with a heroic spirit, and never left it until the June election. He canvassed nearly all of East Tennessee. But, like Johnson and Maynard, he also was absent in Washington when the contest of February had taken place, and none of the glory of that victory can be given to him. In reference to Johnson as well as his supporters, each of the three named—Johnson, Maynard and Nelson—it must be remembered that while they took no part in the canvass preceding the February election, the weight of their names was used in favor of the Union. Neither Nelson nor Maynard, however, had electrified the country during the late session of Congress by a great, stirring speech in behalf of the Union, as Johnson had done, though one year before, on the third day of his career in Congress, Nelson had made an eloquent speech in the House in defense of the Union, which at once gave him national reputation, and which the London *Times* pronounced the "highest product of American oratory." Notwithstanding the ability and boldness displayed by Johnson, Nelson and Baxter, and in a less degree by other Union leaders, no one individual exercised such potent influence upon the minds of the old Whigs of East Tennessee as did Brownlow.

In this critical hour (the spring of 1861) Mr. Johnson's speeches were undoubtedly of great service. They helped to give courage to the timid and constancy to the vacillating of his own party. But I doubt if he made many converts at that late day. All his converts were made previously. Nearly every man had made up his mind in February. At this stage of the canvass (in April and May) the man who had been seized with the blind mania of secession was beyond all argument and hope. It was a time of wild passion and terror. The triumph of the Union men in the February election had been overwhelming. Excepting the influence exerted by the names of these three men—Johnson, Nelson and Maynard—and their generally known position on this question, and the immense influence exerted by Mr. Johnson's speech in the Senate, the credit for this splendid victory is due to local leaders in the several counties and to the patriotic instincts of the people themselves.

In this work, Mr. Brownlow's paper played a most important part. The spirit of that dauntless man pervaded everything. Of all the leaders, Brownlow was both loved and hated as none of the others were. He had a Jacksonian will, and at the same time a kindliness of disposition that linked him to men "as with hooks of steel." No man in East Tennessee at that time moved and swayed friends as he did. This influence was direct and personal. It arose from a mixed love and admiration. Through his paper for months he addressed larger audiences of people than Johnson and Nelson ever commanded. His trumpet gave forth no uncertain sound, but warned every man "to prepare himself for the battle."

So, in the contest of 1861 I hesitate but little in saying that Brownlow, through his paper and by his example and personal popularity, did more to mold and control the Union sentiment of East Tennessee than any other single man excepting Johnson.

The victory of February was won by a set of men comparatively unknown outside of the State, several of whom possessed as much courage and nearly as much intellect as the recognized leaders. Among the many to whom credit should be given may be mentioned Brownlow, Baxter, Trigg, Netherland, Carter, Arnold, Milligan, Fletcher, Taylor, Senter, Butler, Brown, Deaderick, Fleming, Rodgers, Thornburgh, Swann, Staples, Blizzard, Trewhitt, Brabson, Crutchfield, Spears, Clift, Houck, and many others. But by far the larger part of the honor of winning that splendid victory is due to a small number, chief among whom were Brownlow, Baxter, Trigg, Fleming, Arnold, Netherland, W. B. Carter, Taylor, and one or two others. Unquestionably Johnson, Maynard and Nelson helped, at a later day, in the terrible frenzy of the hour, as did many others, to keep the Union men from being stampeded into secession. I distinctly recognize here and everywhere the wonderful influence of Johnson on the Democratic party in that February, as well as in that later June election.

But it was unquestionably the early speakers who did the most effective work—those of December, January and February, who spoke to men who had not yet decided as to their course. The pro-slavery sentiment still dominated the minds of men to such an extent as to make them timid, if not cowardly. An alliance with the Republican party was at first so revolting that even the warm friends of the Union shrank from it. In the face of the hatred entertained by nearly all the Southern people for the Abolitionists, it required, at first, the highest moral courage to oppose the movement in favor of Southern independence.

In order to show in the most conclusive manner to whom the credit shold be given of making East Tennessee loyal, I repeat with emphasis that the Union majority in round numbers was more than six thousand greater in the February election than it was in that of June, though the question was precisely the same in effect in both elections. After the firing on Fort Sumter a considerable number of men fell away from the Union cause. This defection excited some uneasiness, and the local leaders redoubled their energy, for they were determined to save East Tennessee, even if the State were lost. The contest became fierce and determined. It raged from Bristol to Chattanooga, and soon became red hot along the whole line. It is a noticeable fact that the largest Union majorities, the most unanimous Union sentiment in East Tennessee, was in the eight or ten counties around Knoxville, which felt the influence and heard the voices of these less well-known leaders.

By reason of Mr. Johnson's great influence over the Democrats, it must not be supposed that the Whig Union leaders had nothing to do and deserve no credit. Such a conclusion would be most erroneous.

Suppose the canvass of January and February, and I might say December also, had depended on what was done by the East Tennessee representatives in Congress at Washington, and that the local leaders had remained silent, can any man doubt what the result would have been? The Union cause would have been hopelessly lost, and lost, too, beyond the power of man to restore it. It is evident, therefore, that Mr. Johnson alone did not make East Tennessee loyal to the Union, though he did more than any one man, and that he did his part also in keeping it loyal no one will deny. The occasion was grand and full of awful interest. In the presence of momentous events constantly transpiring around him, his faculties and powers seemed to expand. He pleaded with thrilling words the cause of his country. In power, as a public speaker, Johnson was easily the first of the Union leaders in East Tennessee. Never did he make such speeches. He literally took his life in his hand. Whatever may be thought of him in reference to his subsequent acts, he certainly deserved and still deserves the gratitude of his countrymen for this brilliant campaign. The grandeur of the occasion and the stupendous consequences at issue seemed to soften his bitter spirit. He went forward with unfaltering steps, and as the gloom thickened he grew more earnest. That his speeches at that time were masterly efforts, none who heard them ever questioned. At no period of his life was he so great—certainly at no period did he so completely rise above himself. Had he died at the close of this great canvass, he would have lived in memory and in history as the ablest defender of the Union.

When the three members of Congress returned home, as we have seen, the second canvass was on hand. The local leaders were already in the field. The fight had gone on from February almost without ceasing. The members of Congress found the Union men a compact, determined body, solidified and united by the work already done. To attempt to make converts at that late hour would have been almost hopeless. The utmost that could be done was to hold the Union column steady, and prevent stampedes, desertions, and straggling. There was much hard work yet to be done. The startling and rapidly succeeding events daily taking place were calculated to unsettle the minds of men, and it required constant encouragement and support to keep them steady. Under similar conditions, nearly the entire population of Middle and West Tennessee had deserted in a body almost in a day, going over to secession, and so, too, had the large loyal majority in Virginia melted away in an hour. Men were astounded by the masterly boldness of the secessionists, and dazzled and confounded by the audacity with which they played the game of revolution. Day by day the stars in the bright galaxy of the Union were dropping one by one from their accustomed places. Everywhere in the South loyalty disappeared on that black and terrible 12th of April, 1861, but no such falling away occurred in East Tennessee. Scarcely a man wavered.

Lincoln's election, quickly followed by the withdrawal of South Carolina and that of other States, bewildered the people. But Brownlow stood firm and sent forth encouraging messages through his paper. Nearly all the old Whigs took the stump, and with a daring unsurpassed, denounced secession as a crime against the liberties of the people. Thus reassured, the people remained steadfast in their allegiance to the Union.

In estimating the relative value of the Union leaders of East Tennessee, it should be kept in mind that there were four crises in the political situation of this section—the first extending from November, 1860, to the February election in 1861; the second extending from February to the June election. These two were the most important. During the Presidential canvass the influence of Johnson was exerted, whether so intended or not, in favor of the Southern movement. His advocacy of the election of Breckinridge weakened the Union cause, and correspondingly strengthened that of secession. On the other hand, all the Union leaders before mentioned gave their influence, and some of them their active exertions, in behalf of the cause of the Union. But after it became manifest that certain Southern States intended to secede from the Union, Johnson and the other leaders co-operated in a common defense of the Union.

In the third crisis, beginning with President Lincoln's proclamation of emancipation, January 1st, 1863, the leaders divided, and there was never again co-operation between them. Early in this period Nelson, Baxter, Fleming, and Carter, and not long afterward Trigg also, turned away from the administration of Lincoln, and gave their support, and all of them, except Trigg, their exertions, to the McClellan movement. This movement was in effect and in fact an attempt to incite a counter revolution in the North in aid of the greater one then in progress in the South. In Tennessee the contest became bitter and exciting. It was a new crisis in the political affairs of the State. The continued loyalty of the people of East Tennessee depended largely upon the settlement of the new issues that had arisen. The policy of emancipation adopted by President Lincoln was, at first especially, a shock to the minds of many who had been true to the Union. They began to hesitate and waver; some of them denounced the President, and said they had been promised protection for their slaves, and that they did not go into war for the purpose of emancipating them. Some officers even, who had fought bravely up to that time, resigned their commissions, left the army, and denounced the administration and the war. Baxter, Nelson, Carter, and others made haste to denounce the policy of Lincoln, and to give their adhesion to the party opposing him. The breach in the old Union party threatened the most serious consequences to its unity. Many of the rank and file of the Union men became, as they had been in the last days of 1860, uncertain and unsettled as to their duty. But fortunately for the country, Johnson, Brownlow, Maynard, and other leaders took firm and decided ground in favor of the policy of the administration, and by their influence and their exertions saved the party from a serious division. A few men, following the lead of Nelson, Carter, and Baxter, gave their support to McClellan for the Presidency.

The fourth period of serious danger came in 1865, or the early part of 1866, after Johnson became President, and began gradually to withdraw from the Republican party. His steps in this direction were so cautious, and his professions of devotion to the Republican party so profuse, and apparently so sincere, that at first many were misled. He was slow in throwing off the mask in revealing his true purpose. When this at last became so manifest that all men could see it, many Union men who had been inclined to follow him, and who did follow him for a season, turned away and once more became as steadfast as in the days of 1861. A considerable number of loyal men were enticed into his support by flattery, offices, and the hope of reward. But the great body of Union men settled back into the firm support of the principles which they had so patriotically espoused in 1860 and 1861, and for which many of them had gallantly fought. It is a striking fact that not only Mr. Johnson left his friends in 1866, but a majority of the trusted leaders who took part in the contest of 1861—Nelson, Netherland, Trigg, Baxter, Fleming, Carter, and many others, did the same. All the power and patronage of the President were exhausted in trying to secure the following of the patriotic people of East Tennessee, but nothing could blind them or seduce them from their Union faith. During this period the bravest and most conspicuous leader of the Union forces was Mr. Brownlow. When it became necessary again to defend the principles of 1861, he made no compromise with any human being. He quarreled with his old antagonist, Andrew Johnson, and unsparingly denounced him as he had done in 1840 and 1844. For his bravery from 1865 to 1867, during which time the responsibility of leadership rested upon him, the nation can never overhonor him. If he had given way in 1865, and followed the example of the leaders above named, the Union or Republican party of East Tennessee would have been hopelessly divided and destroyed. Mr. Maynard, too, and some of the old leaders of 1861, as well as many new leaders who had sprung up out of the war, deserve honorable mention for their stand for the integrity of the Union party.

It will be observed that Mr. Johnson, while deserving recognition for his efforts in behalf of the Union from December, 1860, to 1865, exerted at two periods all his influence in opposition to it. So also is it true of the other leaders above mentioned, that while they were faithful in 1861, they ceased to be so in

1864. The only prominent leaders of 1861 who remained faithful at all periods were Brownlow, Maynard, Arnold, Milligan and myself. There was never any wavering in the patriotic work of these men. In estimating the comparative *permanent* influence of the different leaders upon the Union cause in East Tennessee, and especially upon the Whigs, the first place is unquestionably due to Mr. Brownlow.

In giving Mr. Brownlow the first place among the Whig leaders in East Tennessee, I do so with a full knowledge of the facts, for I was familiar with all that occurred. Most of these leaders I had known almost from my boyhood. The others I knew thoroughly. I was an active participant in the campaign of 1860. In that which followed the election of Mr. Lincoln, no man was more active than I from its opening to its close. I was therefore in a position to know what each prominent leader did, as well as the value of the services he rendered. The opinion here expressed is based upon actual knowledge of all that took place, from the first public meeting in December, 1860, to the close of the canvass in June, 1861. I also knew the power of all these leaders as speakers, knew their relative influence with the people, and knew the people and the motives which moved and swayed them.

It must be kept in mind that Mr. Brownlow edited the organ of the party; that his paper went into nearly every neighborhood in East Tennessee; that it was read by hundreds, if not by thousands, who were not subscribers. With most of these readers the paper was not only an organ, but an oracle, and they followed its teachings with unquestioned faith. Brownlow's popularity was totally unlike that of the other prominent men. Johnson was strong with his party because of his bitterness, his boldness, and his intellectual strength, but his real friends were not numerous. Nelson was strong by reason of his noble personality—his courage, his ability, and his integrity. But he was a student and never courted applause, nor was he followed by the huzzas of the populace. Maynard was admired for his talents, and like Nelson, for his purity of character. But at that time his personal following was not so great as it became afterward. On the other hand, men were attached to Brownlow by a blind personal devotion, and they followed him with an enthusiastic love, such as the clansmen of Scotland formerly bestowed on their Highland Chiefs. He was the hero of the common people of East Tennessee in 1861, and with them his personal influence far exceeded that of any other man.

Looking back to the canvass of 1861, after the lapse of forty years, it can be seen that the minds of men on both sides were carried away by passion, and were little inclined to listen to reason. They could only see one side, and that in the strongest possible light. Reason was overthrown. I have already pointed out in another work the utter madness of the whole secession scheme—the amazing infatuation and folly of its conception and attempted execution. But strange to say, the Union leaders of East Tennessee, and perhaps elsewhere also, seem to have been carried away with a kind of passion, not so great as that of the secessionists, yet still such as partially blinded them to certain facts forming a large element in the consideration of the questions of the hour. They denounced secession as a crime without a single circumstance to justify it. They overlooked the importance of the repeated violations of the Constitution by Personal Liberty Bills, and the defiance of the Fugitive Slave Law in certain Northern States. In fair discussion of the issue of secession, the consideration of these questions can scarcely be overlooked. Notwithstanding these circumstances a number of reasons can be given why it was most unwise to attempt to dissolve the Union.

Mr. Stephens, in his noted speech at Milledgeville, had discussed this very point. He insisted that the Southern States should not withdraw from the Union, without first making a solemn demand, through a regular Embassy, for the redress of the wrong and the removal of the grievance. He pointed out that this was the course pursued in such cases by independent powers, and that it ought to be adopted in the case of a sister, though sovereign, State, in reference to the violation of the compact of the Union. In substance, this was the answer that Mr. Stephens had given to the demand for immediate secession in Georgia, and it was unanswerable. It was believed at the time that the Northern States could be induced to repeal their laws unfriendly to the institution of slavery. Before the firing on Sumter, Congress had proposed and passed an amendment to the Constitution, which needed only a ratification by a Constitutional majority to render slavery perpetual in the States where it then existed, except by the consent of the people interested in the question. It is therefore insisted that the action of the seceding States was hasty and unwise, in attempting to withdraw from the Union until the last resource of diplomacy had been exhausted. It is evident that diplomacy would have been futile in December. But in February and March, when seven States had seceded and four or five others were likely to do so, a condition had arisen that caused thoughtful people all over the North, as well as in the non-seceding States in the South, solemnly to pause. There was everywhere a demand for a settlement, a compromise, an adjustment by Constitutional provisions and guaranties that would forever settle all vexed questions, and leave the institution of slavery so securely entrenched in the Constitution as to remove all apprehension in reference to its future safety. The great body of the Northern people, in their fright at the appalling prospect of civil war, stood with arms open imploring the people of the seceding States to come back, assuring them of the most ample protection for their slaves. Mr. Lincoln, in his immortal Inaugural Address, in affectionate and pathetic words, entreated the South to stay its hands, declaring, "We are not enemies, but friends." Unless the indications were most delusive, the South could have obtained at that time all the reasonable compensations and guaranties needed. But at this critical hour, when abolition was virtually hushed by the mighty voice of patriotism, evoked by the country's extreme peril, a fatal shot was fired at Sumter, which was heard sounding ominously round the world. As the noise of that shot died away upon the air and upon the sea, all hope of peace died with it.

Secession proved to be from every point of view a sad mistake. If the secession States had waited until they had exhausted every remedy; if the Northern States, after solemn remonstrances had failed to repeal their obnoxious laws; if they had still manifested an unmistakable determination to render nugatory the Fugitive Slave Law, the seceding States would have stood before the world in their fight as the defenders of the Constitution. There would have been much force in the claim that they were fighting to preserve that sacred instrument. Yet in the light of the past, it was an unwise issue to invoke the arbitrament of war. Secession proved to be no remedy for the existing evil, as the Union leaders earnestly insisted it was not. Slavery, the issue of contention, perished in the conflict.

In civil war, such as that of 1861-65, it is most unfortunate for one part of a State to be arrayed against another part, for a minority to be in opposition to a majority. The evil growing out of the division in East Tennessee during the late Civil War can never be estimated. These evils have fallen mainly on the unflinching Union men, and they are likely to continue for generations to come. They were as honest as men could be. What possible motive could they have had for being dishonest in their course? All the prominent leaders, excepting one, were, as their ancestors had been, Southern born. In interest and sympathy, in association and education, they were Southern. All but two were slave owners and friends of the institution of slavery. They had no sympathy with abolition or abolitionists. They believed that secession, whether successful or unsuccessful, would prove a dire calamity to the South. And they were right. The supreme object of the fight—slavery—disappeared while the contest still went on, accompanied by untold evils. These Union leaders today stand vindicated by the result, and by the calm, better judgment of their enemies. The condemnation at the present time of the secession movement by a majority of those engaged in it, ought to be sufficient vindication of those who opposed it.

In giving in the list that follows, the names of the prominent Union leaders in the several counties of East Tennessee no doubt I have omitted many persons worthy of being mentioned. But it must be kept in mind as an act of justice to myself, that, with the exception of Knox and Sevier counties, and Blount to a limited extent, I have had to rely upon citizens of the several counties to furnish me lists of names. So, with the exceptions named, I am not censurable for the omission of names which ought to appear and are worthy of honorable mention. It will be observed that no names are given for Cocke County. The reason is that I have been unable to get anyone to furnish me a list of names, although I have written several letters to prominent men requesting such lists. For the same reason I am able to furnish only a partial list in several counties. It is a source of deep regret that owing to this fact and to my limited space, I am unable to give in detail, or even mention, the services of many Union men deserving recognition. To do so, would swell my book beyond a reasonable size.

NOTABLE MEN OF TENNESSEE 51

JOHNSON COUNTY.—Hon. Roderick R. Butler, A. D. Smith, Rev. Lewis Venable, John H. Vaught, Richard L. Wilson, M. M. Wagner, J. W. M. Grayson, G. H. Shoun, John Murphy, I. E. Northington.

SULLIVAN COUNTY.—Dr. M. W. A. Willoughly, E. A. Millard, Campbell E. Warner, Joshua Hamilton, Hugh Fain, Thomas Fain, John H. Fain, Samuel Pearce, Joel N. Barker, Andrew Gibson, Thomas Buchanan, William Dickson, Andrew Leslie, John Buller, Daniel B. Wegler, William Pearrey, William Mullinix, Rev. Joseph Spurgeon, Eli Anderson, Rev. W. G. Barker, James A. Neal, Dr. Geo. W. Patton, John W. Falls, Samuel Snapp, Samuel Cloud, Dr. R. L. Stanford, James Lynn, G. A. Netherland.

CARTER COUNTY.—Rev. Wm. B. Carter, Nathaniel G. Taylor, Abram Tipton, C. P. Toncry, Colonel J. P. T. Carter, Colonel Daniel L. Stover, Hon. Elijah Simmerly, Jackson Fellers, Colonel John K. Miller, Dan. Ellis, Albert J. Tipton, Samuel W. Williams, Dr. J. M. Cannon, Lafayette Cannon, Dr. A. Jobe, Rev. J. H. Hyder, Samuel A. Cunningham, P. M. Williams, Valentine Bowers, S. P. Angel, S. W. Scott.

WASHINGTON COUNTY.—Judge T. A. R. Nelson, Judge Seth J. W. Lucky, Judge A. J. Brown, Judge S. T. Logan, Judge J. W. Deaderick, Dr. Samuel Cunningham, Dr. Wm. R. Sevier, John A. Wilds, William Dawes, David T. Wilds, S. T. Shipley, Samuel Griffith, Dr. J. D. Gibson, George McPherson, John D. Cox, Henry Hoss, George W. Telford, Dr. W. M. Bovell, E. L. Mathes, Alexander Mathes, Samuel M. Mitchell, W. M. Mitchell, "Addy" Broyles, G. W. Nelson, John T. Baskett, Colonel S. K. N. Patton, M. S. Mahoney, John F. Grisham, Nathan Shipley, John B. Hunt, Hiram Hale, Peter Reeves, Henry Johnson, Samuel H. Miller, Isaac Hartsell, Calvin Hoss, Bird Brown, Edward H. West, M. P. Boring, R. M. Young, William M. McKee, Dr. William Smith, James B. Strain, Payne Squibb, Dr. Richard Humphreys, Ebenezer Barkly, China Marsh.

GREENE COUNTY.—Hon. Andrew Johnson, Thomas D. Arnold, Judge Samuel Milligan, Judge David T. Patterson, R. A. Crawford, Jas. P. McDowel, James Britton, George Jones, Henry B. Baker, M. L. Patterson, Anthony Rankin, Jacob Bible, Chris Bible, Samuel Steel, Leland Davis, Charles Brown, William Brown, William Shields, Samuel Henry, Richard

Susong, Marshal Hartman, Daniel Smith, Samuel Stevens, Abe Johnson, Matt G. Fellers, Bayless Jones, James Jones, Jonathan Easterly, A. W. Walker, William Ruble, John Bible, Billy Bible, George Kinney, Jacob Meyers, Daniel Kelley, Thomas Davis, Barney Cooter, Humphrey Wells, Thomas Johnson, Anthony Moore, James W. Galbraith, David Dobson, Abner Beals, Solomon Good, John Beals, William Ellis, A. M. Piper, William McAmis, T. K. Cox, John McGaughey, William S. McGaughey, Calvin Dobson, Azar Koontz, Neil Hardin, Charles Gass, Jacob Carter, Samuel Keller, William Reed, R. C. Carter, Mordica Harmon, Absalom Gray, Jerry McMillan, Enoch Moore, James Maloney, Abraham Carter, Calvin Smith, Robert Kite, Shady Babb, James G. Reeves, Dr. G. A. Nelson, James F. Nelson, James Lane (pilot and leader of refugees).

HAWKINS COUNTY.—Hon. John Netherland, W. C. Kyle, A. P. Kyle, Hon. Chas. J. McKinney, Hon. William Simpson, A. P. Caldwell, James White, S. D. Brooks, John Blevins, Joseph R. Armstrong, W. W. Willis, Crawford W. Hall, Elias Beal, Radham Chestnutt, H. G. Flagg, Robert Netherland, George W. Huntsman, Judge E. E. Gillenwaters, William Green, Joseph Eckle, James Walker, Hugh Cain, David Kirkpatrick, W. R. Pearson, Harry Vance, William Keener, Richard Morisett.

HANCOCK COUNTY.—Major W. B. Davis, L. W. Jarvis, Henry Tyler.

CLAIBORNE COUNTY.—Vincent Meyers, James J. Bunch, John M. Vanbebber, Wiley Huffaker, E. E. Jones, J. J. Sewell, Houston Sewell, Walter R. Evans, Hugh Farmer, H. H. Kincaid.

GRAINGER COUNTY.—Hon. D. W. C. Senter, Edward L. Tate, Charles C. Smith, James James, C. M. Dyer, George H. Greene, John Brooks, Joel Dyer, Michael McGuire, Harmon G. Lea.

JEFFERSON COUNTY. — Hon. Montgomery Thornburgh, Judge James P. Swann, William Gailbraith, George Hoskins, Samuel P. Johnson, William Harris, George M. Elliott, Samuel J. Newman, M. Looney Peck, Chris C. Carey, Dr. Archibald Blackburn, James Monroe Meek, J. M. Meek, Adam K. Meek, Colonel D. G. Thornburgh, Major Russ Thornburgh.

SEVIER COUNTY. — Dr. R. H. Hodsden, Samuel Pickens, Edmond Hodges, Andrew Lawson, W. C. Pickens, Charles

NOTABLE MEN OF TENNESSEE 53

Inman, Dr. W. H. Trotter, John Trotter, Henry C. Hodges, Wilson Duggan, James M. Murphy, J. C. Murphy, Dr. J. M. Hammer, Wm. Catlett, Dr. James H. Ellis, Daniel Keener, Harvey Keener, William E. Hodges, Rev. James Cummings.

BLOUNT COUNTY.—Rev. Wm. T. Dowell, Rev. John S. Craig, Rev. Thomas J. Lamar, Hon. John F. Henry, John W. H. Tipton, Andrew Kirckpatrick, William J. Hackney, Iredell D. Wright, Captain James Henry, Harold Foster, William McTeer, Montgomery McTeer, Stephen Matthews, Iredel Wright, Spencer Henry, W. L. Dearing, Solomon Farmer, David Goddard, Wm. Goddard, Andrew McBath, Robert Eagleton, W. H. Cunningham, James H. Rowan.

KNOX COUNTY. — William G. Brownlow, John Baxter, Horace Maynard, O. P. Temple, C. F. Trigg, Perez Dickinson, Rev. Dr. Thomas W. Humes, John Williams, John M. Fleming, James H. Cowan, Robert H. Armstrong, Dr. Joseph C. Strong, A. G. Jackson, Judge Samuel R. Rodgers, John J. Craig, E. J. Sanford, James S. Boyd, Samuel Morrow, David Richardson, Thomas Rodgers, Dr. William A. Rodgers, Caleb Baker, David Burnett, Samuel A. Rodgers, Samuel McCammon (Red), Dr. James Rodgers, Jacob Doyle, W. C. Doyle, Samuel Bowman, Peter Derieux, A. C. Callan, Dr. Robert Sneed, W. H. Carter, Andrew Knott, Levi McCloud, Absalom Burnett, James H. Morris, John Tunnell, John Roberts, Thomas Boyd, William Rodgers, James Martin Rodgers, James Sterling, Alexander Reeder, W. H. Swan, James C. Luttell, M. L. Hall, Joseph Parsons, Rufus M. Bennett, Joseph W. Fowler, W. C. Carnes, T. W. Carnes, J. F. Bunker, Calvin Mynatt, Jefferson Harris, ———— Murphy.

ANDERSON COUNTY.—James Ross, John Whitson, John C. Chiles, Wm. Cross, Alfred Cross, Samuel C. Young, Judge D. K. Young, L. C. Houk, D. A. Carpenter, John Leinart, R. H. Coward, W. W. Wallace, James A. Doughty.

UNION COUNTY. — J. W. Baker, John Fuller Huddleston, Francis Huddleston, Christian Ousley, M. V. Nash, Jesse G. Palmer, Emanuel Miller, William Rogers, Kelly Rogers, Isaac C. Dyer, Rice Snodderly, L. R. Carden, William Hawn, R. J. Carr, John C. Baker, John Sharp, Jacob Sharp, Presney Buckner, Isaac Bolinger, Robert Russell, Henry Stiner, Eli Stiner, John E. Sharp, Rev. William Hinkle, B. F. Skaggs, Rev. William Williams, Dr. J. W. Thornburg, J. M. Sawyers,

Isaac Bayless, Dr. S. H. Smith, L. Huddleston, F. P. Hansard, A. McPheters.

CAMPBELL COUNTY.—Hon. F. H. Bratcher, R. D. Wheeler, William Carey, Dr. David Hart, Joshua A. Cooper, Jonathan Lindsay, Reuben Rogers, Dr. John Jones, Alfred Dossett, George McFarland, Elias Bowman, Lew McNew, Miss Sue Carey, Dr. J. H. Agee, George Bowling, J. L. Keeney, Wm. Robbins, Joseph Hatmaker.

SCOTT COUNTY. — Captain John W. Smith, Riley Cecil, James Sanhusky, Joel Parker, Major James S. Duncan, Captain John Newport, Captain Wm. Robbins, "Jack" Brown, James L. Chitwood, Captain Wayne W. Cotton, Captain J. J. Duncan, Captain Dennis Trammels, Bailey Buttram, John Phillips, William Cecil.

MORGAN COUNTY. — Tolliver Staples, Ephraim Langley, James A. Duncan, James M. Melton, John H. Byrd, M. Stephens, John Hall, James Peters, Julian Scott, Samuel C. Hunnycutt.

ROANE COUNTY.—Robert K. Bird (Colonel of 1st Tennessee Regiment), Dr. John W. Wester, Dr. James W. Lee, Samuel L. Childress, Rev. John Y. Smith, Rev. W. P. Lowery, Absalom Adkinson, Samuel Owings, W. J. Owings, Thomas J. Mason, Dr. R. P. Eaton, Mitchell Rose, F. "Cabe" Young, R. W. Boyd, J. T. Shelley, W. M. Alexander, J. W. Bowman, D. F. Harrison, W. S. Patton.

CUMBERLAND COUNTY.—A. C. Yates, F. Kindred.

MONROE COUNTY.—Wm. Heiskell, Daniel Heiskell, Robert Snead, J. F. Owen, D. H. Cleveland, Charles Owen, S. P. Hale, E. A. Taylor, Gilburn Snead, W. H. Dawson, Wm. M. Smith, J. R. Robinson, Samuel M. Johnson.

POLK COUNTY.— W. M. Biggs, J. M. McCleary, Wm. J. Copeland.

McMINN COUNTY.—John McGaughey, Thos. B. McElwee, Charles Cate, Dr. M. R. May, N. J. Peters, A. Hutsell, Judge G. W. Bridges, William G. Horton, Dr. E. Daniel, William Reynolds, Geo. Hutsell, Jacob Gilhut, James Gettys, William M. Sehorn, John H. Slover, David Cleage, Richard M. Fisher, William Burnes, Horace Bryent, Hill Buttram, James Howe, Robert Cochran, E. A. Atlee, Joseph Matthews, Jacob Matthews, M. L. Phillips, Rev. John Wilkins, J. H. Hornsby, Arch Blizzard, Dr. William W. Alexander, Doc Crow, Charles

Bogart, Oliver Dodson, William Dodson, Nathan Kelly, H. Rider, William Bunke, J. H. Magill, the Parkinsons, the Fosters.

BRADLEY COUNTY.—Levi Trewhitt, Dr. William Hunt, Dr. John G. Brown, Allen Master, C. D. Champion, Thos. L. Cate, Stephen Beard, R. M. Edwards, Jesse H. Gaut, John McPherson, A. C. Clingan, P. L. Matthews, D. D. Taylor, John F. Kinchelow, Sidney Wise, J. S. Bradford, A. J. Cate, R. D. Julien, William Pearsley, John Hambright, Ben Hambright, G. R. Hambright, Samuel Parks, James Parks, William Palmer, Montgomery Heebler, John Heebler, James F. Cleveland, Rev. George Julien, Rev. John Julien, Rev. Samuel Julien, Baldwin Cate, Welcome Beard, E. Ramsey, John Blackburn.

MEIGS COUNTY.—T. J. Matthews, Thomas Miller, Andrew Campbell, Thomas Sessell.

RHEA COUNTY.—James W. Gillespie, William Monger, Washington Monger.

MARION COUNTY.—Robert Roulston, David Rankin, G. W. Duane, William Pryor.

HAMILTON COUNTY.—William Clift, A. M. Cate, D. C. Trewhitt, William Crutchfield, A. A. Pearson, John H. James, James R. Hood, E. B. James, Presley T. Lomenic (a noted guide), Hon. Reese B. Brabson, George W. Rider, Jesse M. Ragan, William Crowder, Monroe Masterson, E. H. Cleveland, J. D. Kenner, E. M. Cleveland.

BLEDSOE COUNTY.—General James G. Spears, Hon. Thomas N. Frazier, A. L. Pitts, A. H. McReynolds, Isaac Robertson.

SEQUATCHIE COUNTY.—Washington Heard, Marion Herson.

THOMAS D. ARNOLD.

Born Two Years After Tennessee Became a State—Served Under Jackson—Admitted to Bar, 1822—Defeated for Congress, 1827 and 1829—Elected, 1831, Though Anti-Jackson—Moved to Greeneville—Defeated by Blair, 1835—Elector, 1840—Encounter with Felix Grundy at Greeneville—At Rogersville Next Day—In Congress Again, 1841-43—Second Time, District Changed to Defeat Him—Attitude in 1861—Success in Jury Causes—Peculiarly Emotional Nature.

THOMAS D. ARNOLD stood out by himself with a clear and a distinct individuality. No one altogether like him has lived in the State, and probably ever will. No one could have run the career he ran, and have created the impression upon his generation that he did, without some measure of greatness. He was a native of Virginia, born May 3, 1798—two years after Tennessee became a State—and died May 6, 1870. His father was in humble circumstances, therefore his education was limited. Yet, in after life he had so overcome these disadvantages that his deficiences were scarcely perceptible. When quite a lad he served as a Volunteer soldier in the War of 1812, under General Jackson. Some years later he studied law, and was admitted to the Bar in 1822. Aggressiveness and native ability soon gave him a respectable clientage. His ambition was boundless. In 1827 he became a candidate for Congress against Pryor Lee, a man of ability and worth, but was defeated. Again in 1829 he was a candidate, with the same result. But in 1831 his popularity enabled him to defeat his former competitor, and to secure the coveted prize. In those days parties had not taken on very distinct names. Men were divided into parties by leaders rather than by issues. Arnold was admitted to the bar in 1822. Aggressiveness and native called a Whig. He boldly and defiantly denounced the administration of General Jackson, and made personal war upon him. The overpowering popularity of General Jackson in Tennessee, and this open opposition to him on the part of Arnold, fully accounts for his first two defeats. In 1828 he was an ardent supporter of John Quincy Adams for the Presidency, and in 1832 he again opposed General Jackson, and at that day few public men had the courage to oppose the iron will of the hero of New Orleans. During Arnold's term in Congress, 1831-33, he acquired almost a national notoriety. During this term the Legislature changed his district, attaching Jefferson and Cocke Counties, where his greatest popularity existed, to the first district, then and for a long time previously represented by John Blair. Arnold was too proud spirited to submit to defeat in this manner in his ambitious scheme for Congressional honors. He therefore determined to change his residence to the first district, and to become a candidate against Blair. Accordingly, he moved to Greeneville, and entered the race of 1833 against the able representative who had so long represented that district. The contest was warm and in some respects bitter. But Blair was still too firmly entrenched in the confidence and affections of the people of that district to be overthrown by a comparative stranger and was elected. In 1835 Arnold was again a candidate for Congress, and had for competitors Blair, Wm. B. Carter, and Alexander Anderson. The contest was long and exceedingly animated, not to say bitter, and resulted in Blair's re-election.

After these repeated defeats for Congress, Arnold gave up for the time at least, his political aspirations, and returned to the bar. He soon became one of the leading lawyers of that section, and his practice became large and lucrative. He continued to follow his profession with great energy and industry until the first guns were fired in the notable political contest of 1840. The sound of these shots awakened in Arnold his old political ambition, and like a war-steed he panted for the coming battle. By the unanimous voice of the Whig party of his district, he was chosen Presidential elector on the Harrison ticket. He entered the canvass in February or March with all the enthusiasm of a young man, and laid off his armor only after the victory of the November following. Bravely and efficiently he fought for the success of his ticket, with a zeal unsurpassed by that of any other man. Like an armored knight of old, he was ready to meet any champion, however great, who chose to enter the lists. No Democratic orator came into his district without being forced to encounter that redoubtable Whig. Numberless were the battles he fought, and while he was not always victorious, many were the victories he won.

General Arnold proved in this campaign a hospitable man. He met on the border of his district every Democratic orator who approached, and never left him until he had departed, exchanging with him on the stump such compliments as were then in fashion. With knightly courtesy he welcomed the coming and speeded the parting guest, giving him always a warm reception. I venture to say that no one ever left his district without a vivid recollection of the entertainment he had received. It had been varied, piquant, and highly seasoned.

Among those whom Arnold met in debate was the celebrated Felix Grundy. In 1840 this renowned orator, in returning from his public duties in Washington to his home in Nashville, made a few of his almost matchless speeches in East Tennessee, advocating the re-election of Van Buren. In Greeneville, and at two or three other points, Arnold asked and obtained a division of time. The crowd present at Greeneville was immense, composed almost exclusively of Democrats from adjoining counties. They were the real rampant, shouting type of Democrats, and only a stout-hearted Whig could face such a multitude of defiant stalwarts. But Arnold had no fear, and their shouts did not intimidate him. In order to emphasize the republican simplicity of the Whig party, as illustrated by General Harrison, in contrast with the almost royal pretensions of the Democratic party, so absurdly alleged in that canvass of ridiculous extravagances, Arnold had arrayed himself in a suit of yellow nankeen, with blue, white, yellow, and perhaps red stripes. His appearance was picturesque in the extreme. Grundy was, on the other hand, dressed elegantly and faultlessly—with a flaunting ruffled shirt, the style at that time, with large diamond studs, and wearing a large showy seal ring on his hand. Arnold was thrust forward to speak before Grundy, but after Harvey Watterson, or Hopkins L. Turney, both members of Congress and traveling companions of Grundy. To show the aristocratic habits of the Democratic party, Arnold in his speech, pointed, in a triumphant manner, to the ruffles, the gold ring, and diamond studs of Grundy. Had he been speaking to a Whig crowd on this point, his speech would have been rapturously received. But there were no Whigs present. The royal tendencies of Van Buren, the "gold spoon of fiction," and "Prince John Van Buren's dancing with Queen Victoria," were at that time everywhere proclaimed by Whig orators, and Arnold publicly referred to these. When Grundy came to reply, Arnold was considerably disfigured, and received some severe political wounds. Such wit, such humor, such sarcasm, and such pathos, are seldom heard. Grundy said among other things: "If I were young and handsome as my friend is [ironically], I could wear anything, even the ring-streaked, striped, and speckled suit, like Laban's sheep, in which he is arrayed, and which so admirably suits him, and so well represents the principles of his party. But I am old, my hair is white, my face is furrowed with wrinkles, and it has lost the ruddy bloom of youth so beautifully marked on my friend's face. [Mr. Arnold's face was scarlet.] I am going to my old friends and constituents. I have put on the best I could find as a compliment to them. I wish to show them the highest respect in my power. The best is not equal to their merits. I go to them arrayed in the best possible way, to hide, as far as possible, the hideous ravages of old age." Thus he continued with irony, ridicule, and pathos for half an hour. Before the finish there was not a man in all the vast assemblage but felt that Grundy was paying a most delicate compliment to the proud people of Tennessee by his elegant attire, which Arnold had attempted to ridicule.

In the meantime, Arnold, in his zebra-like suit of yellow nankeen, standing upon the platform, in full view of five or ten thousand people, interjected from time to time, in a loud voice, happy and witty replies. As Grundy, in the most inimitable manner, and with consummate irony, criticised the dress of Arnold, pointing out its resemblance to the diversified principles of the Whig party, the crowd of shouting Democrats sent up a noise that shook the very foundations of the hills around. The sound of ten Niagaras would have been silenced by the shouts of this mighty multitude! But all this did not disturb Arnold. He still continued to "talk back," to interject quick, sharp replies. At length Grundy, turning upon him, said: "General Arnold, you are the noisiest man I ever met. By the old common law, it took two or more disorderly persons to create a riot, but you can create a riot by yourself." But even this did not silence Arnold. A peculiarity of his was that he did not know when he was whipped, and therefore never was whipped. The wounds he received, like those inflicted on the ethereal spirits of Milton, healed as soon as given, and left no pain nor scar.

At Rogersville, next day, Arnold got more than even with Grundy. In his way he triumphed gloriously. Not in the least discouraged by the result of the discussion at Greeneville, he had followed Grundy to Rogersville. The latter was speaking in the court house when Arnold arrived. He had been overtaken by a rain and was muddy and dirty. The thin nankeen suit was wet, and had drawn up and stuck to him as though he had grown in it. Certainly he was a curious sight. Boldly entering the courtroom door, he cried out at the top of his shrill voice: "Here I am again," at the same time demanding a division of time. This was promptly refused. "To the street, to the street!" shouted Arnold to the Whigs. Instantly half the crowd was rushing tumultuously toward the street, yelling and shouting as it went. Quickly Arnold was mounted on a dry-goods box, across the street, opposite the court house where Grundy was speaking. Here he called out for a Whig song. At once a great number of little campaign songbooks were pulled from the pockets of the crowd. Then hundreds of voices, pitched in the highest key, burst forth singing one of the campaign songs of that day, all joining in the chorus. By this time many of Grundy's friends were quitting the court house, attracted by the unearthly noise on the street. The song was followed by three cheers for "old Tippecanoe and Tyler too." Arnold spoke for a while in his vehement, inflammatory manner, then stopping, he called for another refreshing Whig song, and so he went on until Grundy's crowd had nearly disappeared. The latter at length cut short his speech, and hurrying to the hotel, he and his party ordered their carriage, which quickly entering, they started to their next appointment. Arnold was still on his goods box, conducting his varied exercises. Seeing Grundy's carriage approaching, he cried out in an earnest, imploring manner: "Get out of the way, get out of the way there, you common people, or those lordly aristocrats will drive right over you! Get out of the way!" Thereupon a lane was made through the crowd, and the carriage passed on, saluted by another Whig song. Such were the scenes daily witnessed in Tennessee, especially wherever Arnold was present, in the memorable and tumultuous campaign of 1840.*

The prestige won by Arnold, and the faithful work he had done in the canvass of 1840, so endeared him to the great body of his party in his district that, in 1841, he was almost universally looked to as the legitimate candidate for Congress. A feeble effort was made to induce another man to run against him for the nomination and he actually was nominated by a small fraction of the party unfriendly to Arnold. But this man was too sensible, too discreet to accept a nomination with inevitable defeat staring him in the face. Arnold had thus a clear field and was overwhelmingly elected. He served in the Congress of 1841-43 amid the stirring scenes of these memorable years with greater celebrity than he had hitherto attained. It may well be imagined from the aggressiveness and the boldness of Arnold, that his voice was not silent amid the clash and din and uproar of that extraordinary term of Congress, when the dauntless Clay, in the very zenith of his career, was leading the Whig party. Arnold was an ardent admirer and follower of Clay, and, it is said, a warm friendship grew up between them.

Arnold seemed firmly seated in the long-cherished desire of his heart—a seat in Congress. He was popular with the masses, with the voting portion of the Whig party of his district, and but for circumstances beyond his control would

---

*During this canvass Clay visited Nashville to make a speech at the great mass-meeting held there, where it was said forty thousand people were present. S. S. Prentiss was there also. Clay naturally inquired about his old friend and rival, Grundy. He was told that he was making speeches for Van Buren. "Oh, I see," exclaimed Clay; "still following his old profession—defending criminals." Felix Grundy was a most successful criminal lawyer. As he had been Attorney General of the United States under Van Buren, he must have been a good civil lawyer also. Be that as it may, he was unquestionably a very noted orator, possibly the greatest the State has ever had, excepting William T. Haskell. His style of speaking was soft, persuasive and incisive, captivating and irresistible. It was a stream of crystal water, flowing and rippling over a pebbly bottom through green meadows and woodlands, rather than a headlong mountain torrent. A handsome man, of fine person, he possessed every faculty and endowment of the orator. After Hugh Lawson White quarreled with General Jackson, Grundy became the President's defender and his right arm in the Senate. Such gentle, delightful oratory I have never heard. Felix Grundy is one of the men of whom the people of Tennessee are justly proud.

doubtless have had a succession of terms in the House. Other men, however, not of the Whig party, were as anxious as Arnold for Congressional honors. Both Andrew Johnson and Landon C. Haynes had for some time been casting longing eyes in the direction of Washington, and it happened that the former was a member of the Legislature of 1841-42, which re-districted the State. Johnson was artful enough to have carved out for himself a Democratic district, such as suited him, and to cut off from it the County of Jefferson, in which, as before stated, Arnold had his greatest popularity, and to add to it Sullivan and other Democratic counties. Thus, by two Legislatures, Arnold's district had been changed in order to defeat him. He was for the second time, in the midst of greatest popularity, driven to private life by hostile legislation. With decided Whig principles and the avowal of them, there was no earthly chance of his election to Congress for the next ten years in that district, so he returned to the practice of his profession, which he assiduously and successfully followed, with brief intervals, until his death. Once during this time, perhaps in 1855, he was a candidate for the State Senate, and was defeated, but by what majority and for what cause it is immaterial to state.

When secession presented itself in this State in 1861, with all its fury and bitterness, Arnold stood like a bulwark for the preservation of the old Government, endeared to him by services as a soldier in the War of 1812. No man in all the land was more earnest or more unflinching, and few brought to bear in its defense stronger or more persuasive arguments. Everywhere, when occasion permitted, his voice was heard in no uncertain tones, in favor of the Union. His splendid speech in the Knoxville Convention, in May, 1861, of which an account is given in another book, was perhaps the most masterly effort of his life. It was indeed a great speech. Thomas D. Arnold justly deserves mention among the noted union leaders of East Tennessee.

After the close of the War Mr. Arnold continued the practice of his profession with unabated zeal, until his sudden death while attending Court at Jonesboro, in 1870, in the seventy-second year of his age. At this advanced age he seemed to have lost none of the vigor nor force of mind which had characterized him in the days of his early robust manhood. He was still alert, bright, athletic, aggressive. He possessed by nature a wonderful constitution.

Thomas D. Arnold was neither a learned nor an exact lawyer. He knew imperfectly a good deal of law, but this knowledge was fragmentary and detached. He did not know the law as a science nor as a whole, but was an able and successful advocate, in this respect few men in Tennessee being his superior. For twenty years he constantly came in contact with such lawyers as the McKinneys, Nelson, and Netherland, and victory fell sometimes to one, sometimes to another. He was on one side of nearly every important jury case in the courts where he practiced, and no lawyer, however able, expected to gain an easy success over him. Arnold's knowledge of human nature, of the motives, feelings, and instincts of men, was nearly equal to that of John Netherland, and he could play upon these and move men through them with nearly the same success. Wit, admirable raillery, and a remarkable power of ridicule were combined in him with sarcasm of the keenest character. In important cases he rarely failed to draw tears from the jury. In contests, he was capable of pathetic and eloquent appeals. He was tender-hearted, and could weep like a child over the wrongs of his client. By ridicule on the one hand, and impassioned appeals on the other, he constantly excited laughter or tears, while his power of invective was simply terrible. His tongue was as keen as a razor, and his sharp sayings were rained with resistless force, like the discharges of a Gatling gun, upon opposing litigants and witnesses. He had the faculty of seizing upon trivial circumstances, dwelling and harping upon them in his irresistible manner, until he caused the jury to overlook the vital points in controversy. He often thus wrested verdicts from the opposing council when both the law and the facts were against him. A fighter from the start to the close of a case, he never yielded, never gave up, never gave quarter. In every case it was a life-and-death struggle. So when he came in contact with the best lawyers, they expected a contest. He had the courage to say what he thought, regardless of consequences, and he thought of new and unheard-of things. His mind was prolific in new ideas and in new images. Arnold was often eloquent, and in all cases he was forcible and strong. The truth is, nature came well-nigh making him a genius. As it was, it made of him a most successful and dangerous advocate.

When Brownlow's *Whig* was suspended, in October, 1861, and the voice of that brave man was no longer heard through his paper, the Union leaders who still remained in Tennessee became silent. The arrests and imprisonments that were daily taking place warned them that prudence was absolutely necessary for their safety. Arnold, however, formed an exception to this rule. He continued to proclaim his Union sentiments as freely and as independently as before the June election. Although danger encompassed him on every hand, he seemed unconscious of it. In every crowd he praised the old Government and denounced in no halfway terms the Southern Confederacy. It mattered not that Confederate soldiers might be present; they had no terrors for him, and could not silence him. He was impassioned and defiant in his speech. On one occasion, going from Knoxville to his home in Greeneville, on a train filled with Confederate soldiers and officers, he proclaimed his Union sentiments in a vehement manner. Perhaps any other man in the State of Tennessee would have been arrested under the circumstances. His courage and his honesty, however, commanded respect and secured immunity for him. There was something about that lion-hearted old man in his moments of enthusiastic patriotism that was awe-inspiring, even to armed men. His brave and defiant advocacy of the Union from 1861 to 1865, during the terrors of the great Civil War, and amid the persecutions in East Tennessee, was indeed heroic, almost sublime. Alone of his family, excepting one youthful son, he stood for the Union, with a warmth and devotion almost unexampled. Two of his sons were in the Confederate Army, one as a Lieutenant Colonel and the other as a Captain, and yet in his isolation he looked as if he were backed by an army. Undoubtedly his age and distinguished career served to protect him. But more than these, his honesty and dauntless courage constituted his chief shield. No other man could have acted as he did.

When we come to a discussion of General Arnold's personal qualities—and in all cases these make the real man—we are embarrassed, not for want of material, but from the difficulty of so presenting the apparently contradictory facts as to bring into plain view his real character. Anomalous and many sided, he seemed to a casual observer full of contradictions. Yet, if we can find the key to his character, all these can be reconciled and brought into harmony. Ambitious, courageous, impulsive, and belligerent, he was yet kind and tender-hearted. He loved the right and hated wrong. He had at all times a tear for suffering and a sigh for sorrow. He hated deception and hypocrisy and loved candor and manliness. Imagine these qualities united in one person in their utmost intensity, and we have Thomas D. Arnold. They made him, as I have stated, an anomaly, full of tears and sympathy at one moment, a raging storm, or perhaps more appropriately, a furious lion, at another. He could weep at suffering as a woman. An outrage or a wrong threw him into a furious passion. He was bitter toward his enemies, warm and effusive toward his friends. In one moment the most demonstrative friend; the next in a delirium of rage. His forgiveness was as quick as his passion, and his sympathy as broad and universal as human suffering. He could be as gentle as a child, and as terrible as an evil spirit. Arnold was not a bad-hearted man. In passion, and in enthusiasm, he often went to extremes, but these were the result of his boundless and irrepressible emotions. In all he said and did, in all his paroxysms of joy or bitterness, he was honest at heart.

JUDGE JOHN BAXTER.

Rose Rapidly in Profession in North Carolina—Clay Elector in 1844—In Legislature, Speaker of Lower House — Removed to Knoxville, 1857—Rank and Characteristics as a Lawyer—Believed Union Could be Preserved—Bitter Speeches—Favored Moderate Measures at Greeneville Convention—Followed Nelson to Richmond—Influence of Zebulon Vance—Defeated for Confederate Congress by William G. Swan—Co-operates with Secessionists—Arrested at Memphis—Drifts Back Into Union Ranks—1864, Joins McClellan Movement—Attacks Brownlow—1870, Elected to Constitutional Convention—1872, Call to Organize New Political Party—Supports Hayes, 1876—Appointed U. S. Circuit Judge—Summary.

AMONG the Union leaders in East Tennessee in 1861 John Baxter deserves conspicuous mention. He was born in Rutherford County, North Carolina, in 1819, of Irish (probably Scotch-Irish) parents. The education he acquired, which was very limited, he obtained in that county. After following for a time a calling that was not congenial to his tastes, he abandoned it, and began the study of law. At that time it was difficult to obtain a license to practice law in North Carolina, especially in the higher courts, and the standard was high and the examinations rigid. But Baxter passed the ordeal in triumph and while still a very young man was admitted to the bar. He rose rapidly in his profession, and quickly reached the front rank of lawyers in Western North Carolina, a region abounding in able men.

Mr. Baxter was a Whig in politics, and early in life began to take part in political discussions. In 1844 he was presidential elector on the Clay ticket for his district. This was a remarkable compliment to a man only twenty-five years of age. He was subsequently elected two or three times a member of the Legislature, and finally made speaker of the lower House. By this time he was favorably known all over the State, and had much influence with the public men. At the bar he had risen to the very head of his profession in the wide region of his practice.

Notwithstanding Mr. Baxter's success, professionally and politically, and the extensive circle of friends he had won, he was ambitious for a wider field of endeavor than Western North Carolina afforded. Knoxville, Tenn., was at that time justly regarded as a promising town and offered larger opportunities than Western North Carolina for a man of ambition. Accordingly, in the early spring of 1857 Mr. Baxter opened a correspondence with me in reference to locating here. Shortly after, in the month of May, he arrived with his family and servants, having purchased a home before coming. He sought and formed no partnership with anyone, but relied on his own ability to secure professional business. He was then, in point of property, almost independent.

I remember well his first appearance in the argument of a cause. It was in a complicated action of ejectment. His argument before the court and jury was so clear and strong that it marked him at once as one of the leaders of the Knoxville bar, then one of the strongest in the State. From that time forward his success was unbroken. Each year, until he was made United States Circuit Judge by President Hayes for the Sixth Circuit, composed of the States of Tennessee, Kentucky, Ohio, and Michigan, his success was all that his ambition, high as it was, could have desired. He was confessedly the head of the bar in East Tennessee, and I believe he had no equal in the State. His income from his profession after the war was larger annually, perhaps, than any lawyer had ever received in the State. So highly were his services esteemed by litigants that he had only to name his fee.

In his profession Mr. Baxter was a hard-working man, and yet he worked so rapidly, his mind gathered the facts of a case and saw the controlling points so quickly, that he had much time for the society of friends. He dashed off his most elaborate briefs with the ease and speed of familiar letter-writing. Minor points he passed over without notice and went at once to the core of the question, which he fortified and strengthened by authorities and by massive and impregnable arguments. If he had no authorities, if the question was new, he brought all his powerful intellect to show what the law should be declared to be. He attached no sacred reverence to precedents and decisions. If they seemed to be founded on reason and common sense, and to be promotive of justice, he accepted them as law; if not, he denounced them as not law. If a new question was presented for his opinion, he would say what the law should be, and what it was. If the authorities did not sustain his views, he would with the utmost confidence attack them as erroneous. This was not done in a reckless spirit of bravado and opposition, but in the calm confidence of a powerful mind that rested its conclusions on the highest reason.

That Mr. Baxter was a great lawyer, one of the greatest of his day, admits of no doubt. His intellect was massive as well as astute and logical. To compare him with others would be difficult, perhaps invidious, for he was unlike others. There was in him no eloquence, no learning, no adornment of style. He was like a solid block of unpolished granite. Thomas C. Lyon, in his prime, had the reputation, and justly, too, of being one of the ablest lawyers in the State. His arguments on great occasions were lucid, profound, powerful, and clothed in classical, elegant language. But he had nearly run his course, by reason of ill health, before Mr. Baxter came to Tennessee. I doubt whether he was the equal of Mr. Baxter in breadth and comprehensiveness of intellect, though greatly his superior in all kinds of learning. I was too young to compare Mr. Baxter with the two McKinneys, who were in their day masters in their profession. The former distinguished Chancellor, Thomas L. Williams, who had known all the great lawyers of Tennessee for a generation back, such as W. E. Anderson, John A. McKinney, Spencer Jarnagan, Robert J. McKinney, William H. Sneed, Thomas C. Lyon, and others, said to me in 1852 that Judge Hugh Lawson White was decidedly the best lawyer he had ever known in the State. Never having known Judge White except by reputation, I cannot compare Mr. Baxter with him.

As before stated, Mr. Baxter was uneducated. His language and pronunciation were faulty. Brownlow and L. C. Houk overcame this early defect. Baxter and Johnson never did. The truth is, that while Baxter was a hard-working man, he had no taste for general reading.

After Mr. Baxter came to Tennessee he took no active part in political affairs until the threatening aspect of the secession movement aroused him in November, 1860. He was a Whig, a Southern man, and a slave-holder. His personal sympathies were naturally with his brethren of the South. He believed at that time that the Union could be preserved by wise, conservative councils, and by the united action of all good men in the South. Accordingly, in the public meeting held in Knoxville in the latter part of November, 1860, and in the one held later in December, in which both parties took part (of which a full account is given in another book), he proposed and advocated a Conference or a Convention of Delegates from all the Southern States for the purpose of devising some plan of securing the rights of the people of the South, and thus saving the Union. He advocated the same policy in Brownlow's *Whig*. He was unquestionably a Union man. But as his proposition was advocated by the known friends of secession, both in Nashville and Knoxville, and as the Union men in these meetings believed that such a course would strengthen secession and not the Union, they opposed his proposition, and in the end voted it down by an overwhelming majority.

There never was any doubt as to the honesty of Mr. Baxter in his course in these two important meetings, but in the first skirmishes of the great civil conflict, when the ideas of men first began to crystallize into definite forms, he came well-nigh giving a fatal direction to those opinions. Fortunately there were other men present to point out the danger.

In the following January Mr. Baxter was thoroughly alive to the danger which threatened the integrity of the Union. When the Legislature, which was convened by Governor Harris, proposed the call of a convention to pass on the question of the secession of the State, and directed the election of delegates to said convention, Mr. Baxter was unanimously selected by a Union mass-meeting as the candidate for Knox county. He at once, in co-operation with the other candidates, took the stump for the Union. In common with the Union leaders throughout the State, he opposed the proposed Convention, and advised the people to vote it down. This was somewhat in conflict perhaps with his previous position. His speeches were able, argumentative, and extremely bitter. I doubt if any man in the State, not even Andrew Johnson, was so bitter in denunciation of secession and its leaders. He was bold in his speeches to the very verge of audacity.

Mr. Baxter was in no sense, except in wonderful ability, a great speaker. He had a poor voice. He had no fancy; he had no eloquence, except the faculty of grouping facts in a masterly manner, and turning upon them the headlight of his great intellect. And yet he never spoke on a great occasion without producing a profound sensation. If he was deficient in rhetoric, in the power to please the fancy, he possessed in a remarkable degree the mind to convince and move men. In the Spring canvass of 1861, following that of February, Mr. Baxter took an active part in opposition to the separation of the State. Like his former efforts, his speeches were daring and bitter and powerful in the presentation of facts. His influence in molding public opinion in East Tennessee, in both these canvasses, was unquestionably very great. He possessed one quality in as high a degree as any man in the State, a quality of greater value at the time than even splendid ability—absolute fearlessness. In this respect he was the equal of Thomas A. R. Nelson—the very type and model of courage.

While Mr. Baxter had made many threats of continued resistance to secession, in the event the State should vote for separation, yet, when the fact happened, his strong practical sense soon convinced him of the folly, indeed the madness of such a course. Accordingly, in the Greeneville Convention, which reconvened twelve days after the June election, he gave the weight of his influence and his voice in favor of the moderate measures proposed in that body, in opposition to the violent and extreme resolutions presented by Mr. Nelson, which were at first approved by three-fourths of the Convention. Mr. Baxter did his full share in securing the adoption of these peaceful measures, and in thus averting civil war in East Tennessee. He deserves credit for this course, but not more than others. He was not the author of the pacific measures that were finally adopted.

Mr. Baxter was unquestionably one of the great Union leaders of East Tennessee. After Johnson, Brownlow, and Nelson, he deserves as much credit as anyone for making East Tennessee so unflinchingly loyal to the old government, and is certainly entitled to more credit than many of the leaders.

When Mr. Nelson was arrested in August, 1861, on his way North as a member of Congress, and was carried to Richmond, Baxter at once followed him there in order that he might render him assistance. There was no sacrifice Baxter would not make in those days for a friend. While in Richmond he came in contact with Governor Zebulon Vance, and other old friends from North Carolina, and to a certain extent doubtless imbibed their opinions. Vance persuaded him that the true policy of the Union men in such States as Tennessee and North Carolina was to do as he had done—to join the secession movement, to get control of things, and thus check and prevent excesses. Mr. Baxter came home with the idea in his head. But he soon discovered how inapplicable this policy was to the Union people of East Tennessee. They had taken their stand and nothing could move them.

Soon after Mr. Baxter's return he called at my office, and, explaining his views, urged me to become a candidate in the approaching election for the Confederate Congress. This I promptly and decidedly declined to do. He said in reply: "Then, if you will not run, I shall." I answered that neither he nor I, with our opinions, had any business in the Confederate Congress, and that I could not even vote for him, friend as he was, because I could not take part in that election. The result was, he became a candidate, and was badly beaten by William G. Swan, an original secessionist. The Union men would not vote for Mr. Baxter, because they would do nothing that would seem to sanction the validity of the Confederacy; so they kept away from the polls. On the other hand, the secessionists preferred one who had been with them from the beginning.

I am not aware of a single Union man who changed his position on account of Mr. Baxter's abandonment of his old opinions. I have elsewhere said that if every Union leader at that time had deserted his standard and his party, the great majority of Union men would have remained unflinchingly true to the national cause. When the questions involved were new, as in the latter part of 1860 and the early part of 1861, the mass of the people might have been led astray by the example and the teachings of their trusted leaders; but that time had gone by. They had made up their own minds, and no influence could change them. I wish to repeat with renewed emphasis that these Union men were the descendants of the brave Scotch Covenanters, who brought the torch of civilization into this wilderness—a people who never yielded and never surrendered a conviction.

From this time until the spring of 1862 Mr. Baxter co-operated with the secessionists, and was regarded as one of them, though he sometimes criticised their conduct most severely. After the attempt to burn the Strawberry Plains Bridge, in November, 1861, and the successful accomplishment of the burning of five others, when it was reported that the Union men of Sevier County were moving on Strawberry Plains in large numbers in a hostile manner, Baxter took his gun and went with Confederate troops to that point to resist the Union force. The report proved to be a gross exaggeration, as were nearly all the reported gatherings of Union men in a hostile attitude at that time. So, Baxter and his associates came back free from the stain of blood.

In February, 1862, Mr. Baxter started a newspaper of his own in Knoxville called the *East Tennesseean*. The first number made its appearance on the 27th of that month. In an editorial, stating his reasons for issuing a paper, Mr. Baxter said one was "to harmonize the discordant elements among us, and reconcile the disaffected to the Government of the Confederate States." There is no ambiguity in that statement. From some cause, I know not what, only one number of that paper was ever issued.

Some time in the spring of 1862 Mr. Baxter went to Memphis on his own private business, and while there he was arrested as an enemy of the South, and held as a prisoner for some days. He was finally released and permitted to come home. On his return he charged that Governor Harris had had him arrested. After this he quickly drifted back into the Union ranks, and remained there until some time in the early part of 1864. The emancipation policy of Mr. Lincoln, and other acts of his administration displeased Mr. Baxter and other former Union leaders, and they were quick to denounce these measures. They joined in the McClellan movement, to supplant Lincoln as President, and to stop the war. From that time forward, until some time in the 'seventies, Mr. Baxter cooperated with the Democratic party in opposition to the Republican party. He made fierce and bitter warfare on Governor Brownlow, and on his administration of the affairs of the State. He finally went so far as to draw a broadside from the powerful battery of his puissant antagonist, which came well-nigh annihilating him.

In 1870 Baxter was elected a member of the Constitutional Convention of Tennessee, and received the honor of being made Chairman of the Judiciary Committee. This appointment shows conclusively where he stood politically, at that time, for this was as genuine a representative Democratic body as ever assembled in the State. Indeed, Baxter owed his election to the fact that no prominent Republican in his county wished to be in that Convention, so the few who voted in the election voted for him, there being no other candidate fit for the position.

In 1872 Mr. Baxter seems to have become dissatisfied with his party affiliations, for in that year a call appeared in some of the newspapers, signed by T. A. R. Nelson, himself, and a few others, calling for a Convention to assemble on a specified day in Cincinnati, for the purpose of organizing a new political party. Whether this Convention ever assembled, or what it did, is a matter of no general interest, and is therefore passed over.

Some time between 1872 and 1875 Mr. Baxter ceased his wanderings, and came back to his old party, where he remained with more or less steadiness until his death. He supported Mr. Hayes for the Presidency in 1876. That he was sincere in these various changes scarcely admits of a doubt, but they certainly show a mental agility that is somewhat remarkable.

The career of Mr. Baxter in the exalted position of a Judge of the United States Circuit Court has been the theme of both high praise and of severe criticism. As I never appeared professionally before him, and saw but little of him in his capacity of a judge, I leave it to those who were familiar with his mode of administering the law to determine how much of praise or of censure he deserves. Two things will probably be conceded by all, namely, his honesty of purpose and his judicial ability. Prejudice on the part of a judge, however, may sometimes be as fatal as dishonesty would be. One thing was clear to all, that Mr. Baxter on the bench was no mere neutral character. He was a positive force. The tremendous power of his will and intellect was felt in all he said and in all he did.

Riding together one day, in 1859 or 1860, the question arose between Mr. Baxter and myself in regard to the size of fortune that would satisfy each of us. I named a very moderate sum as sufficient for myself. Mr. Baxter laughed, and said it would take ten times that sum to satisfy him. Now, this was not sordidness on his part, but ambition. He was a very prince of generosity in his days of prosperity. He was ambitious for money because it would give him power and influence. Time wore on, and I more than doubled the sum I had named, and when

I reached that point, I retired with a competence, ceasing to strive actively for more. Within a few years after this conversation, Mr. Baxter had acquired one-fifth the sum named. This, with his large income from his profession, and afterward from his salary as a Judge, was sufficient to have made him independent for life, and to have enabled him to leave a fair fortune to his children. But, inflamed with the desire for great wealth, he embarked in visionary speculations, losing heavily.

Judge Baxter was a striking man personally. He was about five feet eleven inches, with powerful body. He weighed two hundred pounds or more. His head was enormous in size. It was admirably proportioned, and his body corresponded with it in the appearance of strength. The head and body were rugged, rather than graceful. His eyes, large and bright, were of a beautiful hazel color. With an expression of kindness they were charming. His face was altogether an attractive one, especially when irradiated with a smile. In the days of his prosperity, Judge Baxter was a delightful companion and a fine conversationalist. He was always the central figure in every crowd. His mind was essentially honest and independent. It sought the light. It had no sympathy with darkness nor devious ways. While Judge Baxter had many faults, he exhibited many virtues and many noble qualities. Certainly he was one of the striking men of his generation. Of the array of remarkably strong men among the Union leaders in East Tennessee, in 1861, it is by no means certain that he was not the very strongest and the most intellectual. He was a notable man among notable men.

REESE B. BRABSON.

Member of Congress—Lawyer—Whig Elector—Vehement Speaker—Spotless Integrity.

IN the Whig delegation in Congress from East Tennessee, in 1859 and 1860, as a colleague of Thomas A. R. Nelson and Horace Maynard, was Reese B. Brabson, from the Third, or Chattanooga, District. He was a native of Sevier County, where he was reared. After finishing his education, he entered the profession of law. He married the accomplished daughter of Judge Charles F. Keith, a prominent jurist of his day, and moved to Chattanooga. Here he followed his profession with success. In 1848 he was honored by his Whig friends by being selected as the Whig elector on the Taylor presidential ticket. He made a canvass of the district with Samuel A. Smith, the Democratic elector, then regarded as one of the most promising young Democrats in the State. Smith afterward achieved considerable success, and made some reputation, as a member of Congress for several terms from the Chattanooga District. On the stump Brabson sustained the Whig cause, and upheld its banner to the satisfaction of his party friends. He was an impulsive and vehement speaker, and pleased the people.

In 1851 Mr. Brabson was elected to the lower house of the Legislature from Hamilton County, and served his constituents faithfully, fearlessly, and with ability. In 1859 he was selected as the Whig candidate for Congress against Samuel A. Smith, the Democratic candidate, and was elected in a district almost invariably giving a majority on the other side.

In the canvass of 1860 he was a warm advocate of John Bell for the Presidency, canvassing his own district for him. In the Congress of 1859-60 he was an ardent supporter of the Union, and never faltered in his course. During this Congress he made an earnest appeal in behalf of the Union. In the dark days of 1861, when so many trusted leaders fell out of the Union ranks, he never wavered nor turned back. He made speeches for the Union, and exerted all his influence for its preservation. As he was at that time, or recently had been, a member of Congress, and a man of spotless integrity, his influence was considerable.

Mr. Brabson's father was a man of wealth, as was also his father-in-law, and from the estates of the two he started life in comfortable circumstances. From his ambition, energy, and popular manners, his career might have become more distinguished than it was, had he not died when he had scarcely reached the full maturity of his power. His death occurred in 1863, in the middle of the Civil War, when he was about forty-six years of age. He was of a warm, genial nature; frank, brave, manly and honest; hence had the faculty of drawing men to him by love as well as by admiration. He was also public spirited, and did much toward laying the foundation of the growth of the flourishing city of Chattanooga.

R. R. BUTLER.

Member of Legislature Eleven Terms — Lieutenant-Colonel — Circuit Judge—Member of Congress Five Terms.

R. R. BUTLER of Johnson County was a comparatively young man during the stormy days of 1861, yet he exerted a decided influence in his county, and possibly beyond it, in behalf of the preservation of the Union. Having been elected to the Legislature in 1859, he was a member of that body when the question of the secession of the State came before it in May, 1861. With unshrinking firmness, he cast his vote against that unwise measure. Both before and after that time he was a brave, outspoken Union man, making speeches in its favor. So outspoken was he, and so powerful his influence among his own people, that he was arrested three times by the Confederates on the charge of treason.

In the latter part of 1863 he became Lieutenant-Colonel in one of the Tennessee Regiments. In 1865, when the Courts of the State were re-established, he was appointed Circuit Judge of the First Judicial Circuit, which position he held for about two years. In 1867 he left the bench in order to become a candidate for Congress, and was easily elected. At different times he has served in Congress, 1867-73, again in 1886. When not in Congress, he has been a member of the Legislature serving six terms in the lower house and five terms in the Senate. It is doubtful whether any other man in the United States can show such a record of Legislative honors. So hopeless of defeating him has it become that no man of his own party will oppose him. He signifies a willingness to serve his constituents, and that is sufficient to secure his nomination and election. He seems to have a life tenure of the office, for no doubt he will be nominated again when his term expires. Besides all this, he served one term on the bench after first retiring from Congress, 1875 or 1876.

It is not surprising that Judge Butler is thus constantly returned to the Legislature, for he is an able and faithful member. Though a bold and outspoken Republican, he is popular with both parties, and can always secure the passage of all measures affecting his constituents. Perhaps no member of that body is so blunt and candid in criticism of the Democratic party, yet all like him personally. He is the Nestor of the Legislature. A strong, clear, vigorous speaker, his information on all political questions is wide and extensive. It is no surprise to those who know Judge Butler that he has acquired and still retains such a tenacious hold on the people of his mountain District, for besides being a man of ability and a very strong speaker, in addition he is simple, affable, approachable, and exceedingly kindly in manner and disposition; yet under all circumstances he is dignified. In person, he is tall and commanding. When not engaged in legislative duties, he still follows the practice of law. But he is much better known as a politician than as a lawyer.

All in all the career of Judge Butler has in it something entirely unique.*

---

*Judge Butler died in the latter part of 1902.

ROBERT K. BYRD.

Bold Leader—Slaveholder—Born in Roane County—Farmer—Entered Into Agreement at Greeneville Convention to Raise Troops—The First Tennessee, Colonel Byrd.

THE boldest, most active, and the leading Union man in Roane County was Robert K. Byrd. He was not a speaker, though he did sometimes speak, but he was a busy and an earnest talker. Positive and confident in his opinions, he encouraged the timid and gave firmness to the vacillating. His boldness and positiveness were a tower of strength in dealing with men in times of danger and alarm. During all the stormy days from December, 1860, till June, 1861—the period of doubt, of fear, of revolution—his clear voice was heard in denunciation of the parricidal crime of secession. A slaveholder himself, the taunting epithets, "Abolitionist," and "Lincolnite," so commonly applied to Union men, had no terror for him. He went bravely and defiantly along the broad way of duty.

Mr. Byrd was born in Roane County, and was a farmer by occupation. In 1861 he was a member of the Knoxville-Greeneville Convention. In the convention he entered into an agreement with Joseph A. Cooper, R. M. Edwards, E. Langley, and Samuel Honeycutt to go home and commence raising and drilling troops in their respective counties. In Roane County, two companies of "Home Guards" were raised, but whether or not by the direct action of Mr. Byrd I am unable to say. On the 9th of August, the State having previously voted in favor of separation and secession, he left home secretly, and by stealth made his way through the mountains to Kentucky, becoming an exile and a wanderer for the sake of his country. On his arrival in this land of refuge, he began enlisting men for the Federal Army among the refugees from East Tennessee, thousands of whom were then as if by common impulse pouring into Kentucky. Roane County, following his example, sent him hundreds, yea, a thousand or more, among them, August 11th, the brave Major H. Crumless, the friend of Byrd. In a month the *First* Tennessee Infantry, of which Mr. Byrd was made

Colonel, was organized, he being the *first* Colonel of the thirty-one regiments which Tennessee furnished to the cause of the Union. Glorious title and distinction! And every one of that regiment had to go to a sister State for the privilege of enlisting.

On his many battlefields—at Wildcat, at Mill Spring, in the capture of Cumberland Gap, at Stone River, in a fight with Wheeler at Kingston, in all the battles under Sherman in the immortal Georgia Campaign, and in many smaller engagements, often commanding brigades, bravely did Colonel Byrd sustain the high honor he had received, and the distinction won by the regiment of being the *First* Tennessee. In August, 1864, he left the army, after three years of continuous service in the field, without a stain upon his splendid record as a brave officer, or a spot upon his reputation as an honorable gentleman and a gallant soldier. He was always ready for a fight, and when engaged in one bore himself with the coolness and courage of one born to command.

Colonel Byrd married the daughter of Dr. James W. Lee. Mrs. Byrd was a woman of heroic spirit—worthy to be the wife of such a man. No one could look into her piercing eyes without recognizing that there was within her fragile form an unconquerable will and a dauntless spirit. She was so pronounced in the advocacy of the Union, and so daring that in May, 1862, she was arrested by the Confederates as a dangerous enemy. By cunning and boldness she eluded her guards and made her way through the mountains into Kentucky, though they were guarded at every pass and everywhere patrolled by Confederate cavalry.

Colonel Byrd departed this life in 1885, deeply lamented by his friends. He was a large, powerful man, of military air and bearing. To this commanding appearance may be attributed in part his influence over men. Added to this he had great boldness and fearlessness. In him was combined every quality for leadership. His was a life of honor, three years of full maturity having been given to the defense of his country.

DANIEL A. CARPENTER.

Born in Kentucky—One of First Volunteer Soldiers—After Number of Engagements, Destroyed Mill at Cumberland Gap—Captured near Rogersville, Taken to Libby Prison and Charleston—Sheriff of Anderson County—Mayor of Knoxville—Pension Agent—Receiver Southern Building and Loan Association—Natural Leader.

ONE of the influential Union leaders of East Tennessee in 1861 was Daniel A. Carpenter. Born in Rockcastle County, Kentucky, in 1837, he removed to Tennessee, 1857. He settled in Anderson County and went into the retail dry goods and grocery business in Clinton. When the troubles of 1861 came on he was an ardent Union man. In July of that year a notable meeting was held in Clinton at which Joseph A. Cooper, Carpenter, and a few other Union men resolved to go to Kentucky and enlist in the Union Army. They pledged one another that whatever might be the course of others, they would give their services to their country. Mr. Carpenter was sent to Kentucky to obtain information, and in a few days returned, having succeeded in obtaining the information desired. Early in August he again went to Kentucky, immediately joining the army. He was one of the earliest refugees from the State, and one of its first volunteer soldiers. He was made 1st Lieutenant in Co. C, 2d Tennessee Infantry, commanded by Joseph A. Cooper.

A year later the regiment was mounted, and Mr. Carpenter was made Adjutant, and in 1862 was promoted to be Major. Most of his service was in Kentucky, Tennessee, Virginia, and West Virginia. He was at the battle of Wild Cat, Kentucky, in 1861; in the battle of Fishing Creek, Kentucky, in the winter of 1861 and 1862; took part in the battle of Stone River in 1862; returned to Kentucky, pursuing General Morgan on his famous raid through Indiana and Ohio; accompanied General Burnside on his march to East Tennessee in 1863; had charge of the advance guard from Williamsburg, Ky., to Lenoirs, on the Southern Railway; from Lenoirs to Loudon he skirmished with the enemy and saw the bridge which crossed the Tennessee

River burned; returned to Knoxville, having charge of the advance guard from Knoxville to Cumberland Gap.

At this time about four thousand Confederates were in possession of Cumberland Gap or the fortifications at that place. General Burnside's command embraced both sides of the Gap, and completely inclosed the enemy. The question was how to procure a surrender without storming the strong fortifications, or the delay of a siege. General Shackelford was in command of the Union forces on both sides of the mountain, General Burnside not yet having come up. Major Carpenter was sent into the Gap with a flag of truce to demand a surrender, and he got far enough to discover that the fortifications were about as they had been left by General George W. Morgan when he retreated from them a few months previous. He further learned from the Confederates that they were short of rations, and that all the corn and wheat they had for bread was stored in a mill situated within the fortifications and rifle pits. These facts Carpenter reported to General Shackelford, giving it as his opinion that a small force could enter the Gap at night, fire the mill, and thus destroy the supplies of the enemy. But in a council of the colonels, commanding the several regiments, with General Shackelford, this plan was rejected.

Afterward Major Carpenter proposed to General Shackelford to volunteer to go inside the fortifications and destroy the mill. This proposition was accepted, the General agreeing to detail, at the request of Carpenter, seventy-five men from the 2d Tennessee, and an equal number from the 9th Michigan Cavalry, with one section of H. Clay Crawford's Battery. The attempt was made and proved entirely successful; the mill and all its contents were destroyed, with the loss of only one man and the wounding of another. Major Carpenter led his men in silence until he struck the pickets of the enemy, when, with a yell and a fusillade of musketry, and the rapid discharge of cannon stationed on Poor Valley Ridge, he rushed forward to the mill, which in a few minutes by means of lighted fagots was in a blaze. The pickets fled in consternation. The noise, the yells, the firing created the impression on the enemy that it was an attack by the whole army. In a brief while the mill was in ashes. Meantime, the enemy's artillery from all the overhanging mountain was thundering forth peal after peal in a tempest of fury, emitting balls and terrific flames of fire.

Major Carpenter, immediately after accomplishing his object, led his men back to camp. The conception of this daring plan, in all its details, originated with him, and he was the successful leader in executing it.

General Burnside arrived the next morning, and Major Carpenter was sent again with a flag of truce to demand the unconditional surrender of the forces in the Gap. The demand was acceded to, and General Frazier, with four thousand men, marched out and laid down their arms.

Carpenter, with a large portion of his regiment, was captured near Rogersville, Tenn., in November, 1863. The privates were sent to Belle Isle and the officers to Libby prison. Here he remained six months, when he was sent to Macon, Ga. After remaining there about one month, he and forty-nine other officers, the highest in rank held by the Confederates, were sent to Charleston, and placed under the fire of Federal guns, commanded by General Foster, who was then shelling that city. There was no exchange of prisoners at that time. General Foster had an equal number of Confederate prisoners brought from the North, and notified General Beauregard, who was then in command, that if he continued to keep the Federal officers in a position where their lives were endangered, he (Foster) would place the Confederate officers on board of monitors and attack the land batteries. General Beauregard replied that in that case he would place the Federal officers he held on the parapets of the fortifications, and if they were fired on, it would be at their peril. Correspondence was then renewed between the governments, by which an agreement was reached that the fifty Confederate officers should be exchanged for the fifty Federal officers, which exchange was accordingly made.

Major Carpenter, after his release in October, 1864, returned to his former home and again went into business. In 1866 he was elected sheriff of Anderson County. He was appointed Collector of Internal Revenue by President Johnson, 1867, with headquarters at Knoxville, and removed at once to Knox County.

In 1887 he was appointed U. S. Pension Agent by President Cleveland, to fill the unexpired term of Governor Robert L. Taylor, and was reappointed by Mr. Cleveland under his second administration. In 1876 and again in 1877, Major Carpenter was elected Mayor of Knoxville.

During the administration of Governor Turney, Major Carpenter was one of his staff officers, with the rank of Inspector General, serving four years.

On the failure of the Southern Building and Loan Association Major Carpenter was appointed receiver by the Chancellor at Knoxville and wisely managed its complicated affairs, extending over most of the Southern States and embracing over two million dollars assets.

In the public trusts held by Major Carpenter his conduct has been marked by the highest intelligence, capacity, and honesty. Few men have held so many responsible positions and left them with so spotless a record.

He is a man of positive convictions, with the courage at all times to speak what he thinks. In conversation he is impressive. His frankness, his sincerity, his power of clear thinking and of plainly and earnestly expressing himself, gave him a marked influence over his neighbors in 1861, when their minds were taking shape in reference to the dissolution of the Union. Daniel A. Carpenter is a natural leader, and was born to command. I have never known one more so. Voice, eye, indomitable determination at once give him ascendency. His courage, too, inspires and awes, and withal he is a kind, good citizen. His reputation is one of which any man may be proud.

ALFRED M. CATE.

In Army—Personally Popular—Actor in Bridge Burning—Escaped to Kentucky—Member of Legislature.

THERE was no better Union man than Alfred M. Cate. His loyalty was manifested both by words and deeds. He proved it by fleeing from a government he hated, becoming a fugitive and an exile, entering the army, and giving three years of his life to the service of his country.

Alfred M. Cate was born in McMinn County, Tennessee, in 1822, and died September 13, 1871. His father was Elijah Cate, and his mother Nettie D. Cate, both of Jefferson County. Mr. Cate's family is large in East Tennessee and exceedingly respectable. In 1861, when the question of secession was agitating the minds of men he was an earnest and bitter opponent of that revolutionary scheme. He was active and unceasing in his opposition, and exerted a large influence in that behalf. His personal popularity and his pleasing address were potent factors in behalf of the Union. By reason of this influence he was largely instrumental in fixing Union sentiments so deeply in the minds of the people of his county that they could never be shaken.

In November, 1861, Mr. Cate was a conspicuous actor in burning the railroad bridges in lower East Tennessee. It will be remembered that this daring project originated in the fertile brain of W. B. Carter of Carter County, that it had the official endorsement of Mr. Lincoln, Mr. Stanton, Secretary of War, and of General McClellan, commanding the armies of the United States; and that its execution was entrusted solely to Mr. Carter. The plan contemplated the simultaneous destruction of all the railroad bridges in East Tennessee, together with the long bridge over the Tennessee River at Bridgeport, Ala.

The destruction of the bridges in lower East Tennessee was entrusted to Alfred M. Cate, a most wise selection. These were the bridges at Bridgeport, Ala., over the Tennessee, two bridges over Chickamauga Creek, one on the road leading from Atlanta to Chattanooga, one on the East Tennessee and Georgia railroad, and one over the Hiwassee River on the last-named road. The burning of the bridge at Bridgeport was intrusted by Mr. Cate to R. B. Rogan and James D. Keener. At the time appointed they repaired to the bridge, but finding it strongly guarded by Confederate soldiers, they were compelled to abandon their design. The destruction of the two bridges over Chickamauga Creek was intrusted to W. T. Cate, a brother of A. M. Cate, and to W. H. Crowder, who were completely successful in their work and escaped without being detected. Mr. A. M. Cate reserved for himself the burning of the larger bridge over the Hiwassee, and the more hazardous undertaking, because it connected two villages situated on the opposite sides of the river, thereby greatly enhancing the danger of detection. He selected as his associates in this daring enterprise Adam Thomas, Jesse F. Cleveland and his son Eli, and Thomas L. Cate, a brother of the leader. All of these men are now dead except Thomas L. Cate, who resides at Cleveland, Tenn., nearing the close of a well-spent life, respected and honored for his virtues and uprightness by a host of friends throughout East Tennessee.

The party headed by A. M. Cate was completely successful. They destroyed the Hiwassee bridge, and returned to their homes without leaving behind the slightest trace by which they could be identified. They were never suspected, and for nearly thirty-five years the mystery of the destruction of these three bridges remained as a secret of the grave. Their neighbors and most intimate friends, even the Union men, meeting them on the streets every day, were no wiser than the Confederate authorities who employed every means and device to ferret out and run them down. Mr. Cate and his associates must have employed admirable skill and cunning in hiding all traces of their tracks. It was well for them that they were guided by a discreet and wise leader, that they were not detected and arrested, for the fury of the Confederates broke out in such a storm of rage that they would as certainly have been hanged as Hensie and Fry were hanged at Greeneville, and as Haun and the two Harmons were at Knoxville. The wildest and the most unreasonable excitement prevailed throughout East Tennessee. The prisons were filled with arrested men. Five men were hanged, and hundreds, perhaps a thousand, sent South without trial, and nearly every one of them on mere suspicion, to languish in filthy prisons, some of them to die.

Mr. Cate, realizing his danger from the outburst of wrath his acts and those of his confederates had created in the country, left his home on the 14th of November, 1861, with about twenty well-armed men, with the view of escaping to the Federal lines in Kentucky. At twelve o'clock that night, before reaching a small Union organization gotten up by William Clift, he was informed that about 1400 Confederate soldiers were approaching from different directions to destroy Clift and himself. Having no sufficient force with which to meet this array against them, Clift and Cate allowed their followers to disperse in the mountains. He himself sought shelter in cliffs and caves, where all his comrades deserted him. He remained there eight days, in bitter cold weather, changing location from cave to cave as safety demanded, seeing squads of soldiers searching for him every day.

Mr. Cate then returned to his home secretly and came very near being arrested. He then set out stealthily for Kentucky, and was forty days and forty nights on the way, traveling over three hundred miles on his second trip, arriving at Sommerset in January, 1862—after nearly two months of wandering and hiding in the hills and mountains since he left his home in November.

Of the hardships incident to the flight of the twice ten thousand Union refugees from East Tennessee, but few suffered more, or showed a higher courage than A. M. Cate. On his arrival in Kentucky he was made a Captain and appointed Commissary, and finally became such in Brigadier-General James G. Spears' Brigade. He remained in the army three years, making a faithful, capable, and honest officer.

In 1865 Mr. Cate, having become a citizen of Hamilton County, was elected to a seat in the Legislature as a State Senator, and in 1867 he was re-elected. This was the reconstruction period of the State, and many important and exciting questions came before the body for consideration. Mr. Cate performed his duty in this and the succeeding Legislature with wisdom and fidelity, shrinking from no duty.

He was a brave and conscientious citizen and public servant, highly esteemed by those who knew him, on account of his integrity and many noble qualities. He was public spirited, and by his fine sense and shrewdness contributed to the public welfare. It was a great misfortune that he died so young.

WILLIAM BLOUNT CARTER.

Great-grandson of John Carter—Washington College and Princeton—Church at Rogersville — Whig—Interview with Lincoln, Seward, McClellan—Bridge Burning—Member of 3d Knoxville-Greeneville Convention—Pocahontas Blood.

WILLIAM BLOUNT CARTER, the subject of this sketch, and one of the noted Union leaders of East Tennessee in 1861, was born in Carter County, September 15, 1820. He was a great-grandson of John Carter, the President of the Council of Five, which administered the celebrated Watauga Association for a number of years with signal success. John Carter was a Virginian, and is believed to have been a Cavalier by descent. The Carter family was both numerous and prominent in Virginia long before the Revolution. John Carter was one of the first settlers on the Watauga, and from his advent became a leading spirit in that infant community. From that day to the present time the Carter family has exercised a leading, at times a supreme, influence in Carter County. By intermarriage the Carters and the Taylors—the descendants of General Nathaniel Taylor—became related, and for three-fourths of a century the influence of these two families dominated that county. With wealth and education, they had more than average capacity, and were, as a rule, guided by high principles. Nathaniel Taylor, the founder of the house in Tennessee, was a Scotch Covenanter—commonly called Scotch-Irish. He was not one of the original settlers, but came at a later day. He served in the War of 1812, and was a Colonel in the battle of New Orleans, winning distinction and promotion by his bravery. From him all the Carter County Taylors are descended. It has always been understood that through Elizabeth McLin, the wife of Landon Carter, a son of John, the Carter and Taylor families inherited the blood of the celebrated Pocahontas of Virginia. Many members of these two families show in their complexion signs of foreign blood. Many of the men have been remarkable for their striking appearance, and the women for their beauty. A certain delicate carving of the nose and chin, and an elegance of face and person, gave evidence of the highest type of manhood and womanhood. William B. Carter, the uncle of the subject of this sketch—the President of the Constitutional Convention of Tennessee in 1834 and three times a member of Congress—was one of the handsomest men of his day. Major General Samuel P. Carter, of the Federal Army in the late Civil War, and later an Admiral in the Navy, was an unusually handsome man. The Rev. Nathaniel G. Taylor, the father of Governor Robert L. Taylor and Hon. A. A. Taylor, —twice a member of Congress,—was distinguished in appearance.

William B. Carter, at an early age, was destined by his fond parents for the Presbyterian ministry. He attended Washington College, Tennessee, then went to Princeton, where he finished his course in the literary and the theological departments. Returning to Tennessee early in the forties, he took charge of a church at Rogersville, where he remained a number of years. Finally, on account of ill health, he surrendered his charge, gave up active work in the ministry, and returned to his old home in Carter County, where he devoted himself to the management of his father's estate, consisting mostly of farms. The Civil War of 1861 found him thus engaged.

As a minister, Mr. Carter was faithful and able. His sermons evinced research and learning, were weighty with thought, and pervaded by intense earnestness. Clear-cut and pointed, they went directly home to the minds and hearts of men. While he employed few graces of rhetoric, his style was remarkably terse, compact, and lucid, and he made men think by the force of his own thoughts.

The Carters and the Taylors had all been Whigs in politics. When the contest of 1860-61 came on, Mr. Carter naturally espoused the cause of the Union, and as he was a man of positive opinions, he gave the Union no half-hearted support. He entered into its defense with all the energy and intensity of determined conviction. When secession swept over the South, carrying State after State into the fatal vortex, finally threatening Tennessee, Mr. Carter took the stump to help arrest its progress, appealing to his neighbors and his countrymen in behalf of the old government with an earnestness and ability surpassed by few men of the Union leaders. Impressive in manner, the occasion and the profound magnitude of the issues involved lent additional solemnity to the warning that fell from his lips, and with all the intensity of an ancient oracle or a Hebrew prophet he pointed out the evils to be avoided.

On the topic of secession Mr. Carter was bitter and uncompromising. When the State voted by a large majority in June in favor of linking its destiny with that of the Southern Confederacy, he remained unconvinced and defiant. In the Greeneville Convention, which assembled after the result of that election was known, he gave his support to the most extreme measures proposed in that body. Being defeated in his policy in that Convention, soon after its adjournment he started North, being perhaps the second refugee from his home. He conceived in his own prolific mind, precisely at what date it is impossible to tell, a daring scheme for the relief of East Tennessee. This was the simultaneous destruction, by fire, of all the railroad bridges in East Tennessee, on the Memphis & Charleston, the Atlantic & Western, the East Tennessee & Georgia, and on the East Tennessee & Virginia roads, including the bridge over the Tennessee River at Bridgeport, Ala. These roads constituted the main line, in the middle South and Southwest for the transportation of troops and supplies from those regions to the Confederate troops in Virginia, and were therefore of vital importance to the South. In September, 1861, Mr. Carter went to Washington, where, having secured an audience with Mr. Lincoln, Mr. Seward, and General McClellan, he laid his plans before them. With his persuasive manner, and his forcible speech, he won them over to his views. The President and the General in command became warmly interested in the project, promising the co-operation of an army to seize and hold the railroads immediately after the bridges should be burned. Both Mr. Lincoln and General McClellan wrote to the Federal commander in Kentucky urging the importance of an independent military expedition into East Tennessee simultaneously with the destruction of the bridges.

Mr. Carter was also furnished funds to meet the extraordinary expenses of this daring enterprise. Its entire execution was left to his discretion. He was to select his own agents to carry out his plans, except that two officers of the army were detailed, possibly at their own request, to aid him, but under his orders. A more suitable man for such a desperate undertaking could not have been found. He was cool, cunning, sagacious, and daring, as well as secretive and resourceful. He knew the country and the people. Before he left Kentucky for East Tennessee, in the execution of his plans, the time for the destruction of the bridges was fixed between him and the Federal commander, General Sherman. General Thomas, with an army, was to move toward East Tennessee, and be ready on the border to march and seize the railroads at the critical moment.

In pursuance of the plan agreed upon, in October, 1861, Mr. Carter started for Tennessee to make arrangements for its execution, and was soon inside of the Confederate lines. No messenger could now reach him. His agents had all been selected to apply the torch to the different bridges. General Thomas, with his little army, had advanced to Barboursville, within thirty miles of Cumberland Gap, and only waited for the appointed hour to pass on into East Tennessee. Now, when all things seemed to be ready, General Sherman, no doubt for good reasons, changed his mind, and ordered General Thomas to retrace his steps. Thus Carter and his agents were left, in the most perilous circumstances, ignorant of the change of plans, to execute alone their daring scheme, and to escape as they could from the enemy's country. Elsewhere the details of this daring attempt are given more fully.*

Mr. Carter, after the partial success of his plans, finding that the Federal Army had not advanced into East Tennessee, as he expected, and as he was assured should be done, with deep disappointment and mortification, secretly threaded his way back into Kentucky. His life would have been worth but little had he been caught at that time, for it soon became well known that he was the leader of the bridge burners. Whatever merit there may be in this military enterprise (for it was a military enterprise, undertaken with the express sanction of the government and with that of the commander of its armies), the credit of its conception belongs exclusively to Mr. Carter. He did his part well toward its execution, and the failure to accomplish the results contemplated can in no sense attach to him. With manly honor he has always refused to divulge the names of those he associated with himself in this perilous undertaking, though many of them have long since been known. All honor to him for this silence!

---

*"East Tennessee and the Civil War," by the author.

After the partial accomplishment of the destruction of the bridges, Mr. Carter, as we have seen, returned to the North, where he waited with ill-repressed impatience, for nearly two years, until the entrance of the Federal Army, under General Burnside, in September, 1863, made it safe for him to return with a happy heart to the home of his birth, the land he loved so well.

In the spring of 1864, the Knoxville-Greeneville Convention again assembled in Knoxville, this being its third meeting. Mr. Carter was present with a number of its old leaders—Johnson, Brownlow, Nelson, Baxter, and Fleming. The gloomy condition of affairs existing at the time of its last meeting, in Greeneville, nearly three years before, had passed away. Men could scarcely realize the change. That imperious power which then dominated the State, and held in subjection the minds of men, had been swept from its confines. The national government now exercised its old dominion and sovereignty over Tennessee. With this change, there had also come a change in the opinions of some of the former prominent Union leaders. I know not the cause of this change—never did know—but some of those who in 1861 were most bitter, were now complaining of the administration, were clamoring for an armistice with the view of treating for peace, were demanding "the Constitution as it was." The Convention lasted four days, and was marked by angry debates and divisions from beginning to close. Mr. Carter was perhaps the leader of the conservative or opposition forces. He was the author of their resolutions. Mr. Johnson, Mr. Brownlow, and Colonel D. C. Trewhitt were the leaders in sustaining the policy of Mr. Lincoln. Finally, Mr. Milligan, the life-long and intimate friend of Mr. Johnson, and probably at his suggestion, seeing that only harm could result from further discussion, moved that this celebrated Convention should adjourn forever. The motion was adopted, and the angry resolutions on both sides were left to die.

Mr. Carter still lives (June, 1901), in the eighty-first year of his age, but alas! a physical wreck.* He has been prostrate for many years, and recently there has fallen on him the additional affliction of total blindness. In a letter to me a few months since he said: "I am still cheerful, and trust in God."

---

*He died in 1902.

His mind burns with the brightness of 1861, when he was a power among the loyal people of his mountain-encircled region.

Mr. Carter was in person tall, straight, slender, and graceful. If he was not in his prime superbly handsome like his brother, Admiral Samuel P. Carter, he was certainly striking in appearance. His peculiar dark complexion, his foreign look, (perhaps due to his Pocahontas blood), his delicate features, his neat, elegant dress, his lithe form and graceful carriage, his soft, musical voice, his bright, keen eyes and peculiar smile, all tended to attract attention, and to cause men to gaze at him. But, above all, his remarkble intellect was the magnet that drew men to him and gave him his power. He was born in the midst of hallowed associations, on the banks of the historic Watauga, the cradle of civilization in Tennessee. Off in the distance, only a few miles, there rises in lofty outline, stretching east and west, a panorama of mountains as grand as ever met human vision. Here John Sevier and John Carter, great-grandfather of the subject of this sketch, had wisely administered for a number of years their new government, the creation of their own minds,—the first free representative government in the Mississippi Valley. Here too, on this very spot, James Robinson and John Sevier had successfully defended the Watauga Settlement against the attack of the powerful Cherokees. Near this spot, September, 1780, the expedition to King's Mountain, under Colonels Shelby, Sevier, and Campbell, started on its long and perilous march through the wilderness of mountains for the purpose of destroying the army of Colonel Ferguson. Surely this is an historic spot. "Ay, call it holy ground!"

COLONEL WILLIAM CLIFT.

Born 1795—A Whig, but Became a Democrat in 1855—Violent Unionist—Defiant of Confederate Government—Wooden Cannon—Agreement with James W. Gillespie — Courier Line Between Knoxville and Chattanooga—In Prison—Atlanta—Escape—Died in Ninety-first Year.

ONE of the most interesting characters living in East Tennessee in 1861, was William Clift of Hamilton County, who was born in Greene County, in 1795. His parents moved to Knox County, where he grew into manhood. In 1828 he married Nancy Arwin Brooks, a daughter of Moses Brooks, who resided near Knoxville. Shortly after this he removed to Hamilton County, settling at Soddy. He invested largely in lands in the neighborhood, which, by reason of the development and growth of the country, became valuable, proving a source of independence to his children. A man of enterprise, he embarked in the construction and operation of a saw and grist mill; he encouraged the building of railroads, and by his influence promoted all schemes calculated to stimulate the growth of the country. In a word, he was public spirited, ever doing his duty to his county and his State as a good citizen.

William Clift was originally a Whig, but in 1855, in the days of Know-Nothingism, he became a Democrat, and remained so for life. In 1860 he supported Stephen A. Douglas for the presidency. When the dark clouds of secession were gathering, in 1860-61, the government had no truer or braver friend than him. He was indeed a violent Unionist. In the Knoxville and Greeneville Conventions, he was a member of the "Business Committee" of thirty, advocating the most extreme measures proposed. As a member of the Committee he helped to report the *quasi* war resolutions of T. A. R. Nelson in the Greeneville Convention, supporting them by a speech. In conversation he was one of the most ultra among the ultraists of East Tennessee in opposition to secession.

After the Greeneville Convention, he became a leader of the Union men for a considerable region of country. These were largely mountain people. His son I. W. Clift, writes me:

"During these trying times my father's home was a refuge to those sharing his sentiments—which were to support the old government at all hazards—and it was not an uncommon thing to see hundreds of stalwart men, men from the mountains, the citadel of freedom, men from the hills, the hollows and the plains, men from all parts of lower East Tennessee, assembled at our home for advice and protection. The writer has seen from five hundred to a thousand men so assembled, and so bold did they become that, right in the heart of the Confederacy, as they were, they proceeded to a military organization. Several companies and a regiment were organized for the Federal Government by my father in Hamilton County, in the summer of 1862."

There was no spot in all East Tennessee, excepting Carter County at the time of the bridge burning, where there was such flagrant and open defiance of Confederate authority as at the home of Colonel Clift. He was the head and soul of it. He flung defiance in the face of the young, haughty and imperious power, as though it were governed by imbeciles and cowards. He openly organized companies of troops, and proceeded to erect fortifications around his house, as if expecting to stay there permanently. He also manufactured a cannon. The tradition is that it was a wooden cannon made by boring a hole in a log of the right size, putting hoops of iron around it and mounting it. The tradition is also that it exploded the first time it was discharged. But I. W. Clift, from whom I have quoted above, says that the report that it was a wooden cannon is in part a mistake. "It was constructed," says he, "of a copper boiler tube, perhaps three inches in diameter, fitted into two pieces of timber split open at the saw mill, the center of each piece grooved out so as to fit around the tube, the timbers put together with the tube in the center, and almost solidly bandaged with iron bands made in the shop."

Such notorious opposition to the Confederate authority could not be tolerated, and accordingly Colonel James W. Gillespie of the Confederate Army, was sent to break up the encampment at Clift's. Instead of attacking and dispersing the rebellious Union men, the two chiefs entered into a treaty of amity and peace, duly signed and sealed by the two high contracting parties, by which they "mutually agreed to let each other alone." Here was a model for the nations which are seeking to settle international disputes by arbitration! Gillespie agreed that the Union people of lower East Tennessee, and especially those who had been so aggressive in upholding the Federal Government, should not be molested, provided they ceased their public assemblies, returned to their homes, and attended to their own affairs. I. W. Clift, from whom I have quoted, says: "This agreement was consented to and signed by all parties, by Colonel Clift and his men, and Colonel Gillespie for the Confederate Government."

Colonel Gillespie, living in the adjoining county, was a neighbor of many of these men, and was a kind-hearted and honorable man. The generous treatment he accorded Colonel Clift's men —indeed, manifested toward the Union men throughout the war, was in harmony with his fine nature. It would have been infinitely better for the Confederate Government if in dealing with Union men the magnanimous spirit displayed by Gillespie had prevailed in all East Tennessee. It would have made thousands of friends, instead of sending tens of thousands of refugees over the border, to return in the course of time as armed enemies.

This agreement between Clift and Gillespie produced peace for a time, but it did not endure long. It is well-nigh, if not altogether, impossible, for antagonistic populations to live together in peace in the same community in time of civil war. There arose in this case mutual distrust, and unrest and disquiet were soon manifest. Mutterings were heard from the Union men of the violation of good faith on the part of the Confederate authorities. This was especially caused by some arrests of Union men. The Union supporters once more flocked to Colonel Clift's house, and open defiance of the Confederate government became as bold as before. It was at this stage of the war that Colonel Clift manufactured his cannon and erected the fortifications around his house. Before these were finished, however, the Confederate authorities sent troops to destroy the puissant power which had lifted its haughty crest in their very midst. The 7th Alabama Infantry approached from the South, and mounted Tennessee troops from the North. These forces coming upon Colonel Clift before he was ready to fight "stampeded all his forces," and destroyed the rising power of the Unionists in lower East Tennessee. It then fell out that each man proceeded to save himself by flight, remembering, no doubt, that

"The paths of glory lead but to the grave,"

and reflecting that the government needed living soldiers rather than dead heroes, they discreetly saved themselves that they might "live to fight another day." There was in all this no disposition to avoid fighting, but at that time they had simply been taken unawares. Colonel Clift, like the old Roman he was, was all fight. He knew no fear.

I do not know of the date of these transactions, but they must have occurred in November, 1861. On the 11th of that month, the Rev. W. B. Wood, commanding the post of Knoxville, telegraphed to Adjutant General Cooper, at Richmond, as follows: "Five hundred Union men now threatening Strawberry Plains; fifteen hundred assembling in Hamilton County, and a general uprising in all counties."

On the same day the Rev. Colonel wrote to General Cooper: "Five hundred Unionists left Hamilton County to-day, we suppose to attack Loudon bridge." Loudon bridge was about eighty-five miles from Colonel Clift's encampment. No doubt these communications had reference to the forces assembled there. The wildness of the statements is not surprising for this was only two days after the railroad bridges of East Tennessee were burned (on the night of November 8th, 1861). The nerves of the Reverend gentlemen were too much shaken for careful sifting of facts.

The alarm created among Confederate troops and Southern sympathisers by the burning of the bridges, indeed, the insane fright that followed, can not be described by word or pen. It would have been laughable as a grand farce, had it not been for the wail of anguish which arose from hundreds of families in East Tennessee, whose fathers, husbands, and sons were thrown into prison on that account. A thousand imprisonments would not measure the number. Despair at once settled on the minds and hearts of Union people. No man, high or obscure, felt himself safe from arrest. The prisons were full to overflowing. The gallows was demanding its victims. Prisons farther South were opening their doors to the Union men of the mountains, who were hurried thither without trial, some never to return. In this state of unsafety, menaced by danger at every step, they almost with one impulse sought safety in flight, and became exiles from a land they loved as life itself.

When the bridges were burned, by preconcerted arrangement, the Federal Army was to have followed into East Tennessee. But the plans were changed the last moment, and the little army of advance was recalled, and ordered to retrace its steps. At the very time the excitement and the alarm were at their height, there was not a Federal soldier within the bounds of East Tennessee except two, and they were hiding and seeking to make their way back to Kentucky. The invading army that was to come was then sadly wending its way beyond Loudon, among the hills of Wild Cat and Rockcastle, toward Camp Dick Robinson. And yet, strange to say, the intense bitterness, and the arrests and imprisonments and occasional executions, continued months after all supposed danger had long gone by. What folly it was to drive these determined Union men, who wished to remain home as producers on their farms, into the ranks of the enemy, whence they finally came back as armed soldiers, with many a wrong to redress.

It was at the time of this excitement that Clift was threatened with an assault by the enemy. His son, from whose statement I have drawn many of my facts, says: "Unfortunately for Colonel Clift the Confederates interrupted him before his gun was entirely completed, and it fell into the hands of the enemy before he had an opportunity to use it. These plans, however, were all interfered with before completion, and all his defenses fell into the hands of his vigilant enemy; his cannon was blown up and himself became a fugitive, hunted in the mountains and hills as Saul hunted David." It was not fair that he was "interrupted" before his gun was completed. He should have had a chance to try it.

It may be remarked that in the battle of Cressy, or Crecy, fought in 1346, between the French and English, the latter used wooden cannons with terrific effect. A late writer thus described them:

"These bombards were small cannons made of wooden staves, clamped by iron bands and loaded with gun-powder and stones, or iron balls. The battle of Cressy was the first in which artillery was used."*

After the disaster to Colonel Clift and his forces, he and most of his men made their way into Kentucky, where he organized the 7th Tennessee Regiment of Infantry. I have the impression that while on his way to Kentucky, or the next spring,

---

"The Story of France," by Thomas E. Watson, Vol. I, p. 203.

most probably the latter time, he and his men had a duel with Colonel A. J. Vaughn's Confederate regiment, at Huntsville, in Scott County, Tennessee, at long range, which resulted in no serious damage to either side. He remained in Kentucky, sometimes drilling his men, and was in the advance when the time arrived for the long-expected and long-delayed march into East Tennessee, for the relief of the Union people was commenced by General Burnside. He was assigned to duty, by written order, under General Shackelford, and by him placed in command of the advance guard and pioneer corps from Crab Orchard, Ky., to Kingston, Tenn. Here he was detailed by General Burnside, and placed in charge of the courier line from Knoxville to Chattanooga. While on this duty, on October 24, 1863, he was captured by a raiding party, and imprisoned for a long time in Atlanta, whence he made his escape, and made his way back through the mountains of North Carolina and East Tennessee, during the extremely cold weather of January, 1864, hiding out by day and traveling at night. He suffered intensely from cold and exposure, from biting frosts, cold rains, and snow. His feet were so frost bitten that he could not wear shoes, and, wrapped in rags as a protection, he arrived at home about the first of February, 1864. The exposures of this trip were almost without parallel in the annals of history or romance. They terminated in a long and severe illness, in which he lost one of his eyes, the sight of the other being greatly impaired. Finally, in August, he again reported for duty, but he was deemed unfit for further service by reason of combined age and affliction. Thus terminated the military service of this remarkable man. He never wavered in his faith in the final triumph of the Union in its mighty struggle.

When the war closed, strife ceased with Colonel Clift. He was the friend alike of those who had worn the blue and of the destitute wearers of the gray. The latter needed and often secured his assistance. How noble it would have been if all persons had acted with the same magnanimous, forgiving spirit toward their late misguided fellow citizens, who were equally honest with themselves in the course they had pursued. Each side, excepting the few ambitious leaders who inaugurated the war, was honest and pursued the right as it saw it. After the lapse of more than forty years men everywhere begin to see that each party from a certain point of view was right.

Colonel Clift was a stern, brave, conscientious man. He made no compromise with duty or principle. He was outwardly in action and speech what he was inwardly in thought and conscience—an honest man through and through. I do not know from what race he was descended, but he was in all his ways of the similitude of a sturdy old Scotch-Irish Covenanter, always seeking to do his duty and God's will. He was a Presbyterian in faith, and a ruling elder in the Soddy Church.

He was a devoted friend of the poor, and his son tells of the cunning methods he devised to give them work. One was this: he would have men prepare the ground for planting corn by the hoe only, although he had numerous plows and teams, in order to lengthen out the job of the dependent laborers. Noble man!

Thus passed the declining old age of this stern man of war, peacefully and calmly, until, in his ninety-first year, like a well-ripened sheaf of wheat, he was gathered to his Father.

GENERAL JOSEPH A. COOPER.

Father from Maryland—Mexican War—Greeneville Convention—Drilled Men on the Farms—Second Refugee—At Cumberland Gap, Chickamauga, Nashville—Internal Revenue Collector at Knoxville—Greatest Union Soldier.

In writing of Union leaders the name of Joseph A. Cooper cannot be omitted. While he was not an orator, and could not dazzle men by beautiful words and phrases, yet withal he was a leader of men. His sharp, quick voice, with its tone of authority, and with a positiveness inborn of strong conviction, made men yield to him. He was naturally but unconsciously imperious, though strictly regardful of the rights of others. His conduct arose from an inward consciousness of strength, and from positive opinions.

General Cooper was born at Cumberland Falls, Ky., November 25, 1823, and came with his father when a child to Cove Creek, Campbell Co. The father, John Cooper, was a native of Maryland and served in the War of 1812. His son was reared on a farm amid the hardships incidental to the frontier life. Schools were few and poor, with the result that he had but little education. But nature supplied a bright intellect, clear judgment, and keen moral sense. In all his instincts he was an honest man, and he had no patience with anything that was not open and straightforward. His spirit was too independent for any concealment or equivocation. These qualities were conspicuous in him through all his eventful life.

Joseph A. Cooper enlisted in September, 1847, as a volunteer, to serve in the army in Mexico. He reached the City of Mexico, in January, 1848, and left it to return home the June following.

After his return, he cultivated a small farm in Campbell County, not far from Jacksboro. In the civil contest of 1860 and in the early part of 1861, he was an attentive observer of passing events. Being an old-line Whig, he naturally supported the Union ticket for the Presidency in 1860. There was no more ardent Union man than he in all the borders of East

Tennessee, and but few private citizens who exerted so much influence. He was a delegate to the great Union Convention in Knoxville. By it resolutions declaring an unalterable attachment to the Union were passed unanimously. When this convention again assembled in Greeneville, Tenn., on the 17th of June, Mr. Cooper was the only delegate from Campbell County. He served on the "Business Committee," consisting of thirty-one members, one for each county, to which was referred, without debate, all resolutions submitted to the Convention, Judge Connally F. Trigg being its chairman. The excitement in the convention was bitter and intense. An overwhelming majority of the members were opposed to submitting to the action of the State in allying its destiny with the fortunes of the Southern Confederacy. There were at first only a few members who were opposed to this mad scheme of resistance. The great body of the Convention could not realize that they had already passed under the rule of a young but powerful revolutionary-military government, amply able to suppress in any quarter of its dominion the first uprising of the people. They were to find this out a little later on. They had not the faintest conception of the strength and the rage of the young giant born at Montgomery only a few months before. Mr. Cooper, in common with his whole committee of thirty, shared in this feeling.

The President of the Convention, Hon. T. A. R. Nelson, had early in its deliberations, submitted a very able paper, entitled a "Declaration of Grievances," accompanied by some defiant resolutions. These resolutions virtually declared the independence of East Tennessee. These papers, along with a multitude of others, were referred without debate to the Business Committee. On the afternoon of the third day that Committee unanimously reported to the Convention the resolutions of Mr. Nelson, with the recommendation that they be adopted. I immediately offered a substitute, which declared our right "to determine our own destiny" in the then pending conflict, that the action of the Legislature in passing an ordinance of secession was unconstitutional and illegal, and therefore not binding upon the people of East Tennessee, and that a memorial be sent to the Legislature asking its consent that East Tennessee be permitted to form and erect itself into a State. After a spirited dabate, lasting all the afternoon, in which a number of the leading members of the Convention participated, and an earnest effort to defeat the substitute, the original resolutions of Mr. Nelson and the substitute, on motion of Mr. Cooper, were referred back to the Committee for reconsideration.* The next morning the Committee, reversing its action of the day before, unanimously reported in favor of the adoption of the substitute. This report was finally adopted by the Convention, in the language of the Secretary *seriatem et una voce* but not without an effort on the part of Nelson and Robert Johnson (son of Andrew Johnson) to renew the fight, in favor of the ultra and extreme measures at first recommended by the Committee.

The antagonistic views of the members of this celebrated convention were reconciled and made harmonious by this measure of peace. The members at last came to a solemn realization of the fact that the two opposing measures presented for consideration represented the issues of peace or civil war for East Tennessee. As Mr. Cooper expressed the situation to me, although in the opening of the convention, he, like nine-tenths of the members, was in favor of fighting on our own soil rather than yield to the Southern Confederacy, he at last saw that such a course would "make East Tennessee a hell."*

In the debate which followed, when I offered my substitute, the persons taking part in the discussion in favor of its adoption were John Baxter, Montgomery Thornburgh, Horace Maynard, A. J. Brown, and myself; those favoring the original resolutions of Nelson, were Thomas D. Arnold, W. B. Carter, William Clift, James P. Swann, V. Myers, and J. T. Davis. When the substitute was presented it was by no means certain in my mind that it would receive a second, so strong was the feeling in favor of violent measures. During the discussion the great majority of the Convention began for the first time to realize that they were madly rushing to their own ruin, if they persisted in the course recommended by the Committee.

The positive character of Joseph A. Cooper was exemplified by a little incident which took place just before the adjournment of the Convention. W. C. Kyle and John Blevins pre-

---

*Mr. Cooper informed me a few days ago (November, 1901) that he made the motion to recommit, a fact which I had forgotten and which does not appear in the published account of the proceedings.

*For a full account of this Convention the reader is referred to "East Tennessee and the Civil War," by the author.

sented a paper protesting "against the action of the Convention," but in what respect they did not say. A motion was made to lay the protest on the table. "Yes," said Cooper, "lay it under the table forever."

Notwithstanding Cooper, for the sake of peace and the safety of the people of East Tennessee, voted for the milder resolutions, his mind seems to have been intent only on war. In the committee room he entered into a secret agreement with Robert K. Byrd of Roane County, R. M. Edwards of Bradley, and S. C. Honeycutt and E. Langley of Morgan, that they would go home to their respective counties and commence secretly raising and drilling soldiers. Cooper returned to Campbell County, and by the 1st of August had organized and drilled more than five hundred men, most of whom afterward joined the Union army in Kentucky. He worked on his farm during the day, and at night traveled from house to house stirring up the Union people, returning the next day to his plow. On Saturdays he met these people for muster in the old fields, in out-of-the-way places, and gave them such instruction in military tactics as he had gained in the Mexican War.

Here was a real leader. Without the gift of oratory, without wealth or the prestige of distinction, or a great name, by the mere force of a superior will, by determination, and by the fire and ardor of burning patriotism, he inspired and led men. Few could have done this.

When the first Confederate troops under Captain Rowan reached Big Creek Gap, Campbell County, Cooper immediately made arrangements to meet and attack them with his mountain men, but by the advice of cooler headed friends decided not to do so. He was not content, however, with his position. He wished to have a hand in the war. If he could not fight the enemies of the government at home, he would go where he could. Accordingly on the 1st of August, in the afternoon, he bade his family good-by, saying: "I am going to the war; I may be gone a year, perhaps three years, or I may never return." That night he began his travel through the mountains, arriving on the borders of Kentucky the next morning. On the day following, hundreds of the men whom he had drilled followed and joined him at Williamsburg.

Joseph A. Cooper, so far as is known to me, was the second East Tennessee refugee who left home with a fixed purpose of entering the Union army. Fred Heiskell, of Knox County, was unquestionably the first. On the 16th day of April he left home, on the 18th he was in Louisville, and on the 20th or 21st, he enlisted in Captain W. W. Woodruff's 1st Kentucky Regiment, serving as a brave soldier to the close of the war.

Cooper enlisted at Williamsburg, Ky., on the 4th of August, and on the same day he organized a company of the 1st Tennessee Infantry, and on the 8th was mustered into service as Captain by Lieutenant Samuel P. Carter, afterward a Major General of Volunteers. The 185 Tennesseeans, besides forming Co. A, were distributed among companies B, C, and H, of the 1st Regiment, and Co. C, of the 2d. Thus Cooper led the way through the mountains as a refugee, was the second volunteer of the State, and organized the first company and was its Captain in the 1st Regiment of Tennessee troops in the Union Army—a record of which his children may justly feel proud. Of the 35,000 Tennessee troops in the Union Army he was the second to enlist, and was Captain of the first company.

Robert K. Byrd was made the Colonel of the 1st Regiment, and commanded it with honor to himself and to the State till near the close of the war. On the 22d of March, 1862, Captain Cooper was made Colonel of the 6th Tennessee Regiment of Infantry, which he had partly raised, and which he commanded with distinction until July 30th, 1864. He was then made a Brigadier General, for distinguished bravery in the terrible battles in Georgia, on the recommendation of Generals Sherman and Schofield.

It would be beyond the scope of these sketches to give in detail the history of the many battles and skirmishes in which Cooper was engaged. I give only a brief outline of them. He was with General George H. Thomas in the decisive battle and victory at Fishing Creek, Kentucky, January 18th, 1862, where the Commander of the Confederate forces, General Felix K. Zollicoffer was killed. Starting from Cumberland Gap in September with 400 men, after a long march of two days, on the north side of the mountain, he encountered the enemy at Big Creek Gap, Tenn., and after a sharp engagement routed them, capturing an entire company of cavalry. The enemy's loss was ten men killed, eight wounded, and ninety-five taken as prisoners, and eighty-seven horses captured. Among the killed were two Captains and an aide of General Smith. Colonel

Cooper received in a general order the special thanks of General Morgan.

In September Cumberland Gap was vacated by General George W. Morgan, who commenced his noted retreat through the mountains of Northeastern Kentucky to the Ohio River. Cooper with his regiment accompanied him, sharing in all the dangers and hardships of the long march. His command was afterward sent to Nashville, and on the 31st day of December, 1862, he was ordered to guard an ammunition train to Stone River, the great battle of that name having opened on the 31st. On the march he was attacked by General Wheeler's Cavalry, which he repulsed, saving the train.

In September, 1863, he arrived in Chattanooga in time for the battle of Chickamauga, and participated in its closing scenes, skirmishing two days with the enemy on Lookout Mountain. He was absent on duty, guarding several points on the Tennessee River above Chattanooga, at the time of the famous battle under the command of Grant. After the battle of Chattanooga he marched to Knoxville, and remained in East Tennessee during the winter of 1863-64, participating in the many skirmishes and engagements with Longstreet's army.

In April he marched to Dalton, Ga., for the purpose of taking part in the memorable Georgia Campaign then just opening, and was assigned to the command of a brigade. Colonel Cooper's brigade was in the battle of Resaca, Ga., losing more than one-third of the effective men of the brigade, either killed or wounded. For more than two months his command was daily actively engaged in one of the most brilliant campaigns on record. It was his gallantry and skill displayed throughout this campaign that induced Generals Sherman and Schofield to recommend Cooper for a Brigadier General.

When General Hood started in the direction of Nashville, and General Thomas' army was detached to follow him, General Cooper, of course, went with it. Arriving with his command near Nashville, he found that Hood's forces had surrounded that city, and that his brigade was cut off. His command could be saved from capture only by a long forced march. He had been on such a march for twelve hours previously, yet his decision was instantly made. Without consulting anyone, he ordered his artillery and command to face about, and at once commenced a march which lasted without rest, all night and part of the next day. He forced a countryman who knew all the roads to guide him under the penalty of death in case of betrayal. Turning southwardly and westwardly he made his way by a circuitous route to Clarksville, distant from Nashville about sixty miles; then crossed the Cumberland River and got on the north side of it. By this winding march he traveled nearly one hundred miles in the retreat. From Clarksville he marched to Nashville, arriving there on the 8th of December, having accomplished this long march in six days, or, excluding the day he rested in Clarksville, in five days, a distance of one hundred and fifty or sixty miles. The report had been published that he and his command had been captured. He was therefore enthusiastically received by the Army in Nashville. This march, in the estimation of military men, was conducted with rare skill, evincing high military ability.

In the battles around Nashville of the 15th and 16th of December, 1864, the troops under the command of General Cooper had a brilliant share. The trophies won by his force were an entire brigade of Confederate troops and two pieces of artillery, after a dashing charge in an open field. "For gallant and meritorious services at Nashville" he was afterward appointed a Major General by brevet.

On the 15th of January, 1865, General Cooper was assigned to the command of the Second Division, Twenty-third Army Corps, and two days later he, with his division, started in a fleet of boats down the Tennessee and up the Ohio, with the view of transportation to the field of active operations in North Carolina, where he arrived on the 23d of February. On the 27th of the same month, by virtue of an order from General Schofield, he was granted a leave of absence, and immediately left for home, from which he had been continuously absent since August 1, 1861. In April he returned to his command, then operating near Goldsboro. After the close of active operations, he was ordered to report for duty at Nashville to General Thomas, commanding the Department of the Cumberland. On the 28th of December, 1865, he was "honorably mustered out of the service of the United States, to date from January 15, 1866."

Thus retired from the Volunteer army one of the bravest and most faithful of the many officers who had conducted to a successful conclusion the greatest war known in history. Returning to his old home, General Cooper settled near Knoxville, on a farm, among his late companions in arms, and among the loyal people who were proud of the glory he had won in the war. Everywhere he was hailed as a modest soldier and hero who had done his duty faithfully. He was regarded as by far the greatest soldier in the Union army which Tennessee produced during the Civil War. Modesty and simplicity of manner added to his merit. There was never any boasting of deeds, nor the least show of vainglory.

During eight years of Grant's administration and a part of Hayes', General Cooper was Internal Revenue Collector for the Knoxville District. In 1880 he moved to Kansas, hoping to better his fortune, for he was always a poor man. He is there engaged in farming at this time (1901), and I am glad to know that he is surrounded in his old age at least with the comforts of life. Recently he visited his old home in Tennessee; he came back to see once more his old companions and to bid them a last adieu. While he was in Knoxville there was a reunion of the survivors of the 3d Tennessee, and of the 6th, which he raised and so long commanded. It was a sad spectacle to see the tears streaming down the furrowed cheeks of those gray-haired veterans, bent with age, as they grasped for the last time the hand of their idolized commander.

General Cooper was positive and outspoken, but within there beat a kind and honest heart. He was true and sincere in all things, and had no patience with pretenses, simulation, or falsehoods in any form. Brave he was as the bravest. Faithful to duty in its minutest details, he always had the entire confidence of his superiors. During a long life he performed every trust committed to him, either as a citizen or a soldier, with the strictest fidelity. Blessed with a clear intellect, he was always able to see the right and to follow it with unfaltering persistence. As a soldier he believed he was in the army to fight, and therefore he was always ready to fight. When a battle was on, he went where danger and duty called. His soldiers caught the spirit of their leader. So well were they trained, and so completely had they caught his mind and spirit that in the battle of Nashville, at the proper moment, without the word of command, they sprang forward, with a common impulse along the whole line, in a charge, sweeping over an open field with resistless might, driving everything before them, and capturing a brigade of the enemy and two pieces of artillery.

WILLIAM CRUTCHFIELD.

Early Settler of Chattanooga—Replied to Jefferson Davis—Sought Safety in Union Army.

ONE of the strikingly unique Union leaders of East Tennessee was William Crutchfield of Chattanooga. His father, Thomas Crutchfield, was a large brick contractor, and resided at one time in Greeneville, Tenn., where William was born. He moved to Chattanooga early in its history, perhaps while that place was still called Ross' Landing, and while William was a mere boy. The father prospered in his new home, becoming the owner of valuable property in the young city and in the country, which ultimately made his children independent. He was a man of shrewdness and much forethought. He built the hotel known for many years as the Crutchfield House, right in the heart of the city, now known as the Read House, but greatly enlarged and improved. It was then the leading hotel of Chattanooga. On the death of the father it was kept by his two sons, Thomas and William.

William Crutchfield was eccentric and peculiar beyond description. He was vehement in manner and impetuous in action. Yet, with all his violence of manner, his heart was as kind and as true as ever beat in the human breast. And he was brave, too, to the verge of desperation.

When the question of secession was presented to the people of Tennessee in the winter of 1861, Crutchfield was fearless and outspoken in his opposition to it, and used all his influence to defeat its accomplishment. He was an ardent Whig, and therefore was most naturally opposed to that mad and unwise measure. His opposition to it gave rise to a dramatic incident, widely talked of at that time, and still remembered by old citizens.

Jefferson Davis, having resigned his seat in the Senate of the United States after the secession of Mississippi, which State he represented, was on his way home and stopped at the Crutchfield House in Chattanooga. That hotel was then owned by the Crutchfield heirs, and was run by Thomas Crutchfield. The facts before me do not make it clear whether or not William was one of the proprietors. The presence of so distinguished a person as Mr. Davis naturally created a desire among his friends, and perhaps others, also, to hear him speak on the great questions then convulsing the country. Accordingly he was waited upon by some of the leading citizens and requested to make a speech. He at first declined, but being urged further, consented to do so. He spoke from a chair in the office or lobby of the hotel. His address was short—probably not exceeding twenty or twenty-five minutes—and dignified, as all his speeches were, and with nothing personally offensive in it. He avowed himself a secessionist, and contended that the States had the constitutional right to secede from the Union at their sovereign will. Judge D. M. Key, afterward Postmaster General under President Hayes, who was a secessionist, and was present, says in a letter to me, that Mr. Davis "made a short talk, very moderate in its character; it had nothing in it personal or offensive in expression or manner."

When Mr. Davis concluded, he, with Judge Key and S. R. McCamy, retired to "a saloon" in an adjoining room, or upstairs, according to another account. William Crutchfield, who had been listening with restless interest while he was speaking, then jumped upon the clerk's counter, and in an excited manner commenced replying. He arraigned Mr. Davis and his associates for deserting their seats in Congress when they were in the majority, and might have prevented any hostile legislation to the institutions of the South. He rebuked him for interfering in the election then pending in Tennessee, by advising the people to vote for a Convention, which was virtually for secession. He said that Mr. Davis, instead of advising Tennesseeans to break up the Union, could better employ his time by advising the people of his own State to pay their honest debts, which they had repudiated. He denounced Mr. Davis in broad terms as a traitor to his country. Judge Key says, on this point: "Mr. Crutchfield did nothing so far as I can remember in inducing Mr. Davis to speak, but he was an ardent Unionist of irascible temperament, who did not mince language when he was aroused. Thoroughly honest and bold in the expression of his opinions, he used vigorous and bitter terms."

Mr. Davis was informed of what was going on while Crutchfield was speaking, and came back to the lobby. About that time, the excitement becoming very great, Thomas Crutchfield, a brother and proprietor of the House, pulled William off the counter, and he and other friends hurried him out of the room. Mr. Davis, again mounting a chair, said that "he understood that a person present had, when his back was turned, aspersed his motives and conduct. That person was no gentleman, and he could afford to have no controversy with him, but if he had a friend who was a gentleman he would settle the matter with him."

According to the account of the affair given by Mr. Crutchfield himself, hereafter referred to, he responded to Mr. Davis by saying: "I am ready to meet you now or any time hereafter." About this time the click of pistols could be heard in the crowd.

Another and somewhat different account of Mr. Davis' reappearance, given by Mr. Crutchfield, but not written by him, was published in the *Canteen*, a paper published in Washington, D. C., in 1891. In reply to the question of Mr. Davis, demanding to know whether the gentlemen present would endorse the speaker as a responsible and reputable man, adding that if they would do so, he (Davis) would hold him responsible personally. Voices in the crowd responded that Mr. Crutchfield was in every way a gentleman. The other witnesses, from whose testimony I have been quoting, say nothing about this response of the crowd. The witnesses differ as to many immaterial points, as it is most natural they should do after the lapse of so many years, but there is a substantial concurrence as to the main facts.

Mr. Crutchfield, according to most of the witnesses, made no reply to Mr. Davis' denunciation and implied challenge. Major Tankersley, a warm friend of Mr. Davis, says he does not think Mr. Crutchfield made any reply to Mr. Davis; if he did, he did not hear him. Judge Lewis Shepherd, who was present, says: "The crowd assembled at the Crutchfield House were mostly admirers of Mr. Davis,—they were hot-headed secessionists,—and when Mr. Crutchfield mounted the counter there were at least fifty pistols drawn and cocked for immediate use. The clicking of these pistols must have been heard by Crutchfield, and he understood that most of them would be used, if trouble ensued, to repel the supposed insult to Mr. Davis. When the latter used the epithet I have quoted he was powerless to resist it, if he had tried. The fury of the men forced him to quit speaking, and forced him off the counter he had mounted."

When Mr. Davis began speaking, Mrs. Davis and Mrs. Thomas Crutchfield, and perhaps other ladies, came downstairs and stood in the doorway to hear him. When Mr. Crutchfield commenced his reply, and the pistols began their ominous clicking, these ladies, says Judge Shepherd, manifested their fright by screaming.

It is stated by one person that "when the excitement was at its height, the lights were blown out, and several pistols fired, though fortunately no one was hurt."

I have thus given the main facts of this affair, as they can be gathered from the statements of the various witnesses who were living at the time they occurred. This scene created quite a sensation at the time it took place, not only in Tennessee, but throughout the South. Mr. Crutchfield in consequence of this difficulty became an object of bitter animosity on the part of the secessionists. A little later on, when they became dominant, and Confederate soldiers were stationed in Chattanooga, or were passing through it, his life was in constant danger, and he had to keep in close concealment. At last he was forced secretly to leave his home at night, and seek safety under the protecting care of the Union army. When that army entered Chattanooga, he returned to his home with it. In the battle of Lookout Mountain he acted as a volunteer aid on the staff of General Grant, and by reason of his knowledge of the topography of the surrounding country he was enabled to render valuable assistance. General Grant always appreciated his services and his singular bravery and devotion to the Union cause, and when he became President he was always ready to show Mr. Crutchfield, or his constituents, any favor in his power.

In 1872 Mr. Crutchfield, though not a politician, was put forward by the Republican party as a candidate for Congress, and was elected by about 1200 majority, in a district usually electing a Democratic representative. His opponent was Judge D. M. Key, afterward successively United States Senator, Postmaster General, and United States District Judge, and, in the language of Judge Shepherd, "one of the purest, best, and ablest men in the country." Mr. Crutchfield served his constituents faithfully and honestly for one term of Congress. Some few years afterward he died on his farm not far from Chattanooga, in the State of Georgia, having the respect and confidence of all who knew him, of both political parties. He died possessed of considerable property. He was an eccentric, erratic man, beyond nearly all men of his day. He was called the David Crockett of his time. Both he and Crockett were natives of East Tennessee, and born in Greene County. On one occasion, while he was a member of Congress, "at the conclusion of a fervid speech of the spread-eagle variety by a member of the opposition, the house was startled by a lusty cock's crow from the desk of the East Tennessee original."

According to all accounts, Mr. Crutchfield was a man of courage. He is spoken of by one who knew him well as a man of "desperate courage." It is equally manifest that he was an upright and truthful, and an honorable and kind-hearted man. This is the character given to him by all his Chattanooga acquaintances, whether agreeing with or differing from him in politics. He was a remarkably generous and noble man in his instincts. Many were his acts of helpfulness to the unfortunate Confederates during the war, and after its close. He opened his purse freely, and gave his time and exertions to relieve their wants. In the language of one of his plain neighbors, "He was a man of right thought." He was outspoken and blunt in speech, and no one was left in doubt as to his opinions. But while he was rough in manner and speech, within there beat a heart that could be touched by every tale of pity, of suffering, or want. He was possessed of noble instincts, which impelled him with irresistible energy in the direction of right, justice, and humanity.

PEREZ DICKENSON AND JOHN WILLIAMS.

Dickenson a Native of Massachusetts—Accumulated Fortune—Ardent Whig—Decided in Stand for Union—Arrested and Discharged—Williams' Family Old and Distinguished—Battle of the Horseshoe—Opposition of John Williams' Father to Jackson—John Williams in Legislature—Fearless Union Man.

Two other prominent Union men deserve, from their standing and influence, more than the mere mention of their names. These are Perez Dickenson and John Williams, both of whom were citizens of Knoxville. The first, a native of Massachusetts, came to Tennessee while, perhaps, in his minority. By shrewdness, industry, and fair dealing he accumulated a good fortune in the mercantile business. He was a man of sagacity and clearness of intellect, as well as of large general intelligence. Few men have possessed better native ability.

Before the Civil War Mr. Dickenson was an ardent Whig, as were nearly all the leading men of Knoxville. In the Presidential race of 1860 he was a warm supporter of John Bell. When the question of secession came up, immediately following the Presidential election, without hesitation he decided what his duty demanded. He unhesitatingly ranged himself on the side of the Union, and from that position nothing could move him. Through all the dark days between June, 1861, and September, 1863—the period of Confederate ascendency in East Tennessee—his heart as constantly turned to the Union as the magnet points to the pole. There was no mistaking his position. While he, like nearly all Union men, was forced into prudent silence during the dominance of the Confederacy, no intelligent man on either side doubted where he stood. In 1861, or early in 1862, he was arrested and taken before Judge West H. Humphreys, presiding in the Confederate States District Court at Knoxville, who released him, there being no evidence against him.

Mr. Dickenson enjoyed in a pre-eminent degree the confidence of the people of East Tennessee as an honest, honorable man, and he was known to the leading citizens of every county and of nearly every neighborhood. At home, in Knoxville, where he resided for two-thirds of a century, he was in the latter years of his life, in the esteem of the people, easily the first citizen. Though the weight of eighty-seven years pressed heavily on his once iron constitution, at the time of his death, in 1901, his eye was not dim, nor his natural force entirely abated. The influence of his example, his words, his name and his high position, in 1861, in favor of the Union, unquestionably entitle him to be ranked as one of the leaders who saved the Union.

John Williams, too, was prominent, and too active in behalf of the Union in 1861 to be omitted from the roll of its leaders. Mr. Williams belonged to an old and very distinguished family. This distinction arose, not from the possession of wealth (though there was a considerable amount of that in the family), but from splendid endowments and noble achievements. It would be tedious to name all the persons in this family who have filled distinguished positions in North Carolina and Tennessee.*

But to me the best thing about the Williams family was, not its honorable lineage, not its ability, not the distinction won by so many of them through the holding of high offices, so faithfully and so worthily filled, but the spotless integrity, lofty honor, and unfaltering courage in doing right, manifested by them in all positions and conditions of life. John Williams, the father of the subject of this sketch, was a lawyer by profession. In the war with the Creek Indians, in the celebrated battle of the Horse Shoe, he commanded the 39th United States Infantry, under General Jackson, and this regiment, under the lead of Williams, first scaled the breastworks which decided that battle. His conduct on this occasion has always been regarded as most heroic.† Subsequently he became United States Senator, and served one term. He was afterward appointed Minister to one of the South American Republics.

In Tennessee he was the head of the opposition to General

---
*Richmond Pearson Hobson, one of the heroes of Santiago, is descended on his mother's side from Colonel Joseph Williams of North Carolina, and also from General James White, the founder of Knoxville, being the great-great-grandson of each.

†Thomas H. Benton was Lieutenant Colonel of this regiment, and Sam Houston an Ensign, or a Lieutenant.

Jackson, which culminated in the first defeat of that imperious man in the presidential election of 1836, when the State cast its vote for Hugh Lawson White, the brother-in-law of Williams, in opposition to Van Buren, the favorite of Jackson. The only man in the State, of courage, ability, and popularity sufficient to withstand the power of the great hero of New Orleans was Colonel Williams. This he did as long as he lived, and in the end successfully. In courage he was the equal of Jackson, with none of his objectionable traits, and with some noble qualities which the latter never possessed.

John Williams, the younger, and the son of Colonel John Williams, was three or four times honored by an election to the lower house of the Legislature of Tennessee, from Knox County. In 1861 he was serving in that capacity, when the question of the secession of the State came up for consideration in that body, during its two extra sessions, and he, with unfaltering courage, voted against every proposition looking to that end. His vote was recorded with the small minority of brave men who, amid the storm and delirium of the hour, voted against the ordinance of secession. No man in the State was more outspoken or more bitter in his opposition and denunciation of this movement. He was earnest and unequivocal in his course, and made no compromise. The whole movement was absolutely wicked in his estimation. He renounced it everywhere, never concealing or withholding his sentiments. Even after the State had voted to secede, and Confederate armies had occupied the country, in the presence of soldiers and officers, both publicly and privately, he at all times proclaimed himself a Union man. No other man in Knoxville dared to do this. There was but one other man in East Tennessee, after Brownlow left in March, 1863, who openly avowed his adhesion to the old government, and this man was Thomas D. Arnold, elsewhere described. The very audacity of these men seemed to secure immunity for them. Other men would have been arrested and hurried off to prison, but Mr. Williams was never arrested, though he was included in the warrant issued against Mr. Dickenson and myself, December 25, 1861.

Mr. Williams was not only a brave, stalwart Union man, but he was a gentleman of the highest type of the old school—frank, manly, open, noble. There was no deceit, nothing false in him. He was as true as the laws of nature. In consequence of these qualities, men could always trust him, and his influence in shaping and molding the opinions of his neighbors and acquaintances, in the shifting, changing condition of public opinion in 1861, was considerable. He was no speaker, but a worker and a fine talker, his name lending strength to any cause that he espoused. In an eminent degree he possessed the qualities most needed in the terrible times of 1861—determination, and a courage that knew no retreat. His family has just cause of pride in his record as one of the best and truest Union men in the South.

JOHN M. FLEMING.

Born in Hawkins County—Educated at Emory and Henry College—Takes Charge of Whig *Register* in 1855—Supports John Bell—One of Three or Four to Oppose Secession—Elected to Legislature in 1861—Humorous Letter on Fall of Nashville—Secretary of Knoxville-Greeneville Convention — Supports General McClellan — Opposes Reconstruction Measures—Superintendent Public Instruction—Editorial Work—Encounter with John Mitchell—Controversy with Phelan.

JOHN M. FLEMING was the youngest of the Union leaders of East Tennessee. He was a son of the Rev. David Fleming, of the Methodist Episcopal Church, and was born in Hawkins County, Tennessee, about the year 1833. He was educated at Emory and Henry College, Virginia, and soon after his graduation settled in Knoxville. In 1855 he was invited to take charge of the old Knoxville *Register*, a Whig newspaper that for many years had exercised great influence in its party in East Tennessee. Mr. Fleming was a good scholar, and wielded a facile pen, and it soon became evident to the public that a young man of more than ordinary ability had made his appearance. From the very start he wrote pointed and telling articles. His style was chaste, his facts strong, and when he chose to indulge them, his wit and humor were excellent, and he soon came to be regarded as a brilliant young editor. Continuing in the editorial profession until 1858, he obtained license to practice law, having studied under John Baxter. After coming to the bar, he was taken into the office of his preceptor as a partner.

Mr. Fleming, as may be inferred, was a Whig in politics, and took some part in the canvass of 1860 in behalf of John Bell. In the spring of that year he had attended the Baltimore Convention as a delegate, and had cast his vote in favor of that distinguished statesman. In the latter part of November, 1861, when the spirit of secession first began to manifest itself in Knoxville, Mr. Fleming was one of the brave men who helped to organize opposition to it, and who openly met and resisted the first approaches of disloyalty. In the two public meetings which occurred about that time in Knoxville, and in the public discussion that took place, he was one of the three or four men who openly opposed secession. He helped to defeat it in its purpose to gain an ascendency in Knoxville and Knox County. Although on account of youth and lack of previous services he was less conspicuous than a number of other Union leaders, it can be safely affirmed that Fleming's opportune opposition to secession in its very beginning, in these two public meetings, was in the end as valuable and wide-reaching as were the labors later of any one of the Union leaders of higher distinction, except possibly three. The check given to secession, and the confidence inspired in the friends of the Union by these early meetings, can never be overestimated. Mr. Fleming has never received, and perhaps never will, the credit he deserves for his share in them. During the two canvasses that followed, in February and May, he took an active part against the alliance of the State with the Southern Confederacy. He spoke wherever his services were in demand. While not a great orator, he was an exceedingly entertaining and instructive speaker. His information on all public questions was full and minute, and he had the faculty of presenting his facts in the most lucid form. His speeches abounded in facts and arguments, presented with clearness, and when occasion demanded with wit and humor, and but for a little sharpness and shrillness of voice, he would have been a very successful speaker.

In 1861, after the State had voted in favor of secession, Mr. Fleming was elected as a representative to the Legislature from Knox County, and served during the ensuing sessions. That he was forced by this position and these surroundings apparently to support the Southern Confederacy in the Legislature admits of no doubt. Yet his Union friends knew perfectly well how he was in heart. Indeed, it seems to have been well understood in Nashville that he was still loyal to the old Government, for while acting in the capacity of representative, he was arrested by the Confederate States Marshal on a charge of disloyalty to the Confederacy.

It was during this session of the Legislature that Mr. Fleming wrote his celebrated letter, which placed him in the estimation of all who have read it among the best humorists of the country. Fort Donelson had fallen, and the Federal Army under General Buell was approaching Nashville. Governor Harris, the Legislature, all the public functionaries of the State, and the secession citizens of Nashville were thrown into the wildest panic.

They were attempting to save themselves by hurried flight. Mr. Fleming witnessed all these things, and wrote an account of them, which, in some way, got into the newspapers. In point of humor, it would do credit to Mark Twain.

Some time in 1862, or early in 1863, Mr. Fleming left East Tennessee and became a refugee in Kentucky. While there he wrote a second letter, which was published in the newspapers, giving an account of a similar panic which had occurred in Knoxville previous to his departure upon the reported approach of the Federal Army. This letter also gave further evidence of Mr. Fleming's talents for humorous writing.

He acted in 1861 as the Secretary of the Knoxville-Greeneville Convention, and faithfully reported the proceedings of that body, which were put into form and published under his supervision. He was also a member of the Secret Union Executive Committee, appointed by the Greeneville Convention. He remained true to the Union and to the administration of Mr. Lincoln until the spring of 1864, when he joined Nelson, Baxter, and other Union leaders in support of General McClellan for the Presidency in opposition to Mr. Lincoln. He opposed the administration of William G. Brownlow as Governor, and also the Reconstruction measures of the Republican Party. He finally became a full-fledged Democrat, remaining so to the end of his life.

In 1871, after the restoration of the Democratic party to power in the State, he was appointed State Superintendent of Public Instruction by Governor John C. Brown. At one time he was also a prominent candidate for the Democratic nomination for Governor, and his chances of success seemed fair. He probably would have received the nomination, but for certain irregularities in his personal habits. At one period, since the war, he again returned to his editorial work in Knoxville, and in this capacity he became known throughout the State as one of its most brilliant writers. Unquestionably he was one of the most accomplished editors the State has ever possessed. His versatility enabled him to employ in his work the most varied talents. While emphatically peaceable in his disposition, as an editor it was unsafe to attack him. In controversy, there was but one man in the State at that time who was his superior, and that was William G. Brownlow. Mr. Fleming was always wary and cautious, and avoided arousing the old lion of the Knoxville *Whig*. On one or two occasions, he did venture to cross the path of Mr. Brownlow, but the latter, with one short pithy paragraph, secured silence. A short time previous to the War, John Mitchell, the celebrated Irish Patriot, as he was styled, in conjunction with William G. Swan, started a newspaper in Knoxville, advocating the most extreme Southern views. In some way Mr. Fleming and Mr. Mitchell became involved in a controversy. The wit and ridicule which Fleming bestowed upon Mitchell were more than that impulsive Irishman could endure. He accordingly assaulted Mr. Fleming on the street, but no serious damage resulted to either party. Perhaps a more noted case of the power of Mr. Fleming was the controversy which occurred at a later day between him and James Phelan, a member of Congress, and a former editor at Memphis, and a late historian of Tennessee. Phelan in his history cast serious reflections upon some of the early inhabitants of East Tennessee. Fleming took up the gauntlet in behalf of his own people, and overwhelmed Phelan with facts and ridicule. The latter became exasperated, and in desperation challenged Fleming to mortal combat.

After the war, at intervals, Mr. Fleming followed the practice of his profession. If he had been constant and persistent, his efforts would have been crowned with great success. It cannot be said that he was ever a great lawyer. His time was so divided between journalism, politics, the law, and the superintendency of public instruction, that it is no wonder that he did not become eminent in a profession requiring unremitting attention. But he certainly possessed a legal mind of a superior order. He was capable of high achievements in this direction. He had remarkable memory, quick apprehension, nice discrimination, and the power of profound thought. To win high distinction, he lacked only industry, persistence, and high distinct purpose, sustained by unswerving determination. Yet Mr. Fleming, notwithstanding his idle habits, sometimes did achieve considerable success when his heart and mind were warmly enlisted in a cause. He won justly merited reputation at the close of the war by the ability he displayed in the defense of some Union soldiers charged with murder, by raising the question, and arguing it with ability, as to the jurisdiction of the State Courts in a case of the kind. The case was prosecuted from one court to another, both State and Federal, until it finally reached the Supreme Court of the United States, where Fleming's position was sustained, and consequently the prisoners were finally discharged. John Baxter used to say that few if any men in the State had such intellect as Fleming. This was the opinion, possibly in a modified sense, of all who were familiar with his capacity. While he possessed fancy, wit, and humor, reason was the dominant quality of his mind. These were helps, but they were subordinate to his judgment. Lacking in assiduity, he was naturally averse to hard labor, and could not bring himself down to continuous study. Doubtless he felt that he could accomplish with little study what required great labor on the part of ordinary minds. He was fond of general reading, and became exceedingly well versed in most of the elegant literature of the day, but for the dry details of the law he had no taste. He was an amiable, delightful companion, and enjoyed with great zest the convivialities of social life. It followed, therefore, that he had many warm personal friends. It must be confessed, however, after all that has been or can be said, that he failed of the high destiny for which his abilities qualified him. No one has ever questioned that he was prodigally endowed by nature with high intellectual gifts. But with all his gifts he was deficient in moral force, and could not resist temptation, finally becoming a victim of intemperance. He had many lovable traits, but alas, he had his failings.

Mr. Fleming is one of the three men who remain of the prominent Union leaders of 1861. It is melancholy to add that he is a wreck of his former self, both physically and mentally.*

---

*The above was written while Mr. Fleming was still alive. He died in 1900.

ANDREW J. FLETCHER.

Attended Washington College—Practiced Law in Newport—State Senator—Difficulty with Mason—A Refugee—Secretary of State—Candidate for U. S. Senate—Speech in Defense of State Administration—Origin of Term "Carpet Bag."

ANDREW J. FLETCHER, born in Carter County, Tennessee, June 21, 1820, was descended from Revolutionary stock,—his grandfather having lost his life in the battle of Brandywine. Andrew, the son of John and Leah Fletcher, was educated at Washington College, and afterward taught school in Elizabethton, at the same time studying law with Alfred D. Taylor. He was admitted to the bar, practicing his profession a short while in Elizabethton, and finally settled in Newport, Cocke County. Here he became a successful lawyer, being engaged in nearly every important case on the dockets of the courts, and extended his practice into some of the adjoining counties. In 1859, for the sake of better schools for his children, he removed to Greeneville.

While residing at Newport, Mr. Fletcher was induced by the Whigs to become the party's candidate for State Senator, for the district composed of the Counties of Greene, Cocke, Sevier, and Blount, and was elected by a handsome majority. His competitor was the celebrated Thomas D. Arnold, an old lawyer and experienced politician. The canvass became exceedingly bitter and personal. General Arnold was an expert in the use of language calculated to stir the blood of an opponent, and all his canvasses—and he had had many for Congress—were directly personal. Yet he found in Fletcher, a man who could give as well as receive hard blows. The canvass, while not distinguished for dignity and high-toned courtesy, was rendered famous by its bright encounters, the wit and sarcasm, and the biting retorts of two men skilled as mental athletes. Fletcher made as Senator considerable reputation as a man of talents. One of his speeches attracted much attention, as a specimen of argument, research, and wit. He came out of the Legislature with a greatly enhanced character as a man of ability.

Two years after his first race he was again a candidate for the Senate in the same district, but was beaten by Lloyd Bullen. In 1860 he unfortunately became involved in a difficulty with Robert Mason, of Greeneville, in which the latter was killed. The trouble grew out of a law suit in which Fletcher was counsel. Mason attacked Fletcher and followed it up with great violence. Investigating the facts immediately after the occurrence, as counsel for Fletcher, I became convinced that the killing was a clear case of self-defense, and the court and the prosecuting attorney must have also taken this view, for the defendant was never brought to trial. After remaining on the docket for a few terms, the case was dismissed. Fletcher was not, in the ordinary sense, a fighting man, much less a desperado. He was sober, peaceable, but with courage to defend himself when attacked.

When the Civil War came on, Andrew Fletcher, being a Whig, naturally took decided ground in favor of the Union. Taking the stump he pleaded for the preservation of the old Government, denouncing in no measured terms the insane scheme of ambitious men to disrupt it. Wherever heard his speeches produced a marked effect. He set men to thinking. He cited facts, weighty and momentous, that gave pause to the minds of men. His utterances were sharp and pointed, piercing to the very marrow of the question.

When the bitterness of the adherents of the South became so great that it was dangerous for pronounced Union men to remain at home, in East Tennessee, Fletcher became a refugee, and with a large party sought safety in Kentucky. He endured the hardships of a long journey through the pathless mountains, inspired by love of his government. After wandering as an exile from place to place, he finally settled in Evansville, Ind. By special request of President Lincoln, he made a number of speeches for the Union cause in the Northwest. In 1864 he also made speeches in Indiana and Illinois for Lincoln and Johnson.

When Tennessee was reorganized in 1865, he returned home, and was elected Secretary of State, which office he held for three years, at the expiration of which time he was re-elected, and held the office until the Democrats got control of the State, and defeated him in 1870. Mr. Fletcher then purchased a farm near Cleveland, and settled down for the practice of his profession. Unfortunately, he died in July, 1870, his useful life cut short at the age of fifty, in the very meridian of his fine mental powers.

In 1867 Mr. Fletcher was a prominent aspirant for a seat in the United States Senate, before Governor Brownlow announced himself as a candidate. It is no disparagement to his worthy competitors, Maynard, Cooper, and Fletcher, that through the overwhelming popularity of Brownlow they were all defeated. No man in this State, however worthy, could have had the remotest chance of success against him.

In June, 1867, while Secretary of State, Fletcher made a notable speech at Cleveland, Tenn., on the "issues of the canvass" in the State, in reply to one made a month earlier by John Baxter. William G. Brownlow was at that time a candidate for re-election as Governor, being the unanimous nominee of the Republican party. The dissatisfied spirits of the old Republican party, who had joined in the McClellan movement, and had supported President Johnson in his attempt to divide and destroy the party, nominated Emerson Etheridge in opposition to Brownlow. Etheridge took the stump and prosecuted one of the ablest and bitterest canvasses ever made in the State. He was then forty-seven years of age—in the very prime of vigorous intellectual manhood. From the Mississippi to the Mountains in the East, his burning words of denunciation were heard. John Baxter, his inferior in eloquence, but his superior in intellectuality and courage, took the stump in support of Etheridge, and in an exceedingly malignant speech arraigned Brownlow's administration. Judge John S. Brien of Nashville, an old Whig leader, also joined in the crusade. At no time excepting in 1861 has the State been so stirred by angry passion as during this canvass of 1867. Governor Brownlow was disabled from speaking by the partial loss of voice. It therefore fell to the lot of his Secretary of State, Fletcher, to defend the administration, in shaping the policy of which he had had much influence. He made but a single speech: that was sufficient.

The speech of Mr. Fletcher created a sensation throughout the State. I read it on its first appearance, and have recently reread it. The second reading has confirmed my first opinion—that it is a complete and masterly vindication of the State Government under Governor Brownlow, as the conditions then existed. It was bold in utterance, perspicuous in statement, skillful in argument, thorough in detail, caustic in condemnation, and withal, even-tempered, as of one who spoke from a consciousness of right, fortified by an irrefutable array of facts. It is the best defense of Brownlow's administration ever made, and the only one needed. The flood of misstatement and falsehood which was pouring in rapid currents over the State was dissipated by the clear and lucid statement of facts taken from the records.

Mr. Fletcher was one of the first, if not the very first, in the State to denounce the hordes of greedy office-seekers who came from the North in the rear of the army in the closing days of the War. He was ready to welcome the genuine settler, but for the adventurer who came to prey on the people of the South he had an undisguised contempt and hatred. In a speech in Nashville he had the boldness to use an expression that has since become national, in reference to this class of men. He said:

"No one more gladly welcomes the Northern man who comes in all sincerity to make a home here, and to become one of our people, than I, but for the adventurer and the office-seeker who comes among us with one dirty shirt and a pair of dirty socks, in an old rusty carpet bag, and before his washing is done becomes a candidate for office, I have no welcome."

This was the origin of the term "carpet bag," and out of it grew the well known term "carpet-bag government."

A. J. Fletcher was an honest and truthful man; upright in all the relations of life. His example and influence were on the side of law, order, morality, and religion, and he always stood ready to do his duty as a good citizen. His courage, moral and physical, was of a high order. There were no concealments, no double dealing, but directness in all transactions. His ability was much above the average even among men counted clever. His quick mind was clear, logical, well balanced, and capable of the nicest thought and discrimination. As a lawyer, he studied cases thoroughly, mastered them, and was never caught unprepared. His adversary always knew that he had to do his best to win his cause. He labored under the disadvantage of always having lived in little towns, where there were poor libraries, and but little stimulus to high endeavor. If he had been more favorably situated for development and self culture, there can be no doubt of the fact that he would have become a distinguished Tennessee lawyer. As a writer, his style, while not elegant, was felicitous and lucid. He went in a few words, both in speaking and writing, right home to the point. He had the faculty, unfortunately, of saying, in a few words, sharp and pointed things, sometimes producing laughter, and sometimes leaving a sting behind. His sarcasm was bitter, his wit enlivening or annoying, according to the object of it. Mr. Fletcher was either a hearty, genial, sunshiny friend, or an open, defiant enemy.

LEONIDAS C. HOUK.

Born in Sevier County—Appearance Before Judge Alexander—Read Law at Night—Encounter with Foote in 1861—Contradictory Qualities—Member of Johnson Convention—Career in Congress.

ONE of the unique characters of East Tennessee, somewhat after the type of David Crockett, William G. Brownlow, and Thomas D. Arnold—all of the same section—was Leonidas C. Houk, who was born and reared in Sevier County, the place of the nativity of John H. Reagan, now of Texas. Mr. Houk's father died when he was a mere boy, leaving him in extreme poverty to shift for himself. The only education he had was acquired in a two months' course in an old field schoolhouse, where the teacher was but one degree above the boy in scholarship. At an early age he learned the cabinetmaker's trade, and worked at it a few years. About the time he was grown he became a Methodist preacher, but soon abandoned that calling and turned to the profession of the law. It may be suspected that the work of the ministry was too repressive for his naturally elastic, bounding spirits.

Mr. Houk's introduction to the bench and the bar took place about 1853, when he was still a boy. In the Circuit Court at Maryville a criminal case was called against someone for shooting at a mark within two hundred yards of a public road. A bright, good-looking boy stepped forward to answer to the charge. Judge Alexander, who was presiding, asked if he had counsel. He said no, that he wished to submit. A witness was called, who testified to the facts. These showed plainly that the offense was wholly inadvertent, committed in ignorance of any such law. The Judge fined him in accordance with the statute. I was sitting in the bar and had become interested in the boy. I arose voluntarily, urging the Court to be merciful, suggesting that he was a mere youth, ignorant of the law, and would have to pay the fine and costs by hard labor, and that it was a case for the exercise of the greatest clemency. The Judge, though strict in the enforcement of law, was kind-hearted, and concluded, with the consent of W. G. McAdoo, the State's

Attorney General, to let the boy off with a nominal fine, Mr. McAdoo agreeing to remit his fee. By this time the good looks of the defendant and his bright replies had made him quite a favorite with the bar. This incident perhaps first suggested to young Houk the idea of studying law. He more than once referred to it in after life, and always in grateful terms. It made him my lifelong friend.

Two years later, as Governor Neill S. Brown, William G. Brownlow, Judge John S. Brien, and I were on our way to Sevierville to make political speeches, we overtook a boy on foot going to the meeting. As we came up he hailed us with some jocular remark. We halted, and on approaching, he recognized me, and reminded me of the incident in Court at Maryville. I had forgotten him, but not the incident. Here was the sprightly boy once more, now nearly grown into manhood. We took him into our conveyance and carried him the balance of the way to town. Governor Brown and Judge Brien were quite struck with him, not dreaming, however, that he would some day become the leader of his party in the State.

In 1859, or early in 1860, L. C. Houk, now grown, came into my office, and told me he wished to read law. He said he had no money with which to purchase law books; that he wished to borrow them from me; that he intended working during the day and reading during odd hours at night. I gave him a book, perhaps Blackstone. From time to time he came over on horseback from Clinton, where he then resided, distant eighteen miles, to get a new book, taking it back in his saddle bags. In a few months he was a full-fledged lawyer with his sign hanging out in Clinton. He used to laugh heartily about his first case. Shortly after he went to the bar, he had an advertisement put in the newspapers, something like this: "Special attention given to the collection of debts." It so happened that Jesse Ayres of Knox County had a note on him for a small amount, say five dollars. He enclosed the note to Houk, in a letter, telling him that he sent him for collection a note on one L. C. Houk, directing him to collect it and remit the proceeds. Promptly came a reply, saying: letter enclosing the note on one L. C. Houk had been received, that the gentleman had been seen, and that the note, amounting principal and interest to $6.33, had been promptly paid; that the fee for collecting was ten dollars, and crediting the account with that amount left a balance on fee of $3.67, which Mr. Ayres would please remit at his earliest convenience!

Ayres, as we can well imagine, was thunderstruck at the turn things had taken. Of course, this was simply one of Houk's characteristic jokes. No man paid his debts more willingly than he when he had the money, which was not always the case.

Young Houk was bright and witty, at times almost impertinent in his boldness. He made himself felt and heard wherever he went. He was embarrassed in the presence of no one. In 1861 the celebrated Henry S. Foote was sent by the secession leaders of Nashville into East Tennessee to make speeches to convert the Union men to secession. He had been until recently a Union man himself, and it was therefore thought he would have great influence. Among other places, he went to Clinton to speak. That was Houk's peculiar territory, and mere youth as he was, he suffered no man to make disunion speeches there without an answer. Accordingly he demanded of Governor Foote a division of time. Foote was almost breathless with astonishment at the audacity of this boyish-looking fellow demanding a division of time with him who had debated with Clay, Webster, Benton, Davis, Yancey, and others. But being a man of high courtesy, he readily granted the request. Foote made his regular speech—high-toned, able, and full of elegant civility. Houk followed with the confidence and assurance of a veteran. He knew all the points of the Union side perfectly, as well as all the weak places on the other side. With daring boldness and sometimes with rudeness of speech, he arraigned the secession party, enlivening the debate by happy anecdotes, and by sallies of wit aimed at the Ex-Senator and Ex-Governor.

As Houk went on with his speech, Foote was filled with amazement at the shrewdness, the extent of information, the happy hits and the cool impudence of the young village politician. Sometimes he would suddenly start, as was his custom under great excitement, as if to assault the speaker, and then resume his attitude of astonishment. This episode was such a surprise to Governor Foote that he could not tell which to admire the more, the bold assurance of the young man, or his sprightliness. Out of it there sprang a warm friendship between the two men.

I need hardly add that Mr. Houk was an enthusiastic Union man in 1861. He made Union speeches in his own, and perhaps in some of the adjoining counties. In the Greeneville Convention in June, 1861, he was a member of the Committee of thirty-one, called the "Business Committee," and as such favored the violent and extreme measures proposed. Some time after the August election, in 1861, seeing that all was lost at home, he quietly crossed the mountains and sought refuge in Kentucky. Here he enlisted in the 6th Tennessee Regiment of Infantry, of which he was made Colonel. In about two years he resigned from the Army. In 1865 he was a member of Andrew Johnson's pretended Convention, which assumed to amend the Constitution of the State. He was one of the few persons present—I do not say delegates, for there were no regularly appointed delegates there—who had the courage to oppose the alteration of the Constitution in that irregular and illegal manner.

After the State was reorganized and restored to its former relations with the Federal Union, Mr. Houk was elected Judge of the Circuit Court of the circuit embracing the county in which he resided. This office he held until about 1870, when he resigned, resuming the practice of law. In order to have a larger field of professional labor he moved to Knoxville, later forming a partnership with Henry R. Gibson. These two made a strong firm. In a short time their business became large and profitable. Mr. Gibson was already a good lawyer, and Judge Houk by hard study rapidly became one. They soon became one of the leading firms in East Tennessee. Judge Houk developed qualities hitherto not supposed to belong to him—industry, and the ability of patient and thorough investigation both of law and facts. He not only could seize and understand the most profound legal principles, but it afforded him the most sincere pleasure to be engaged in their investigation. Legal discussions, no matter how abstruse, excited his liveliest interest.

Mr. Houk unquestionably had a legal mind of a high order. Had he remained a few years longer at the bar, he would have become one of the foremost lawyers of Tennessee. He could state a legal proposition with the most exact precision. This was the more remarkable when it is recalled that he had no education, and had never studied the standard law books, except in the most cursory manner. Even when on the bench, where he studied little and frolicked a great deal, he sometimes wrote opinions in important cases which astonished the profession. An able jurist who had made much reputation on the Supreme bench, and who did not like Houk, on reading one of these opinions, remarked to the author: "It is amazing where that man learned his law. He never studies, he never reads, he has no education, and yet he writes better opinions than we can after studying all our lives, and they are besides written in as exact and as good English as we college graduates can use."

The clear, terse, and generally correct language, of both Houk's written speeches and of his legal writings, was something astonishing, considering his almost total want of education, something Andrew Johnson and Judge John Baxter, with all their ability, never acquired.

In 1878, just as Houk was beginning to make for himself a reputation as a lawyer, and had begun to accumulate property, he was, unfortunately for himself, tempted by favorable circumstances, to enter the arena of politics. The field was open to go to Congress, and though contrary to his first inclination, as I happen to know,* he finally yielded to the temptation. He became a candidate, and was easily elected in the strong Republican district of which Knoxville is the center. For seven successive terms he was elected, generally with an increased majority. In each race he had opposition, sometimes bitter and determined, but his hold on the public was such that he could never be defeated. Were he alive to-day, he would still no doubt be in Congress. But before the commencement of the seventh term, he died suddenly in Knoxville, June, 1890, in the sixty-sixth year of his age.

Leonidas C. Houk exhibited qualities that seemed contradictory. For example, he was a stalwart in politics. His speeches and utterances toward the opposite party were often bitter and defiant, and always positive, and yet at times he manifested a moderation perfectly inconsistent. During the violence and the bitterness of the period from 1865 to 1868, he disagreed with his party as to two important measures: disfranchisement and negro suffrage. He believed that the disfranchisement of the se-

---

*Before the question came up for final determination he urged me to accept this position, and offered to use all his influence for me, which offer was declined.

cessionists should have been limited to those who were the active leaders in the secession movement, to those who had held office under the old government, and to those who accepted office under the Confederacy, including officers who served in its armies. He believed it was bad policy, as well as harsh and unjust, to exclude from the ballot box the thousands of privates in the army, and peaceable private citizens who had taken no active part in inaugurating the revolution. This was unquestionably so. Whether Judge Houk ever expressed these views publicly, I know not, but he certainly entertained them and expressed them privately. When the question of enfranchising the colored race of the State was first presented for consideration and adoption, he openly and publicly opposed it. In a circular addressed to the voters of the Second Congressional District, in 1867, he arraigned Mr. Maynard, his competitor, because he favored colored suffrage. All can now see how level-headed Houk was in reference to these policies.

The conduct of Judge Houk, in 1869, in the race for the Governorship between Senter and Stokes, was not so divergent as it at first appears. He gave his earnest support to Senter, and made speeches in his behalf, when it was well known that there existed an agreement, either expressed or implied, that the election laws, in reference to those laboring under disfranchisement, were to be disregarded in the approaching election, on the condition that these persons voted for Senter. This they generally did. While firm in his opinions, and an unfaltering Republican, Houk was personally generous in his feelings toward his political enemies. He had not, as stated, approved of the wholesale disfranchisement of the secessionists in 1865; therefore in that respect he was consistent in supporting Senter. But helping openly to overthrow the laws of the State presents quite another question. I choose not, at this late day, to enter upon its discussion, since those laws were very sweeping in their application, and the result reached was what had to come soon anyway, and the sooner the better, perhaps.

Judge Houk was ardent and impetuous in temperament, open, and bold in speech. He practiced little concealment of any kind. Feeling strongly, in the heat and excitement of debate, he naturally expressed himself strongly, even bitterly. But withal, he possessed a big, warm heart, and in private life all this bittterness entirely disappeared, except against his personal enemies. Even toward the latter he was magnanimous, and ready to forgive on the first indication of friendship. His sympathy for suffering was of the tenderest. Indeed his heart in its tender affection softened at all suffering, all sorrow, all want. He would borrow from a friend five or ten dollars for some immediate need, and give half of it to the first object of charity he met on the street. His tender heart could resist no appeal. It was the knowledge on the part of the people of this generous nature, of this undoubted sympathy with the hardships of the toiling masses, that gave him a hold on the affections of the people without a parallel in our section except that of William G. Brownlow.

Judge Houk seldom made a mistake in politics. He was wise in forethought. A prominent, aspiring man from an adjoining county once wrote him a very indiscreet letter, proposing some kind of a political partnership. The proposition was well calculated to produce a sensation if made public. Houk afterward was telling a friend about this episode, when the latter asked: "What did you do? Did you answer the letter?" "No," replied he, with a cunning smile, "I put nothing on paper. I carefully filed the letter, got on my horse and rode to his county to *talk* the matter over!" As long as Judge Houk lived, he kept that letter, and held it *in terrorem* over that man. One of his habits, like that of William G. Brownlow, was to preserve all letters, whether from friend or foe, never knowing when a present friend might become an enemy.

Leonidas C. Houk had great fondness for the humorous side of life. This made him a favorite in social circles and on the streets. Men delighted to listen to his ever overflowing good humor constantly bubbling up and breaking out in his speeches, as well as in private conversation. This was nearly always genial and kindly. When he appeared on the streets, he was sure to be surrounded by a crowd listening to his cheery, fresh, original remarks. These were not mere idle jests, but thoughts seasoned and flavored with sparkling humor. With all his flow of good feeling, there was mingled a keen wit, sharp and pointed, but, like his humor, nearly always good-natured. For years, perhaps yet, his bright sayings as a boy were quoted in Sevier, Blount, and Anderson counties, where he had resided. Seldom, if ever, did any man either at the bar, on the stump, or in Congress get the advantage of him in the play of wit, humor, or repartee. He rarely used this wit to wound and seldom in sarcasm. His nature was too kindly for the infliction of pain.

No one who knew Judge Houk ever questioned his ability. He had a well-rounded intellect, equally strong in every direction. He could comprehend almost at a glance the most difficult questions. But more than this, he could hold a question before his mind until he turned upon it all the concentrated light of his reason. His mind was not only logical, it was astute and discriminating. In a word, there seemed to be nothing, in intellectual effort, that he was not naturally equal to.

It may be strange for me to state that Judge Houk was exceedingly fond of the deeper problems of theology. He delighted in discussing these. He understood the leading tenets of every denomination in the State. When he had a little leisure, which seldom happened in the latter part of his life, he was fond of reading. He was especially fond of deep philosophical, ethical, or religious works. Does this sound strange to the reader? Let it be remembered that Judge Houk was a thinker, an investigator, and was naturally religiously inclined. He had the most devout reverence for all things sacred. The strength and the breadth of his intellect led him to the belief that the stupendous and harmonious wonders of creation were not the result of chance, but the work of an infinitely wise and omnipotent power—an Almighty God! At home he was a regular attendant at the Methodist Episcopal Church, of which he was a member.

In his later years, Judge Houk when not engaged in a canvass, or in mingling with his friends, was an earnest worker. The amount of work he could do and the rapidity and ease with which he threw it off, were astonishing. When on the point of opening an important canvass, he would, in a few hours, dash off with his own hand, a speech which would be the keynote of the campaign, and deliver it nearly exactly as first written. He knew in advance what he wanted to say, and in his logical mind every thought presented itself in its natural order. There was no confusion of ideas, nor obscurity of meaning.

In his own State he was a leader, not a follower in politics. For years before his death he was the leading man in the Republican party in Tennessee. He generally wrote or largely dictated its platforms, and made the opening speech, indicating the lines along which the battle was to be fought. His judgment in regard to the issues to be presented in a canvass was almost unerring. He knew what would prove popular and what would prove otherwise. He scarcely ever committed an error in this regard. Springing from the humble walks of life, it would be expected that he would exhibit more or less demagogism in his opinions and speeches. On the contrary he was exceptionally free from this spirit. He had the independence to think for himself, and to avow his opinions openly before the people. Where there was likely to be a difference in opinion, he trusted to his ability to convert them to his views.

Judge Houk possessed in the highest possible degree a sensitive, delicate organism. His feelings and sensibilities were most acute. His nervous system responded to the lightest touch, and thrilled at the slightest harshness. He was the subject of extreme exhilaration or of extreme depression. And this, beyond a doubt, largely accounts for his failings. A cold, sluggish nature is deeply moved neither by passion nor appetite, neither by success nor disappointment. Higher natures need something to restore or keep alive their exaltation. They crave and must have stimulation, either mental or sensual. It thus comes to pass that genius is too often allied to great failings.

Judge Houk had his failings. The world knew them. He knew them, admitted them, and lamented them. And "grievously" he "answered" for them. They were buried with him. Let the silence of the grave cover them.

HORACE MAYNARD.

Born in Massachusetts—Graduate of Amherst—Professor in East Tennessee University—Defeated for Congress by Churchwell in 1853—Elector for State at Large in 1856—Elected to Congress in 1857, 1859, and 1861—At Disadvantage Among Southerners—Went Into Kentucky After August Election, 1861—Attorney General of the State—Twice Elected to Congress in the '60's—In 1865 Defeated for U. S. Senate—In 1872 Elected to Congress from State at Large—In 1874 Defeated for Governor by James D. Porter—In 1877 Appointed Minister to Elected to Congress in the '60's—In 1865 Defeated for U. S. Senate—by Howell E. Jackson in 1881—Ability—Oratory—Personal Characteristics—Rank as a Lawyer—Early Political Experiences—Last Days.

ONE of the distinguished Union men of East Tennessee, in 1861, and in fact the most distinguished after Johnson, Brownlow, and Nelson, was Horace Maynard. He was not perhaps in ability quite the equal of one, or possibly two of these, and yet he was no ordinary man. Nature had been bountiful in the bestowal of mental gifts on him. These had been improved by all that a finished education and hard study could do.

Horace Maynard was a graduate of Amherst College. When he entered college he put the letter "V" prominently above the door of his room. When he became the valedictorian of his class the meaning of the mysterious letter was explained. After his graduation he located in Knoxville, Tenn., and was for a number of years a professor in the East Tennessee University, now the University of Tennessee. Among the public or professional men of his day, in Tennessee, he was one of the ripest and most polished scholars. Indeed, in broad culture, but few college professors anywhere were his superiors. This gave him in some respects an immense advantage over his compeers.

Mr. Maynard was born in Massachusetts. The fact that he was born in that State was a drawback to him in his political career in the South. I believe he always felt that such was the case, especially after the fierce sectional strife arose. To this feeling may perhaps be attributed, in part, the extreme caution which always characterized his course and utterances in public life. He seemed sensibly to realize that the Southern people would not tolerate in a native of Massachusetts the boldness of speech that they accepted in a native of the South. Hence his words were often marked by a certain hesitation. But, independent of this fact, he was by nature wanting in that openness and independence which were so conspicuous in Brownlow and T. A. R. Nelson.

Mr. S. S. Prentiss, when he first went to Mississippi, was conscious of the disadvantage he labored under as a Northern man, and he fought duels as he said in order to secure the respect of the people, and to avoid contempt and insults.

In politics, Mr. Maynard was an old-line Whig before the war. In 1853 he was nominated for Congress by the Whig party in the Knoxville district. His competitor was William M. Churchwell, a man of wealth and of great shrewdness. By the use of money and other means not to be commended, Churchwell succeeded in overcoming a good Whig majority and in being elected. Maynard, it must be confessed, was far from being popular at that time. In proof of this I give the vote in Knox County, his home:

Maynard, Whig	1760
Churchwell, Democrat	1210
Henry, Whig candidate for Governor	2308
Johnson, Democratic candidate for Governor	787

In the Presidential canvass of 1856 Maynard was selected by his party as one of the electors for the State at large. Ignoring the bad treatment he had received in 1853, he magnanimously took the stump, and canvassed the State with great earnestness and ability. This conduct on his part greatly endeared him to his party, and gave him a popularity not possessed before. In 1857 he was again nominated for Congress without opposition in his own party, and was elected by a small majority. In 1859 and in 1861 he was re-elected, no one in his own party opposing him.

Mr. Maynard's career in Congress during these six years was not distinguished by any striking display of ability such as he possessed. He was regarded as a man of much more than average capacity, but he by no means became a party leader. In 1859, during the long contest for Speaker, however, he at one time received sixty-five votes for that position, a very high compliment. John A. Gilmer of North Carolina, distinguished as he was, could command only thirty-six votes. Each of the parties, the Democrats, the Republicans, and the Americans, had its own candidate.

From 1860 to the spring of 1861, the great absorbing topic, both in Congress and out of it, was the impending crisis on the slavery question. He that was the boldest, and the most defiant in the utterance of his opinions, whether on the one side or the other, was the man who gained the greatest notoriety.

I have placed Mr. Maynard among the Union leaders in 1861, and he deserves that position both by reason of his ability and his reputation, yet in a true sense he was deficient in some of the elements of leadership. A leader in times of revolution must have courage, audacity, and enthusiasm, as well as ability. Ability Mr. Maynard certainly had, but not the other qualities in high degree. While not deficient in a reasonable share of physical courage, in that infinitely higher quality which enables a man not only to face danger, but to defy public opinion, and inspire others with his own great spirit, he was not distinguished. Yet I repeat, that I think this was in part due to the fact that he always felt the disadvantage among a Southern people of having been born and educated in the North. When we add to this his natural caution, we can see how it operated on his mind. It would be in vain to deny that he had warm admirers, but in the later years of his life, after he had risen to greater eminence he had a much more devoted personal following.

After Mr. Maynard's return from Congress, some time in April, 1861, he took the stump and rendered able service in behalf of the Union. His speeches were earnest and strong in arguments and facts. But it was not arguments that were then needed. It was courage—enthusiasm—leadership. Arguments did not hold the timid or the wavering. The agency of the revolution was terror. In the wild whirl and frenzy of passion, reason lost its way. In times of great danger, "on the perilous edge of battle," men needed the example of courage, not polished sentences. The contagion of daring, like the contagion of fear, quickly spreads from man to man. Many of the men who early rushed into the Confederate Army were moved by sudden fear —the apprehension of some great disaster that was impending— they knew not what.

I would not underestimate the services rendered to the Union cause by Mr. Maynard. They were unquestionably great. His name and high character, as well as his ability, were of the highest value. But the opinions of the Union men were already fixed long before he returned from Washington, as was shown by the February election. When he returned he did not change them, but simply, with the assistance of others, helped to hold and confirm them. For this he deserves the gratitude of his countrymen, especially when so many others were false and faithless.

At the August election in 1861, notwithstanding the State had seceded in June, Mr. Maynard was voted for and elected a member of the Congress of the United States by the Union men. He remained in the State until the day of election. He managed on that day to be in Scott County, which lies on the border of Kentucky. When he had thus finished his canvass and arranged all his plans, he took his horse, crossed over into Kentucky, and went on to Washington at his leisure. Not until Burnside had redeemed East Tennessee in September, 1863, was he permitted to return to his home. At the opening of the next Congress he was sworn in as a member of that body, not on the certificate of the Governor, but on the certificate of the loyal sheriffs of the different counties, who certified that he had received a majority of the votes cast.

When Andrew Johnson was Military Governor of Tennessee, Mr. Maynard was appointed by him Attorney General of the State. After the State was readmitted into the Union, he was again elected a member of Congress, and at the next election he was re-elected.

1865, before the State was recognized by Congress as entitled to representation in that body, Mr. Maynard was a candidate for a seat in the United States Senate. He was defeated by eight votes by Judge David T. Patterson. At the same session Joseph S. Fowler was elected to fill the other seat in the Senate. Looking back at these results, at this day, they certainly seem most surprising. Mr. Maynard was entitled to this position both by reason of ability and services. Neither of these men was distinguished for superior ability, though both ranked above the average. Neither of them by virtue of services had any strong claim on the party. Patterson, like Johnson, was an old-line Democrat, and had supported Breckinridge in 1860. He made no speeches for the Union in 1861—indeed he could not make a speech. Neither had Mr. Fowler rendered any service that gave him a claim on the State or the party for such a high honor. The election of Patterson can be easily accounted for; he was the son-in-law of President Johnson. It was fortunate for Mr. Johnson that these two men were elected Senators, for on the impeachment trial they both voted for his acquittal.

The election of Patterson over Maynard was an error and a wrong. True, he was a man of fair ability, and a worthy gentleman. He had made a most excellent Circuit Judge, but he had not built up the Union party and had no claims upon its honors. After a few months in the Senate, he went back to his life-long love—the Democratic party. Mr. Fowler was a worthy man, but he also had done nothing to merit such a distinction. Recently from Ohio, he was not identified with Tennessee except for a brief period. Mr. Maynard would have been elected but for the influence of Mr. Johnson, and he would have reflected honor upon the State in a much larger measure than either of the others.

In 1872, a member of Congress had to be elected from the State at large in Tennessee. Mr. Maynard was nominated for this position by his Republican friends. General B. F. Cheatham was put in nomination by the Bourbon Democracy, and Andrew Johnson became a candidate of his own volition. The canvass was an interesting one as well as a remarkable one. Cheatham had been a brave and distinguished General in the Confederate Army, as well as a gallant Colonel in the Mexican War. He was a plain, blunt, honest man, who was always ready in war for a fight. He believed that war meant fighting. He was no speaker and was of very moderate ability. The three canvassed the State together. Johnson, of course, had his own policy to defend, and so far as he was concerned, spent his time in defense of himself and in attacks on his enemies. Cheatham made short, sensible, but gentlemanly speeches. Maynard was fair, honorable, and exceedingly dignified. His polished sentences and elegant bearing were in marked contrast with the coarse, strong, bitter language and harsh manner of Johnson. In none of his previous canvasses had Mr. Maynard made so much reputation as a public speaker. He won golden opinions from all parties. The contrast between the two men was marked. In this canvass Maynard reached the zenith of his fame and popularity. It was admitted by all parties that in eloquence and dignified bearing he rose far above Johnson. He never appeared so well. The result was that he added immensely to his reputation, while Johnson lost. I need hardly add that with a divided Democracy Mr. Maynard was easily elected. In 1874 Mr. Maynard was the Republican candidate for Governor against James D. Porter. He was defeated, almost as a matter of course, in a Democratic State. In 1875 he was appointed Minister to Turkey by President Grant. He represented this government with dignity at the Court of the Sublime Porte, though nothing arose during his official term demanding special diplomatic ability. At the end of about five years, D. M. Key, the Postmaster General under President Hayes, was appointed United States District Judge for Tennessee, and Mr. Maynard was recalled for the purpose of taking the place thus made vacant in the cabinet. The duties of this office he discharged efficiently and faithfully until Mr. Cleveland came into power. This closed the public life of Mr. Maynard. In 1881 he was a candidate for U. S. Senator, and was beaten by Howell E. Jackson, after a very close race, the Democrats being in a majority. From this time till his death, May 3, 1882, he spent his time quietly among his old friends in Knoxville. He never seemed so agreeable, so happy, and pleasant as after his retirement. As the sunshine of a bright closing day settled about him he took more than usual interest in good works. Whenever called on he delivered graceful lectures to Sunday schools or prayer meetings, seeming to realize that the stormy scenes of political life were over, and that the time for rest and peace and preparation had come. He delighted in going quietly around among his old friends, sitting down and having with them long familiar talks. Many people now saw Mr. Maynard in a new light,—in that of the quiet Christian gentleman, with a well-stored intellect and a heart out of which had been taken all traces of bitterness and passion. The night before his death, a friend and myself were with him, at his own house, until a late hour, on important business connected with the University of Tennessee, of which institution we were all trustees. As this gentleman, who was a strong Democrat, and I walked home together that night, the wisdom, the deep earnestness, the utter absence of all prejudice, and the intense desire to do what was right, on the part of Mr. Maynard, were subjects of remark by both of us. He was then apparently in perfect health, with the promise of several years more of usefulness. In thirty hours or less after we left him, he passed suddenly away from heart failure at the age of sixty-seven years.

The community was startled by the unexpected news of his death. On the day of his funeral there had never been such a concourse of sorrowing people on the streets of Knoxville, except on the occasion of the death of Ex-Senator Brownlow, a few years earlier. His sudden demise in the full maturity of his powers, and in the enjoyment of perfect health, deeply touched the public heart.

The private life of Mr. Maynard was singularly pure and free from reproach. I do not recollect ever having heard him charged with a single questionable act in point of morals, and in all his stormy political life he maintained his consistency as an upright member and a ruling elder in the Presbyterian Church. In all things he was extremely regardful of the truth. His life conformed to his professions. In his dealings he was honest and just, always rendering to others what was their due, while in his public life no temptation could seduce him from the path of honor and honesty. The best proof of his absolute integrity is found in the fact that he died with only a moderate estate, notwithstanding that he had had a large practice as a lawyer before he entered public life, and that during all the time he was in the public service—about twenty-five years—he lived in the simplest manner, and with the strictest economy.

In ability Mr. Maynard was above the average of even able men. His mind was remarkably quick, incisive, and penetrating. It was more: it was strong, comprehensive, and brilliant. Few men thought more quickly or more clearly. There was no flaw, no weakness in his intellect. It was well-rounded,—bright, broad, and deep. And yet I do not mean to say that he was massive intellectually, for he was not. But he certainly had a clear, bright mind, of great force and rare power. His head was large and decidedly intellectual in outline. Fred Douglass, in speaking of him, once said he had a "three-story head." His eyes were as black as could be, and wonderfully bright, sparkling like coals of fire. I do not think the world ever saw a full manifestation of his mental power. There were certain hindrances to this in his nature—caution, timidity, modesty,—

some characteristic—which always restrained him. His greatest exhibitions of power were at the bar.

In oratory Mr. Maynard always ranked high in Tennessee. He possessed some of the first qualities of a fine orator. He was tall and straight in person, and if he was not graceful, he was not ungainly. His voice was uncommonly deep and strong, rather musical, and with a wide compass and great power, pleasant in all its variations. In imagination he was sufficiently gifted to adorn his argument with enough rhetoric to relieve it from dryness,—weaving beautiful threads of gold into his web of facts. When he wished he could be almost as effective as Rufus Choate, but without the dazzling display of W. T. Haskell, of our own State, whose marvelous eloquence will never be forgotten by those who heard him.

Besides person, voice, intellect, and a chaste fancy, Mr. Maynard, as I have already stated, had culture of a rare order. This gave him the use of the best and choicest language. All his words were skillfully chosen, and all his sentences were polished and rounded ready for the press. Few men, of little or of great renown, spoke such pure, perfect, beautiful English. The thought was always good; the language exceedingly felicitous.

In addition to these qualities, his mind was stored with useful information as well as with elegant learning, and all that adds to the graces of oratory. He was a thorough classical scholar, with a memory that was never at fault, so he could draw at times on his varied and almost boundless resources.

To give point and effect to his arguments, he had at his command humor, keen wit, and a biting sarcasm. It is doubtful, however, whether this last quality is not, in public speakers, a source of weakness rather than strength. It certainly is, if used often. In early life Mr. Maynard used these gifts, especially his sarcasm, a great deal at the bar, and with terrible effect. Toward the close of his career he seemed to have mellowed down very much, and the use of severe or offensive language was seldom heard from him.

I could name several orators in Tennessee who excelled Maynard in popular effectiveness, but none of them was his equal in pure, lucid, and classical English. Governor James C. Jones was a marked illustration of the former class. He was rather a shallow man, but by reason of his dashing manner was unquestionably one of the greatest popular orators of his day. And yet Mr. Maynard was no ordinary speaker. He sometimes rose for a moment into the loftiest strains of brilliant oratory. It always seemed to me that he was capable of doing so at all times. I think it possible that his taste and his culture, acquired in early life by study and in teaching, became a positive drawback to him as an extemporaneous speaker.

As a lawyer Mr. Maynard stood high, his legal ability never being questioned. Almost as soon as he was admitted to the bar, he was rated by his fellow lawyers as an able member of the profession. He at once went into a full practice, at least as full as the measure of legal business then warranted. In the preparation of his cases he spared no labor. When the trial came on he was master of his case, fighting with intense earnestness for his client. In this theater there appeared most conspicuously the learning of the lawyer and the skill and shrewdness of the advocate. He was wary, vigilant, artful, and able.

He unquestionably possessed a mind capable of the finest analysis and the clearest reasoning. In the argument of his cases, whether before the court or a jury, he was strong and clear. His addresses to the jury were forcible and shrewd, and full of fire and vehemence. Often they were bitter and withering. Here he gave full vent to his wit, sarcasm, and his irony, frequently displaying a high order of eloquence, and often illustrating with happy effect the point in issue by some beautiful classical allusion. It was in these extemporaneous speeches before juries and courts that Mr. Maynard's highest efforts were made. Here, in my opinion, he displayed greater ability than he ever did in politics. I always questioned whether he did not commit a mistake in quitting the bar. Certainly he could have won the highest eminence in this field. His ability was sufficient to have won fame for him beyond the limits of the State, if an opportunity had presented itself.

Mr. Maynard came to the bar in the golden era of the profession in East Tennessee. John A. McKinney, the elder, still lingered at the bar with his distinguished ability. Robert J. McKinney had just reached the meridian of his well-earned fame. Thomas A. R. Nelson, though still young, had nearly attained the zenith of his successful career. Gray Garrett, of Tazewell, was still noted for his wit, his exact learning, and for his incisive logic and power. William H. Sneed was now in the full vigor of his prime, and in the exercise of those quick and strong faculties which made him so formidable an antagonist. And Thomas C. Lyon, next after Mr. Maynard the most cultured man at the bar, was then also in the full possession of those splendid powers which made him, in the estimation of many, the ablest lawyer in the State. Certainly he was excelled by few. These were all great lawyers, recognized as such throughout the State at that time, and they still hold place in the memory of this generation.

Mr. Maynard in his wide circuit came in contact with all these, and notwithstanding the high standard of ability they formed, he was able to make a reputation but little inferior, and in some respects superior to any one of them. He did this, too, in only a few years, for he left the bar to enter Congress after only about ten years of practice, and never returned to it. His career as a lawyer is indeed remarkable and brilliant.

During the first few years of Mr. Maynard's life at the bar he was abrupt and unamiable, and often offensive in his manners, snapping men up without hesitation. Many were the persons he stung and wounded by his biting sarcasm or pungent wit. But few men whom I have known were so savage and so bitter toward witnesses and the opposite parties in his cases; and sometimes his assaults were simply terrible. In his younger days his manner toward his fellows was cold and stiff, which explains in part his early unpopularity. But once in politics he outgrew this habit. In his early days he was in fact a typical Massachusetts man, and not a Southerner, in his manners.

Never, perhaps, did an honest man make more enemies than he in early life. He had a few friends that were attached to him, a few who admired his ability, and only a few. Yet notwithstanding all this, his legal practice was large. Said a prominent Democrat, the Hon. Peter Staub, Consul to Geneva under Mr. Cleveland: "I voted twice for Mr. Maynard. I never liked him, but always *admired* him on account of his *talents* and the *purity of his character.*"

Time passed on. He began to make Whig speeches. That made him friends. It brought him also more in affiliation with the people. In 1853, as we have seen, he was nominated for

Congress, and was badly beaten in a Whig District. Seldom have the vials of slander and defamation been more freely and unjustly poured out than they were on him on this occasion. He took his defeat meekly, complained not, made further sacrifices for his party, and in this way began to grow stronger. In 1856 in the face of his recent ill-treatment, he canvassed the State for the Whig party. In 1857 he was again nominated for Congress, and this time was elected. Many of those who disliked him in 1853, through sympathy or from better knowledge of him, now supported him. He, too, had learned by experience. The "common herd," as he had called the plain people, with whom he said in one of his essays while a teacher in the University he "desired no fellowship," he at length learned to respect, and to treat with the consideration they always demand of those who seek their suffrages. By this time he had found out that the "few choice spirits" he desired as "associates," could not elect a man to a seat in Congress. The prejudice created by his manners and by these foolish articles, not written seriously perhaps, began to die away, but it did not entirely disappear until his last years in Congress, or until his triumphant race for that position against Andrew Johnson.

By long dependence on the people Mr. Maynard learned in a tolerable manner how to mix with them—how to win their personal esteem. But there always remained traces of his early stiffness and apparent coldness. I cannot say whether he was really cold and indifferent or not. I once thought in his younger days than he was. In the latter part of his life I saw so much that was sunshiny in him that I doubted the correctness of my former judgment. He was capable of acts of rare kindness, but always in a quiet, unostentatious way.

Mr. Maynard died in his sixty-eighth year, when he apparently had many years of usefulness before him. At the time of his death he was the most eminent citizen of the State, and the leading Republican of the South. He had outlived the prejudice which once existed against him, and had become the idol of his party. Travel anywhere through the State, and always a sentiment of deep attachment, or of sincere admiration was found to exist for him. At his name, the eyes of the Republicans sparkled, and their hearts swelled with pride and enthusiasm; while it called forth from Democrats words of praise for his great ability, his many virtues, and the exalted purity of his life. There was not, in fact, a black spot, or a serious blemish on his character. And as time goes on, I predict that his name and his fame will not die out, in this State, but will grow brighter. The people will remember with something of romantic interest the young New Englander who came among them to identify his fortune with theirs, and who, unaided and alone, and by his conspicuous integrity, energy, and superior abilities, rose to be one of the most honored citizens that ever lived in the State.

Mr. Maynard's life showed that a man could be a successful politician without losing his honesty or his religion, or becoming a demagogue. His influence was always healthful; his example and teachings helpful. Young men learned from him constant lessons of virtue and goodness, and an inspiration to an effort after a better and a brighter life.

All through Mr. Maynard's active public life, he was the object, beyond that of most public men, of malignant abuse on the part of his political enemies. Nothing was too bitter or too mean to be said of him. During much of his political life he lived in an atmosphere of storms and darkness—his life a veritable tempest. But as time went on, so much that was pure, so much that was honest and of good report was seen in him, that these clouds of slander and abuse cleared away. His own demeanor also had been becoming milder and gentler, and his opinions broader and higher, until at last he stood for the highest type of a pure and exalted citizen and sincere Christian. The contrast between the apparent coldness and the storms of his early life, and the gentle warmth and the soft calm of his later days, gave perhaps especial emphasis to the tranquillity and the sweetness of this last period.

I remember a total eclipse of the sun which occurred away back in the 'seventies. Awe-inspiring darkness gradually crept over the earth until it seemed that night had come. After awhile the sun came out from its obscuration in its full splendor, and again poured its light on the earth. The day was the very perfection of softness and beauty; the air balmy and serene. Not a leaf stirred. It was like those soft, bewitching, dreamy days that are often seen in the winter in California or Southern Texas. When evening came on, the sun sank beneath the western horizon in a sea of gold. Then, there shot up behind it a flood of purple and golden light, that filled all the western sky.*

Thus it was with Mr. Maynard. In his early political life he had his eclipse. There was almost total darkness. But this passed away and his evening came on; peaceful, cloudless, beautiful. And as he sank to rest, there was left behind the memory of a well-spent day and the light of a serene and beautiful sunset.

---

*This figure comes to my mind from the fact that a son of Horace Maynard, Washburn Maynard, then a young naval officer, now a Commander in the United States Navy, was at my house, which stood on an eminence, during this eclipse, making observations, perhaps for the use of the government. He has since become famous by reason of his learning, but especially because he fired the first shot in the late Spanish-American War.

JOHN McGAUGHEY.

Exponent of Justice and Goodness—Arrested near Athens—Provost Marshal—Raised Union Regiment.

THE sketches of the Union leaders of East Tennessee would be incomplete without a notice of the venerable and lamented John McGaughey of McMinn County, who was known by character all over East Tennessee, and by public men throughout the State. He was distinguished wherever he was known for purity of life and unstained integrity. In his own county his name was connected with every enterprise for the upbuilding of her people, in moral, intellectual, and material advancement, and he stood as the highest and foremost exponent of all things just and good and worthy.

Mr. McGaughey was an ardent old-line Whig, a noted type of those grand men, of whom there were so many of wealth and intelligence in East Tennessee, representing the best thought, the highest culture, and the broadest patriotism. When the Civil War came on, by education as well as by tradition he naturally preferred the glory of a broad nationalism to a narrow and bitter sectionalism based upon undying hatred of the North. He was, therefore, an unflinching friend of the Union. He was opposed to dividing a country naturally one, united by a common glory, a common interest, and by a common destiny.

Tall, grave, and dignified, he was a noted man wherever he appeared. Whenever he opened his lips, he spoke words of wisdom and truth. Seldom has any community been blessed with a better citizen or a nobler model of a man.

Yet, so bitter was the spirit that inspired the South, or rather I would say the baser sort of Southern men (for there were examples of mercy and magnanimity among the better class even here in East Tennessee, and very many from a distance), that a gang of outlaws, in 1863 or 1864, arrested this good and harmless man, in or near Athens, in McMinn County, and carried him off, inhumanely treating him, and then murdered him in the mountains at Hiwassee Gap. This was one of the saddest incidents in the Civil War in East Tennessee, being only one of hundreds that marked the suffering, the cruelties, and, in may instances, the barbarities, that befell Union men. I do not either directly or by implication charge this crime on the Confederate authorities, but expressly exonerate them from it, for the facts are, as I understand, that this inhuman deed was done by a lawless gang of Confederate guerrillas; but the *spirit* which inspired it, I regret to say, encouraged the bitterness of secession.

Mr. McGaughey was Provost Marshal at Athens, with the rank of Lieutenant, at the time of his arrest. He was engaged in raising a regiment for service in the Federal Army. The force which arrested him was under the command of a man named Graham—a thousand strong, it was said—from the State of Georgia.

On returning from Athens the force divided, and a part of it went to Madisonville, where it arrested Mr. Joseph Devine, and took him off into the neighboring mountains, where he also was cruelly murdered. Mr. Devine had taken shelter on the approach of the enemy in the cellar of Dr. Upton's house, and finding difficulty in getting him out, he was promised the treatment of a prisoner of war if he would surrender. Thereupon he accepted the terms offered him. He was also a Provost Marshal, with the rank of Lieutenant in the Federal Army, and was also engaged in recruiting a regiment for the Federal Army.

SAM MILLIGAN.

College Career—Physique—Influence with Pupils—Elected to Legislature in 1841—Re-elected in 1845—Read Law in Interval—Quartermaster in Mexican War in 1846—Greeneville *Spy*—In 1857 Defeated for Congress—In 1861 Aggressive for Union—In 1865 Appointed to Supreme Court of Tennessee—Appointed to Court of Claims in 1868—Influence Over Andrew Johnson—Personality.

SAM MILLIGAN, as he always signed his name, was my college mate and lifelong friend. I shall therefore speak of him with affectionate regard and possibly with undue partiality. He was born in Greene County, of humble but upright parentage, about the year 1814. At the age of sixteen he became a schoolteacher. Soon after that time, perhaps about 1834 or 1835, he entered old Greeneville College, then under the Presidency of that estimable man and accomplished scholar, Mr. Henry Hoss. By what chance the subject of our sketch conceived the idea of acquiring an education is altogether unknown. He lived in a very obscure part of the county, where there were at that time only occasional schools. Some unknown cause must have fixed his young mind with the ambition of becoming something above the conditions then surrounding him. The most trivial circumstances often determine the calling and the destiny of men.*

While at this college, Sam Milligan pursued his studies with assiduous devotion. The tall, pale, intellectual student soon attracted the attention of the president and of his fellow students. It was at once seen that he was no ordinary young man. The students were startled one day when the president announced that he would not be surprised if young Milligan should some day become a member of Congress—an honor at that time bestowed only on men of worth and ability. The news went

---

*I well remember, in my own case, that the accidental possession and reading of a small abridged edition of Locke's "On the Human Understanding" while I was in camp as a soldier in the Cherokee Nation, in 1838, amid the dissipations of camp life, led me to the settled conclusion of entering upon a regular college course as soon as I should return home, and of studying law, which purpose I unswervingly carried out until I had a law license in my pocket in 1846.

round among the boys, and from that time Milligan was regarded by them as an extraordinary person. From time to time, he assisted the president in teaching, or taught a short term school in the country to raise means to defray his expenses. I remember two such schools it was my good fortune to attend, one a class in arithmetic, another a three months' school in the neighborhood.†

Mr. Milligan was in Greeneville College perhaps three or four years, until the College finally went down about 1838, the president, Mr. Hoss, having died a year or two previously. So popular was Milligan as a teacher that the three months' school above referred to was largely attended, the best young men of the country for miles around coming to it on foot and on horseback. On the termination of that school in November, 1838, Mr. Milligan and four or five of his pupils, among whom was myself, went to Tusculum College, now Greeneville and Tusculum College, a few miles away, to renew their studies under Samuel W. Doak, D. D. Here Milligan continued his studies until 1841, when the unexampled honor of being nomi-

†I venture to give an account of the schoolhouse known as George Linty's, two miles from Greeneville College, in which the latter school was taught. The house was made of hewn logs, instead of round logs, as was usual in those days. The singular part of the house was its interior arrangements. It literally had a hanging chimney in the center of the room. By some means long beams were fastened to the joists and the rafters, extending a few feet above the roof and down to within four or five feet of the fireplace. These beams widened out from the roof toward the floor like a funnel. Across the beams laths were nailed. Then the chimney was stuccoed, not with lime plaster, but with red clay mud. This chimney was altogether unique. It was supposed theoretically and scientifically that the smoke from the fireplace, which was immediately under the chimney, would ascend and escape at its mouth on top, upon the principal suction. That theory held good so long as there was no disturbing element, but when there was a breeze or current from the door, the smoke refused to obey the laws supposed to govern it, and went out into the room, entering the eyes, throats, and nostrils of the pupils. Then what a scene of sneezing, coughing, and wiping of eyes took place! The seats, made of slabs, or puncheons, were ranged around the fireplace, which was immediately below the chimney, facing inward. There was another peculiar feature in this schoolhouse. On three sides of it a log was cut out, leaving an opening of about one foot in width. Instead of filling this opening with sash and glass, sheets of white writing paper, well greased on both sides to facilitate the admission of light, were pasted over the opening, and through this aperture the schoolhouse received its light. And, after all, it was not such a very bad light. Was there ever such a schoolhouse in the interior as this? Now, let it not be supposed from this description that this schoolhouse was in the wilderness, for it was situated in one of the best neighborhoods in Greene County that had been settled sixty years before.

nated as a candidate for the Legislature while still a student, was conferred upon him. Perhaps no such occurrence can be found in the history of the colleges of the country. He was easily elected, because the Democratic party, which had nominated him, was in a decided majority in his district. After serving in the Legislature as the colleague of Andrew Johnson, he returned to his studies and was graduated in 1843.

Sam Milligan was in College at least eight or nine years. This is partly explained by the fact that he had engaged in teaching school, and had lost one year or more in canvassing for the Legislature and in attending its sessions. But he was a deliberate man, never in a hurry about anything. His mind did not gather knowledge rapidly. He was, however, so thorough in all he did and in all he acquired that he never lost what he had once gained.

In 1845 he was re-elected to the Legislature. In the meantime he had been reading law, nominally in the office of Robert J. McKinney. In this year (1845), probably while at Nashville, he obtained a license to practice law, and after the adjournment of the Legislature returned to Greeneville, where he located. When the Mexican War broke out in 1846 he was appointed by President Polk a quartermaster in the army, with the rank of Major, and served first at Vera Cruz and afterward at Jalapa. Returning home at the end of the war, he resumed his professional life in Greeneville. In 1849, he married Miss Elizabeth Howard, an accomplished young lady of an old and excellent family of Greeneville. Some time after this he became the editor of a Democratic newspaper called the Greeneville *Spy*. Some years later he was appointed by the Governor or the Legislature a Commissioner on the part of Tennessee, to settle an old dispute as to the boundary line between the State of Tennessee and the State of Virginia, which duty he efficiently discharged. In the year 1857 he was an unsuccessful candidate for Congress in the first district, the conditions then existing not being favorable to his election, notwithstanding his great popularity. In the intervals, he pursued his profession with the greatest industry and with high success, considering that the dockets were not then crowded with business. In every case in which he was employed, he was conscientious and unsparing in the use of all honorable means in the discharge of his duty to his clients.

When the war broke out between the States in 1861, with the full concurrence of his judgment, he followed the leadership of his lifelong friend, Andrew Johnson, and gave a warm and earnest support to the cause of the Union. He was appointed by the Legislature in 1861 a delegate to the Peace Congress, which assembled in Washington, the object of which was, as its name implies, to preserve the peace of the country. In the preliminary struggles in the State of Tennessee over the question of secession, Mr. Milligan exerted all his influence, both in private and on the stump, in behalf of the preservation of the Union. His ability, his high character, and his great popularity were potent factors in preserving or creating a loyal sentiment in the minds of the people where he resided.

Mr. Lincoln, soon after his inauguration, appointed Mr. Milligan an associate Justice of the Supreme Court of the Territory of Nebraska, which office he declined.

In the election of 1861, Mr. Milligan was elected a delegate to the Constitutional Convention proposed by the Legislature, but which was negatived by the people in the February election. After the time had arrived when it was unsafe for Union men to express their sentiments, Mr. Milligan, like most of the other leaders, became quiet and ceased to make opposition to the Confederate Government. And yet there was never an hour during the period intervening between June, 1861, and September, 1863, when his heart did not turn fondly to the old government. In 1865, when the war was drawing to a close and Tennessee was virtually redeemed from the domination of the Confederate Government, he was appointed one of the Judges of the Supreme Court of Tennessee under the newly organized State. It should be stated, however, that in the so-called Constitutional Convention which assembled in Nashville in the winter of 1865, Mr. Milligan took a leading part, and largely drafted the amendments to the Constitution. He held his position on the Supreme bench until 1868, when, without any solicitation on his part, he was appointed by President Johnson a member of the Court of Claims, at Washington, which position he held until his death, April 20, 1874.

In the beginning of the political career of Andrew Johnson, Mr. Milligan was his warm supporter and admirer, and as they were associated together afterward in legislative duties, and in many a hot political contest, they became warm friends. Finally

Mr. Milligan became the confidential adviser of Mr. Johnson, and this relation continued for twenty or twenty-five years. He was undoubtedly during all this time the most intimate friend to whom Mr. Johnson gave his confidence. No two men could have been more unlike than they were in every element of character. And yet Mr. Milligan possessed the very qualities and qualifications that Mr. Johnson needed. He was educated, trustworthy, and discreet. His judgment was sound, his information extensive, and his fidelity unquestioned. He was consulted by Mr. Johnson upon all new and grave questions, and no doubt he often changed the views and purposes of his great leader. He had the frankness and the manliness to speak the truth and to give honest advice. Among those who knew them well in their own county, it was always understood that either Mr. Milligan prepared or revised all the important documents coming from Mr. Johnson's pen. It has often been asserted that he prepared the first message of President Johnson to Congress, but from an intimate knowledge of both men I incline to the opinion that this is true only in part, and possibly not true at all. It is unquestionably true, however, that during the long and stormy political career of Mr. Johnson, he leaned with confidence upon Mr. Milligan for advice and assistance. Johnson had one other confidential friend, mentioned elsewhere, John Jones, residing in Greene County, who was sometimes taken into their confidential consultations.

In the discharge of his duties as a lawyer Mr. Milligan was faithful and laborious. His cases were always thoroughly prepared. His arguments before the courts were clear and learned. While he was not so elaborate and forcible in these arguments as Mr. Nelson, nor so exact and exhaustive as Robert J. McKinney, he was as clear and pointed as either of them. He possessed in an eminent degree a legal mind, capable of the nicest distinctions, and the clearest apprehension of the principles involved in his cases. As a judge he was eminently just and impartial, as he saw the law and the facts. His opinions have stamped him as an able jurist.

It is not, however, in the capacity of a politician, a lawyer, or a jurist that he presents his highest and most admirable traits of character. His public life was more open and more dazzling, but it was his splendid personality that gave to him his highest attractiveness. As a student, a lawyer, and a private citizen, it was the conspicuous virtues of the man that made him altogether unlike his fellows. In college he was always the pet of his teachers, and the favorite, if not the idol, of his schoolmates. He was so gentle, so patient, so amiable and so obliging that everyone loved him. If the younger scholars needed assistance in working an example in arithmetic, or a problem in algebra, or help in the construction or translation of a sentence in Latin or Greek they went to him. He was kind in aiding them,—cheerfully stopping from his own studies for this purpose. The older scholars found in him a genial companion, an intelligent adviser, and an example of all that was commendable. His superiority was ungrudgingly acknowledged without the slightest mixture of jealousy. When we add to this his kindliness, his warm, sunshiny disposition, his helpfulness, and his unchanging sweet temper, it need not occasion surprise that he was such a favorite. During the five or six years that I was in college with him, and on the most intimate terms, I can recall no occasion when he was angry, or when he spoke an unkind word. He certainly possessed human passions and human prejudices, but they were kept in perfect restraint. Nothing could disturb his ever-present serenity.

In after life, however high or exalted his position, he exemplified constantly the same winning, noble qualities that distinguished him at school. He was unpretentious in manner and conversation.

Mr. Milligan was not a great orator, but was a very impressive speaker, earnest, lucid, and persuasive, possessing some fancy, which he held in such complete subjection to his intellect that it seldom appeared in his speeches. His mind was eminently logical and philosophical. He was a thinker. His high intellectual head indicated thought, rather than imagination. He was a classical scholar, and well read in the great works of prose and poetry which add so much to the power of a public speaker. He had decided taste for all works of beauty and thought, and yet at all times he was devoted to his profession, and indulged in these only for recreation.

In demeanor, Judge Milligan was grave, sedate, and retiring, with a quiet, thoughtful, and contemplative air. His modesty and humility were so excessive that he seemed to be always shrinking from observation, yet in private there was a strong undercurrent of fun and merriment bubbling up in playful good humor. In college he took no part in the sports and games of the students, yet in private, his ear and heart were open to their joys and their griefs, to the tales of their sports and their amusements. All sought him, all followed him, all delighted to be with him. By a sort of magical power, he drew all persons to him who came within the influence of this spell. Now, what was the secret of this? He was not showy, not brilliant, not dazzling, not effusive, not demonstrative. A single word will explain it all—it was *goodness!* Tennyson has expressed it in these lines:

> "Howe'er it be, it seems to me
> 'Tis only noble to be good;
> Kind hearts are more than coronets,
> And simple faith than Norman blood."

Sam Milligan's life was one long round of modesty, humility, gentleness, and peacefulness. He uttered no harsh words, gave no wounds, was guilty of no questionable acts. His conduct in all things was upright and noble. He absolutely had no enemies. He was a peacemaker, "Blessed are the peacemakers." He came out of all his political contests, however heated, with the good will, the esteem, and admiration even, of his political opponents. He was just and honorable in all things. He might have stood up before all the world and said, as Samuel of old did to the assembly of Israel: "Whom have I defrauded? Whom have I oppressed? Whom have I wronged?" and no one could have answered his challenge. Altogether I think he was the best man I have ever known—he had fewer faults and more virtues. He was indeed a beautiful character. Would that I could paint his life as a picture, and show it to the world, just as he lived it. How pure, how fresh, how dewy— like a garden of flowers in the early morning.

> "His life was gentle, and the elements
> So mix'd in him, that Nature might stand up,
> And say to all the world, 'This was a man!'"

JOHN NETHERLAND.

Born in Virginia—Educated at Tusculum Under Doak—Two Years in Franklin, Tenn.—State Senator in 1833—Elector for State at Large in 1848—Defeated by Harris in 1859—Constantly in Politics—Jury Lawyer—Personal Characteristics.

AMONG the prominent Union leaders of East Tennessee in 1861 was John Netherland, of Hawkins County. Of this remarkable set of men, he was by nature, in some respects, perhaps, the most remarkable. In person he was more striking than any one of them. He was endowed with a native intellect scarcely inferior to that of the ablest. He possessed qualities for winning popular favor superior to any of his associates, excepting one. His personality was captivating. Mr. Netherland was born in Virginia, September 20, 1808, and died in Rogersville, Tenn., October 4, 1887. He was educated at Tusculum Academy, now Greeneville and Tusculum College, under old Dr. Samuel Doak, and read law under Judge Samuel Powell. Before he was twenty-one years of age, he obtained a law license, and soon thereafter located in the town of Franklin, Middle Tennessee, where he remained two years, then returning to East Tennessee. In 1833 he was a State Senator from the First District, and in 1835 represented Sullivan County in the Legislature.* In 1836, though quite a young man, he was Presidential Elector on the White electoral ticket, and cast his vote in the Electoral College for that venerable statesman. In the division of parties in the country, in 1835, he became an ardent Whig. In 1848, he was elector for the State-at-Large on the ticket for General Taylor, and cast his vote for him as President. In 1851 he was elected to the Legislature for the third time, and served with distinction in that body. In 1859 he was selected by the general voice of his party throughout the State, as the Whig candidate for Governor against Isham G. Harris, the then Democratic incumbent of that office, but was defeated by a considerable majority. His

---

*By the Constitution of 1796 a man was eligible to a seat in the Senate at the age of twenty-one.

aspirations were always high. In 1847 he was a candidate before the Legislature for United States Senator, but was defeated by the Hon. John Bell, then in the zenith of his power and popularity. In 1870 he was a member of the Constitutional Convention of the State.

During all his life John Netherland took a prominent part in politics. In every canvass, whether personally an applicant for office or not, he was zealous in behalf of the success of his party. Because of his great sagacity, his advice and his counsel were constantly solicited by the leaders throughout the State. His knowledge of men, and his shrewdness as to the effect of party measures were so well known, that his opinion had great weight. No man in the State had a keener perception of what would prove popular and what unpopular in a canvass. He knew the people, their instincts, and their thoughts. Even Andrew Johnson could not fathom the popular mind more perfectly than he. He possessed a fund of common sense and forethought, in this regard scarcely equaled by any of our public leaders.

The strong position which Mr. Netherland won in the councils of the State, and in the estimation of its distinguished men, and the reputation which he achieved as a lawyer, prove that he was no ordinary man. In olden times, in Tennessee, only men of real ability and great popularity were selected for the higher positions of honor and trust. The very names of the Whig leaders in the State, Bell, Jones, Foster, Brown, Campbell, Henry, Gentry, Etheridge, Nelson, and Maynard, prove that men of mediocrity were not put forward. There was such an array of talent that inferior men were not sought for the high positions. The selection of Mr. Netherland as the Elector for the State at large, in 1848, at the very time of the high noon of greatness in the State, proves that he was regarded by his party as one of its ablest defenders. And his almost unanimous nomination for Governor, in 1859, against Governor Isham G. Harris, the most adroit Democratic politician, excepting Andrew Johnson, in the State, was an emphatic endorsement of his ability.

His pre-eminence as a jury lawyer was well established. His circuit embraced large portions of the first and twelfth judicial districts, extending from Sullivan County to Campbell, along the northern border of the State, a distance of more than one hundred miles. In these circuits, he constantly came in contact with the best legal talent in East Tennessee, possibly in the State. At every court, and in every important case, he had to encounter such lawyers as John A. McKinney, Robert J. McKinney, Thomas A. R. Nelson, Thomas D. Arnold, William H. Sneed, Horace Maynard, Grey Garrett, and Robert H. Hynds. These were all first-class lawyers in some department of the law, and some of them in all departments. Thomas A. R. Nelson, for illustration, was not only a technical lawyer, but he was also a jury lawyer. Yet Mr. Netherland, for more than twenty years, held the unquestioned supremacy as a jury lawyer throughout the length of his large circuit. Certainly no mean distinction.

Another fact must be taken into consideration. Mr. Netherland's position in this respect was won solely by natural ability. He had but little literary culture, and never worked assiduously. He knew little of books, either in his profession, in history, or in general literature. He was familiar with few books—the Bible, Shakespeare, Byron, and Burns were his favorites. He was not thoroughly posted on the current events of the day. He read newspapers, but read them hurriedly and cursorily. Yet so retentive was his memory that he had a fair knowledge in reference to nearly all passing events. He had but little of the philosophy of political economy. From his calling and associations, he necessarily knew something about the science of government, though he never gave it much study. His reliance at all times was upon his strong common sense, and in this he was exceptionally superior. His power and success as a jury lawyer were all due to his natural ability. His addresses, before juries and on the stump, were plain, simple, and unadorned. There were no flights of imagination, no displays of rhetoric. He addressed the minds of men, not their fancy. His success lay in the use of his intellect, power of analysis, happy illustrations, remarkable clearness of statement, and skillful massing of facts. In the knowledge and judgment of human nature, of the motives which sway men, of their passions and prejudices, he was almost phenomenal. He could play upon the passions of jurors as an artist plays upon the strings of a violin. Yet he was no demagogue. Never was he accused of any thing dishonorable, either in the use of arguments or in appeals to juries. Trusting in his ability to win his causes, he disdained to resort to little or unworthy tricks. In the selection of jurors, he seemed to know intuitively whether the person presented for election or challenge was the kind of man he needed in the particular case. He read the countenances of men as an open book. He knew everybody in the wide region where he practiced, knew their history, their prejudices, their peculiarities. Hence he was scarcely ever mistaken in his choice. It was indeed a bad case where he did not win a verdict before juries.

Mr. Netherland was an upright man. While artful and shrewd in accomplishing his ends, outwitting those with whom he came in contact, it cannot be said that he resorted to questionable means. He was indeed the very prince of good fellows—genial, sociable, delightful. His fund of anecdotes was inexhaustible, and his manner of telling them inimitable. He delighted in his leisure hours—and he was rarely much pressed for time—in having around him a crowd to whom he told innocent stories, and recounted reminiscences. He was a wit and a humorist. Humor bubbled up in him like a perennial spring. All his speeches abounded in it, yet it was only used to illustrate weighty facts. In repartee and sarcasm he was rarely surpassed. To illustrate: an old lawyer friend between whom and himself there had always been a little jealousy, but great intimacy, were in the habit of indulging their wit upon each other, sometimes in rather rough terms. They were both together at court in the presence of two or three friends, among them myself, when they began to rally each other. Said this friend to the company: "Mr. Netherland is the closest man I have ever known. If he were traveling along the highway and came to the forks of the road, and one fork led down to perdition, and the other up to Paradise, and he had to pay toll of ten cents along the road to the Celestial City, he would refuse to pay it, and would take the road to the regions below." "Yes," said Mr. Netherland, quick as thought, "if you were already in Paradise in Abraham's bosom, and some boon companion were to shake a bottle of liquor at you from the bottomless gulf, and say, 'Come down and let us take a drink of good old whiskey together,' you would say 'Farewell, father Abraham,' and at once start for the regions below." This colloquy ended the conversation without ill-feeling on the part of either.

I have noted that Mr. Netherland would not confine himself to hard study. He often did himself injustice by the habit of relying upon his natural ability. An illustration of this is given by Governor Harris, in accounting for his success over Mr. Netherland (the race in 1859). Harris said that when he heard that Netherland was to be his competitor, knowing his reputation as a man of ability and his skill as a public debater, he felt a little uneasy as to whether he should be able successfully to meet him on the stump. He therefore went to work, preparing himself thoroughly for the discussion of every public question that was likely to arise between them. Harris entered the contest, therefore, armed at every point for their joint debates. When the canvass opened, it soon became evident to everybody that Harris had the advantage over Netherland in detailed information upon the issues involved in their discussions. The result was while in natural ability Netherland was the equal of Harris, he did not gain the advantage over him that his friends expected, and was not elected Governor.

And yet, in his old age, Governor Harris told a mutual friend, that so fertile were the resources of Mr. Netherland, that, in this canvass, in order to keep upon his feet, he had to be more cautious than with any other antagonist he had ever encountered. Netherland could, in fact, turn the most serious charge of an opponent, or destroy the force of it, by a shrewd answer or by his wit and irresistible humor, and he seldom failed to do this.

In person, Mr. Netherland was tall and slender, being fully six feet high. His body was straight, round, very symmetrical and graceful. In his younger and better days he dressed in faultless manner, which set off his person to advantage. His head was large, round, and intellectual in contour. His face could hardly be called handsome, and yet it was of such a character, so well molded, that he would everywhere impress the beholder. The face had something of sternness, and yet, he was neither stern nor sour. He was, however, a man of determination, and this the face indicated. He could not be moved from his purpose when once fixed, by any ordinary opposition. Wary and cautious in committing himself in favor of new measures, he always weighed carefully all considerations and consequences. He never ran off after new theories until he fully saw the results that were to follow. Hence he seldom committed the errors which politicians so often have to lament. He had, however, often to regret the use of his wit and sarcasm. He once remarked to me that these talents had been a drawback, instead of an advantage in his public life; that in moments of excitement, he had often inflicted wounds which rankled, making enemies of those against whom they were directed. This is perhaps always the case when these weapons of speech are heedlessly used.

When the Southern States, in 1860 and 1861, began to withdraw from the Union, Mr. Netherland, being an old-time Whig of very decided conviction, naturally espoused the cause of the Union. It were needless to say that his influence among his thousands of friends in the region where he lived was very great. He was earnestly for the preservation of the Union, and took the stump in its behalf, in his own county. When the election of February, 1861, was ordered, and a Constitutional Convention was proposed to determine the status of Tennessee in the great conflict then pending, Mr. Netherland, by common consent was turned to as the ablest representative of the Union party to be sent to that Convention. After canvassing the county, he was elected by a large majority. But as that Convention never convened, being defeated by the people at the ballot box, in common with all other Union delegates, he never took his seat. In the succeeding canvass, upon the straight and direct question of separation, or no-separation, Mr. Netherland remained unflinchingly on the side of the Union. His standing and ability gave him great weight in holding East Tennessee loyal to the government. He deserves therefore to be ranked as one of the prominent Union leaders of East Tennessee. But as he was not so active as some others in the great fight that took place in the spring of 1861, the same honor cannot be claimed for him in the success which followed, that rightfully belongs to those whose efforts covered a wider field.

Mr. Netherland was a member of the celebrated Knoxville-Greeneville Convention. He took no active part in its deliberations, but singular to say, the only speech in that body, given even in brief terms is his. It was wise and patriotic and doubtless made an impression. It was spoken early in the deliberations; he earnestly advised moderation and conservatism. In the subsequent proceedings Mr. Netherland took no active part. But it was evident from his speech that he was opposed to any wild, revolutionary measures. Thus he stood firm and determined in his opposition to secession to the closing scenes of the agitation. Throughout the long months that intervened between June, 1861, and September, 1863, Mr. Netherland's sympathies were all on the side of the Union. He was, however, prudent and conciliatory, and demeaned himself in such a manner as to escape arrest, or to avoid bringing upon himself any serious odium on the part of the authorities of the Southern Confederacy. In the Spring of 1864, when a majority of the Union leaders of East Tennessee conceived it to be their duty to separate from the Administration of Mr. Lincoln, and unite in a conservative course in favor of the election of General McClellan, he united with them. From that time until his death he co-operated with and supported the Democratic party. The little faults of Mr. Netherland were so overshadowed by the multitude of his good qualities, that no friend would venture for a moment to suggest them. So striking were his qualities, so lovable was he personally, so superior in point of intellect, that long after most of his contemporaries shall have been forgotten, his name will be an endeared household word among those who remember him as he was in his prime, and his wit, his sayings, and his kindly deeds will descend as pleasant recollections. What man who once knew John Netherland intimately,—that warm, genial, sunshiny nature,—can ever forget him!

THOMAS A. R. NELSON.

His Phenomenal Rise at the Bar—An Old-line Whig—Nelson and Haynes Canvass of 1858—First Speech in Congress, December, 1859—Nelson and Johnson in Tennessee, Spring of 1861—Re-elected to U. S. Congress—Captured and Taken to Richmond—Letter Published on Return to His Home—Attitude Toward Lincoln's Proclamation of Emancipation—Attitude in 1872.

AMONG the great Union leaders of East Tennessee in 1861 Thomas A. R. Nelson was not the least. In all that was manly and brave, he had no superior. If courage, ability, and honor are qualities that make a leader in dangerous times, then this man was born to lead.

Mr. Nelson, a native of Roane County, East Tennessee, obtained his education at the University at Knoxville. When quite young he obtained a license to practice law. Very soon after this he moved to Jonesboro, in the eastern part of the State, where he settled to practice his profession. The bar of that circuit was at that time an unusually able one, perhaps equal to any, if not one of the strongest in the State. It embraced two lawyers, John A. McKinney and Robert J. McKinney, who had no superiors in the State. Besides these, there were Seth J. W. Lucky, afterward both Circuit Judge and Chancellor; Jacob Peck, a former Judge of the Supreme Court; Alfred Taylor, John Kennedy, General Thomas D. Arnold, John Netherland, John Brabson, and others.

Soon after the settlement of Mr. Nelson in Jonesboro, he was appointed prosecuting attorney for the circuit embracing that town. As such, he had constantly to measure his strength against that of the able men I have just named. They soon found that it required all their ability to meet the strong, brave young man who had so suddenly risen up among them. He underwent no long probation at the bar, as most young men had to do in that circuit, but leaped at once into a full practice, taking his place by the side of the older lawyers. In nearly fifty years of observation I have seen no parallel to his early success.

There was much, however, in Mr. Nelson that seemed to explain his phenomenal rise at the bar. He possessed fine natural talents. These had been polished and strengthened by education, and by most diligent study. He had a splendid constitution, and could endure almost incredible labor. In his profession he knew no rest, no relaxation, no cessation from work. In the preparation of his cases, every authority bearing on the points at issue was examined and full notes were made of it. He had a strong, deep, commanding voice, which at once arrested attention. But above all, he was the most ambitious of men. To excel, to deserve success, rather than to gain a mere empty triumph, spurred him to almost superhuman efforts. But all this toil, all this boundless ambition was regulated and controlled by the keenest and the highest sense of honor and right and the most sacred regard for truth. I doubt if any man during his whole life for a moment questioned either his veracity or his honor. He possessed one other quality, without which there would have been a weak place in his character, and this was an undaunted courage that knew no fear. This courage was so conspicuous that it was never questioned.

With all these qualities there were united frankness, openness, directness, generosity, sympathy, and magnanimity, and rarely has any man possessed these in a higher degree. It can at once be seen that a man endowed with such attributes would soon impress himself favorably on a brave people like those of East Tennessee. Soon he was regarded as the very impersonation of all that was brave and manly. And so it came to pass that men never dreamed of anything little or mean or unworthy in connection with the name of T. A. R. Nelson.

All this is high praise, but it falls short of justice to this remarkable man. There was in him a combination of high qualities such as is seldom seen united in any single individual. His defects were small in comparison with his splendid characteristics. It may be safely said that no man in the State ever commanded the confidence of the people more unreservedly and more universally. Even his political enemies, in times of high excitement, never doubted his honesty and his good faith, and but few of them personally disliked him. Though the most positive of men, and the boldest and severest in the denunciation of wrong, he made few enemies. So thoroughly did he impress men with the idea that he spoke alone from honest convictions, that utterances which would have given the deepest offense if spoken by others, gave none coming from him. He was tolerant of the opinions of others, and his own manly and frank words were always received in good part.

Mr. Nelson was an old-line Whig. In the exciting canvasses of 1840 and 1844 he took an active part, and established a high reputation as a debater and orator. In 1850 Senator Bell procured for Mr. Nelson, from President Fillmore, the appointment of Minister to China. But as the acceptance of this office, high and honorable as it was, involved the sacrifice of a large practice, and as the salary was only $6,000 a year, he promptly declined its acceptance. In 1851 General William B. Campbell, the Whig candidate for Governor, became ill, in the midst of the joint canvass of himself and of his competitor, Governor Trousdale, and Mr. Nelson was selected to take the place of General Campbell on the stump. In this position, with characteristic self-denial, he canvassed a large part of the State with marked ability. Campbell was elected, and with him a Whig Legislature, thus securing for the party a United States Senator. Mr. Nelson became a candidate for this office, and was beaten by Ex-Governor James C. Jones, after a long and somewhat bitter contest. Jones had made himself famous by his celebrated contests with and triumphs over James K. Polk for Governor of the State in 1841 and 1843. In 1859 he was elected to Congress from the first district, after an animated and noted canvass with Landon C. Haynes. This is one of the memorable canvasses of Tennessee. Mr. Haynes had the reputation of being one of the finest Democratic orators in the State. He was a fluent speaker, and possessed all the arts of a skilled politician. His voice was remarkably musical; his manner pleasing and his fancy exuberant. A few years before he had run against Andrew Johnson for Congress, and, though beaten, he was the most perfect match Johnson had perhaps ever met. Haynes was an adept in the very mode of speaking that his great rival had always used so successfully.

The discussions between Nelson and Haynes were able and high toned. Indeed, no man would have ventured to violate the rules of gentlemanly propriety in a canvass, or a debate, with T. A. R. Nelson. He was so fair and honorable himself that he universally secured the respect of and honorable treatment from his competitors. Great crowds were attracted to the meetings of these two able men, and followed them from point to point. The partisans of each claimed the victory. In argument and the marshaling of facts, Mr. Nelson was the superior; in mere declamation, perhaps Mr. Haynes had the advantage. The district being Whig in sentiment, the former was elected. He took his seat in Congress on the 5th of December, 1859. Two days afterward, while the election of speaker was pending, he made his début in that body, and at once won national fame. In his speech he gave utterance to the most devoted attachment to the Federal Union. It was received with boundless enthusiasm. During its delivery he was interrupted almost constantly by questions from Southern Democrats, and always with discomfiture to the questioners. Mr. Garnett of Virginia, and Mr. Lamar of Mississippi, had made hot, fiery Southern speeches. When Mr. Nelson arose, his voice at once arrested the attention of the House. He proceeded to discuss the political situation with great moderation and fairness, but with perfect candor and independence. As he advanced he warmed up, and began to utter with great energy sentiments in favor of the preservation of the Union. Finally he burst forth in a magnificent appeal for our glorious united country. It was such an overflow of eloquence as schoolboys delight to declaim. The applause in the galleries, and finally on the floor, became uncontrollable.

When Mr. Nelson resumed his seat, Roger A. Pryor, the former celebrated editor of Virginia, rose to reply. He was the Hotspur of the House, and a man of ability. His speech was in that arrogant style then peculiar to Southern "Fire-eaters." He evidently did not know and had not heard of Mr. Nelson. No one knowing him would have ventured to indulge in an insulting manner toward him. In one of his first sentences he spoke of his "indignation" at the sentiments just uttered by Nelson. Pryor's speech throughout was in keeping with the manner and tone so common at the time in the South. Among other things he criticised Nelson because he had eulogized the Union, but had said nothing in defense of the Constitution. In his rejoinder Mr. Nelson was exceedingly happy on this point. He said:

"If I mistake not, it is the common sentiment of the secessionists of the South, that they talk about the Constitution, but say nothing about the Union. When I talk about the Union, what do I talk about? I talk about that thing which is the result of the American Constitution." (Loud applause upon the floor and in the galleries). "I speak of the larger idea; when I say I am in favor of the Union, that carries everything along with it; and it carries everything else with it that any patriot in this land should desire to support."

Mr. Pryor used some expressions in the course of his speech which Mr. Nelson construed as a threat. When the latter commenced his rejoiner, he said "that in anything I have said, or may say, I am competent to protect myself against any assault, either in the House, or out of it."

A line or two further on he added: "I have no apprehension either from the person or the arguments of the gentleman, if anything he has said can be dignified by the name of argument."

Those who have seen T. A. R. Nelson in a passion can imagine with what a lofty and undaunted tone of defiance he uttered these words.

This rejoinder to Pryor was nearly as long as the original speech, and was even more pointed.

Thus, on his third day in Congress Nelson became famous. His speech was the sensation of the session. Perhaps not more than two or three speeches in the last forty years had produced such a stir, and not one by a new member. The newspapers everywhere praised it. And yet it was not specially a great speech. It was the occasion, the spirit, and its manner that made it great.

The Baltimore *Patriot* headed its notice as follows:

MR. NELSON'S GREAT SPEECH.

In another column we give the *National Intelligencer's* brief report of this most extraordinary speech. It fell like a thunderbolt on the House. . . . Mr. Garnett of Virginia, it seems, led off in a set disunion speech. He raved and threatened and stormed, and went on like someone just out of Bedlam. It was followed by Mr. Lamar of Mississippi in pretty much the same strain.

When these Locofocos had given vent to their passion, Mr. Nelson, one of the noble little band of twenty-three Americans in the House, arose. He is slightly lame, we are informed, and this is his first appearance in a deliberative body. He had scarcely raised his voice before it began to ring through the hall in a way that silenced all talking. Every eye was turned upon him. The galleries were crowded to excess.

Turning from them (the disunion speakers) he appealed to the friends of the Union on that floor, and called on them to rise in their majesty and rebuke the rank treason that was now daring to raise its sacrilegious hand against the existence of our blessed Union. At this point he launched forth in vindication of the Union, and with such effect and power that the galleries and the very House itself gave way to the most immoderate applause. . . .

Mr. Pryor, the new member from the Petersburgh District, arose in reply to Mr. Nelson. He, too, began with an attempt at domineering, and after vaporing for a while sat down.

Mr. Nelson returned to the charge, and said he was no duelist, but was ready to defend himself in that House or out of it. Poor Pryor, in a little while, found himself utterly prostrated. This time the galleries and the House got almost beside themselves, and yielded up to the influence of their feelings in the applause of this wonderful speech with a perfect abandonment. The effect of the speech upon the House, says our informant, was almost dissolving. . . .

We cannot refrain from thanking Mr. Nelson for thus keeping down the arena with the flag of the Union in his hand and unfolding it over the heads of the disunionists.

The Honorable Jere Clemens, editor of the Memphis *Enquirer*, and ex-United States Senator from Alabama, writing to his paper from Washington, December 15, 1859, said:

I but repeat what is on the lips of every man in this city when I say that no member of either branch of Congress has won so much renown as Mr. Nelson.

The Louisville *Courier*, then a Democratic paper, said of Mr. Nelson:

The passage between Mr. Pryor, the young member from Virginia, and Mr. Nelson of Tennessee was a little sharper than either bargained for. The dose administered was decidedly unpalatable. Experience is a severe physician. We find comfort, however, in the thought that its severity tends only to keep people "from waking up the wrong passenger." Nelson was waked up through mistake. If it be agreeable to him, he will be allowed to slumber through the present Congress. It is hardly probable that anyone will venture to arouse him.

The Louisville *Courier* was correct. No man ever dared to arouse Nelson after that memorable day. That was the only time he ever served in Congress. In 1861 he was re-elected, but as will be more fully explained hereafter, he failed to reach Washington to take his seat.

Those who knew Mr. Nelson well can readily realize with what overwhelming power of voice, passion, argument, and eloquence he crushed Mr. Pryor. In his first sentence almost, Pryor stirred the deep spirit within him, by speaking of his "indignation" and by the undertone of superiority which he manifested. Pryor aroused in the very outset all the latent powers of that remarkable man, who, under excitement, became a raging lion. Ordinarily Nelson was gentle and amiable, but under provocation, he became a storm, a tempest.

During the Presidential canvass of 1860 Mr. Nelson supported Bell and Everett. He made many able speeches in behalf of the Union. But it was during the canvass of the spring of 1861, while the question of secession was still pending in Tennessee, that the ability and matchless courage of Mr. Nelson shone more conspicuously than at any period of his life. Seldom did any public man display higher courage, and rarely greater ability. The times were perilous and startling beyond anything in our history. His life was in daily peril. From the day he arrived at home, from Washington, in March, to the close of the canvass in June, he was on the stump, arousing the people to the dangers that threatened the country. He canvassed his own district, the first, thoroughly, and then came to the second, going over it county by county, extending his labors even into the third district. Everywhere he was greeted by vast crowds of people.

During the latter part of the canvass he and Mr. Johnson had joint appointments and they traveled and spoke together. Seldom has there been witnessed such courage, power, and eloquence as were daily exhibited by these two able men. Mr. Johnson, for once in his life, ceased to be a partisan, and became a statesman. Setting aside the ways of his previous life, he rose into the dignity of a broad, bold, great man, full of earnestness and words of wisdom. Never did he appear so much of a man! The appalling dangers which surrounded the country seemed to rid him of all narrowness and make him for the time a patriot.

But while the people flocked to hear these orators, Nelson was their favorite. They listened with admiration, and even with enthusiasm, to the words of Johnson, because he gave expression to their sentiments, but they turned to T. A. R. Nelson as their hero. He commanded their confidence more fully perhaps than any of the great leaders. Brownlow had their love; while Johnson had neither the love, nor the full confidence, of a majority of the Union people.

The explanation of these statements, which may seem strange to people unfamiliar with the facts, is plain and simple. Mr. Johnson was a Democrat, while a majority of the loyal people of East Tennessee were Whigs. These Whigs had always hated Johnson. Even now they could not fully forgive him and looked upon him with more or less suspicion. They regarded him as a cold, haughty, selfish man. While the common people of his party clung to him with tenacity and admiration, because he was the ablest defender of their opinions in the State, he had but few warm friends who were attached to him personally.

As to Mr. Nelson, his life had been so pure, his conduct so lofty and free from selfishness and baseness, that he was universally respected and admired as one of the noblest of men. It is true he had led a remarkably busy professional life until the last two years. He had never resorted to the arts of mere politicians to gain popularity. He did what was right, and uttered what he believed, and only that, whether it made or lost friends. He was always, and on all occasions, a noble, conscientious, brave man. These qualities secured for him almost universal admiration.

In another chapter I have given a full account of Mr. Nelson's part in the Knoxville-Greeneville Convention. Both his ability and his courage were conspicuous in that Convention. I, however, think that the Union men of East Tennessee have always had cause for thankfulness that the policy he advocated did not prevail. It would inevitably have plunged our section into civil war, short lived, no doubt, but destructive and terrible in its results to the Union people.

Notwithstanding the fact that the State had voted on the 7th of June in favor of "separation," elections were held in all the counties of East Tennessee in the following August for members of Congress and of the Legislature. Mr. Nelson was a candidate in the first district, and was of course re-elected. Soon after the election, he, in company with one of his sons, and one or two guides, set out on horseback from Jonesboro, for Kentucky. He had gone as far as Lee County, in Southwest Virginia, when he was suddenly confronted by a company of Confederate homeguards who had been sent out to intercept him. He was arrested and at once sent to Cumberland Gap, and thence to Richmond. On his way to Richmond, at Abingdon, Va., he was joined by John Baxter, who, on hearing of the arrest of his friend, at once volunteered to go to his assistance. On their way to Richmond they were joined by several members of the Confederate Congress. All of these treated Mr. Nelson with great consideration. On his arrival at Richmond he was not placed in close confinement, but put on his parole of honor.

Mr. Nelson was so conspicuous for ability and high character that it at once became an object with his former friends at Richmond to win him over to their cause. It was well known to them that threats, intimidation, or force would be utterly unavailing. All the power of the Southern Confederacy would not have made him yield one iota. This was well known. Instead, therefore, of treating him as a felon and a traitor, he became the object of the most assiduous and delicate attentions. Flattery and kind consideration would do what force and ill treatment could never do. Leading men paid him court. During his stay there he "was visited by various members of Congress and other public men connected with the Southern Confederacy." He was finally persuaded that he had misapprehended the object of the Confederates in sending armies into East Tennessee. At length he was induced by flattery or legitimate arguments, to address a letter to President Davis dated August 12, 1861. In this letter, after expressing his sincere desire "to preserve the peace and quiet of East Tennessee," he says, among other things:

"I ask to be discharged from a vexatious prosecution, that I may return home peacefully, to follow my private interests and pursuits, assuring your Excellency that I will not, either directly or indirectly, by counsel, advice, or action, encourage, aid, or assist the United States Government to invade, or attain success in the present struggle with the Confederate States, nor will I counsel, or advise others to thwart or cripple the Confederate States in the pending contest with the United States, nor will I do so by my own acts.

"In view of the increased majority in the election which has just taken place in Tennessee, I shall feel it my duty, as a citizen of the State, to submit to her late action, and shall religiously abstain from any further words or acts of condemnation, or opposition, to her government."

To this letter Mr. Davis replied on the 13th of August, reminding Mr. Nelson that he had "made promise" that he would "as a citizen of Tennessee submit to her late action, and religiously abstain from any further words or acts of condemnation whatever, or opposition to her government." He goes on further to inform Mr. Nelson that he had ordered his discharge from custody.

This correspondence was published by Mr. Nelson after his

return to his home, in a letter addressed to "the People of East Tennessee," dated August 17, 1861. In this letter he said, with characteristic frankness and boldness:

"I shall offer no plea of duress; because neither the Southern Confederacy, nor any other earthly power, could have compelled me to make an agreement which my judgment and conscience did not approve in the situation in which I was placed."

Further he said: "While I did not promise allegiance nor active support to the Southern Confederacy, and will not advise you to assume any obligations contrary to your convictions of duty, I feel perfectly free to say that the failure of the Government of the United States for four long months to sustain us in our position, its apparent inability to do so since the battle of Manassas, within any reasonable time, the deliberate action of our State in the August election, the assurance of public men that no test oaths or drafting measures will be adopted or required; the mutual hatred that has grown up between the antagonistic sections of the Union, and the recent confiscation laws which have either been adopted or proposed on both sides, as well as other causes, have painfully impressed my own mind with the belief that unless some wondrous and improbable change is effected, our beloved Union is gone forever, and it is our duty and policy to submit to a result which, however we may deplore it, seems to be inevitable.

"Aware that my advice as well as my motives may be liable to misconstruction, I would still most respectfully recommend to my friends the propriety of abstaining from all further opposition or resistance to the Confederate authorities, or the action of our own State. * * *"

Although Mr. Nelson had enjoyed in a larger degree the confidence of the Union people of East Tennessee than any other leader, and though this letter was intended to reconcile them to the new government, there is no evidence that it effected a change in a single mind. The loyal men remained as they were before, stubbornly, but silently, defiant and bitter. They had heard his bitter denunciation of secession on the stump; they had heard him read his terrible arraignment of it in "The Declaration of Grievances" in the Greeneville Convention, they had heard him urge them to arm in defense of their constitutional rights, and to resist, if necessary, even to the shedding of blood, and they saw, in their plain mental vision, no greater reason for co-operation with the Confederates in August than they had seen in June.

Yet I would not censure Mr. Nelson. He was a pure, brave, honest man. From his great courage, no imputation of fear can possibly be made against him. Perhaps most men, under similar circumstances, would have acted as he did. And yet I cannot but regard this act as an error. He cannot, however, be held responsible for it. No doubt he placed his honor in the keeping of his friends, and they led him into this position.

An incident is said to have occurred at Richmond which showed the high honor of Mr. Nelson. He was urged by two, and perhaps more, of his warm personal friends, to take his seat as a member of the Confederate Congress, by virtue of his election in August to the United States Congress. This he most positively declined to do. John M. Fleming, at that time, and for a number of years afterward, the law partner of Mr. John Baxter, the counsel and friend of Mr. Nelson, is my authority for this statement. On the return of Baxter from Richmond, he told Fleming that he and Governor, now Senator, Vance, of North Carolina, tried to induce Mr. Nelson to do as I have stated above. Mr. Nelson could not have done this without criticism on his conduct.

On his return to his home and after publishing his letter, Mr. Nelson, in compliance with his promise to Mr. Davis, remained quiet until September, 1863, after General Burnside had entered and occupied East Tennessee. He then made his appearance in Knoxville, where he afterward remained. No one who heard him talk doubted his loyalty at this time. During his retirement he seems to have had revived within his bosom all of his old love for the Union, and his hatred of the Confederacy. About the time of the entrance of the Federal Army there appeared in a small printed volume two political poems, written by him, entitled respectively "Secession" and "East Tennessee," with copious notes. Both the poems and the notes were exceedingly caustic and bitter. The notes were in the scorching style of Brownlow. The following is Note 8, taken from Mr. Nelson's poem. It is copied to show how bitter he was in 1863:

The Conscript Law was passed to keep the Southern army together. Thousands who had volunteered to serve twelve months were forced into the three years' service. In executing the law, in East Tennessee, Union men and women were whipped, and the latter sometimes hanged, to make them tell where the conscripts were secreted. Many were shot, and nothing was more common than to bring them tied and handcuffed into the little towns. At Knoxville conscripts were whipped, compelled to wear the ball and chain, and, in some instances, hanged for desertion. . . .

The following is Note 11:

Poor old Virginia! Land of politics and pride and victim of traitors! The Cotton States were too smart for her, and transferred the war to her sacred soil. She rushed into it without cause, and her fields are desolate, her bosom a graveyard! She has nothing left but the Resolutions of "98."

From the time the Federal Army became permanently settled in East Tennessee, Mr. Nelson engaged actively in the practice of his profession. The proclamation of emancipation by Mr. Lincoln gave offense to him. His mind was conservative in its constitution, and filled with reverence for existing forms. He could not see how, under the exercise of the powers of Commander in Chief of the Armies, in the time of war, the authority could be found to emancipate the slaves of those in rebellion against the government. He denied the right and the authority. Once started in the course of opposition, he soon found other points of objection, until finally he became anti-Republican in politics. After the death of Mr. Lincoln, when the quarrel arose between Congress and Mr. Johnson as to the plan of Reconstruction, Mr. Nelson most naturally took sides with his old friend. And when impeachment proceedings were instituted against the President, the latter at once turned to his distinguished friend as one of his counsel. No doubt he sought Mr. Nelson on account of his legal ability, but also because, since the dark days of 1861, he had been his personal as well as his political friend. In this hour of trouble no doubt Mr. Johnson wished to have near him a trusted friend, in whose honor and fidelity he could fully rely and trust his inner thoughts. It was a great honor and distinction to be called upon to defend a President of the United States before the august tribunal of the Senate.

In 1870, when the Democratic party gained the ascendency in Tennessee, Mr. Nelson was nominated and elected one of the six Judges of the Supreme Court, or Court of Appeals. While on the bench he delivered in the case of Smith vs. Brazelton, reported in 1st Heiskell, his celebrated and learned opinion in which it was held, contrary to former decisions of the State, that the Southern Confederacy was a *de facto* government.

Reluctant as many of the Republicans were to accept as correct the doctrines of this opinion (which was but a reaffirmance of the decision of the Supreme Court of the United States) it is so fully sustained by authority now that it will hardly be called in question hereafter. It must be confessed that the war waged by the Confederate States was more than a mere insurrection. It was a great uprising of one section of the Union against the other section, with a "boundary marked by lines of bayonets which could be crossed only by force; south of this line it was enemies' territory, because it was held in possession by a hostile and belligerent power."

Judge S. T. Logan, who was for some years after the war a partner of Mr. Nelson, and was at one time Judge of the Circuit Court of Knox County, tells a humorous story in reference to this decision. Soon after it was delivered Mr. Nelson asked him what the people were saying about it. "They are saying a great deal," he answered. "Among other things they say that Jeff Davis, after four years of fighting, with all his armies, was unable to establish the Southern Confederacy, but that you with a few bold lines of your pen have succeeded in *setting it up*." Mr. Nelson was not much pleased with this pleasantry.

After serving on the Supreme Bench for eighteen months, he voluntarily resigned, and returned to the practice of his profession in Knoxville. Why he resigned was never certainly known. It was given out that the salary was not sufficient for the support of his large family, which was probably true. Privately it was intimated that two members of the court had offered indignities to him in their consultations, which he would not submit to, and yet which he could not resent in a becoming manner without a public scandal, and a reproach upon the highest judicial tribunal of the State. He therefore preferred to resign. Whatever may have been the reason, it can be safely affirmed that he was influenced by that high sense of duty which controlled his whole life.

In 1872 Mr. Nelson seems to have lost some of his love for his late associates. He had partially "come to himself," as appears by a call signed by him and Mr. John Baxter, and others, for a convention to meet in Cincinnati to organize a new party. Whether this Convention ever met, or what it did, if it did meet, I have thought it of sufficient importance to hunt up. Not very long after this, Mr. Baxter, after wandering a long time, came back to the old fold, where he remained through the remainder of his life. Mr. Nelson no doubt would ultimately have done the same thing, if he had lived longer.

For nearly forty years the friendship between T. A. R. Nelson and William G. Brownlow was warm and intimate. During a large part of this time they were neighbors, first in Jonesboro, and afterward in Knoxville. Until 1864 they belonged to the same political party. There was never any serious breach in their intimate relations. In 1847 this friendship was strained for a short time, over a religious controversy then existing between the Rev. Dr. Frederick A. Ross and Mr. Brownlow, as to Methodism and Calvinism. A correspondence took place between Brownlow and Nelson, in which each expressed himself with frankness, but with praiseworthy moderation, after which the difficulty and the threatened coldness passed away. No two men understood each other better than these two, and each knew the strength of the other, and the consequences involved in a quarrel. Each knew the ability and the high mettle of the other, and therefore naturally dreaded an encounter. Besides there was no real cause for a quarrel.

In 1849 Mr. Brownlow, in advocating the nomination of Mr. Nelson for Governor, said:

"Mr. Nelson was mainly instrumental in getting us to take charge of the Elizabethton *Whig* ten years ago, which he knows was reluctantly done by us at the time. He has been our friend when a friend was needed—when we were surrounded by mobs, and pursued by assassins by day and by night—and such friendship we are not the man to forget nor lightly esteem."

While Mr. Brownlow was in the Senate an incident occurred, which showed the reliance of Mr. Nelson upon the years of friendship. The son of Mr. Nelson had unfortunately gotten into a position where it was necessary for him to give a bail bond for a large sum. Mr. Nelson wrote a note to Senator Brownlow asking him to sign this bond, saying that he no doubt could get a number of men to sign it, but he preferred asking his old friends. This was at a time when they differed widely in politics. Scarcely had Mr. Brownlow received this note before he hurried off and was on his way to sign the bond.

There is something touching, and pathetic in these strong, determined men, so long intimate and tender friends, at last diverging and separating in their political courses, but continuing friends to the last, ever ready, as in the days of their vigorous manhood, to do for each other acts of kindness. Such was the brave Nelson and such the ever-faithful and kind Brownlow.

The statement that Mr. Nelson possessed a high order of intellect deserves some explanation. He unquestionably had a strong mind, but he was so honest that it made him slow and cautious in his mental operations. He arrived at conclusions on important questions only after the most careful reflection. On new questions he would express no opinion until he had looked into them most carefully and thoroughly. But in his investigation he overlooked no important point. When his mind reached its conclusions, it rested on them in perfect confidence and security. In his arguments as a lawyer before the courts and juries he was elaborate and diffuse. He overlooked no important point in his cases.

It is almost useless to add after what I have said as to his characteristics, that in his intercourse with his professional brethren, with his clients, and the bench, he was a model of fairness, courtesy, and noble bearing. I believe that he was never even suspected of a dishonorable act during his professional career, much less guilty of one. His enemies even would have entrusted their lives—their all—to his honor and his keeping.

In August, 1873, T. A. R. Nelson died at his home in Knoxville, of cholera, in the sixty-first year of his age. When stricken down he was in the full possession of all his mental and physical powers, and had the reasonable assurance of many years of usefulness and activity. Thus passed away a man, the like of whom, we shall not, in all probability, see soon again. Time had apparently somewhat softened and mellowed his fiery spirit. The vaulting ambition which once filled, but never marred, his soul, seemed to have been somewhat subdued, and he appeared only anxious to discharge his duty as a citizen and a Christian. He had for many years been an active and earnest member of the Presbyterian Church. At the time of his death he was an active worker in the Sabbath school of the Second Presbyterian Church of Knoxville, of which he was a member. He and Mr. Maynard were members of the same Church, and like Mr. Maynard, one of his last acts was to deliver an able address before the Church on the Bible. Both of these great men spent their last days in good works, as if prescient of the coming end.

DeWITT C. SENTER.

Active in Influence for Undivided Country—Father Prominent—Speaker of Senate and Governor—Later Years Passed in Retirement.

DeWitt C. Senter of Grainger County deserves honorable mention for the part he bore in the great political contest of 1861. Previous to that time he had become somewhat prominent as a young member of the celebrated Legislature, elected in August, 1859, which by the passage of the ordinance of secession of May, 1861, assumed to vote Tennessee out of the Union. Amid the wild excitement of Civil War, Mr. Senter, with unflinching courage, stood with the little band of Spartan heroes—who voted "no" on that fatal measure. At home, too, in his own county, his voice and active influence were earnestly given in behalf of an undivided country. It was to local leaders like Butler, Brown, Staples, Houk, Senter, and others, who worked so earnestly and bravely in their respective counties in the winter and spring of 1861 that the great Union victories in East Tennessee were due in a degree not generally recognized. They worked with earnest determination among their neighbors and friends, where they had the greatest influence, with telling effect. Never was there a greater mistake made than to assume that a few great leaders alone won the marvelous Union victories in East Tennessee. This honor belongs, though in greatly unequal degrees, to a great number of persons, some of them distinguished throughout the land, and some entirely unknown to fame beyond the limits of the State, and, in some cases, beyond their own counties. But for the exertions of local leaders, led by a few prominent men, Johnson, Nelson, and Maynard would have found the battle lost when they returned from Washington in the spring of 1861.

DeWitt C. Senter was a son of William T. Senter, who died some time before the Civil War. The elder Senter was a Methodist minister of considerable celebrity from 1830, or earlier, to 1850. He was a member of the Constitutional Convention of 1834. In the political canvass of 1840, like Governor James C. Jones, he suddenly sprang into great notoriety by his ability as a stump speaker. Wherever he spoke he aroused the wildest enthusiasm. He had a spicy, incisive, thrilling kind of eloquence precisely adapted to the hot temper and bitter violence of that abnormal period of political fermentation. He was, in fact, singularly pointed, caustic, and effective in speaking. In some respects he was superior to James C. Jones in a political discussion. Woe to the man who fell into his hands in 1840. He had no mercy on a political opponent. He would launch at him a torrent of wit, argument, and denunciation, in rapid speech and thrilling tones, that was apt to overwhelm him. At a great mass meeting at Brushy Creek, in Washington County, in October, 1840, I heard him almost annihilate a certain politician who had the temerity to demand a hearing and to appear on the stump. The celebrated Virginia-South Carolina orator, William C. Preston, who was present, was greatly interested in Senter's wild eloquence. He hung upon his words with intense delight.

In 1843 William T. Senter was elected to Congress as a Whig from the Second District. But except in the heat of a canvass he was of a phlegmatic temperament, and therefore he made no especial reputation as a debater in that body. He needed opposition to kindle the fire of his genius.

When Tennessee was reorganized in 1865 DeWitt C. Senter was again elected to the Legislature. In 1867 he became a member of the Senate and was made its Speaker. When William G. Brownlow resigned as Governor in February, 1869, in order to take his seat in the United States Senate, Mr. Senter became Governor of the State by virtue of the Constitution. At the approaching election he was naturally a candidate before the people for the office he then held. William B. Stokes, who had served with some reputation in the Union army as Colonel of a Tennessee Regiment, became a candidate also. The nominating convention split after disgraceful scenes of passion, and both candidates were separately nominated by their respective friends. The excitement throughout the State became great and surpassingly bitter. A joint canvass between the two candidates followed, distinguished for its personalities and want of dignity and propriety. The administration of Governor Senter had not been sufficiently fortunate to escape criticism. A majority perhaps of the Union men ranged themselves on the side of Colonel Stokes. From the first Governor

Senter began to pander to the feelings and prejudices of the late secessionists. Before the close of the canvass he openly declared in favor of their enfranchisement. The election laws of the State, restricting the elective franchise, were openly disregarded and violated by Senter's friends, and those lately laboring under the disability of disfranchisement went to the poles and voted as freely as the Union men. Senter was elected by a large majority, receiving the entire vote of those lately in arms against the government. A Democratic Legislature was also elected. Thus the State, through the open violation of the law on the part of Governor Senter, passed back into the hands of those who had carried it into secession in 1861. A Constitutional Convention was speedily called, and every vestige of the unfriendly legislation of 1865-1869 was erased from the statute book. Governor Senter gave the late secessionists the opportunity they desired at the ballot box, by openly disregarding the election laws, and it would have been amazingly strange if they had not joyfully accepted it.

At the end of the term of Governor Senter the Democratic party came into power in the State by an immense majority. He retired to private life on a farm near Morristown, from which he never emerged, though possibly not exceeding thirty-seven or thirty-eight years of age. The Democratic party had no further use for him, and the Republicans did not forgive him for his course in 1869. He recently departed this life on his farm. After his retirement he never took any active part in politics, though I believe he still claimed to be a Republican.

His administration has never been a source of pride to the people of the State. Hungry and rapacious men swarmed around him in search of spoils. The public service was lowered and corrupted. But the Democratic party has been blind and silent as to its faults, because to Senter they owed their enfranchisement, and their restoration to power in the State. He was mainly elected by Democrats and became on this account their Governor.

Governor Senter was unquestionably a man of excellent natural ability. If he had been a student, and had remained in public life long enough for the full maturity of his fine powers, he might have become a somewhat remarkable man. He was rather a handsome, striking-looking person. His voice, in the glow and fervor of debate, like his father's, was peculiarly thrilling. Like his father, also, when aroused, he was animated, pointed, and aggressive, but I hardly think he was so caustic, so incisive. While in many respects he was much like his father, he was never the latter's equal. On the whole, Governor Senter had that in him which might have been developed into more than ordinary power.

GENERAL JAMES G. SPEARS.

Early Struggles—Clerk of Circuit Court—Happy Marriage—A Democrat—Delegate to Knoxville Convention—Daring Operation—Led His Regiment at Fishing Creek—In Battle at Murfreesboro—Hot-headed—A. L. Spears, His Son, a Brave Officer in Union Army—a Lawyer.

GENERAL JAMES G. SPEARS was born in Bledsoe County, Tennessee, in 1816, and died at Braden's Knob in the same county, July 22, 1869. From his infancy his road in life seemed rough and hard. He was the eldest of five children, and the burden of supporting the family rested on his shoulders, his father having lost the bulk of his estate in speculation. It is the same old story told of Lincoln and Johnson and Garfield, and of many other great men, and being daily repeated in actual life by ambitious, brave boys—of aspiration, of toil, disappointment, struggles with poverty, and finally of success achieved. As remarked by his faithful wife, "It seemed as if it was his misfortune always to get hold of the rough end of everything, and he viewed everything in that light—that if it was not a hard road to travel it was not worth going." This was the key to his mind—courage, persistence, ambition. Every obstacle on his way must be swept aside. Success is certain with a man of such a will.

After young Spears became of age he acquired a meager education by his own efforts. He was fond of reading and embraced every opportunity to gain knowledge. After leaving school he studied law, and located at Pikeville, Tenn. In 1848 he was elected Clerk of the Circuit Court and served two terms in that capacity. After the expiration of his terms as Clerk, he resumed his profession as a lawyer. He must have had considerable aptitude for making and saving money, for about 1851 he bought a farm near Pikeville, built a house on it and moved to it, and put his colored people there to cultivate it and take care of his fine stock, of which he was very fond. In 1849 he married Miss Adeline K. Brown, daughter of William L. Brown of Bledsoe County, who still survives her husband, loved and respected for her own virtues, as well as honored as the relict of a man in many respects of no ordinary mold. This marriage proved to be a happy one. Mr. Spears spoke of his wife with great tenderness, and often said that "if he wanted to marry a dozen times he would court the same woman every time." His children consisted of five sons and one daughter. They were A. L. Spears of Jasper, N. B. Spears of Pell City, Ala., J. Brown Spears of Pikeville, W. D. Spears of Jasper, James G. Spears, Jr., and Mrs. James Robertson of Sequachee City. All are still living, except Colonel A. L. Spears, who died in 1900.

General Spears was in politics a Democrat. In 1860 he supported Stephen A. Douglas against John C. Breckinridge, the regular Democratic nominee for President in Tennessee—the disunion candidate of the South. Mr. Lincoln was elected, and Mr. Spears was willing to abide by his election rather than have a disruption of the Government. He was a delegate to the Knoxville Convention in May, 1861, and afterward to the more important meeting of that body in Greeneville in June. He was a member of the Business Committee, consisting of thirty-one members, to which were referred all important resolutions.

There was no member of these bodies who was more bitter and extreme in his opinion, not even Colonel William Clift. He therefore favored the violent measures proposed by a distinguished member of that body, which were at first unanimously reported for adoption by the Committee. He returned home not entirely satisfied with the pacific policy finally adopted by the Greeneville convention.

After returning home, like nine-tenths of the Union men, it was not his desire nor purpose to take up arms against the Southern Confederacy, but to remain at home a quiet spectator of the great strife. But he was not permitted to do this. Learning that a warrant for his arrest for disloyalty to the South had been issued against him, some time in the early fall of 1861, he, in company with Colonel D. C. Trewhitt and others, secretly left their homes, and passed through the mountains into Kentucky—the land of refuge for fleeing, persecuted loyalists of East Tennessee. Here he raised a regiment among the refugees and became its Colonel.

While at Cumberland Gap he undertook a bold operation, such as his daring spirit delighted in. Leaving the Gap, he marched to the North side of the mountain, and crossing Log Mountain, he turned westwardly, and pushed on through the mountains to Big Creek Gap, distant by this indirect route some forty or more miles from his starting point; then he pushed on to Wallace's Cross Roads, distant twenty-odd miles farther, and eighteen miles from Knoxville. Here he surprised a Confederate force, and scattered it in confusion, killing, wounding, and capturing sixty-five men. He returned by the same route to Cumberland Gap without the loss of a man.

It is impossible to follow Colonel Spears with details in his various marches and battles of the next three years. It can only be briefly mentioned that he led his regiment in the battle of Mill Spring, or Fishing Creek, and by his bravery contributed to the first decisive battle on the part of the Federals in the War. Soon after this event he was made Brigadier General of Volunteers, in recognition of his bravery. He was with General George W. Morgan when Cumberland Gap was captured, and had a conspicuous part in the skillful maneuvers by which it was accomplished. He was also with him when the latter was forced to abandon Cumberland Gap, in the fall of 1862, to avoid capture by the superior forces of General E. Kirby Smith at the time he and General Bragg jointly invaded Kentucky. General Spears helped to conduct the celebrated retreat from Cumberland Gap, through northeastern Kentucky to the Ohio River, during which the Union forces were constantly harassed by the enemy in front, in the rear and on the flanks, and subjected to extreme want of water and food, a single drink sometimes costing five dollars.

General Spears had an honorable part in the battle of Murfreesboro, and also in that of Chattanooga, besides participating in many skirmishes. Wherever he was he bore himself bravely. When President Lincoln issued his emancipation proclamation, he denounced it as illegal and unauthorized. He was represented as saying, at that time, a great many insubordinate things, but I will let his good wife, tell the tale and the result in her own language: "He thought the Government could be preserved without altering the Constitution. He went into the war to support and uphold the old constitution, and he was not the man to go against his principles. He would stand by them, let every other man take his own course. Through the jealousy of some of his officers his sentiments were reported to the President, and charges were preferred against him, which caused Mr. Lincoln to order an investigation, which led to a dismissal from the army."

This was an unfortunate ending of the honorable military career of General Spears, which every true friend of his regrets. But there was nothing in it positively disgraceful to him. He had not shown cowardice in the face of the enemy; he had not betrayed his country. He was brave in battle, but hot-headed, impulsive, and obstinate in what he thought was right. His violent temper and courage in the expressions of his views carried him too far, and as an officer his conduct became insubordination, which under the Articles of War could not be tolerated. He could have resigned, but this his proud, defiant spirit would not allow him to do in order to escape the consequences of his acts. Thus he showed himself to be brave to desperation in the very extremity of his fortunes.

No man ever doubted the courage of General Spears. In addition he was manly and honorable, while the career he ran shows that he possessed remarkably strong qualities. He was the first volunteer officer from Tennessee who was made a Brigadier General. This was early in 1862, and only a few months after he had entered the service. Even General Joseph A. Cooper, who finally won the first place as a distinguished officer among Tennesseeans, did not receive a Brigadier's commission until the summer of 1864, nearly three years after entering the service.

General Spears, after leaving the army returned to the practice of his profession and to the work of regaining his fortune, which I infer had been a considerable one at the outbreak of the war. His health also was impaired by the hardships to which he had been exposed in his campaigns, and he never fully regained it. His life ended, as before stated, July 22, 1869, in the fifty-third year of his age.

A few words as to A. L. Spears, his eldest son, who also was a soldier and an officer in the Union Army. This young man, aged eighteen, was a student at Emory and Henry College, Va., when the war broke out, and was in sentiment and sympathy with the South. It happened that he heard the Hon. John. B. Floyd boast, in a speech, I think, that he had, as Secretary of War, stripped the North of arms and sent them South for the use of those in insurrection against the United States. This baseness of Floyd was so shocking to the honor of young Spears that he immediately determined to leave college and enter the Union army. When he got home, however, his services were needed to take care of the family and the estate, his father being on the point of going to Kentucky to join the army. He accordingly concluded, by the direction of his father, to remain at home. After staying there a few weeks or months, he found himself the object of such suspicion and persecution that he was compelled to seek safety in flight to Kentucky, notwithstanding his father's orders to the contrary.

In Kentucky he at once entered the army. In a short time he was appointed the Adjutant of his regiment, and continued in this position until the close, or near the close of the war.

He was with his regiment in all its battles, including Sherman's Georgia Campaign, on every field, displaying the qualities of a brave and noble soldier. After the war ended he studied law and followed that profession with great success, accumulating a large estate. In person he was large, tall, and fine-looking. He was well informed, and a most delightful conversationalist. He was broad and liberal in his opinions, and altogether a most striking and attractive man.

BENJAMIN TOLLIVER STAPLES.

Family Among Settlers of Jamestown—Taught by Parents—Leader in Cumberland Plateau—Defeated Twice for Legislature—Activity in Behalf of Union—Raised a Regiment—Wounded and Taken Prisoner—Tortured and Shot—The Mountain Man—"Tinker Dave."

BENJAMIN TOLLIVER STAPLES, one of the leaders of the people on the Union side in 1861, was born in Morgan County, Tennessee, December 24, 1817, the youngest of fifteen children. His father, John Staples, at the age of eighteen, was a soldier in the Revolution, and served through the entire war. He was with Washington at Yorktown, and witnessed and shared in the crowning glory of the surrender of the British Army. His family were among the early settlers of Jamestown, the first cradle of English-speaking people on this continent. John Staples moved with his family to the gold fields of Georgia, where he lost a considerable fortune, and then came to Morgan County, Tennessee, a poor man.

Tolliver Staples—the name by which he was generally known—though a man of good education, never went to school a day. He was taught by his parents, both of whom were educated. Before his twentieth year, he was employed by the County Surveyor as an assistant. Afterward he became County Surveyor himself, which position he held for a number of years. In addition to surveying he also farmed and raised stock.

At the breaking out of the Rebellion and for some years previously, Staples was Clerk and Master of the Chancery Court of Morgan County—an office requiring for the proper performance of its duties highest fidelity. In 1853 and again in 1855 he was a Whig candidate for Representative in the Legislature for the District composed of the Counties of Morgan, Scott, and Fentress, and though the district was largely Democratic, he was each time defeated by less than one hundred votes.

In 1860 Tolliver Staples was an ardent friend of the Union, and a supporter of Bell for the Presidency. When the Civil War was inaugurated, true to the teachings of the Whig party, he remained an unflinching friend of the old Government. He canvassed Morgan County, and devoted all the energies of his mind and body to defeat the insane and unwise measure. He was a delegate to the Knoxville Convention, called, it will be remembered, to aid in defeating the secession of Tennessee. His activity in behalf of the Union and his outspoken opposition to the Southern Confederacy led to his arrest in November or December, 1861, and his incarceration in jail at Knoxville. This was after the bridges on the railroads were burned, at that time of universal gloom and terror, when the prisons were overflowing with Union men, and the scaffold so frequently had its victims.

After his release he made his escape into Kentucky and thence to Nashville. Here, he and others obtained authority to raise a regiment of Tennessee Cavalry for service in the Federal Army, of which Isham Young became Colonel; R. A. Davis, Lieutenant Colonel; J. S. Duncan, Major; and of which he was appointed Adjutant. On the 17th of March, 1863, he and Colonel Davis, Major Duncan, and a few soldiers encountered a Confederate force at Pine Knot, Kentucky, where he was wounded and taken prisoner, his horse being killed. Major Duncan was also killed, and Colonel Davis wounded, though the latter succeeded in escaping. Staples was carried to Monticello, Ky. On the 22d he was given in charge of the command of the noted Confederate guerrilla, Champ Ferguson, to be taken to Knoxville. The guard took him about fifteen miles on the road toward Albany, Ky., where he was cruelly and inhumanely abused, even tortured, and finally shot.*

Thus while a prisoner was a brave and a noble man foully murdered. This killing excited widespread sorrow and indignation at the time, and is even yet recalled with horror.

Benjamin Tolliver Staples deserves mention, because of the wide influence he exerted, in 1861, on the people of a large part of the Cumberland Plateau. The brightest and brainiest man in all that region, he was also earnest and active. On all questions of the current politics of the day he was well posted,—he was a fluent talker, and was full of action and enthusiasm. A

---

*This is the account given of this affair by Samuel H. Staples, a son of Tolliver, who is a reputable lawyer living at Harriman, Tenn., and a Democrat, and the account corresponds with that current at the time and prevailing since.

mountain man of extraordinary mentality, of positiveness and energy, he was also endowed with courage, keen moral convictions, and a physical frame of the power and strength to command universal respect—a born leader among a mountain people.

In 1860 and 1861 he was an uncompromising Union man, taking a deep interest in the political discussions of the time, and powerfully influencing the mountain people whose confidence he enjoyed. With a unanimity seldom witnessed, except in the County of Sevier, the people of this region were Union men. In the June election, on the question of separation or no separation, the vote in Morgan County in its favor was only thirty-eight and in Scott nineteen. I have not the figures before me as to the vote in Cumberland and Fentress Counties, but it was overwhelmingly in favor of no separation, approximating the unanimity of Morgan and Scott. These people are brave, generous, and, in the main, lawabiding. No such family and neighborhood feuds, often extending over whole counties and resulting in frightful shedding of blood, as those in some of the neighboring counties in Kentucky and in West Virginia, exist or ever have existed in this section. Nor is intoxication or illicit distilling as prevalent as would be expected in a mountain region. Indeed the latter is almost wholly unknown. In morals the people are remarkable, considering the lack of schools and of the advantages of an old civilization.*

---

*When I was a candidate for Chancellor in 1870, my competitor, an able lawyer, did not receive a single vote in Scott County. I had canvassed in 1860 these mountain counties, except Cumberland, as elector on the Bell-Everett ticket. Again, from 1870 to 1878, I held courts in them as Chancellor (excepting Cumberland), a part of the time in all of them, and for the whole time in one of them, and thus had a good opportunity of knowing these people. During all that time I never heard of any general lawlessness, nor have I since. One of my courts, that of Fentress County, was about ninety miles from my home in Knoxville, every foot of which I was compelled to make on horseback. But I enjoyed my trips immensely, with venison and wild turkey as my meat. Here I met Captain Dave Beatty, or "Tinker Dave," as he was commonly called, the celebrated partisan or guerrilla commander of an independent company on the Union side during the Civil war. He operated in this mountain region and was the terror of all the Confederates. I venture to tell how I quieted him. The first day I opened court in Fentress County he took a conspicuous position near me, and in a short time commenced interrupting the proceedings by loud remarks in reference to them. He seemed to think it his duty to give his opinion about all matters that came up, as had been his habit. I admonished him gently that he must keep quiet. The admonition did not silence him. The third time he interrupted the court with his advice I said to him in a firm but kindly manner: "Captain Beatty, when you were in command of a company in the army and gave an order, you expected and required it to be obeyed without argument or talking back. There was but one captain in your company. Now, I am captain in this court and the Sheriff is my lieutenant. There is but one captain here, and the privates must not interfere." He quickly said: "I am shut pan," and became perfectly quiet from that moment. He afterward said to me at my hotel: "Judge, you are right; there cannot be two captains for one company." I never had any trouble with him afterward, and we became good friends. He was a brave man and in many respects a good private citizen.

DR. JOSEPH C. STRONG.

Earnest Friend of Union—His Father in U. S. Navy—Family Prominent in Social and Business Affairs—Aided Union Guides—Strong Family Dates in United States from 1630.

IF there was anywhere a better or more earnest friend of the Union than Dr. Joseph C. Strong, of Knox County, I should like to know who he was that I might in these pages devise some special honor to his memory. This generation does not and cannot comprehend the courage it required in the South, after June, 1861, to be a Union man,—the sacrifices he made, the sufferings he endured, the dangers he was exposed to, and the reproaches and the obloquy he had to bear. And strange anomaly, the men who were false to our Government, and fought but failed to destroy it, with supreme arrogance assume that they are better than the men who were always true and faithful!

The immediate ancestor of Dr. Strong was Dr. Joseph C. Strong, a native of Massachusetts. He was a surgeon in the U. S. Navy. When President Jefferson adopted his foolish scheme of gunboats for the defense of the commerce and our coasts, he virtually destroyed our navy, and Dr. Strong therefore resigned his position, and in 1802 came South and settled in Knoxville, Tenn. He became and so remained for many years an eminent physician in that city. On his death in 1838 he left several children, and a considerable fortune. The Hon. Charles Ready, the eminent lawyer, and for a number of years a distinguished member of Congress from Middle Tennessee, married one of his daughters. Others married prominent business men. His descendants are numerous, and are among the first in the society and in the business circles of Knoxville. Among them is the well-known, public-spirited, and wealthy citizen, B. R. Strong, so highly esteemed by his fellow citizens of Knoxville for his uprightness. Two brothers, Gideon and Joseph, own the magnificent farm of the late Dr. Strong on the Holston River, the old homestead, twelve miles East of Knoxville, and they are model farmers, prosperous and wide awake, and are among the best citizens of East Tennessee in every way. The descendants of Dr. Strong do honor to their long line of honorable ancestry.

Dr. Joseph C. Strong lived in the country on the fine farm we have just mentioned. He was an educated gentleman, a slave holder, a practicing physician, and a man of intelligence, and possessed of a good estate. He was therefore naturally calculated to exert a wide influence among his acquaintances. In the February and June canvasses, 1861, he was an open, active, and avowed friend of the Union. But even after the State had aligned itself with the Southern Confederacy, he did not cease to work, nor grow faint-hearted. His farm was directly on the Union "trail" to Kentucky, and was the point for crossing the river for the refugees from Sevier County and a part of Knox, under the leadership of the famous guide Spencer Deaton. Dr. Strong knew all about their movements, and aided them in every conceivable manner in making their escape. His farm was a resting place for Deaton in passing to and from Kentucky. On one occasion Deaton was in Strong's barn when a Confederate regiment passed by on the public road within forty or fifty yards of the place where he was silently watching it. Dr. Strong's house was a secret place for the delivery of letters brought by Deaton from refugees in the army to their families in the neighborhood. This faithful guide—one of the most noted in East Tennessee—who successfully piloted through the mountains thousands of fleeing Union men, was at last captured in the latter part of 1863 or early part of 1864, carried to Richmond, condemned as a spy, and hanged in Libby Prison. It was astonishing how bold and reckless these pilots became in their operations. I recollect seeing and talking with Deaton on the streets of Knoxville in 1863, while the Confederates held possession of that place. I did not then know he was engaged as a pilot for Union men. He, and all of his calling, led desperately hazardous lives, and their services to the Union refugees, and to the Union Army as well, were invaluable.

If we seek for a much older family than that of the Strongs in the United States, we shall have to go back to Massasoit, the dusky king of the Narragansetts, or Powhatan, Emperor of the Virginians, for their ancestor Strong landed from the good ship, *Mary and John*, in Nantasket, in May, 1630. An examination of the date of the landing and the name of the vessel on which he arrived discloses the coincidence that he and Matthew Grant, the direct ancestor of Ulysses Grant, came over from England on the same vessel. The *Mayflower* had arrived in New England nine years earlier, but nine years is but a speck of time in nine generations of men. The Strongs can claim for their family a venerable antiquity in the United States. The passengers on the *Mary and John* settled at Dorchester. As from one of them has sprung a president of the United States, we are encouraged to hope that a like good fortune may befall some one of the descendants of other passengers.

NATHANIEL G. TAYLOR.

Grandfather Owned Immense Estates—Graduated at Washington College and Princeton—Became a Minister—Distinguished Appearance—Rare Gifts—Raised Funds for Relief of Destitute People of East Tennessee—Aided by Rev. Dr. T. W. Humes—Elector, 1860.

NATHANIEL G. TAYLOR, one of the prominent Union leaders of East Tennessee in 1860 and 1861, was born in Carter County, in December, 1819. He was the son of James P. Taylor, a bright lawyer in his day, and the grandson of General Nathaniel Taylor, who came from Virginia at an early day and settled in Carter County. General Taylor was the owner of an immense landed estate, amounting to tens of thousands of acres, lying in the mountain regions of East Tennessee and Southwest Virginia. He was a man of wealth, and lived in fine style for his day. In the battle of New Orleans he commanded a regiment of Tennessee troops, and distinguished himself by valor and splendid soldierly bearing.

The family of Nathaniel G. Taylor, the subject of our sketch, was wealthy and influential on both his father's and his mother's side. His educational advantages were of the first order. He took a course at Washington College, Tennessee, and then a second course at Princeton, where he was graduated about 1842. He intended becoming a lawyer, and had perhaps entered upon the study of law, when an incident happened in 1843, which changed the whole tenor of his life.

One Sabbath night, during a camp-meeting at Brushy Creek, at or near the present town of Johnson City, Miss Mary Taylor, a beautiful and lovely young lady, a sister of Mr. Taylor, and two young college mates of mine, John Miller from North Carolina, and David Gillespie of Rhea County, were conversing together in the door of one of the cabins, when they were all suddenly stricken down by a terrific flash of lightning. Miss Taylor and Mr. Miller were instantly killed; Mr. Gillespie, after weeks of suffering, finally recovered. This terrible calamity threw a gloom over the assemblage gathered at the camp ground. The news of it spread over the country and drew an immense crowd to the meeting. Religious feeling became deep and intense. Two or three days afterward Mr. Taylor arose near the pulpit, and with graceful and highly dramatic action and pathetic voice, delivered a surpassingly fervid, impassioned, and thrilling religious exhortation. Coming as this address did, when all present were already under a spell of profound excitement, the effect was electrical. The sea of human beings was stirred as if it had been swept by a tempest. I often heard Mr. Taylor afterward, in the days of his maturity, but never heard him surpass, or even equal, this effort made at the age of twenty-three. Soon after this incident he became a Methodist minister.

Mr. Taylor was endowed in many respects with rare gifts. His person was remarkably striking. Though of only medium height, there was an elegance, a rotundity, and a dignity about it that at once commanded respect. His face was highly striking. There was in it a foreign look that gave him a most distinguished appearance. Perhaps it was the blood of Pocahontas reappearing in him. His whole person was marked by a refinement indicating high breeding. We say this about horses and cattle, and why should we not say it about man, highest and noblest created thing? His voice was strong and clear, and in its higher tones ringing and musical. His language was always chaste and elegant. He had a rich fancy, but his good taste and education held it in check. There was seldom anything in his speeches of an extravagant character; or that bordered on bombast. He possessed humor and sometimes indulged it, but he never descended to buffoonery. As an orator, when he had the proper spur and incentive, he was superior to his celebrated brother-in-law, Landon C. Haynes. For rough work or boisterous talk, I admit he was not Haynes' equal. It was perhaps well that Mr. Taylor did not follow the law. He neither had the industry nor the taste for a profession of any details.

The people of East Tennessee owe to Mr. Taylor's memory a lasting debt of gratitude. In 1864 he originated the idea of securing some relief for the people of this section, who were already in great need of the common necessaries of life, and were likely to become in the near future almost absolutely destitute. This state of want was the natural result of the occupation of East Tennessee by three armies—General Longstreet's in the upper part, General Burnside's in the central, and General Sherman's in the lower part. Toward the close of 1863 the destitution was becoming alarming. About this time Mr. Taylor, moved by his sympathy for the people, and of his own will, went North to secure aid for the suffering people. He began the work alone, by making public speeches, soon attracting volunteers to his aid. In Boston a great public meeting was held in Faneuil Hall. Mr. Everett, Governor Andrews, and indeed nearly all the leading men of the city attended, and took seats on the platform. Mr. Taylor made a splendid, thrilling speech, in which he pleaded with all his nature for relief for his countrymen in the valleys and mountains of East Tennessee. Mr. Everett followed in one of his beautiful, masterly addresses. That of Mr. Taylor was hardly inferior to that of Mr. Everett. The result was that a plan was organized, and committees were appointed for raising money in the New England States and elsewhere. Money poured in by thousands to the committees. All over New England many women and even children vied with one another in their generous contributions. Philadelphia and other cities caught the contagion, and in a few months the sum of over one hundred thousand dollars was raised. This money was judiciously laid out from time to time by these committees, for provisions, shoes, clothing, etc., and forwarded to an Executive Committee at Knoxville, and distributed through local committees to all the Counties in East Tennessee. These supplies were sold at about cost to those who were in want and were able to pay for them, and this money reinvested in other supplies. To the destitute supplies were given gratuitously. Thus by the happy conception of Mr. Taylor, and in his noble efforts, aided by Mr. Everett and other philanthropic gentlemen, were the people of this section saved from great suffering and perhaps a famine during the years 1864 and 1865.

It is a gratifying fact, highly honorable to the venerable president, the Rev. Dr. T. W. Humes, and to the other members of the local Executive Committee at Knoxville that these large supplies, amounting in the aggregate to perhaps $200,000, were all distributed without reward, and the accounts closed on settlement with Northern agents, without any complaint, or even suspicion of speculation, corruption, or favoritism.

Mr. Taylor deserves for his canvass in 1860, as elector for

the State at large, on the Bell-Everett ticket, more than a passing notice. He seemed to be deeply impressed with the danger which threatened the Government. I heard at one time, and this was concurrent testimony of all who heard him, that in his discussion with W. C. Whitthorne, at Knoxville, his speech was a remarkably brilliant and masterly effort, so far as it applied to the question of secession. It produced at the time a great sensation among scholarly men. A week or two later I heard the discussion between the same parties at Tazewell, but on this occasion his speech was less remarkable. How he sustained himself at other places I do not know, but I think well, and sometimes splendidly. The question of disunion was one well suited to his peculiar talents.

Mr. Taylor was a man of uncertain and unequal moods. It required a great theme, a great occasion, and a present stimulus or inspiration to call out his powers. His temperament and mind were rather phlegmatic. They needed shaking up and arousing. When they were quickened into activity, he was always successful. Indeed under the proper conditions he was a most chaste, graceful, and eloquent orator. He, however, was under all circumstances dignified, scholarly, pleasing, and honorable, and on some rare occasion he had but few, if any, superiors as a speaker.

Personally Mr. Taylor was a delightful gentleman. He was gentle, genial, and cheerful. His temper was even and placid. He loved ease and tranquillity. While he loved political honors, he scarcely possessed the ceaseless energy necessary for high success in that field of endeavor, and yet he was frequently a candidate for office. In 1849 he was a candidate for Congress in the first district against Andrew Johnson, but there being a good Democratic majority in favor of his competitor, he was defeated. In 1853 he was again a candidate, against Albert G. Watkins and Brookins Campbell, the early rival of Mr. Johnson, and his competitor for the Legislature in 1837 and 1839. Mr. Campbell was elected, but died while serving his first term. Mr. Taylor again became a candidate, and was elected to fill out the unexpired term of Mr. Campbell, defeating Mr. Watkins. In 1855, and again in 1857, he was a candidate, but was defeated by Mr. Watkins. In 1865 Mr. Taylor was successful in his race for Congress. After the expiration of this term, he was appointed by President Johnson Commissioner of Indian affairs, which office he held until after the Administration of General Grant came into power. In 1852, and again in 1856, Mr. Taylor served as an elector on the Whig ticket.

In the canvass of 1860 he was Elector for the State at large, and rendered splendid service for the Union cause by his eloquent, earnest speeches. At a little later period, when the question of secession came directly before the people of Tennessee, he gave his powerful voice and influence in opposition to that movement. Yet he was not so active in his opposition as a number of other men, though equally as earnest. He was an old-line Whig, and the Whig party in Tennessee at first, at least, was almost solidly arrayed against secession.

Mr. Taylor was the father of Hon. A. A. Taylor, who was elected a member of Congress three times from the celebrated first district of Tennessee, so long represented by Andrew Johnson. He was also the father of Governor Robert L. Taylor, so distinguished as a stump orator and a humorous lecturer. The latter is now one of the most successful lecturers, in his line, in the United States. As a delightful orator he is without his peer. It was simply amazing how many beautiful, happy, unrivaled little speeches he made as Governor at Nashville, during the Centennial Exposition in 1897. Each was a rare gem of beauty. His voice, his words, his manner were the perfection of art.

Nathaniel G. Taylor deserves to be held in grateful remembrance by his countrymen for his many noble virtues, his pure life, and his exalted example. He deserves to be remembered especially by the people of East Tennessee for the splendid work he undertook alone in 1864, in securing funds and provisions for the needy and starving people, to thousands of whose homes and firesides famine came so near, and was relieved or averted by his efforts.

MONTGOMERY THORNBURGH.

Studied Law—State Senate Three Terms—Attorney General—Active in
Conciliation—Confined at Tuscaloosa.

A brief, but honorable, and at the same time a sad story in the end, is the one I have to tell of Montgomery Thornburgh. He was born in Jefferson County, Tennessee, in 1817; and obtained a limited education in New Market, at his own home. He was a farmer by profession in the early part of his life, before he entered political life and studied law, though he sometimes assisted his father in his tanyard in the wintertime. In 1845 he was elected to the State Senate, although he seems to have been but twenty-eight years of age at the time. He was also elected to the Senate in 1847 and in 1849. In all his legislative career he was faithful and independent in the discharge of his duties. He must have had, and indeed did have, popular ways and manners as a candidate, for he was opposed, at least, in his last race, by strong and winning men. He was always strong and pointed on the stump as a speaker—never elegant and polished, but with his sledgehammer blows and with his plain common sense, he accomplished more than ornate speech would have done.

About 1850 Mr. Thornburgh obtained a license to practice law and was admitted to the bar. In 1851 he was elected Attorney General of the Twelfth Judicial District, and on the expiration of his term of office, he was re-elected. I have been told by his family that he was elected Attorney General three times, but as each term was six years, and as the two would have extended his time to 1862 or 1863, I believe they are mistaken.

As a prosecuting officer Mr. Thornburgh was vigilant and able, bringing out the evidence before the court and jury with great skill, and arguing the facts with vigor and power. After his many years of experience in criminal trials he became a strong jury lawyer.

In all the social relations of life Mr. Thornburgh was a gentleman of integrity and of high moral deportment, warm and genial in his friendships, and just in all his relations. He had many warm friends, because he was a big-hearted, as well as a big-bodied man. He was over six feet high, and weighed about two hundred and twenty pounds.

In politics Mr. Thornburgh was an earnest Whig. When the exciting contests of 1860 and of the early part of 1861—preludes to the Civil War—were everywhere filling the minds of men with anxious forebodings, he most naturally adhered to the party whose watchword was the Union and the Constitution. Subsequently, when the question of secession came directly before the people of the State, and the dark shadows of the tempest of revolution were appearing, he threw all his mind and powers in behalf of peace and the Union. He made speeches in favor of abiding in the old Government, and used his utmost influence in behalf of that policy. When, however, the people of the State voted in favor of separation, and separation became an established fact, he yielded a quiet submission to the supremacy of the Confederacy. He was a member of the Greeneville Convention, which met after the final vote on the question of secession, and in that body he both spoke and voted in favor of peaceable resolutions and measures. I think it is true that, at all times, he advised submission on the part of the people to the new government.

After the burning of the bridges in November, 1861, Mr. Thornburgh was greatly exercised in his mind over the sad condition of the Union men, many of whom had been led by overzeal and undue confidence into rebellious acts against the authorities over them, and hundreds of whom had been thrown into prison. From these causes his mind was most anxiously engaged in the work of conciliation. I saw him and consulted with him more than once, and I can recall no one who more earnestly desired the tranquillity of the Union portion of the population of East Tennessee.

Notwithstanding the pacific disposition of Mr. Thornburgh and his earnest efforts to prevent an outbreak among the Union population of the country, in the month of May, 1862, he was arrested by the Confederate military authorities on the charge of disloyalty and taken to Knoxville. At the same time William Galbraith, Samuel P. Johnson, and James Monroe Meek were arrested in the town of New Market. In a short time they were all sent South to Tuscaloosa for confinement. After remaining there a short time, Mr. Thornburgh (and I believe the others) was sent to Macon, Ga. The hardships of travel and of prison life, the bitterness of arrest, and the odium of confinement among a population every one of whom detested a Union man, soon told on his proud spirit and robust constitution. Disease laid hold of him, and in July his strength yielded to his gloomy surroundings. Thus passed away, amid the horrors of military prison life, the spirit of one of the best and most honorable of the noble Union men of East Tennessee.

DANIEL C. TREWHITT.

Lawyer—Chancellor—Circuit Judge—Mind Clear and Quick.

THE subject of this sketch was a young man engaged in the practice of law in Hamilton County when the Civil War broke out in 1861. He was born and reared in Bradley County, East Tennessee. The well-known lawyer and highly esteemed citizen, Levi Trewhitt, was his father, whose sad death in a Southern prison is still talked of and remembered with sorrow by thousands of East Tennesseeans. In his old age he was seized, and after being in close confinement some time at Knoxville, he was carried off to prison at Tuscaloosa, thence to Mobile, without a trial, for no other crime except being a Union man. One of the deepest stains on the character of the Southern Confederacy is the treatment of this innocent old man.

Daniel C. Trewhitt was a Union man in 1861, and as such he canvassed Hamilton County, making speeches against secession. He was a pointed and incisive speaker, clear and logical, and full of earnest conviction. His speeches therefore had considerable weight in shaping the opinions of the people of Hamilton County. He was so active and outspoken against secession that he had to flee from his home and seek refuge in Kentucky in 1861, when the Southern Confederacy became dominant in Tennessee. There he enlisted in the army and was made Lieutenant Colonel of the 2d Regiment of Tennessee Infantry, and afterward he became General Spears' Adjutant-General, Morgan's Division. He was a most capable officer, and well suited for the position he held.

In 1865 he was appointed Chancellor for the Chattanooga Chancery Division, and held the Chancery Courts until 1870, when the new Constitution went into effect. He then went back to the bar, and practiced law until 1878, when he was elected Circuit Judge for the Chattanooga Circuit. In 1886 he was re-elected, and held that office until his death, January 4, 1891, having served as Chancellor and Circuit Judge altogether nearly eighteen years.

Both as Chancellor and as Circuit Judge he was considered

by the members of his profession an able and an impartial presiding officer. He grasped and solved the questions coming before him for determination with almost intuitive knowledge. His mind was singularly clear and quick. It did not require a moment's deliberation for him to decide all ordinary questions. The result was that he dispatched business with great rapidity. He was endowed by nature with the mind of a high grade lawyer and an able judge. With all this he was honest, and loved justice, and was quick to discover it. He was in fact an exceptionally able and upright judge.*

---

*I applied to one of Judge Trewhitt's near relatives for fuller information concerning his life, but was unable to obtain it.

JUDGE CONNALLY F. TRIGG.

Born in Abingdon—Defeated for Congress in 1853—In 1855 in Partnership with Author—Delegate to State Convention in 1861—Favorite with Union People—Left Tennessee in 1861—Took Part in Gubernatorial Canvass in Ohio in 1863—Appointed U. S. Judge in 1864—Crowded Docket—Sympathizes with Those Lately Opposed—U. S. vs. Moses Gamble—Never Severe.

CONNALLY F. TRIGG, one of the prominent Union leaders in East Tennessee, in 1861, was born in Abingdon, Va., in the year 1810, and died in Bristol, Tenn., April 25, 1880, at the age of seventy years. He belonged to an old and highly respectable family. In some way he was related to the Campbells, the Prestons, and to most of the old families of Abingdon, a town famous for its aristocracy. In 1833 he obtained license to practice law, and at once entered upon his profession. He became a good lawyer, and secured a fair share of the business there was at that time in Southwest Virginia. The business in the Courts was not large, and there were many able lawyers to share it. Mr. Trigg had a natural fondness for politics, and often took part, as a volunteer, in political canvasses. He was an ardent Whig. In 1853, perhaps, he was urged by his friends to become a candidate for Congress, and yielded to their solicitations. His competitor was the somewhat noted Fayette Mullins—made famous by the pen of William G. Brownlow. The contest was hot and exciting, and became for the time being somewhat celebrated, at a distance. But as Mullins was backed by a Democratic majority, Trigg was defeated. Notwithstanding this defeat, he gained considerable celebrity in this canvass, by the ability he displayed as a debater and orator.

In 1855 Mr. Trigg removed to Knoxville, Tenn., where he entered into partnership with me. This partnership lasted until 1859. Mr. Trigg was an able, clear-headed, exact lawyer. He had by nature a fine legal mind. He never seemed to read much, and yet he was well grounded in all the leading principles of law demanded in the profession in the region where he resided. He was a skillful pleader under the old

Common Law forms. I saw his learning and his ability tested in every kind of a case—in cases involving hundreds of thousands of dollars, in every conceivable question of law, in complicated actions of ejectment, in exciting murder trials—and in all he was equal to the most exciting demands. And yet he disliked labor. Trigg was hardly the equal of Baxter, or Lyon, or Sneed, and yet he was not greatly their inferior. In the forcible presentation of facts, indeed he was the superior. He was somewhat peculiar in this, that he was nearly equally strong in all departments of professional action.

After the removal of Mr. Trigg to Tennessee, he took no part in politics until January, 1861, when the exciting scenes of secession in the Southern States called him from the quietude of his profession. When the Legislature called for the election of delegates to a State Convention, to which was to be submitted the solemn question of the secession of the State, the Union people turned to him as one of those delegates. He was nominated unanimously to represent the Counties of Knox and Roane. He immediately entered the canvass with the most intense earnestness and enthusiasm. His speeches were able, daring, and aggressive. If anyone in the State was more bitter and unsparing in denunciation of the secession movement than he, I fail to recall such a person, unless it was Mr. Baxter. Trigg was in fact an ardent, bold, uncompromising Union man, with the courage to proclaim his opinions in terms sometimes startling. His fearlessness and bravery in those trying days made him a fit companion of Johnson, Nelson, Baxter, and Brownlow. As a public speaker he was but little inferior to the best of them—perhaps only to Johnson and Nelson. While inferior to Baxter in mental power, he was decidedly his superior in effectiveness as a speaker. And, while inferior to Mr. Maynard in well-rounded periods, he was decidedly his superior in the bold portrayal of the mad scheme to disrupt the national Government. When he warmed in his speeches, his whole mind and soul seemed to be on fire. As his excitement grew in intensity, and with wild dramatic action of body and voice, he reached some startling point, his audience would be roused into a state of wildest excitement.

Mr. Trigg was a gallant man, who would neither give nor submit to an insult. He possessed in a high degree a genial, sunshiny disposition, and his nature was essentially equable and gentle. And yet on the stump, and before juries, his whole being seemed charged with electricity.

He was certainly an effective, powerful, popular speaker. He had no imagination, nor was he a polished orator, but he possessed earnestness, ardor, action, thought, and conviction. This intense ardor, this dramatic action was strange in him, for off the stump, he was deliberate, unexcitable, indeed almost phlegmatic.

In the canvass of the winter and spring of 1861 Mr. Trigg made a considerable reputation, and became a great favorite of the Union people. He justly deserves to be ranked as one of the ablest of the Union leaders. In both the Knoxville and Greeneville Conventions, he was Chairman of the "Business Committee," to which was referred all resolutions. In consequence, he took no part in the discussion on the floor, and hence it is impossible to say how he stood in the latter Convention on the exciting question that divided that body. It is probable that, like three-fourths of the members, he at first favored the ultra-war-like resolutions of Nelson, since, without any dissent, he reported them to the Convention for adoption; but that he afterward changed his mind in favor of the "Substitute" finally adopted. Whether or not this be true cannot be certainly known. It is very well known that Mr. Trigg was calm and level-headed. As a member of a secret committee with him I had an opportunity of knowing that after the Greeneville Convention he used all his influence in restraining Union men from any violence or resistance to Confederate authority. I know further that soon after that Convention, he and his committee suppressed and prevented an outbreak of Union men in one of the counties of East Tennessee.

Mr. Trigg was known after the State seceded as a determined Union man. He became restless and dissatisfied under the new government. He may have been, and no doubt was, uneasy as to his personal safety. I know of no prominent Union man who was not. So, in the fall of 1861, he determined to make his escape into Kentucky. This purpose was communicated to a few intimate friends. One night he mounted his fine blooded saddle horse, and rode off alone toward Kentucky. After one or more narrow escapes from capture, in three or four nights' travel, he reached a place of safety inside the Federal lines. He remained in the North until 1864, when he returned to the State to open his courts, having been appointed by President Lincoln Judge of the United States Courts for the District of Tennessee. In the gubernatorial canvass of Ohio, in 1863, he took a prominent part as a speaker in behalf of Governor Brough, with fame to himself. After the close of the canvass the prominent Union men of Cincinnati gave him a banquet as a testimonial of their high appreciation of his services on the stump.

When the United States Courts in Tennessee were opened by Judge Trigg he found crowded dockets and a vast number of cases demanding attention. These involved grave questions growing out of the Civil War. There were confiscation cases, treason cases, and revenue cases, all involving new legal questions. He brought to the consideration of these questions judicial fairness, and unfailing patience. I do not recall that a single decision of his upon these war questions was ever overruled. It would have been remarkable if he had given universal satisfaction. He did not. There was much complaint that his decisions were all favorable to those lately hostile to the government. The public mind was greatly excited, and the evil passions aroused by the late Civil War were still dominant, but in the light of experience and reason, it is manifest now that decisions that tended toward peace and good will were wisest and best for all classes.

Not many months passed after Judge Trigg ascended the bench before it became evident that his sympathies and feelings were all on the side of those to whom he had been lately so hostile. This was the more striking when it was considered that he was not a fickle, emotional man, a man of hot impulses and bitter prejudices, but the very reverse. He was conspicuous for his fairness, his coolness, and his tenacity of opinion. And yet he changed, and never returned to his old life-long party affiliations. No one ever knew the reason. Perhaps he did not himself. Possibly the subtle influence of social recognition and position, then as now, so strong in the State, silently and even unconsciously, touched his ambition, or his pride, and did its potent work. It is not ungrateful even to a judge to receive the flattering attention of the powerful and the rich, and to find the doors of elegant and hospitable homes at all times open to him.

It is a somewhat singular fact that the five Union leaders of East Tennessee—Johnson, Nelson, Baxter, Carter, and

Trigg—who were the most implacable in 1861, should all have found themselves in 1866 and afterward in full fellowship with their old enemies. In some cases the change can be easily explained, but in others it cannot be.

Among other novel cases that came before Judge Trigg at Knoxville was that of United States vs. Moses Gamble, for treason. Under an Act of the Legislature, Governor Harris appointed Mr. Gamble, an agent in Blount County, to seize and bring in to the Confederate authorities all arms belonging to the people. This act was designed to disarm Union men. Mr. Gamble was a Union man, and accepted the office in all probability only to avoid being suspected by his Confederate neighbors. He discharged his duties with gentleness and kindness. Nevertheless he had to take some arms from his neighbors, and this gave offense to the Union men. When the United States Court was opened, he was indicted for these acts, being charged with waging war against the United States and of giving aid and comfort to its enemies. The trial before the court and jury consumed two days. I appeared as counsel for the defendant. The law as expounded by Chief Justice Marshall in the celebrated case of the United States vs. Aaron Burr was relied on for the defense. Judge Trigg charged the jury in that way, and it accordingly returned a verdict of not guilty. The case is unique; it was the only trial in the county for treason, so far as I recall, growing out of the great Civil War in 1861-5, and this, too, the trial of a Union man. Many indictments were found against persons engaged in hostilities against the Government, but all were dismissed. This was best. No stain of bloodshed for treason tarnishes the fair record of the United States. This is an imperishable monument to the magnanimity of the triumphant party.

In inflicting punishment on the violators of the law, Judge Trigg could never find it in his heart to be severe. His kind nature was pained and shocked at the thought of suffering. Every violator of the law found in him, if not a friend, a sympathizer. He punished the guilty, but with the utmost humanity.

In person Judge Trigg was tall, slender, erect, and athletic. He was highly sociable in disposition, generous and magnanimous. He had his faults, but where there was so much that was good, so much to love, let the faults be forever covered by the mantle of charity.

DAVID K. YOUNG.

Born and Lived in Anderson County—Circuit Judge—Exceptional Land Lawyer—Arrested—Captain of Tennessee Artillery—Good Financier.

It is with pleasure that I write of my more than fifty years' friend and companion in my profession, Judge David K. Young. Away back in our careers, and later, too, when the lengthening shadows were being cast toward the East, together we rode and chatted and merrily laughed at passing incidents, or recalled from the silence of the past those of other years. Together we traversed the pleasant valleys and climbed the rugged mountains in pursuit of our profession. Together we slept in log cabins and ate corn bread, such as is made only in good mountain homes, and feasted on fresh venison and wild turkey. Together we ascended the eastern slope of life's journey, and together we are now far down on the western, while our companions who started with us, some a little earlier, some a little later, have one by one dropped out by the wayside, and we are left almost alone to finish our brief remaining course.

And our other friend and companion, in later years, the third of the trio—Judge William A. Henderson, the most genial, the brightest of men, the life of every company—should have a notice in these sketches, but alas, in early years he wandered down into "Dixie's land to take his stand, and live or die for Dixie," and therefore, can have no place in this gallery of familiar faces!

Judge Young was born in Anderson County, his present home, January 1, 1826. He was the son of Samuel C. Young, a most respectable old citizen, whose father was a native of the Highlands of Scotland. In 1849 he obtained license to practice law, and settled in Clinton, the county seat. From that day until the present time he has been continuously connected with the bench and bar of Tennessee, except a brief period during the Civil War. During all that time he has maintained, as a lawyer, judge, and man, a position of considerable eminence.

He was Circuit Judge of his circuit from 1873 to 1886, once by appointment to fill a vacancy and twice by the election of the people. During this time, or a part of it, he was by statute assigned to hold the Chancery Court in five of the counties of the circuit.

As a judge he was courteous, prompt, and impartial, and as a lawyer, ready, faithful, and honorable. His speeches at the bar were models of brevity, clearness, and earnestness, never wearing out the court or jury by long, noisy declamation. As a land lawyer his attainments are exceptionally good.

In 1861 Judge Young, being an old-line Whig, was naturally an earnest advocate of the Union. He was active in its support. He and L. C. Houk, then a very young man, were the only Union speakers residing in Anderson County. Soon after the Confederate troops entered that county, he was arrested by them as an influential leader, and held a prisoner for a while. In 1863, after the occupation of East Tennessee by the Federal army, he organized and was made Captain of Battery D, 1st Tennessee Artillery, assigned to the heavy artillery, and placed in command of Fort Johnson, which was the capitol at Nashville. He was under the command of General W. T. Sherman. He remained in command of that Fort until he was appointed Attorney General of the 2d Circuit, which office he held until the latter part of 1868, faithfully performing the duties thereof.

Judge Young lives about one mile and a half from Clinton, on the famous farm known as "Eagle Bend." It is one of the finest farms of the State, comprising many hundreds of acres, a large part of which is rich bottom land on the Clinch River. Here he is surrounded by every comfort and luxury that an uncorrupted taste can desire. His heart, however, is in his profession, and it has never been particularly fascinated with rural affairs. He has given up the management of the farm to a large extent to his son, James Walter Young, who divides his time between scientific farming and the cultivation of literature. Judge Young has been particularly fortunate as a financier, and has by his shrewd judgment built up the largest fortune ever made by a lawyer in East Tennessee, possibly excepting Judge Robert J. McKinney. And this, as in the case of Judge McKinney, has been made honestly and by judicious economy.

Judge Young still delights in the mountains; he still attends their courts. He is a good horseman, and when the term comes around, true to his early habits, he can still be seen, as fifty years ago, mounted on a good horse, setting out for these courts, and he must be a good horseman, whether young or old, who can keep pace with him, or ride as far in one day. He is a remarkably preserved man for his years—young, vigorous, and cheerful, and playful as a boy. In none of his ways, nor yet in his looks or action, does he seem an old man.

JOHNSON AND TEMPLE RACE FOR CONGRESS IN 1847.

Attracted Great Interest—Democratic District—Temple Young, Unknown, Inexperienced—Johnson's Position Impregnable, but Record Vulnerable—First Debate, July 11—Lively Contentions—Disaffection Toward Johnson—Temple's Letter to W. G. Brownlow—Temple Had Good Voice—Ardor, Enthusiasm—Johnson Approaches Competitor to Withdraw — Fifteen Appointments — Less than Three Weeks' Campaign—No Personalities—Notice in Brownlow's Paper—Enthusiasm Over Temple at Washington College Among His Fellow-Students—Political Conditions—Temple Fought Johnson with His Own Weapons—Whig Leaders Stood Aloof from Temple—Time Too Short to Overcome Inertia of the Whigs—They Were Too Indifferent to Go to Polls—Johnson's Majority 314—In the County Canvassed Thoroughly by Temple His Vote Largest Ever Given a Whig—Temple Changed Residence to Avoid Politics.

THE race of Andrew Johnson and myself for Congress in 1847 excited considerable interest in the district at the time it was taking place, and still greater interest throughout the State immediately after its result was known. It is still talked of to this day—more than fifty-six years after the event. Unquestionably this was mainly due to the prominence of Mr. Johnson, and the unexpected result of the election. The distinguished position which he afterward attained has naturally stimulated a curiosity to learn every incident connected with his strange and most extraordinary career. I know therefore that I shall but meet a general desire by attempting to give even at this late day some of the leading facts in reference to that race.

The first Congressional district of Tennessee had been Whig in politics from 1836. It was represented in 1842-43 by Thomas D. Arnold, an old and bitter anti-Jackson Whig. At the same time Andrew Johnson was a Senator in the Legislature, and in laying off the Congressional districts, under the new apportionment, he had a new district carved out for himself, which was Democratic by about fifteen hundred majority. It was his ambition to go to Congress in 1843 and fill the place he had created expressly for himself. But in fixing up the new district, Abraham McClellan, another Democrat, who had represented an adjoining district several terms as it had been previously constituted, was transferred as it were to Mr. Johnson's district by attaching Sullivan County, his home, to it. Mr. McClellan wished to continue in Congress, but Mr. Johnson, by his aggressiveness, silenced and drove him off. Mr. Johnson was therefore easily elected in 1843 over John A. Aiken, an eloquent and worthy man who ran as a United States Bank Democrat. When the canvass of 1845 came around, a new and brilliant star, glittering with scintillations, Landon C. Haynes, rose in the horizon, crossing in its course the orbit of Mr. Johnson. A collision was imminent, and while passing fearfully near, they missed actual contact for the time being. To drop the figure, Mr. Haynes, after threatening awhile and showing a warlike spirit, deferred his race until 1847. In the meanwhile Mr. McClellan and his large kindred and friends were again watchful, active, and expectant, but they finally retired with mutterings and inward curses against Mr. Johnson. Thereupon W. G. Brownlow, a Whig, became a candidate against Mr. Johnson, and was defeated, as Mr. Aiken had been.

When 1847 came around it was confidently expected that the ambition of Mr. Haynes could no longer be repressed. At the same time the aspirations of Mr. McClellan were by no means extinguished, but Mr. Haynes was by very much the more potent and had the larger following. For a long time, Mr. Haynes, while a *quasi* candidate, hesitated whether to be or not to be an avowed one. It was universally expected he would announce himself. Mr. Johnson all along had expected it, and on the faith of that belief, and in order to fence against it, he committed in the late Congress the most stupendous political blunder and party crime of his life. Finally, late in the canvass, Mr. Haynes withdrew his pursuit of Congressional honors to the less ambitious but more certain one of a Senatorial seat in the Legislature, followed by the speakership of that body.

Thus Mr. Johnson was left with a clear field. There was no longer any danger of Democratic opposition, and equally as little, apparently less, indeed, from the Whig party. The old Whig leaders did not covet certain defeat. Some of them, indeed, had promised Mr. Johnson that he should have no Whig opposition. While it was yet considered certain that Mr. Haynes would be a candidate, and more certain that no Whig would be, Mr. Johnson, feeling that he held an impregnable position, went over the district in the early days of the canvass, in his pride of might and defiance of temper, denouncing, almost by name, the leaders and their friends who were opposed to him, as an upstart, mushroom aristocracy, who were striving for selfish ends to put him down, and foist one of themselves upon the people. He delivered long harangues in Jonesboro against the Blairs and Haynes, and in Blountville against the McClellans, Gammons, and their friends.

While the situation was as I have described it, Neill S. Brown, then a Whig candidate for Governor, came along in the latter days of June, making speeches, and suggested to me to become a candidate for Congress, saying there never had been such a chance for a bold young man to make reputation as that district presented, and earnestly urging me to become a candidate. A little later Mr. Brownlow, and then another gentleman, without concert, urged me to this course. I was then residing in Greeneville, near the home of my ancestors, twenty-seven years of age, with a law license less than a year old, and with virtually no business. At first I was awed at the idea of encountering Andrew Johnson, and quite as much so by the thought of the amazement of my friends at my temerity. To rush in the face of such majority, against such a man, with little experience on my part, and young and unknown, looked on its face like foolhardiness. But I was ambitious, full of bounding young blood, and cared little for the consequences. What if I should be beaten? I would have excitement and a lively time—the joy of youth. I knew I would receive blows and wounds, but I knew equally well that Mr. Johnson was not invulnerable, and from my well-filled quiver, however feeble my arms, I expected to be able to inflict some wounds also. This was the confidence of young manhood. In middle life no consideration would have induced me to make that race. Perhaps I was emboldened in this course by the recollection of a little encounter between us in 1840, while I was in my minority, in a young men's Whig meeting in Greeneville, where the occasion, the audience, and the circumstances were all unfavorable to Mr. Johnson, in which I had gained my first popular applause at his expense.

So I announced myself as a candidate about the 6th or 7th of July. I almost immediately set out for Jonesboro, where I issued a circular, and then went to Taylorville, the seat of

Johnson County, where Mr. Johnson had an appointment to speak on Monday, July 11th, the first day of Circuit Court. The crowd assembled to hear Mr. Johnson was moderately large, but few people knowing I was a candidate. Mr. Johnson opened the discussion; he simply referred to the fact that I was present, and a candidate, and would speak. At the conclusion of his speech, I rose, under some embarrassment, and made my first speech, not so much a reply to his as a general arraignment of him and his political course. I charged him with voting in Congress for a proviso to a resolution in effect censuring General Taylor for his conduct in the Mexican War. I also arraigned him for voting, in effect, against increasing the pay of private volunteer soldiers in the Army in Mexico, from seven to ten dollars per month. I pointed out that while he was receiving eight dollars *per day*, and living in ease and luxury as a member of Congress at Washington, he was voting against paying the poor volunteer who was fighting our battles in a torrid climate as much *per month* as he was receiving *per day*.

But my highest arraignment, the most telling one and the most excruciating to Mr. Johnson, was his attack on the administration of President Polk and on those in authority under him. In a speech made in the last Congress, on the 2d of February, 1847, on a proposition made by Mr. Polk to levy a tax on tea and coffee, as a war measure, Mr. Johnson opposed it, and among other things, said:

"But, in conclusion, I must be permitted to say, I wish to Almighty God that the whole American people could be assembled in this city; that there was some kind of amphitheatre constructed, capacious enough to contain the whole voting population of the United States, and that they were convened for a short period of time, and the veil that now conceals from their view the many abuses could be drawn aside, and they be permitted to take one calm survey, one full and dispassionate view, of all the secret springs of the entire proceedings of things under this Government, of all the intriguings of officers in authority from the highest to the lowest. I will not say they would lay violent hands upon an edifice designed by its founders to be so sacred and perfect in all its parts, and tear it into a thousand pieces. I will not say they would rush upon it in a state of precipitancy with the resistless and devastating fury of some mighty tempest; no, I have too much confidence in their forbearance to believe so for a moment. But I feel well assured of one thing, and that is, they would rip up and tear off some of those funguses that have been fixing, and have fixed themselves upon the vitals of this government for years gone by; they would turn some mighty stream through the Augean stable until it was thoroughly cleansed from the abominable filth that had been preying on the life blood of the republic too long."

In my circular and in my speeches, I said in substance, that my competitor ought to know whether these things were true or false, for he was there among them, and understood the "secret springs of their entire proceedings," and was one of them. With a pious, heavy heart, he pours out bitter lamentations that "the veil which conceals the many abuses could not be drawn aside," and the people be permitted to take one dispassionate view of all "the secret springs of things" under the Government, of all "the *intriguings of officers in authority from the highest to the lowest.*" His indignation is kindled and swells in his bosom at all the evils he sees, and in his high and pure emotion he summons the whole American voting population to assemble in the capital of the nation to view the scenes he would disclose, and he exclaims that but for the people's forbearance they would rush upon the sacred edifice "with the devastating fury of some mighty tempest, and tear it into a thousand pieces," pulling down its grand towers, and walls and pillars, and leveling them with the dust! He says that those in authority "from the highest to the lowest" are "intriguing," that is, they are scheming or plotting to accomplish things in an underhanded and secret manner for their own corrupt purposes and not for the public good. He says all the cabinet officers—Marcy, Bancroft, Buchanan, Walker, Clifford, and your own Cave Johnson—that the thousands of subordinate officers under them, and above all that your own President, your favorite, for whom you have so often voted and shouted and thrown up your hats, your idol, James K. Polk, is thus engaged in corrupt intriguing!

I said further, in substance: "Mr. Johnson says he did not mean to include the President in his charge; that the word "from" excludes and leaves him out. I care not how this is. If the President is embraced by the words in the charge, then he is one of the corrupt intriguers. If he is not included, then he is guilty of fostering, protecting, and keeping in office a set of men, every one of whom, from the highest to the lowest, is engaged in the work of corruption! What a charge! What a multitude of scoundrels! All are corrupt, all from the highest to the lowest! No man can believe it, except on the authority of my competitor! *He* says it is true.

"But he says in explanation, that he is no grammarian, that he did not understand the exact import of the language he used, that he did not intend to embrace the President in his charge. Those who are stupid and credulous enough to believe these explanations can do so—I do not. But admit the truth of his explanation, and what a pitiable and deeply humiliating attitude does he occupy? He now represents, and is again a candidate to represent a proud and an *intelligent* constituency in Congress, and yet he is so *ignorant* by his own showing, that, when he would *praise* his *party, he slanders and defames it!* Democrats! Can you vote for such a man? He has insulted you by defaming your President before the whole world, and by making the most sweeping, universal charge of corruption against the administration of Mr. Polk ever made by a man out of a madhouse. He has furnished arguments to his enemies which everywhere throughout the land are used against him.

"This unprovoked, this cruel, this terrible, this universal charge of corruption against Mr. Polk and his administration, against the whole Democratic party, indeed, is unparalleled in its spirit and vindictiveness. What was the motive of it? Was my competitor expecting Democratic opposition, and was he bidding for the Whig vote of the district?"

These were the substance of the comments, and in many places, the very words, with many others not recollected, with which Mr. Johnson was arraigned in my canvass. I was a good reader, and I read and commented on each charge with emphasis and with audacious boldness.

From Johnson County we went to Sullivan, where we filled three appointments in the country. Monday, July 19th, found us in Blountville, the county seat of Sullivan, the most thoroughly Democratic county in the State, with only a handful of Whigs. It was Circuit Court day. The people were there—a very large crowd—from all parts of the county. I was a stranger to nearly all of them, but they had heard of our canvass and were eager to hear us. It was Mr. Johnson's day to speak first. I knew that this day was "big" with my fate; I felt keenly the responsibility, but I was getting a little accustomed to speaking and to lively contentions. I therefore braced myself up for a supreme effort.

Mr. Johnson made his usual speech of one hour and a half in length, but he was not himself. Perhaps it was because he knew there was a widespread disaffection there in reference to him. His speech did not awaken any enthusiasm. The people listened, but were silent. I made a speech of the same length as Mr. Johnson's. While I read extracts from his speech in which he denounced the administration, and commented in bold terms on it—the substance of which in part is given above, but not its spirit—there was a visible sensation in the crowd. It was too evident to escape observation that there was deep indignation against Mr. Johnson. So high did this feeling rise that while I was speaking, and holding up Mr. Johnson in bold terms and in a defiant manner to the gaze of the people, one Democrat cried out in a loud voice "Give it to him!" and many expressed their approval by smiles and laughter. Mr. Johnson rejoined in a half hour's speech and I did the same to his. The speeches were hot and spirited throughout. I was aggressive and frequently on the border-line of the offensive. Mr. Johnson on the contrary, was angry and on the defensive. My friends were "jubilant" as a gentleman who was present— now an old man—expressed it to me recently.

While at Blountville I had time to see the condition of the Democratic party, and time to think and to form my plans for the campaign. The old recognized Whig leaders of the district were in Blountville, in attendance on the court. They did not attend the speaking nor come near me. They gave me no advice, no encouragement. I was, therefore, left alone to fight my own battle. They were honorable gentlemen, and two of them at a much later period became my warm friends, and one of them solicited a law partnership with me. I had not consulted them about becoming a candidate. If I were disposed to be uncharitable, I might say they did not view with complaisancy the thought of a young man so suddenly growing into prominence and leadership. I will not say this, for they were "all honorable men."

The situation was this: A great many Democrats, especially Blair's, McClellan's, and Haynes' friends were displeased with Mr. Johnson. Indeed, they never did like him. They did not desire his defeat, for a Democratic representative was needed in Congress to support Mr. Polk in his war, but they did desire his humiliation, by his receiving only a bare majority. In a letter to W. G. Brownlow, dated July 18th, from Blountville,—the original of which I have, which was preserved by him, and since his death handed to me by his son, Colonel J. B. Brownlow,—I mapped out the canvass in part as follows:

"The true policy in this canvass between Johnson and me is to conduct it in such a way as not to *alarm* the Democrats. If they become alarmed, they will rally to the support of Johnson. If, on the contrary, they think there is no danger, and they are not made *mad*, they will suffer him to fight for himself, and will not care much whether he is elected or not. Therefore don't *abuse* him much, do not make the charge that he is an *infidel*, nor *boast* that I will be elected. The battle must be fought *secretly*. The factions in this district must be artfully *appealed* to and *managed*. I can manage some of them, and my friends must do the rest."

In a second letter of the 20th to the same person, which is also in my possession, I wrote:

"Johnson and I had a warm time here yesterday. My speech took well with the Democrats. They say, 'Lay on, Nancy,' and one of them told me while I was speaking to give it to him. He spoke out in a loud voice. They all want him punished, and several of them told me that they *wanted Johnson to beat me just one vote*. This desire, and it is general, will beget indifference and neutrality. I direct my friends everywhere to make no noise and to let on to the Democrats that there is *no chance* of my election. It will throw them off their guard, and the election will go by default. *You must adopt this course* (in your paper). No excitement is the motto. But the Whigs must understand it. * * * * I am almost certain, that, if my friends play their part right, I can be elected. There never has been such a state of things as exists in this country at the present. I receive nearly as much attention from the Democrats as Johnson does. *Work in secret!*"

In pursuance of this policy I never boasted on the stump of having any chance of being elected, although confident of election, nor consented for Brownlow's paper,—the only Whig paper in the district, and only a weekly at that,—to do so. But I commenced a strenuous system of private work, by letters and private conferences, which was kept up night and day until the election. I rode, I wrote letters, I talked all over the district. How much work I did—how many secret conferences held with Democrats—no man, except myself, will ever know, for I shall never tell.

The relations of Mr. Johnson and myself were formal and distant, although outwardly they were friendly. His bitter spirit was stirred to its depths by the daring arraignment of him I was making every day. His manner was therefore cold and haughty, and I returned it in kind.

I had a good voice, I spoke with ardor, earnestness, enthusiasm, and boldness, such as to fix attention. I hurled my charges against my competitor with taunting and almost vindictive assurance. Mr. Johnson in his speeches, said nothing derogatory to my understanding or my honor, but he criticised my college manner of speaking. I was slender and stood very erect, and therefore he spoke sneeringly of my carriage. It was little and contemptible in him, but I suffered him to continue it, for I knew he was hurting himself more than he was me. But I laid it up in my heart, and returned these things with more than interest in other ways. In a word, war existed between us in all things, but not open and flagrant.

Only twice during our canvass, was Mr. Johnson pleasant to me. Once on Sunday, in going to Blountville from the country where we had stayed all night together, and once in traveling together in the night, from Fall Branch to Greeneville—our mutual home. On both occasions he was very gracious. His motive was obvious. On both these occasions he used all his influence and flattery to induce me to withdraw from the race. He told me in his gentlest and softest tones that I had already made what I had entered the race for—reputation—and that I had better retire while my laurels were still green. Finally he told me in order to intimidate me, that if I ran on he would *disgrace* me, by beating me worse than he had ever beaten any one of his competitors. I made him no answer, for I wished him if he was sincere, to remain of the opinion expressed. But young as I was I saw through all his tender solicitude for my character. I knew he was *scared.* The idea of the bitter, implacable Andrew Johnson begging his competitor to withdraw to save him from disgrace!

The appointments for speaking were made by Mr. Johnson—

only fifteen in all—before I became a candidate. In four of the counties we spoke once only in each, and in two of them not at the county seat. He had been speaking all the summer. Therefore, excepting Sullivan, I had no chance to see, nor to be heard by, a large majority of the people. The canvass opened July 10th and closed August 4th.

At Jonesboro, two days before the election, we had a very hot time, the discussion being nearer personal than anywhere else. The discussions were always animated, spirited, and stirring. We had up to that time conducted the discussions on a decent, not to say a high, plane. There were no charges other than political made by either of us. I had no political record, and my private character could not be attacked. Mr. Johnson's private character was not bad at that time. If I had been disposed—and I was far from being so—to assail his character, I would have had little material for such course. So, while our discussions were always hot and exciting, they were never marred by vulgarity or personal abuse—not a word of it. At Jonesboro, besides holding up and exposing his record, I reminded the people of his speech in that town, in which he had denounced the venerable John Blair—revered both for his age and his virtues, and the distinguished position he had so long held, as a member of Congress—and the Jonesboro Democratic leaders, as mushroom aristocrats, and had almost defied them in his proud haughtiness. That speech was made when he expected Mr. Haynes to be his opponent. John Blair and his brothers, as well as Mr. Haynes, and a number of prominent Democrats, resided in Jonesboro, all of whom, or nearly all, were opposed to Mr. Johnson. For this he subjected them to the kind of discipline he was in the habit of using on the McClellans and Gammons in Sullivan County. This point—his denunciation of the "Jonesboro ring of aristocrats"—aroused all his fire, and being too independent to deny the charge and afraid to justify it he turned upon me with savage bitterness, for he now wanted the votes of the odious ring. While he did not assail me personally, he was bitter in manner. In hunting around for something to say, he turned to the Mexican War—which formed a topic of discussion every day, and which I denounced as both unjust and unconstitutional in its inception, yet was in favor of its vigorous prosecution—and twitted me for not being in the army fighting. I retorted by telling him, as he knew full well, that I had volunteered and raised a company, and that its organization had been delayed by the interference of his tools and underlings until the quota called for in the State—three regiments, I believe—had been made up, thirty thousand men having volunteered. I then ask him why he was not in the army; why he had not resigned his seat in Congress to raise a regiment and go to Mexico and fight in *his* war, as his fellow members of Congress, Baker and Bissell, two Whigs, from Illinois had done. I do not recollect whether or not I told him, but the thought was the most natural for the occasion, that the difference between $8 a day and $7 a month which he wished the poor soldier to get, may have influenced his conduct in keeping out of the war.

Altogether this discussion, from the beginning to its close, was red-hot—on the very border of the fighting line, and yet there was no personal abuse. Brownlow, in his paper of the following day, spoke of that discussion, as follows, it being his second notice of me, the first being only ten lines long, and not complimentary:

"Messrs. Johnson and Temple, the candidates for Congress, spoke here on yesterday at the court house for near five hours, the Whig candidate, Mr. Temple, leading off. The large court house room was full. Temple did lift the ticks off of Johnson at a rate that was really distressing. He showed up his votes in Congress—his opposition to Polk; and his hatred of the Jonesboro leaders. The Jonesboro leaders enjoyed the showing up. Johnson tried to laugh off the blows of Temple, but they got so hot toward the close that Andy got black in the face.

"We must say, in justice to Temple, that the Whigs were delighted, and had no idea of his ability on the stump till they heard him. No man had met Johnson in his district before, in our hearing, who has held him as uneasy as Temple did. And this we believe the Democracy are free to admit."

So bold and audacious had I been in my speech at Jonesboro, and so much harassed and exasperated was Mr. Johnson that he told a friend, and it was repeated to me, that if I acted toward him in the same way the next day, he would chastise me. Well, I had expected him to attempt that that day, but he did not. The next day we were to speak at Braylesville, near old Washington College, where I was graduated less than three years before. It was the day before the election. All college exercises were suspended, and the President—my warm friend—and students, all turned out to hear us. The crowd was large; my friends were in the majority and full of enthusiasm. I had the closing speech—an advantage I highly appreciated, especially at that place. I was in high spirits, while Mr. Johnson seemed depressed. In my speech, I kept my temper perfectly, and yet I was equally as aggressive and to some extent more offensive than on former occasions. To the extent of my ability, I did not spare Mr. Johnson. I was greeted with so many signs of appreciation that I was encouraged in my effort. My most worthy friend, Dr. W. M. Bovell, laughed immoderately, and shouted out: "Give it to him! Give it to him!"

Mr. Johnson was very fond of showing off his little learning and he always had some scraps of it, in history, or more frequently on mythology, which he repeated in solemn pomp, at the conclusion of his addresses. One of these was a beautiful and pathetic story, and a true one too, but not as he told it, in the life of the unfortunate Regulus, a Roman General who was captured in Carthage,—one of the noblest examples of stern Roman patriotism to be found in all history, entitling him to be ranked with the elder Brutus, or Cato,—which he told in his softest, most impressive manner. He had been repeating it for several days, but he had the story all wrong, and when told truly, it did not fit his point at all. I knew all the time he was telling it wrong, but I concluded to wait until we got to Washington College, in the presence of the professors and students, before exposing him. Sure enough, in his stately peroration, he told the Regulus story. In my reply, I corrected his history, and showed its total inapplicability to the point he was making, and then turning to him, and pointing my finger at him, I said in the most scornful manner: "Now, sir, go and *learn* history before you presume to *teach* it to an intelligent people." Mr. Johnson seemed to be stunned as if by a blow, but he could neither say nor do anything. And with this incident the canvass closed, so far as speaking was concerned. My friends all went away exulting and rejoicing.

I would not and could not be so presumptuous as to leave the impression on the mind of the reader that I was the equal of Mr. Johnson on the stump. How could I have been at the age of twenty-seven, with little experience in speaking, while he was known to be one of the ablest stump speakers in the State! It is true, I worried him, galled him, and excoriated him until he sometimes became desperate, and frequently had the advantage of him in popular estimation. But it must be kept in mind, in justice to him, that he was at that time weighted down by a great load—that fatal speech against Mr. Polk's administration—the specter of which would not "down," conjure it ever so sweetly. Day by day his inward spirit cried out:

"Avaunt! and quit my sight! Let the earth hide thee!"

And still, he had to listen to that speech, which was freezing up his very soul, and causing "his two eyes," like "stars," to "start from their spheres." He dared not deny it, he was too haughty to retract it, he was afraid to justify it; he could only plead ignorance,—that he was no grammarian! Oh! the height and depth of his humiliation!

It should be stated in explanation of that speech that at the time of its delivery, and at the time he was going over the district denouncing McClellan and the Blairs, he expected Landon C. Haynes to be his next competitor. The Whigs, after two unsuccessful efforts, had despaired of beating Mr. Johnson. The old, prominent Whig leaders were unwilling to run when defeat was certain. Mr. Haynes, after his brilliant word-painting canvass of 1844, as a Polk elector, had many friends who were pressing his claims, and he was himself anxious to run. Everybody expected him to do so. The Whig leaders of Hawkins County had promised Mr. Johnson, as it was afterward well understood and believed, that he should have no opposition in the Whig party in 1847; that is, no Whig competitor. This accounts in part for the fact that they turned a cold shoulder to me at Blountville and throughout the canvass. It was also reported and believed to be true, that in consideration of this support of Johnson, his friends were to permit a Whig to be elected from that county to the Legislature, and one was elected by a good majority, though a Democratic county, running ahead of Brown, the Whig candidate for Governor, and myself.

Mr. Johnson's calculations, when he had made that speech, under the supposition that Haynes was to be his competitor, were wisely made in view of the facts then existing. It was a bold bid for the Whig vote of that district, which he would have gotten as a general rule, as he got it in his race with Haynes four years afterward. While he would have gotten the Whig vote generally, he would also have received the solid Democratic vote of his own county, Greene, and a large majority of the party in Hawkins and Cocke, and a considerable vote in the other counties. These would have elected him easily. But Haynes declined, after vacillating a long time, probably having seen the game that was to be played by Johnson. My becoming a candidate disturbed all these plans and calculations and threw all into confusion. Johnson had a Whig to face, and the specter of his speech, prepared for a Democratic opponent, rose up every day to torment him, while the Whig votes he expected to secure by it came to me.

Now, a few words as to myself. I was unmerciful to Mr. Johnson because he assumed a haughty air of superiority toward me. His manner was stern and often discourteous. He never spoke a kind word to me nor did a gracious act. He invariably called me his "Juvenile Competitor," uttered with a sibilant sound. I determined to punish him and to the extent of my ability not to spare him. I knew how he had hacked and bullied old Matthew Stevenson and Brookins Campbell, two of the gentlest of men and as worthy as ever lived in the State, and my spirit arose against such treatment. From a long knowledge of Mr. Johnson I knew there was but one way to meet him—to fight him with his own weapons. I was the first person, and excepting Mr. Haynes, the only person, who ever fought him in this way.

When I became a candidate I had no fixed idea of being elected. I saw in the race, fun, excitement, training, reputation, at least notoriety, with hard knocks, bruises, and scars, with a faint chance of success. My young heart leaped at the prospect. While I was at Blountville, I became thoroughly convinced of my election, if I could overcome the universal opinion that there was no chance. To boast, as Johnson was doing, and to deny his claim made every day, that he was going to be elected by the largest majority of his life, would alarm the Democrats, for it must be kept in mind that they did not desire defeat, but his punishment by giving him only a bare majority. Not to boast, and not to deny the unfounded claim of Johnson, was leaving my friends without the stimulus of hope. Notwithstanding the difficulties of the non-alarm policy, I determined to adopt it. I had no one to consult in Blountville in whose judgment I had confidence. The old leaders were standing aloof from me. As it was, I worked privately as few men could have done to overcome the inertia of the Whigs, and to convince them that I could be elected. My labors were incessant night and day, but the time was too short and the incredulity of the Whigs too great for one man. I convinced very few. Perhaps I alone had full confidence. In one of the counties I spent half an hour with its Whig leader, my warm personal friend, in laying the facts before him, when he remarked: "Oliver, I should rejoice at your election as much as any man, but really I can see no chance." That man could have set, by a word, twenty leaders of influence, to riding over the country the next day, working for me. The result was that enough Whigs from that county stayed away from the polls to have elected me, or nearly so.

Johnson and I were the only two men in the district who fully understood the condition of things—both of us knew that I would be elected, if there was a full Whig vote. When he was boasting every day that he would disgrace me by an overwhelming majority, he knew as well as I did that he was politically prevaricating. I think I may say with truthfulness that I was the only person in the district, except Snapp, Rutledge, and Millard, and one or two other young men in Sullivan County, who worked in the earnest confidence of my election.

Well, Johnson was elected by 314 votes, his usual majority being reduced from ten to twelve hundred. Although he had won the race, the result was everywhere regarded as *my triumph*. He was mortified, chagrined, and overwhelmed with shame. On Friday afternoon, the day after the election, the returns from the eastern counties having been received in Greeneville, it was believed that I was elected. The people insisted on our making our acknowledgments to our friends in little speeches. When it came to Mr. Johnson's turn, he shed tears, and almost broke down with emotion. The next day the returns came in from Hawkins and Coke Counties, which gave the election to Johnson. Hawkins was the county where the Whig leaders, for purposes of their own, had promised or made a compact with Mr. Johnson that he should have no Whig opposition. In each of these counties the expected Whig majority fell short. In Sullivan, the only county I canvassed thoroughly, even in parts of it, where I spent more than a week, and made five speeches, I received the largest vote ever given to a Whig, larger than General Harrison's, or Jones', or Clay's.

After the election, the Whigs from nearly every county, commenced sending word that if they had dreamed that there was "any chance" they could have brought to the polls, of the stay-at-home voters, nearly men enough in every county to have changed the result. "Too late." They also insisted that I should repeat the race two years hence, and that they would elect me. Too late. The bird had flown. They had lost their only chance. Johnson had learned a lesson, and my common sense told me that he would never repeat his error of 1847, and he never did. He was as docile and as tractable in the next Congress under party leadership as he had formerly been recalcitrant. The result was, he was re-elected, in 1849, over the eloquent and accomplished Nathaniel G. Taylor, not by 314 majority, but by the usual Democratic majority.

I need not attempt to disguise the fact that this race gave me considerable reputation throughout the State— a reputation entirely disproportioned to any ability or merit of my own. My daring arraignment of Mr. Johnson, his vulnerable record, the unexpected closeness of the election, together with my youthfulness, gave an unwonted *éclat* to the result. At no other time in his life could Mr. Johnson have been attacked so mercilessly and yet so successfully as then.

As for myself, not long after this, being offered a favorable partnership by the generous William H. Sneed, of Knoxville— due no doubt to my late race—I left the first district, where I was born, reared, and educated, and where I had many dear friends, and removed to Knoxville, largely, I confess, to get out of politics and to avoid another race, which I plainly saw would result in defeat. The only chance to defeat Mr. Johnson had been thrown away, not by reason of any objection to me, but by the inertia of the Whigs. In that race I might easily have been elected by from five hundred to one thousand majority. But I can declare truthfully that I never seriously regretted my defeat. Even then I feared that an election would prove an injury to me. Since then I have never been tempted to seek Congressional honors, although many opportunities have occurred for obtaining them. I never regretted my race, as I can trace to it, directly or indirectly, the source of the most important honors and successes, however inconsiderable, I have attained in life.

MEREDITH POINDEXTER GENTRY.

Born in North Carolina in 1809—Removes to Tennessee in 1813—Early Education—Extensive Reader—Studied Law—Elected to Legislature, 1835—In Congress, 1839—Powerful Debater—Opinions as to His Ability as an Orator—Runs Against Johnson for Governorship in 1855—Contrast of Their Characters—Defeated by Johnson—In Retirement on His Farm—A Union Man Until Sumter—Then a Secessionist—Elected to Confederate Congress—Loses All His Property Through Failure of Confederacy—Died in 1866.

THE period from 1833 to 1860 was the high noon of greatness in Tennessee. There was during that time a perfect constellation of glittering stars to be seen in the heavens. At the first-named date, Andrew Jackson, that splendid luminary, although fast passing from his zenith to his nadir, still held on his brilliant course. The venerable Hugh Lawson White, although "hastening to his setting," still stood high in the heavens. The eloquent Felix Grundy gave no signs of diminished brightness. But while these older men still lingered and held the public eye, there appeared above the horizon a younger set of men, little less great than those just named, who were destined to shed their brilliance upon the State and the nation. Among these I mention James K. Polk, John Bell, Ephraim H. Foster, Bailie Peyton, Spencer Jarnagin, Cave Johnson, Aaron V. Brown, James C. Jones, Gustavus A. Henry, A. O. P. Nicholson, Meredith P. Gentry, Emerson Etheridge, William T. Haskell, Andrew Johnson, Isham G. Harris, Thomas A. R. Nelson, William T. Senter, John Netherland, Landon C. Haynes, and Horace Maynard.

Of these distinguished men Meredith P. Gentry was one of the greatest and perhaps the most striking. He was born in 1809, in North Carolina, and was therefore one year younger than Andrew Johnson. In 1813 his father, who was a wealthy planter, moved to Tennessee, and settled in Williamson County, his son being then four years of age. Young Gentry completed his academic education at the age of fourteen, never having had the advantage of a college course. After that time, until he was twenty, he improved his mind while working on his father's farm by an extensive reading of history, poetry, and general literature. His memory was retentive, and it never lost what it had acquired.

Shortly after he came to the years of manhood, he delivered a fourth of July address, which was greatly admired and gave promise of his future renown. He studied law, I believe, but it seems he gave it up. From 1835 to 1839, he was a prominent member of the Legislature. A committee composed of Mr. Gentry, Mr. Grundy, and Mr. Topp submitted to the Legislature in 1835 an exhaustive report in favor of the State's lending its aid, by the issuance of bonds, to a system of macadam roads. Under an act passed in conformity with that report, Middle Tennessee became dotted over with macadamized roads, and several millions of bonds were issued for that purpose, which now constitute, directly or indirectly, a part of the public debt of the State. East Tennessee never availed itself of the liberal terms of that act, not a single mile of road having been built under it.

In 1839 Mr. Gentry was elected a member of Congress, and with the exception of one term, when he declined being a candidate, he remained in Congress until 1853—twelve years. He soon made his début in Congress. His first speech was in favor of receiving—not granting—the prayer of petitions from the North for the abolishment of slavery in the District of Columbia. This speech attracted universal attention. He was no abolitionist, being a large slave holder himself, but he insisted that to petition Congress was a constitutional right on the part of the citizen, which could not be denied. His second speech was on the subject of securing the freedom of elections, and the restriction of executive patronage. This was one of the ablest speeches of that Congress, and was widely read and distributed. At this time he was only thirty years of age.

During his subsequent terms Mr. Gentry became one of the most powerful debaters and distinguished orators in the lower house of congress. Mr. Alexander H. Stephens said of him that very few members "possessed so much political knowledge, or were so ready in debate." He further said that his eulogy on Mr. Clay, though impromptu, was "apt, powerful, and pathetic." In his diary, John Quincy Adams, a member of the House several years with Mr. Gentry, pronounced him the finest orator of that body. A distinguished member of Congress from Pennsylvania, who served with him, and who often heard Mr. Clay, said that he (Mr. Gentry) was the only man he had ever heard who had a better voice for speaking than Mr. Clay. Having heard both Mr. Clay and Mr. Gentry, the latter several times, I cannot concur fully in this opinion. So far as I am aware, the opinion for seventy-five years has been well nigh universal that no man's voice in this country was so musical, so fascinating, so magnificent as Mr. Clay's.

Mr. Gentry unquestionably had a very grand and a very extraordinary voice. It was clear, ringing, and far-sounding, like the bugle's thrilling notes, and at the same time it was deep, musical, and powerful. In his ordinary mood, it could be heard distinctly at a great distance. He spoke with the same ease both to himself and his hearers that characterized Mr. Clay, and in both speakers in the "very torrent, tempest, and whirlwind of their passions," as Hamlet advised his players, they manifested a "temperance that gave it smoothness." But to my ear, the indefinable, the bewitching, the flute-like music of Mr. Clay's voice surpassed that of Mr. Gentry's.

Mr. Gentry was a phenomenal man nearly every way. His person was majestic, though not over 5 feet and 11 inches high. It was robust, manly, dignified, and highly impressive. Anyone beholding him would have been struck with his proud, kingly bearing. He had a grand, stately stride, as if above fear, and conscious of his own dignity and worth. His face, to my mind, was handsome and attractive, having a most benignant expression, and being suffused with the ruddy glow of good health and high living. Mr. A. S. Colyer, in an article a short time ago, said of him that he always regarded him as the most accomplished orator in Tennessee. "He was the most comely man I have ever seen on the platform. * * * His voice was music * * * His head was intellectual and his features regular and nicely chiseled into classical forms. In quickness of apprehension, and in the power of generalization, his mind was nearly of the first order. He needed not to study a difficult subject. His intellect mastered and illumined it at first sight. In the expression of his ideas, he was wonderfully lucid, forcible, and striking. They were sharp cut, incisive, glittering; they were direct, pointed, and unambiguous, and came from his mind with the force of a ball projected by some powerful agency. He wore his opinions and his principles as he wore his face—uncovered. In the avowal of his opinion he was frank and candid, and open as the day. He would have scorned as cowardly and dishonorable any concealment or any equivocation. No public man of his time was so bold and independent. He cared infinitely more for his honor and his self-respect than for promotion, or place, or popular applause. Withal, there was an honesty, a heartiness, a whole-soulness, a don't-care independence in his speaking that won all hearts. As we shall see presently, when he proudly said in his last speech in Congress, "I defy you all," he only provoked sympathetic laughter. He was so honest and good-natured that the most daring expressions gave no offense.

As an illustration. In 1849-50, W. G. Brownlow was pressing the claims of two or three friends on the new administration, for appointment to offices, through Senator Bell. Mr. Bell was not succeeding as well as Mr. Brownlow wished. The latter became a little impatient at the apparent indifference or slowness of his old friend, and wrote him a sharp letter on the subject, and probably wrote an editorial in his paper complaining of his conduct. Mr. Bell showed this letter to Mr. Gentry, who knew of the efforts he was making, and the difficulty in the way of procuring the offices for the friends of Mr. Brownlow. Thereupon he sat down and wrote Mr. Brownlow explaining these difficulties, and averring that Mr. Bell was doing all that any human being could do, and wound up by saying: "Now if I were in Mr. Bell's place, I would write to you and tell you to go to h—l." Mr. Brownlow showed the letter to friends and only laughed heartily at it.

As above intimated, Mr. Gentry's power of generalization showed his masterly intellect. He could annihilate a labored piece of casuistry by a single sentence, or blast an argument by a sarcasm, or a witticism. Thus Mr. Johnson once arraigned him for voting while in Congress, to pay the hotel bill of the celebrated Louis Kossuth, the great Hungarian exile, while in Washington as the invited guest of the nation, although he himself had voted with Gentry in inviting him there. In reply Mr. Gentry indignantly turned upon Mr. Johnson, and with contemptuous scorn, explained: "Is this Tennessee hospitality to invite a man to your house to stay a few days, and then tell him when he is leaving, 'Sir, I want you to foot your bill; you must pay for the liquor you have been drinking'?"

He could gather up and throw into the form of an aphorism a whole argument in a case, embodying its very essence and spirit. This was well-nigh genius. Mr. Calhoun possessed this faculty in a high degree. But Mr. Calhoun was a scholar and a student all his life; Mr. Gentry was never a student, nor had he high scholarship.

Mr. Gentry was generally considered an eloquent man. In the sense in which Haskell, Henry, Haynes, N. G. Taylor, and many other Tennessee orators were considered eloquent, Mr. Gentry had no high claim to such a distinction. He was not florid, much less turgid in speech; he used but few flowers of rhetoric; he did not turn his imagination loose to roam at will through the pleasant fields of fiction. There were no brilliant coruscations of fancy; there were, however, of thought and genius—dazzling and startling by their boldness. But in the sense in which Webster and Clay were eloquent, and Mr. Calhoun sometimes so (as Mr. Benton says), Mr. Gentry deserves to be ranked very high as a great orator. In the same category may be ranked the illustrious Chief Justice Marshall, who was said by one of his contemporaries, I believe Mr. Madison, to have been the most eloquent man in his speeches he had ever heard. Of the three great men—Webster, Clay, and Calhoun—contrary to what is the popular opinion, especially of Mr. Clay, Mr. Webster was by far the most ornate, and often indeed florid, in his style and diction. Many of his speeches, or parts of them, were highly embellished with beautiful pearls of rhetoric, and all of them were more or less so. Some of them were gorgeous with beautiful imagery. He clothed his magnificent thoughts in the rich drapery of elegant classical learning. But these were but the accessories, used in the embellishment of the great thoughts he uttered. Mr. Calhoun's speeches were never adorned in this way. They were expressed in a simple, terse, compact, crystallized form, always in aid of and in subordination to the most rigid reasoning. Mr. Clay was always ardent, fervid, glowing and impassioned and eloquent in manner, but he seldom ventured in his senatorial speeches into the higher regions of imaginative oratory, so common with Mr. Webster. And from the fragments of the speeches of Alexander Hamilton which remain—the greatest genius of the Revolutionary epoch, and perhaps of any epoch in our history, and indeed, in the opinion of the celebrated

Talleyrand, the greatest of the age in which he lived—we may class him as an orator in this respect more after the style of Mr. Calhoun than that of Mr. Webster.

The eloquence of all these great men consisted in the happy and vivid illumination of questions of government by the light shed upon them by their great intellects, expressed in the clearest, and choicest words, and in the most earnest, natural and fascinating manner. It was as the light of the X-ray poured upon these questions. In this sense Mr. Gentry was an eloquent man. He was gifted with the power of striking thought, vigorous expression, felicity of language, earnestness of manner and conviction, and with a voice and manner in the highest degree attractive and dramatic. Running through it all, there was the evidence of high and noble purpose. When seen in one of his highest efforts the minds of men would involuntarily say, "Behold, what a man!" His speech flowed in a deep, rapid, unceasing silvery current. He was always grand in manner and sometimes when strong emotions stirred him, he was as an irresistible tempest.

If the forcible presentation of great ideas in vigorous and lucid terms; in a manner earnest, fervid, and flowing; with a voice of surpassing beauty; and with a mind all on fire with his subject,—if these constituted eloquence, Mr. Gentry was certainly an eloquent man.

But after all, it was not his gifts intellectually and physically, nor his graces of speech, nor his grand manner, but the great soul of honor within him that marked the difference between him and most other men, and made him what he was—an ideal. No earthly consideration—not even to obtain the presidency—would or could have induced him to do a little, a mean, or a dishonorable act. Thus, in his canvass for Governor with Andrew Johnson, in 1855, he suffered his competitor to go all over the State "nagging" him with low innuendoes, without taking any notice of them, except contemptuous silence. When urged to retaliate, he said with lofty pride: "I know the rules of honorable debate among gentlemen, and my sense of self-respect forbids me to violate them, even if my competitor does do so. I cannot have a wrangle every day on the stump with my competitor, if the result is the loss of my election." And he adhered to that high ideal to the close of the canvass, never doing or saying anything that would not pass current in the highest court of chivalry.

Indeed Mr. Gentry dwelt in the pure atmosphere of honor and truth and noble purpose—on the very mountain tops, where the murky and miasmatic vapors of envy, slander, falsehood, and littleness never ascended, and where the vision swept the whole boundless horizon.

In 1852 Mr. Gentry arose in his seat in Congress and delivered one of his characteristically bold speeches, in which he announced his purpose of not supporting General Scott for the presidency in the event of his nomination by the approaching Whig national convention. He was an ardent old-line Whig, a follower of Mr. Clay, and a friend of John Bell. He had followed the leadership of Mr. Clay in 1850 in support of his compromise measures, and was a devoted friend of the Union. He feared that General Scott was not in good faith a friend of those measures, and charged that he was under the influence of Mr. Seward, and that if nominated he would owe his nomination to him. He charged that General Scott had permitted "Mr. Seward to seize him and wield him as a warrior wields his battle-ax, to cleave down into the dust Fillmore and Webster, and all the patriots of the North who sustained him."

Mr. Gentry went on to say:

"Any gentleman who dreams that any Southern State will cast its vote for General Scott in the next presidential election, dreams, in my opinion, a dream that will never be realized.

"I suppose for this I am to be a proscribed character, an excommunicated Whig. Well, gentlemen, I defy you all. [Laughter.] I only insist that no man shall denounce me until he can show a better Whig character in the past than I can. Observe this condition and I am willing for you to say what you please. I acknowledge to a proper extent allegiance to the party. But I owe a higher allegiance to my country than any party can impose. I should consider myself a traitor, recreant to all the interests of those who honored me with their confidence in sending me here, if I would for a moment cooperate in producing such a result as I have described. What shall I do? Why, I am very much troubled about it. It is a painful idea to contemplate. It is exceedingly painful for a man to stand as I stand, and who has stood as I have stood, to be separated from his party, and to be brought in antagonism with those with whom he has associated; and therefore I have been recurring to my early reading of poetry to find some consolation, and I have determined to adopt the advice Cato gave to his son:

> "'My son, thou oft hast seen
> Thy sire engaged in a corrupted State
> Wrestling with vice and faction; now thou seest me
> Spent, overpowered, despairing of success;
> Let me advise thee to retreat betimes
> To thy paternal seat, the Sabine field,
> Where the great Censor toiled with his own hands,
> And all our frugal ancestors were blest
> In humble virtues and a rural life.
> There live retired and pray for the peace of Rome;
> Content thyself to be obscurely good.
> When vice prevails, and impious men bear away,
> The post of honor is the private station.'

"I will go home. [Laughter.] In a sequestered valley in the State of Tennessee, there is a smiling farm, with bubbling fountains, covered with rich pasturage and fat flocks, and all that is needful for the occupation and enjoyment of a man of uncorrupted tastes. I will go there and pray for 'Rome.'"

The country was startled at this speech. The Whigs were confounded. His own friends in Tennessee, who loved him with warmest devotion, were overwhelmed with mingled sorrow and surprise. However, unlike some other prominent Tennessee Whigs, Mr. Gentry neither supported Pierce, nor took any active part in opposition to General Scott. He quietly cast his vote for Mr. Webster. Like the great Achilles, he now retired to his tent to brood over his imaginary wrongs, while the Trojans and the offended gods, as the great poet tells us, slaughtered the Greeks. Thus for two years this brilliant man remained in self-appointed retirement, on his magnificent bluegrass farm in Tennessee. But in 1855, when there was a demand for the greatest leader in the Whig party, in response to an almost universal call, he came forth from his retreat, and once more became the idolized leader of it. He was nominated for Governor of the State by the Whigs, now calling themselves the American, but popularly called the Know-Nothing party. Andrew Johnson, then Governor, was the Democratic candidate. The contest was exceedingly bitter on the part of Mr. Johnson, as well as on the part of the people; it was indeed malignant and furious; but Mr. Gentry in the presence of this raging sea of wild and angry passion, everywhere in his speeches preserved a dignified self-respect and a grand equipoise in bearing. Neither by words nor acts did he do anything that he could not have answered for before the august tribunal of history. His speeches were masterpieces of argument and dignified eloquence, occasionally enlivened by humor and the most refined but withering sarcasm.

Of his power, the following illustration may be given:

Mr. Johnson on one occasion, and possibly on more than one, twitted him with having ceased "praying for Rome," and having left his retirement on his "Sabine farm," and come forth in search of office. Mr. Gentry showed in reply that Mr. Johnson had been a candidate for office many more times than he; that so anxious had he (Johnson) been to be a candidate, that two years before, he had cheated Andrew Ewing, who was the choice of the party, out of the nomination for Governor and had forced himself on his party. And as for himself he had not announced himself a candidate until it became manifest, by public meetings and the press, that a majority of the people desired it. He told the following anecdote illustrative of the reason why he was not then on his farm praying for the good of his country: A fearful drought once afflicted Spain. For a whole summer the earth was parched up with the heat without one drop of rain; the streams dried up, the cattle were dying, and many of the people also were perishing. Then a body of Catholics, headed by a devout priest, traveled over the country praying for rain. One day they came to a field particularly needing rain. The priest looked at it a moment, and then raised his hands and closed his eyes, but said nothing. Opening his eyes he again carefully surveyed the field and again closed them and raised his hands, but said nothing. For the third time he carefully surveyed the field and then said: "Brethren, praying will do no good for soil so cursed and blighted as this has been. This field must have *Manure*."

Mr. Gentry with wonderful humor, said: "Tennessee does not need prayers. There is a curse resting on the State which has marred its fair face, and parched and dried up its prosperity. I have come forth from my retirement and my prayers to help remove this curse. This curse is Andrew Johnson." As Mr. Gentry made the application, my informant, who was present, and a distinguished Johnson Democrat, says it was the most powerfully dramatic piece of oratory, as well as the most withering he had ever heard from the lips of a man.

Mr. Johnson was elected and Mr. Gentry defeated. In another place, I have described this canvass, and discussed Mr. Gentry and Mr. Johnson in full, and cannot therefore go into these matters now.

After the defeat of Mr. Gentry in 1855, he retired to his farm, where he lived a quiet life until 1861, though still comparatively young. He loved his ease. If not an indolent man, he was certainly far from being a pushing, ambitious one. He had none of the restless ambition which characterized Mr. Johnson. If he had been inspired with the latter's vaulting love of power, and endowed with temperate and industrious habits, his fame would have filled and echoed throughout the land. But he was unfortunately addicted to the excessive use of liquor—a habit so often the companion of genius. In my time I have seen the lives of the four most brilliant and gifted men in the State marred, and their brightness obscured, and that of at least three of them blasted by this fatal habit; and two of them cut off in the full meridian of their glory as if by an untimely "killing" frost. But notwithstanding the habits of Mr. Gentry, men loved him with something akin to idolatry. He was so grand, so noble, so magnanimous in bearing, so true and generous in action, so bright and genial in his life, so pure and transparent in purpose and lofty in aim, and so dazzling in speech and conversation that men could not but love

"Where every god did seem to set his seal
To give the world assurance of a man."

When the Civil War came on, Mr. Gentry, in common with Mr. Bell, and the old Whig leaders of the State, was a Union man. He left his retirement and made a few speeches, two or three perhaps, in favor of the Union, and in opposition to the Harris movement. But when Fort Sumter was fired on, contrary to all reason, like Mr. Bell and other Middle Tennessee leaders, he plunged into the raging current of secession and drifted off into the sea of blood. Afterward Mr. Gentry became a candidate for the Confederate Congress, was elected, and served as a member for one term. He made but one speech in Congress, and that was in opposition to enforcing the conscript law in East Tennessee. On account of ill health he broke down before finishing it. He urged that men who were in favor of the cause would volunteer, that those whose hearts were not in it would not fight. He recalled how Tennessee had earned the title of the "Volunteer State," by the conduct of her sons ever since the days of the Revolution, and that they needed no conscription to make them do their duty if their hearts were in the cause. This, his only speech, as one of his colleagues said, showed that he was the great orator of the Confederate Congress.

From the testimony of his intimate friends who are yet alive, and who knew his thoughts and feelings perfectly, it can be safely affirmed that the heart of Mr. Gentry was never on the side of secession. His judgment, too, condemned it as an act of supreme folly. When it first started, he warned his neighbors that it would be disastrous to the South, and could in no conceivable manner benefit anybody. After the war he said to an old and ardent admirer: "I sympathize with my neighbors and kindred who were in the Confederate army; I always deplored secession. I knew it was no remedy for any real or imaginary grievance. I always felt that secession would result in evil, and only evil, to the South. The war ended as I anticipated it would from the beginning, but after I espoused the cause, I did all I could for it. * * * I sympathized with my neighbors and kindred who were in the Confederate army." These words reveal the cause of the strength of secession. Sympathy with friends and kindred became the bond that united the South. Tens of thousands of men who had no heart for secession, did have a heart for their neighbors and kindred. This almost universal fellowship and sympathy drew men together in behalf of a cause which one-half of them disapproved. "One touch of nature makes the whole world kin."

Who shall condemn the feeling, so commendable, and, under the circumstances, so sublime?

The celebrated Henry Watterson in February, 1894, delivered a lecture in Washington to an immense crowd. Among other things he said that the brutalities which he had seen when a child inflicted on Southern plantations upon the negroes, had given him a horror of slavery, and that he loved the Union and was opposed to secession. He said in substance: "You will naturally ask why I joined the rebellion, which was started to perpetuate slavery. I can only reply in the words of Meredith

P. Gentry, of Tennessee, who was long a member of Congress from that State, and the greatest orator of his generation in Congress. After Gentry had served in the Confederate Congress, General Rousseau, of the Union army, while his troops occupied the county in which Gentry resided, dined with him one day. Gentry said he had always loved the Union, never believed that a State had a right to secede, never believed that secession would be otherwise than ruinous to the South, never believed that it could be a remedy for any evil, either real or imaginary, but, said Gentry, 'a d—d old worm-eaten, rickety, stern-wheel boat, Secession, came along, and, contrary to my feelings and warnings, my friends, neighbors, and kinsmen, all rushed pell-mell aboard. I looked around, and saw myself alone on the bank of the stream, and they were pulling in the gang plank. I shouted to the captain: "Hold on! Hold on! I'll get aboard too, and we'll all go to hell together."''"

On one occasion a crowd of original secessionists surrounded Mr. Gentry, and asked him if the States could not peaceably secede. He replied with that lofty eloquence and power of condensation so peculiar to him: "Peaceable secession! My God, gentlemen! Do you think this Union can be peaceably dissolved? No rivers of blood will flow, but seas incarnadine will mark and eternize the mighty conflict." This awful prophecy was uttered before a gun had been fired.

Mr. Gentry was not a party leader. Perhaps he did not wish to be. Certainly his honesty, his independence, his habits and thoughts did not qualify him for leadership. Besides, he was too indolent, he loved his ease and his pleasures too much for such a position.

During the war, in a moment of folly, he sold his fine farm, in which he had only a life estate, and received in payment Confederate notes and bonds. When the Confederacy went to pieces, both he and his children were left impoverished. He was afterward advised by his old friend Dr. John W. Richardson, the father of James D. Richardson, the present distinguished Member of Congress from Gentry's old district, that, as the consideration given for the land was Confederate money, and his children were minors, he could recover it back, under the recent decisions of the courts of the State. Gentry proudly straightened himself up and said: "I staked my fortune on the losing card, and we will starve before we will plead the baby act, or take advantage of a technicality in law." He lived only a short time after this, dying in 1866. But he still lives in the hearts of his countless friends, Union men and secessionists alike.

Mr. Gentry was one of the few Southern men who was not pardoned by President Johnson, and who would not ask for a pardon. This did not arise from any hatred of the Government, for he never hated it, but his proud spirit would not stoop to ask for any favor at the hands of a man for whom he had so much contempt as he had for Andrew Johnson. As one of his admirers stated it, "Gentry would have been crucified rather than ask a pardon of Andrew Johnson."

Perhaps in one or two grand qualities, other men in the State equaled, possibly in some excelled Mr. Gentry; Foster, Peyton, and Nelson were his equals in courage; Henry his peer or above him in elegant accomplishment; Haskell his superior in brilliant rhetoric; and Bell and Jarnagin in logical analysis and far-seeing statesmanship. But in Gentry there was a combination of grand qualities, with no great defects, seldom united in one man, and certainly not in any of these distinguished men. All in all, he was the grandest and the noblest, and by nature one of the greatest, if not the very greatest, excepting Andrew Jackson, of Tennessee's distinguished men. The greatest Roman said, "I am always Caesar." So, too, he was always the same proud, generous, magnanimous Gentry.

THE RACES OF JONES AND POLK IN 1841 AND 1843.

Jones' Limited Education—In Legislature, 1839—Nominated for Governor by Whigs in 1841 at Age of Thirty-two—His Personality—His Opponent, Polk, Highly Educated and an Experienced Politician—Polk Not a Great Orator—Jones Not a Buffoon—His Debates with Polk—Polk's Personality—Polk's Secret Trip to East Tennessee—Discovered by Jones—Jones' Stinging Reproaches—Jones' Election—Jones in United States Senate, 1851—Votes to Repeal Missouri Compromise—Becomes a Democrat—Polk's Nomination for Presidency—A Strict Party Man—His Election.

THIS sketch was written in response to a letter from a friend which contained the following paragraph:

"I hope you will now tell us all you can about Governor James C. Jones. He is one character in Tennessee politics I can't understand. * * * How was it possible, having little education and no experience as a public speaker, for him to meet and cope with such a man as Polk, whose knowledge of public affairs must have been up to that of Jim Blaine in his day."

Now, here is a question that has long puzzled the politicians of Tennessee, and one as to which perhaps no large number of them would give the same answer. The impression seems to be gaining ground at this day, among the younger generation of men, that Jones' triumph over Polk was owing to what may be summed up in one word—his buffoonery. There are other equally objectionable qualities attributed to him, but this term will probably convey the general idea. With all deference I cannot concur in this opinion.

I heard Polk speak once or twice in 1839; I heard both Polk and Jones speak three or four times in their joint discussions in 1841 and 1843; and I heard Jones several times afterward. I therefore became tolerably familiar with their style of speaking.

First, briefly, as to the history, appearance and characteristics of Jones. He was just thirty-two years of age in 1841, when he was first put forward as a candidate for Governor. He was a farmer, with limited education, never having been to college a day, so far as I know. In 1839 he was a member of the Legislature of Tennessee. His first speech that attracted attention was made in Nashville in 1840, at a meeting ratifying the nomination of Harrison for the presidency. In the succeeding canvass he was one of the electors on the Harrison ticket. And in 1841 he was nominated for Governor by the Whig party, as the competitor of James K. Polk, the most adroit and successful stump speaker, as Mr. Phelan says, in the southwest.

Mr. Jones was 6 feet 2 inches high and weighed 125 pounds. He was not, as supposed by some, a "gangling, gawky," loose-jointed man, swaying like a reed in the wind. On the contrary, he was straight, round and erect in body, and elastic in movement. "He walked with a precise, military step," says one who has described him. In a word he had the physical form for the grandest and most effective oratory, such as was possessed by Mr. Clay, Mr. Calhoun, and in the most marvelous degree by Tennessee's greatest orator, that prodigy of genius and brilliancy, William T. Haskell. Jones' complexion was swarthy, which gave him a peculiar and decidedly distinguished look. He was dignified in bearing, and always dressed like a gentleman. In conversation he was sociable and genial. But his voice was his organ of consummate power. It was deep, solemn, melodious, flexible and of the widest compass, not musical like Mr. Clay's, not of the clarion ring of Gentry's, not like the shrill piercing notes of Haskell, but always charming, delightful, high sounding, and even flowing. But before I heard Mr. Jones, or knew much about him, knowing the power of Mr. Polk, I was uneasy about the result of a joint discussion between them, but the moment I heard his solemn and impressive voice in his opening remarks, in tender allusion to the death of one of his children, I was reassured and all fear of the result was forever gone.

Let the reader bear in mind that I am not now considering Jones as a statesman, but as a popular stump speaker, and with reference to his races with Polk. And let it be kept in mind also who and what his competitor was. Mr. Polk was a graduate with the highest honors of Chapel Hill; he had been in Congress fourteen years, and twice Speaker of the House, as well as Governor of the State for two years. Everywhere his high ability was acknowledged. In Tennessee he stood in the same class with Grundy, White and Bell. Being a diligent student, his information on all political topics was very great. As a debater and stump speaker he was considered, after his memorable canvass of 1839, the foremost man in Tennessee. He had wit and humor, the power of mimicry and ridicule, and the art of telling anecdotes all at his command, as well as the most effective oratory. With these he had cunning, subtlety, ingenuity, and sophistry, which could make "the worse appear the better reason." He had defeated Governor Newton Cannon in 1839 for Governor by three thousand majority, thus revolutionizing the State. In his canvass with Cannon he ridiculed his competitor until even the latter's enemies felt sorry for him. He told anecdotes, laughed at him, mimicked his manner of speaking, perverted the facts and finally drove him from the stump.

I do not say that Polk was a great orator. In the highest sense he was not. He had no imagination, without which to some extent the highest results of oratory cannot be achieved. But I do say he was a consummate debater, pleasing and entertaining in a marked degree, and capable of holding an audience spell-bound for three or four hours at a time, as he did in 1839. He discussed questions with the mental grasp of a statesman, and with a manner that commanded and held the attention, not infrequently, however, with unfairness and always with the bitterness of a partisan. He repeated all the filthy and false charges then so common against the Whig party. He dwelt upon the slanderous charge against Mr. Clay, of "bargain, intrigue, and corruption," in the presidential election of 1824.

Jones in his speeches not only bore himself with a confident, masterly air, but he filled his followers with the same feeling. They were happy, buoyant, enthusiastic. While the speaking was going on they laughed and shouted and then went away full of joy and exultation. Mr. Polk had made such splendid speeches in his brilliant canvass in 1839, so masterful and overwhelming were they, so grandly and triumphantly had he swept over the State, that he confounded the Whigs, and carried dismay into their minds. So confident and supreme had he been in manner when he swooped down on his enemies, that they dreaded him, and fled from him as the birds flee when the falcon is abroad. It was therefore with a feeling of timidity and defeat, already in their hearts, that they ventured out at first to the discussions between the all-conquering Polk and the unknown Jones. They expected him to win victories again, as he had always done over every opposer.

Now, I do not wish to be understood as saying that Mr. Polk did not in the canvass of 1841-43 make able, yes, surpassingly able speeches. Nor do I mean to say that Mr. Jones' speeches were equal to his in breadth and depth and statesmanship, nor that Jones always gained what may be termed overwhelming victories. These battles between them were always desperately fought, with enough ability, ingenuity, and effective oratory to give each side in the early canvass reason for claiming the victory. But very soon the impression produced on men's minds was that Jones had the advantage of Polk, and this impression grew until finally it became general. The discomfiture of Polk at last was evident in the countenance of his warmest friends. They did not boast as of old, they were not filled with boundless enthusiasm as they once were, they did not burst the very heavens with shouts and yells, as they did in 1839, when Polk was warming them up by portraying the Whigs in his most lively colors, nor did they go almost into convulsions of laughter, with tears streaming down their cheeks, as they did when Polk mimicked good old Newton Cannon and Bailie Peyton two years before.

The fact that Jones was daily gaining the advantage in popular estimation was manifest, by the additional fact that Mr. Polk was becoming irritable, that he was always complaining, that he was mad indeed. His doleful complaints, with the absence of the exuberant flow of spirits seen in 1839, told as plainly as an outburst of wailing could have done the bitter anguish he felt at his daily defeats. His party also were greatly depressed throughout the State. After the debates were over, his friends wore long, solemn faces, as though they had just returned from the funeral of a dear friend. They were peevish and out of humor. An incident is related by Phelan, the historian,—no friend of Jones,—of a man from Sommerville who was naturally good-tempered, and who on returning from one of these discussions, was asked what Polk had said. He answered fiercely, "Polk made an ass of himself, talking sense to a lot of d—d fools!" "And Jones?" "Jones—Jones! I don't know what Jones said! No more does anybody else. I know this much. If I were Mr. Polk I would not allow anyone to make a laughing stock of me." In addition to the sneers of his political enemies, the Democratic newspapers through the State were filled—were boiling over—with articles abusive of, and most derogatory to, the talents and conduct of Jones.

In the meantime, with the most placid temper and equanimity, Jones went on in his triumphant career, daily gaining victories before vast assemblies, such as had never been seen in the State, except during the ever memorable canvass of Ephraim H. Foster in 1840. The truth is, his speaking career was marvelous. He kindled in his followers a boundless enthusiasm, stirring the very depths of their souls with a sublime confidence, courage, hope. He at all times seemed in air and bearing an invincible conqueror. He laughed at the piteous complainings of Mr. Polk, and aggravated him to still greater display of irritability and peevishness.

This was the man that Jones, the farmer, the unknown, the comparatively inexperienced, was to meet in debate and overcome, or be himself destroyed. And when I say that in two of the most memorable and protracted canvasses ever conducted in the United States Jones did most signally overcome and triumph over his redoubtable opponent, I but reaffirm what was then the opinion of a majority of the people of the State and now of all.

Jones had great humor, great power of ridicule, great facility in turning a point against an adversary, imperturbable good temper, strong confidence in himself, a graveyard solemnity of voice and face, and apparent consciousness of mastery in his air and manner that helped to bring him victory. He was not a statesman in knowledge nor intellect. Yet, on the contrary, he was not a mere political puppet, a clown nor a mountebank, amusing his audience with tricks and grimaces. He had respectable ability and in a certain sense very superior ability, and could discuss, and did discuss, the questions of the day with clearness and force. His presentation of them was in the most plain, plausible, and fascinating manner. As before stated, but few public speakers I have heard had such an impressive, delightful voice, and none a better one, except Mr. Clay and possibly Mr. Gentry. He spoke with ardor, enthusiasm, and with immense earnestness. He fired his words with great rapidity and precision, and with a distinct enunciation. As they flowed from his lips there was no hesitation, no halting, the words and sentences following each other without a break or a pause in their rapid current. His voice, at all times clear and distinct, swelled, with grandeur when the dignity of the subject demanded it. He was emphatically a dashing, captivating orator, indeed wonderfully so.

The opinion I have expressed as to the decided ability of Jones is the one generally entertained at the time he was making his fame. Lately there has been a disposition, by men who never heard him speak, to underrate, to belittle him. This does injustice to the memory of Mr. Polk as well as to him. I repeat that Jones was not a statesman, that he was not a great man, except in a qualified sense. But at the same time I declare that he was a marvelous stump orator, especially in hurly-burly encounters in joint debate, in times of high political excitement. I further venture the opinion that any other Whig in Tennessee, except Jones—Bell, Peyton, Foster, Gentry, Henry—able and distinguished as they were—would have failed to triumph over Polk, or would have been discomfited by him. Foster was worsted by Aaron V. Brown, Henry by Johnson, and Gentry, great as he was, scarcely maintained his reputation with Johnson.

There was something in Jones—I cannot analyze it, I cannot fully explain it—that peculiarly fitted him for hot aggressive contests. He seemed to delight in the noise and clangor of battle. The happy combination of voice, person, humor, good temper, earnestness, ardor, clear statement, remarkable fluency, a vocabulary never at fault, quickness in seizing weak points, aptness of expression, and a remarkable facility in telling anecdotes—these were in part the qualities he possessed and the instruments he used with such phenomenal success in his great contests with James K. Polk. Attack him wheresoever, or howsoever his adversary might, he was always able in some way to repel the attack. His resources never failed, and he always used them with an air of supreme confidence that he was absolutely right—that there could not possibly be two sides to the question. He was a master in fencing, equally expert in parrying a blow, or making a thrust. He fought with all the means at his command—anecdotes, raillery, burlesque, humor, facts, arguments, or solemn appeal. When he saw the enemy entrenched in a strong position, it mattered not to him whether he made a feint or a flank movement, or opened with heavy artillery, or charged with the very lightest arms, provided he drove him from his position, and sent him flying from the field. The rapidity with which he answered the points of his adversary was one secret of Jones' triumphs. He spent but little time in answer to any point, and then passed on to another and another, and so of all, and when through with them, he had time to make counter attacks. His confidence in himself never failed. Then, he did what many speakers fail to do; when he made a good point he drove it home, with tremendous force and with a triumphant air.

Jones as a stump speaker was not specially noisy. He spoke with much ease to himself, with a clear, loud voice, and with distinct articulation and enunciation, and therefore he could with ease be heard on the outskirts of a large crowd. There was no great physical exertion on his part, wearying to himself and painful to his hearers. His speaking, while it was most animated and dashing, yet had a smoothness that took away all sense of uneasiness on the part of his audience. Polk was the more violent of the two. Even in telling his anecdotes, in his humor and in the utterance of his deepest emotions and passions, there was in Jones an air and manner of gentleness. There was never any shrieking, any piercing cries, any unnatural postures, any horrid contortions of face or body. He was in all his moods as dignified as any humorous and anecdote telling public speaker can be.

What then was the secret of his power? It was (in part) his voice, his delightful manner, his easy, flowing speech, his clearness of statement, his boldness in the avowal of opinions, his ingenuity in turning points against his adversary, and his inexhaustible humor which kept his audience at all times in sympathy with him. These explain only in part the ascendency of this man over the minds and hearts of men. There was in fact a kind of hypnotism that brought them under his spell. He got down in the very life and hearts of the people. It was the seasoning and the dressing of the food that he served, together with the delightful service of it, and not the dainty and superior quality of the material, that gave to it its flavor and its piquancy.

Polk, having equal faculties for speaking with Jones, and in the highest—the intellectual—being his superior, it is evident that the signal victories of Jones were won by his superior skill and power in the use of those faculties.

But if an inferior man, with scarcely an equal average equipment in all the arts of speaking, could gain, day by day, in two long canvasses such decided victories as to be acknowledged by nearly all men then, as well as now, surely such a man must have been more than common. It will not do to account for this discomfiture, in more than two hundred pitched battles, of one of the confessedly greatest debaters of the State, by the cry of buffoon, clown, mountebank. The mere statement of these facts, while not placing Jones on the highest plane of intellectuality, does elevate him to a respectable position in that regard, and to the first place as a joint debater before popular assemblies. It was an intellectual impossibility for such successes to have been achieved without more than common ability. It is inconceivable, if Jones were only a political juggler. At his advent in the political world, he was regarded with wonder, and still the wonder grew as he continued his triumphal career for two years.

The desire to know more of Mr. Polk is most natural. But few of this generation ever heard him speak or ever saw him. He was scarcely of medium height, being not more than 5 feet 7 or 8 inches tall. He was slight in body, but trim, straight, and graceful. His head was large with a decidedly intellectual cast, and his eyes were very large, of a brown or hazel color, very striking and handsome and with a benignant expression. In dress he was faultlessly neat. Indeed I considered him a very handsome man, at least a very distinguished looking one. Notwithstanding his delicate body, he was capable of the greatest physical endurance, as was evident from the almost incredible amount of labor he performed in his three canvasses of the entire State in 1839, 1841, and 1843. His voice was loud and good, though his intonation was somewhat unusual, but not disagreeable. He spoke with fluency, clearness, earnestness, and rapidity. More, he spoke with elegance, and with great pointedness and power. As a debater, in the presentation and marshaling of facts he was ingenious, lucid, and masterly. This was his strong point. Very seldom has any public speaker been able to present a long array of facts so impressively, and at the same time so attractively and with such irresistible power. Andrew Johnson could not have done so, because he did not possess the charm of manner, the elegance of language, the lucidness of statement, nor the compactness of argument. In a word, Mr. Polk was universally regarded in his day as a very great public speaker and a most skillful debater. Looking back at his canvass of 1839, I very much doubt whether there was a man in the State, on either side, who could have produced such a profound impression on the public mind. As before remarked, after his defeat by Jones, he never seemed to have the position as a man of rare ability that he previously had, and I think in this regard injustice has been done to his memory. It is an acknowledged fact that while he was President he was master of his own administration, and shaped and guided its policy as he thought best. It was stronger and accomplished more than William Henry Harrison's, or Tyler's, or Taylor's, or Fillmore's, or Pierce's, or Buchanan's, or Hayes', or Arthur's, or Benjamin Harrison's, and possibly even Monroe's. He was in fact Prime Minister as well as President. By a war, brought on by his own act, he added to our dominions a vast territory of incalculable value.

Mr. Polk was but little spoken or thought of for the Presidency, outside of Tennessee, previous to his nomination in 1844. His nomination came about in this wise. The Southern Democrats, under the skillful leadership of Mr. Calhoun, had determined to annex Texas to the United States, and to that end they had determined also that Mr. Van Buren, who was by long odds the most prominent candidate for that position, and who was openly opposed to annexation, should be defeated in the nominating convention. For this purpose they artfully secured the adoption of the rule requiring two-thirds of the delegates to make a nomination. That killed Mr. Van Buren's chances, as it was designed to do, for in no contingency after his letter in opposition to the annexation of Texas, could he get the requisite two-thirds with the solid South against him. Much less could General Cass, the next prominent candidate, get a two-thirds vote. Therefore after balloting and balloting in vain for these two men, Mr. Polk's name was presented, as had been previously arranged, and his nomination put through with a shout.

Mr. Polk's election was but little less anomalous. Mr. Clay, the opposing candidate, had taken early in the canvass, in his

Raleigh letter, decided ground against the annexation of Texas. Later on, in what was called his Alabama letter, with the view of reconciling his friends in the South, some of whom were discontented with his position—the feeling in favor of annexation becoming daily stronger and stronger in that section—he modified or changed his position, by saying he would be glad to see Texas annexed, provided it could be accomplished, without war with Mexico, and without national dishonor, and with some other conditions. That letter defeated him. The election ultimately depended upon the vote of the State of New York. The race there was very close. The Abolitionists—then a mere handful—held the balance of power. They were displeased with Mr. Clay for his change of position. They were violently opposed to the annexation of Texas, because they saw in it the extension of slavery and the growth of the slave power. They therefore deliberately cast their votes for Mr. Birney, their own candidate, and withheld them from Mr. Clay, with whom they agreed in general in politics, and thus gave by a very small plurality the vote of New York to Mr. Polk. If they had voted for Mr. Clay, as most of them intended doing previous to his second letter, he would have carried the State of New York and been elected. Thus the small band of Abolitionists of New York secured the election of Mr. Polk, the open advocate of annexation, and the defeat of Mr. Clay, the enemy of that scheme, or at least a doubtful friend. Every vote cast for Birney in the existing conditions was a vote taken from Mr. Clay, and, in its effect, a vote for Mr. Polk. But annexation was bound to come in spite of Mr. Clay and Mr. Van Buren, and in spite of the Whigs and Abolitionists. It was the "manifest destiny" of the country, guided by the genius of Mr. Calhoun and the Southern Democrats. The country, and especially the South, demanded the liberty of sharing in that magnificent territory enriched by the blood of Milam, Crockett, Travis, Bowie, and Hanning, and won by the valor of Houston.

Mr. Polk's private character was exceptionally good. There was not a blot nor a stain on it. He was gentle and lovable. When he made the canvass of 1839, Bailie Peyton, then a distinguished Member of Congress, was to have been his opponent, as he (Peyton) himself said in substance in a speech in Greeneville. I never knew why he was not, but suppose Governor Cannon would not get out of the way. If Peyton had been the candidate, the result almost certainly would have been different. He was a fiery, daring, stirring speaker, with infinite humor and wit, and considerable eloquence. He had the courage to dare and the will to do anything that his judgment approved. He was not the equal of Polk in statesmanship, nor as a debater, but he possessed a dash, a brilliancy, a manly bearing that more than made up for the lack of these, and which Polk would have dreaded more than he did Jones. The wit and humor of Peyton were irresistible. Besides, he was a noble and chivalrous gentleman of the highest type. The reaction against Jackson in Tennessee began in 1835, and resulted in giving the vote of the State to Hugh Lawson White for President, and then in 1837 to Cannon for Governor, and was still going on in 1839, when Polk arrested and checked it for the time being. But it was only checked. It again swelled into majestic proportions in 1840, when Harrison rode in triumph on the crest of the tide of popular indignation, and carried the State by thirteen thousand majority.

But to hasten to a conclusion. Polk was a small and apparently a delicate man. But he was vital with energy and ambition. His endurance was almost phenomenal. He entered the contest of 1841, determined to win, but he soon found he had a competitor very different from good old Governor Cannon. The two ambitious competitors opened the canvass in Wilson County in March. Soon they were in East Tennessee. They canvassed the State, county by county, from Johnson to Shelby. In some places, and possibly at all, they spoke five hours a day. In those days there were no railroads, and therefore they had to travel altogether on horseback or in private conveyances. They spoke every day, and generally had to go twenty-five or thirty miles to reach the appointment for the next day. What an immense strain on the vital powers!

In the canvass of 1841, the speaking apparently closed beyond the mountains. But Polk secretly made a second list of appointments for himself in East Tennessee, and slipped off to fill them. While he was on his way, driving furiously forward to reach them, Jones was informed of, or suspected his design, and he also immediately set off for the distant appointments—nearly three hundred miles away. Jones, whip in hand, spurred onward night and day, giving neither sleep to his eyes nor slumber to his eyelids. What was the surprise and confusion of Polk to find Jones at his first appointment, ready to reproach and taunt him, as he did, with telling effect, for his cowardice in trying to avoid meeting him face to face. Jones thus gained an additional advantage over Polk. In the last days of August I heard them on this flying trip, before a great crowd, at Bull's Gap, near the corner of Greene, Hawkins, Jefferson, and Grainger Counties. Jones was bold and confident, having the air of a conqueror. Polk, on the other hand, was careworn, irritable, indeed mad, as his party was mad all over the State. He complained in doleful tones of Jones' levity and want of dignity in the debates, in telling anecdotes. Jones retorted by reminding him of how he drove poor old Cannon almost distracted with his stories, his mimicries, and his grimaces two years before, and how gay he then was, and how dignified and sedate he was now.

It was at Bean's Station, I believe, that an incident happened which was never forgotten by those who were present. Polk was complaining, as usual, of the levity of Jones' discussions, and said that if a stranger from another State should happen to be present he would not dream that his competitor was seeking the high office of Governor, judging from his manner, but would suppose he was acting the leading part in the ring of a circus. "Yes," said Jones, in his reply, "I will accept the position assigned to me by my competitor of master of the ring, will get down into the sawdust, with whip in hand, and bring out the pony, but my competitor must perform the other part—wear the spangles, put on the red cap, and take the place of the little fellow that goes around on the pony. When I raise my long whip [raising his hand as if in the act of cracking it] and crack it, and give the word of command, then go." In a moment he shouted, "Go!" The crowd caught the idea, and imagining they saw Polk flying around the ring on the pony, in wild uproar cried out, "Monkey, Monkey! Baboon, Baboon!"

Such a scene as followed, it is rarely given to mortals to witness—the wild, tumultuous laughing and yelling that seized and held the crowd! That afternoon the people went home laughing, they awoke the next morning laughing, and for a long time afterward, whenever they thought of Polk with a red cap flying round the ring in a circus, they continued to laugh.

Polk was petrified. It is believed he never rode the pony afterward, nor attended another circus!

The two canvasses of 1841 and 1843 were exceedingly exciting. Very large and eager crowds everywhere greeted the speakers. Curiosity and expectation stood on tiptoe! The discussions were more than animated—they were hot, spirited, intensely earnest. They awakened the keenest and the most bitter interest throughout the State. Finally this interest spread beyond the State, and extended to the outer borders of the Union. These contests, in their duration, though not in the greatness of the subjects discussed, were the most marked political campaigns ever conducted in this country. Treating the two canvasses as one, they lasted eight months of active speaking, with nearly two hundred pitched battles. The joint debate, justly so celebrated, between Lincoln and Douglas, embraced just seven days.

Mr. Jones' speaking was simple, direct and straightforward. He never played with metaphors or figures of speech. There was no attempt at great oratory. There were no eagle flights, no grand pyrotechnic diplays. It was addressed and adapted to the average intelligence of Tennessee audiences of that day. The plainest mind could comprehend him. He did not shoot above the heads of his audience.

I need not say that Jones was elected Governor in both these elections. In popular estimation he became a political hero. His name was often mentioned in connection with the vice-presidency. In 1851 he was elected one of the Senators of the United States from Tennessee. As far back as 1839, he had proclaimed himself for Mr. Clay for President. This was at the time when Mr. Clay was still suffering from the enmity of the overshadowing influence of General Jackson. In both of his canvasses with Polk he daily declared himself for Mr. Clay for the presidency, and called on his competitor and indeed dared him to name his candidate for that position among the Democrats. At Jonesboro, as John S. Mathes relates, while Jones was daring Polk to name his candidate, old Adam Broyles spoke up in the audience and said he would name the candidate and the next president also; it would be James K. Polk! And sure enough it was!

Jones' devotion to Clay suffered no abatement while that

patriot lived. After he became Senator, during the protracted illness of Mr. Clay, he was daily at his bedside—one of the few having that privilege—and in his last moments he was standing by when the spirit of that great patriot and statesman took its flight from the earth.

In 1854 Jones, as Senator, voted for the repeal of the Missouri compromise measure, along with every Democratic Senator of the South, except Sam Houston, and separated himself from his colleague, John Bell, thus swapping horses while crossing a stream. He from that time forward was a Democrat. He once had declared that there was a great chasm—dark, deep, and wide—that separated him from the Democratic party, which it was impossible for him to cross, yet somehow or another he got over it.

The claim made by some at this time that Jones was a mere shallow clown is contrary to both history and tradition. Men can believe a good deal, but not everything. If those who persist in saying that Jones was a mere mountebank would admit that while he was not the equal of Polk in argument, or logic, in learning and statesmanship, in breadth of intellect and knowledge of public affairs, yet that he possessed an active, versatile, dexterous mind, great readiness and resources in debate, and wonderful power in turning points against an opponent, I could readily agree with them—indeed I have already said the same things. But when they attempt to make of him a mere ninny, almost a shallow fool, they set at naught the judgment of the tens of thousands of persons all over the State who heard him, the intelligent as well as the ignorant; they set at naught the tradition which has come down to this day, and they make of Mr. Polk a *very weak man*, to be vanquished in two hundred debates by such a buffoon and simpleton.

The subsequent career of Jones was not specially brilliant. In 1848 he supported Taylor for President and in 1852 he was one of the special champions of General Scott. This was the canvass (that of 1852) in which John H. Crozier, William G. Swan, James and William Williams of our own State, and Toombs and Stephens of Georgia, quit the Whig party, and went over to the support of the Democratic party. It was the canvass in which Gentry and Brownlow refused to support Scott, but cast their votes for Webster without ceasing to be

Whigs. The action of all these was based on the ground that Scott was not believed to be true to the South on the Slavery question.

As before stated, Jones was elected in 1851-52 to a seat in the United States senate and served one term. In 1856 he abandoned the Whig and joined the Democratic party, although he had once boasted that there was a great chasm—deep, wide, and impassable—that separated him from that party. Yet with supreme agility he bounded over it!

I am asked what became of Jones, after his retirement from the Senate, and his wonderful bound across the impassable chasm described by him. The answer is briefly given. When he retired from the Senate, he was last seen slowly, sadly passing down the decline on the other side of the chasm, disappearing below the political horizon, hastening to his early setting, and no man ever saw him more politically.

To abandon figures of speech, Mr. Jones' political career closed with his term in the United States Senate, which was not brilliant. He lived but a few years afterward, dying in the very maturity of his powers, leaving many friends in the State to mourn his loss, among whom were many old Whigs, who remembered with gratitude the glories of 1841 and 1843.

The effect of the defeats of Mr. Polk for the Governorship of Tennessee was the obscuration of his fame for a brief period. But the still potent influence in his behalf of his faithful friend, General Jackson, and the ever devoted friendship of his other Tennessee friends, exerted at a critical moment, when there was a deadlock in the national Democratic convention between Mr. Van Buren and General Cass—neither candidate being able to secure the requisite two-thirds vote—Mr. Polk's name being suddenly sprung on the convention, secured for him the nomination and subsequently his election to the presidency. Notwithstanding his elevation to this high office, and the acquisition by his administration of very large and valuable territory, and notwithstanding the administration was marked with vigor, and by the adoption of measures of momentous consequences to the country, Mr. Polk has never been ranked in statesmanship with our great presidents. I think, indeed, that injustice has been done him by his countrymen. One reason of this was the fact that he was always a partisan in his official acts. He was never able to lift himself above party into the serene heights of liberal statesmanship.

He had been an active participant in the exciting and tempestuous scenes of Jackson's administration, and a part of Van Buren's; he had heard himself reproached and denounced by the fiery Whig leaders—Prentiss, Marshall, Wise, Peyton— he had keenly felt the refusal of the Whigs to give him a vote of thanks when he was about to retire from the Speakership of the House, and he knew that S. S. Prentiss, amid the thundering applause of his political friends, had denounced him in the House as "the tool of the President and of his party," and although a very amiable man in private life, he could never forgive his political enemies for these wrongs, and he carried this feeling into the presidency.

DISTINGUISHED PERSONAGES OF LAST GENERATION WHOM I MET OR KNEW.

Andrew Jackson—General Winfield Scott—James K. Polk—Bailie Peyton—Felix Grundy—John J. Crittenden—William C. Preston—John C. Calhoun—President Taylor—Henry Clay—General Brooks—Joseph E. Johnston—General Hardee—General Garland—Albert Sydney Johnston—General Harney—General Sam Houston.

In the following account of the distinguished national personages whom I met or knew, the first in order of time, and perhaps in durability of fame, was Andrew Jackson. In 1835, while he was President, he was passing through East Tennessee, in his own carriage, on his way from Washington to the Hermitage, when he stopped for a day in Greeneville, with his friend, John Dixon, a merchant of that place. News had been circulated in advance that he would be in Greeneville on that day and therefore the country people turned out in large numbers to see him. He held a reception, and the people passed him, one after another, and had a chance to shake his hand, and some of them to have a moment's conversation with him. I was then a boy, but I fell in line, and had the honor of receiving a graceful bow from the most dignified and august man of that generation. To see him once was to remember him forever. His air of majestic imperiousness, though united with the most princely and gracious manner, struck a kind of awe into the mind of the beholders. If ever a man was born to command men at first sight, he certainly was. Men involuntarily yielded him leadership. His very presence—I might almost say his terrible presence—excited awe—inspiring respect mingled with admiration.

The next national character I saw was General Winfield Scott. In 1838 I was a volunteer soldier under him in the Cherokee nation during the Indian disturbances, and holding an honorable position it became my duty to carry a dispatch from Red Clay, Ga., to him at his headquarters at Charleston, Tenn. During my stay I saw him mounted on a splendid large, black horse, in full uniform, followed by some or all of his staff, taking a ride. It is useless to say, as all persons already know, that he was an unusually tall and large and magnificent man— a figure of chivalry, or romance. Richard, the lion-hearted, as painted by Sir Walter Scott, in his flashing steel panoply, going into gay tournament, was not to the eye grander in carriage or in mien than General Scott when mounted on his powerful charger. Several years after this I was taken to his headquarters in Washington, and introduced to him by an officer and a comrade of his in the War of 1812. We were received with impressive politeness, and spent a half hour with him in friendly, but dignified conversation. He doubtless was unusually complacent on that occasion, as the presidential canvass of 1852 was then only six or eight months ahead, and he made no concealment of the fact that he would be a candidate for the Whig nomination. In this conversation he used the expression, "the rich Irish brogue," so much referred to in the succeeding canvass, but whether or not for the first time I cannot say. His great weakness was his excessive vanity and love of show; hence his nickname, "Old Fuss and Feathers." Excepting his weakness and his foibles in this and in other respects, and his haughtiness he was a man of the highest merit and of first-class military ability. He displayed his military ability conspicuously in two wars in Mexico and in that of 1812, when he was only a very young man. His campaign in Mexico, from Vera Cruz to the capital, considering the smallness of his army, was one of the most remarkable triumphs of military genius of our history.

In 1839 I first saw James K. Polk and heard him make a notable speech of nearly three hours' length, in Greeneville, as a candidate for Governor. I often heard him afterward in 1841, and 1843, in his celebrated discussions with James C. Jones. Mr. Polk was unquestionably a man of a high order of ability and of very great power as a speaker. He dealt with facts and ideas with great fluency, skill, and force. But few men equaled him in the power of holding men, by clear and convincing presentation of political issues. Nothing but the phenomenal power of Jones, in his own peculiar way, could have triumphed over him. The country has never given Mr. Polk his due for ability, neither as an orator nor as a statesman, nor has Tennessee done so since his defeat by Jones.

In 1837 or 1839, I heard Bailie Peyton speak. He was

then a very handsome young man, in the meridian of his fame, and a brilliant member of Congress. He and Harry A. Wise had led in the house the fiercest assaults ever made on Jackson and on Van Buren's administration. He was a game, noble, chivalrous, brilliant man, ever ready for a fight, or to assist in a matter of honor. In later years I knew him well.

In 1840 Felix Grundy, returning from Washington in company with Senator Hopkins L. Turner and Henry Watterson of the house came through East Tennessee, making speeches in favor of Van Buren. They spoke at Greeneville before an immense assemblage. Of course Grundy was the "observed of all observers." He was one of the greatest orators in a certain way this country has ever produced, fit to be, as he was in his young days, the rival of Henry Clay. His eloquence was soft and gentle and persuasive, moving an audience with a bewitching and irresistible fascination. On this occasion the scene was enlivened and rendered in the highest degree picturesque by the appearance on the stand of General Thomas D. Arnold, who demanded a division of time on behalf of the Whigs, which was granted, but he was sandwiched in between Watterson and Turney on the one side, and Grundy on the other. Such a scene of wit, ridicule, sarcasm, repartee, and occasional eloquence as occurred between Arnold and Grundy I never have witnessed. I do not pretend to describe it here. The soft and gentle eloquence of Grundy still lingers in my mind as one of my most cherished recollections. Some one (was it Homer, in reference to the eloquence of Ulysses?) has compared this kind of eloquence to the gentle falling of snow.

In that same year, 1840, I heard John J. Crittenden make one of the greatest speeches of his life, to an audience which was estimated at the time to be forty thousand, at the great interstate mass meeting at Cumberland Gap, held by the people of Kentucky, Tennessee, Virginia, and North Carolina. I afterwards met him two or three times in Frankfort and in Washington. He had the reputation in his day, and I think he deserved it, of being second only to Mr. Clay and one or two others, both in oratory and statesmanship. He was an amiable and a lovable gentleman and one of the purest and noblest statesmen of his generation.

In the same year I met and twice heard William C. Preston, the great Virginia-South Carolina orator, at a Whig mass meeting at Brushy Creek camp ground, now Johnson City. The first day he spoke in advocacy of the Whig cause, and in favor of the election of General Harrison, and the second day on the battle of King's Mountain, the anniversary of that event occurring on that day. Mr. Preston was unquestionably an orator of nearly the first magnitude, ranking but little below Mr. Clay, in the power to stir men's blood, and above him in the classical beauty of his diction. He was most imposing in appearance, being very large and portly, and about 6 feet 5 inches in height. His hair was sandy colored, with the ruddy complexion of his grandfather, Colonel William Campbell, and of his ancestors, the Campbells (Argylies) in Scotland. He came legitimately by his eloquence, being the great-nephew of Patrick Henry. Unquestionably he was one of the grandest orators of this country.

In 1845 John C. Calhoun stopped in Greeneville for a night, on his way to his home in South Carolina from the springs in Virginia. He was traveling with his servants in his own carriages. Some young law students, studying under Judge R. J. McKinney, among them myself, called on him to pay our respects, but quite as much to see so great a man and hear him talk. He received us most graciously and kindly, and talked to us for half an hour or longer, he choosing such subjects as he knew would interest young men. He poured out an incessant stream of information and thought, clothed in the most terse, lucid, and striking language. We listened to him as to a sage or an oracle. In my lifetime I have met no man who impressed me more with his pure intellectuality. In appearance he was tall, straight, and slender, and of a most graceful personage, and, I thought, handsome. In appearance he was my ideal of what I deem a statesman and a great man should be. His dress was faultless black. In a word, everything about him—his person, his features, his face, his dress—were refined and in the best taste, such as one would expect in a man of delicate organism and the purest intellectuality.

In 1850 I made my first trip to Washington, going by way of Chattanooga and Charleston, and traveling alternately by boat and by railway. While in Washington I attended one of President Taylor's receptions. His frank, simple, cordial manners were strikingly refreshing. He grasped the hand and expressed delight at seeing one with an energy equal to Roosevelt at the present time. It was the warm-hearted greeting of an unaffected soldier. I was quite as much struck with the elegant manners and the unostentatious simplicity of the dress of the daughter, the first lady of the land, Mrs. Bliss, who was doing the honors of the White House. She wore a plain, a very plain, crossbarred lawn, absolutely without trimmings or ornament. And yet it was so neat and fit her fine person so well that I thought she looked quite queenly.

I saw Mr. Clay, Mr. Webster, and Mr. Benton—the three most distinguished characters then in Congress—very frequently. Mr. Calhoun had just died a short time after delivering his last, and one of his greatest, speeches on the absorbing questions of 1850. As I went on I met his remains, with the funeral escort, in North Carolina. Indeed he was dying when he made his last speech, and I believe it had to be read by some one for him. I saw every day for two or three weeks, Senators Seward, Berrien, Badger, Mason, Clayton, Bayard, Soule, Houston, Rusk, Crittenden, Davis, Foote, and Bell, and Representatives Toombs, Stephens, Douglas, Corwin, and all of the great men of that time. I heard a part of the speech of Alexander Stephens on the admission of Oregon as a State. Mr. Toombs was by his side, all excitement, prompting and making suggestions to him. The house was all alive, and showing the most intense interest as the eloquent little Georgian delivered his fearless speech. At the time I was sitting beside Andrew Johnson. He remarked to me that Stephens was a greater man than Toombs.

One of my life-long regrets has been that I did not avail myself of the kind offer of a Member of Congress to go with him to call on, and be introduced to, Mr. Clay (and perhaps Mr. Webster also). I very foolishly felt timid about appearing in the presence of so great a man, and therefore postponed going from time to time until too late. But I had the privilege of a greater pleasure—that of hearing Mr. Clay deliver one of his set and greatest speeches. A short time before my arrival Mr. Webster had made his great and patriotic speech of the 7th of March, which so provoked the rage of the Abolitionists, and which finally put him out of public life, and caused his premature death.

At the time of the intense excitement in the country, in 1849, and the threatened secession of the Southern States, Mr. Clay came forth from his voluntary retirement, and re-entered public life, going into the Senate, with the avowed purpose of trying to save the country, as he had done in 1820, by offering a compromise of the differences between the North and the South. After many measures and resolutions had been offered in Congress, and much angry debate, a committee of thirteen was appointed, of which he was chairman, to which were referred his and other resolutions. After anxious and long deliberations, Mr. Clay at length submitted a report embodying his plan of a compromise, which in substance, after a long debate, was adopted, not as a whole, as proposed, but in separate bills.

It was upon these measures, involving the peace of the country and the integrity of the Union that Mr. Clay, after due notice, arose in the Senate to open debate. For hours before, the Senate gallery (it was the old Senate chamber) was packed with people anxious to hear the great orator and venerable Senator. I was there early and got a good seat, where I could both see and hear the speaker. For two or three hours he held the Senate and galleries spellbound by his matchless eloquence. The most profound silence prevailed, lest the listeners might lose a word that fell from his honeyed lips and persuasive tongue, save only when a pleasant colloquy took place between Mr. Mason and him. I need not say that he was the most graceful orator, the most perfect in action, the most easy and natural in manner, the most frank and fearless in the avowal of his opinions, and that his voice was the richest and the most melodious I ever heard, and at the same time that he was the most courteous to his fellow Senators. This would be but repeating what has been said of him by millions of people for fifty years. His voice, whether in its highest or its lowest notes, was music itself—it was indeed grander and sweeter than music. After the lapse of more than fifty years, I can yet distinctly catch its sound and feel its thrill in my own mind. It has been said often that Mr. Gentry of this State had a better voice than Mr. Clay. Mr. Gentry unquestionably had a grand voice. It rang out like a bugle, sweet, loud, and sonorous. But it lacked the divine melody, the soul enrapturing symphony of the voice of Mr. Clay.

Perhaps after all it was not the marvelous voice, the superlative distinctness of enunciation, the grace of action, the naturalness of manner, the easy flow of apt words and bright thoughts, the sincere and earnest conviction that captivated all audiences in Mr. Clay, so much as the inner spirit of the man—his greatness of soul, his high honor, his open frankness, his courage, his warm heart, and his wonderful power of catching and holding, as if by a spell, the fancy and the hearts of men. Thus, for a life time he was loved and idolized by a large part of the American people as no other leader ever was. His very name sent a thrill through their hearts.

Next after his melodious voice and wonderful gracefulness of manner, I think the effect of his oratory was owing to the surpassing distinctness of his utterance and enunciation; you could hear nearly every letter in his words. For example, he pronounced California as it is divided thus Cal-i-for-ni-a, without halting on the letters or parts, and with the rhythm of music.

He spoke with the vigor and fire of young manhood. There was no cessation in his flowing sentences, no halting, no hesitating for words or thoughts. His oratory was kept sustained and at high tide throughout, like the current of a full and mighty stream.

In a few months after hearing Mr. Clay, I heard the celebrated Tom Marshall speak. He was considered, and was in fact, a great orator—sensational, erratic, and emotional. He was a type of the brilliant orators, after the style of William T. Haskell, though I thought him inferior. His too partial friends, however, considered that he was the equal of Mr. Clay. He doubtless thought so himself, for he attacked the latter in a powerful speech in Lexington, I believe, their mutual home. Mr. Clay answered him and afterward neither his friends nor Mr. Marshall himself ever entertained that opinion.

Mr. Clay's oratory was of the simplest character, except his grand and impressive manner. It was earnest and full of life and vehemence, yet in the very "torrent, tempest, and whirlwind" of his speaking, there was a "temperance" that gave it "smoothness." Every sentence, as uttered by him was alive with thought and passion. That wonderful voice and his magnificent, yet simple manner, were back of all and through all. There was not the slightest effort at what is supposed to be brilliant oratory, no skyscraping, no eagle flights, no flinging of rainbows across the heavens. His own mind was burning with great thoughts, and he was deadly intent on telling them to others.

Much of the so-called flights of fancy in public speaking is not to convey ideas, but to conceal the want of them. We have had great floods of this in Tennessee. "How stale, how flat, and unprofitable."

In 1850 I spent six months in Texas, in an official capacity that brought me into intimate relations with officers of the regular army stationed there. I became well acquainted with General Brooks, commanding that department, then the most important in the United States; with Colonel Joseph E. Johnston, Colonel Hardee (afterward general), with General Garland, the son-in-law of General Worth, with the daring General Harney, the successor of General Brooks, as department commander, and was introduced to Albert Sydney Johnston. Colonel Joseph E. Johnston was then, as he was after he had won his fame as one of the greatest generals of the Civil War, modest, quiet and gentlemanly, and a man of great intelligence. He was considered by the officers one of the most promising men in the army. General Harney was then a little past his prime. He had won considerable reputation in the Mexican war, as a daring and dashing cavalry officer, and in fighting Indians on the frontier. As he was from Tennessee, he was naturally drawn to me, and we became fast friends. He was a giant in size, being 6 feet 6 or 7 inches in height. His wife was a St. Louis lady of great wealth. The result was that he lived on the frontier in great extravagance. The most elegant and costly dinner I ever attended was given by him in honor of our commission. He was indeed a big-hearted as well as a brave fellow.

But the most celebrated person I met in Texas, and I met many, was General Sam Houston. He made a speech in Houston on the Fourth of July, 1851, the day I arrived there, returning home. The next day I traveled with him on a boat to Galveston, and put up with him in the same house, where we were together for two or three days. Of course I had heard him speak in Houston. As a speaker he was strong, rough and effective, but not an accomplished or eloquent popular orator. But the fighting qualities in him made his speeches quite attractive. He struck right and left with ponderous force at his enemies. He openly hurled defiance at them and damned them to perdition. When he got through with them there were not many fragments left. No man had warmer friends or more pronounced enemies. I was told by scores of men that he was an arrant coward, and that he skulked in the battle of San Jacinto. Even the late admiral of the Texas navy, while it was a republic, enlivened the passengers on our crowded stage coach, going from Houston to Austin, for a whole day denouncing him as a coward, and in every way as dishonorable and unworthy. Many others, indeed a large majority of persons in Texas, of equally as much standing, believed and affirmed that Houston, while not a saint, was a pure patriot, a brave soldier, and justly entitled to be called the defender and the father of the republic. Through a pitiless storm of abuse and detraction he proudly held on his way, the central figure, and by long odds the foremost man in Texas from 1836 to 1861. No ordinary man could have withstood and triumphed over such bitter and long continued opposition.

WILLIAM GANNAWAY BROWNLOW.

CHAPTER I.

Brownlow a Native of Virginia—A Mechanic—Methodist Preacher—Established *Tennessee Whig* at Elizabethton, 1838—In 1839 Removed to Jonesboro, Paper Taking Name Jonesboro *Whig and Independent*—Editorial Contest Between Haynes and Brownlow—1849, Removed Family and Paper to Knoxville—Bitter Quarrel with Knoxville *Register*—Controversy with John H. Crozier, William and James Williams, and William G. Swan—In 1860 Circulation of Whig 14,000—Personal Characteristics—Public Spirit—As a Public Speaker—Influence in 1861.

Of the Union leaders in East Tennessee, in 1860-61, the next after Andrew Johnson in national importance and political influence was unquestionably William Gannaway Brownlow, a native of Virginia. He was a unique and a remarkable character. Like Mr. Johnson, his early education had been incomplete, but he possessed a natural ability which enabled him to overcome this deficiency much more completely than the former ever did. By reading and association with others he acquired to a considerable extent the graces and diction of an educated man. He also, like Johnson, had been an apprentice and a mechanic, having learned and worked at the trade of a carpenter when quite a young man. But unlike Johnson, he was not always ostentatiously parading this fact before the world. He was not ashamed of his early calling, but never felt the need of constantly proclaiming it. There was not in his nature the slightest trace of the demagogue. He never found it necessary to array one class against another in order to gain popularity. He was always the friend of the poor and helpless, and they all knew it, not by his words, but by his daily acts of beneficence. While he did not obsequiously court the rich and the powerful, he was uniformly just toward them, and never for political or personal effect sought to array laboring men against them. He was just to both classes, and had the respect and esteem of both.

Early in manhood Mr. Brownlow became a Methodist preacher. In this capacity he soon became distinguished. His fame spread far beyond his immediate circuits. He was unprecedently aggressive against every sin and vice, and against every creed he did not like. His motto was, "Cry aloud, spare not." With an unparalleled audacity he attacked systems, creeds and sects, and all offending persons. This, of course, soon brought him into bitter controversies. One of the first of these was with a Baptist minister named Humphrey Posey of North Carolina. Finally a libel suit was the outcome of this controversy. In a book published by Mr. Brownlow in 1838 he immortalized poor old Posey, and then turned him over to the gaze of posterity. This book is entitled: "Helps to the Study of Presbyterianism." It was both personal and controversial. In it the Presbyterians came in for the larger part of his attentions. That was a period of almost universal controversy and disputation among religious sects in East Tennessee and Southwestern Virginia. Men fairly burned with zeal for their respective churches, and were almost ready to die for their faith, though they preferred seeing their religious enemies die. In this there was more hot blood than grace, charity, or good will.

Mr. Brownlow early became the champion of the Methodist Church in the South, and so continued until approaching age began to quench the fiery ardor of his younger days. Any attack on his own church was sure to call forth from his facile pen a scathing reply not easily forgotten. For this purpose he generally used the columns of his own paper, but when the controversy became exciting, by reason of the importance of the question involved or the greatness of the opposing controversialist, he resorted to serial magazines of his own.

In these controversies Mr. Brownlow always sustained himself to the satisfaction of his Church and his friends. Generally, when he got through with his adversary, by the use of reason, facts, ridicule, and sometimes cartoons and abuse, there was not much left of him. He had the faculty of always making any cause he advocated appear to be right to his admirers. This was talent, not to say genius. In the popular mind he always triumphed.

In the Church Brownlow's influence was all powerful. In 1832, at the age of twenty-seven, he was elected a delegate to the General Conference of the Methodist Church, which assembled in Philadelphia. Perhaps it is remembered by but few persons of this generation that Landon C. Haynes, one of the Senators from Tennessee in the Confederate Congress from

1861 to 1865, started out in life a Whig and a Methodist preacher. It finally came about that he and Mr. Brownlow had a bitter quarrel, and through the influence of the latter he was silenced and turned out of the Church. Mr. Haynes then became a Democrat and the editor of a village paper, and finally a lawyer. A fierce and terrible newspaper war followed between these two remarkable men, which lasted for many years. This was in Jonesboro, Tenn., at that time their mutual home. Mr. Haynes was a bright, witty, showy, and an aggressive man. He was a fluent and skillful orator.

Mr. Brownlow's first connection with the press was as editor and proprietor of the *Tennessee Whig*, the publication of which he began as a weekly, at Elizabethton, Tenn., in 1838. From the first number this paper uttered no uncertain sound. One of the old mottoes flying at the head of his paper was: "Independence in all things; neutral in nothing." His paper was stalwart in its advocacy of Whig principles, and from the first its bold and fearless utterances attracted attention. The vigor and originality of his style, the fierce and daring attacks made on all kinds of wrong, the astounding boldness with which he attacked men and measures, soon established the reputation of the paper and gave notoriety to its editor far beyond the banks of the beautiful Watauga, the home of the first settlers of Tennessee, where it was published. Let it be remembered that this paper was issued from a little out-of-the-way mountain village of not more than two hundred souls, and with scarcely fifty houses. At that time, and indeed for many years afterward, Mr. Brownlow fairly wantoned in his strength, his courage, and in the wild excitement of personal controversy.

In 1839 Brownlow moved with his paper to Jonesboro, a larger town, about twenty miles west of Elizabethton. Here the paper took the name of the Jonesboro *Whig and Independent*. Jonesboro was the oldest town in the State, and contained from seven hundred to one thousand inhabitants.

The Jonesboro *Whig* was a five-column paper, about twenty-five inches long, published at two dollars per annum, if paid in advance, three dollars if paid within the year, and four if paid afterward. Through this little paper, published once a week, its editor gained a national reputation, even away back in 1840. No parallel to it can be found in this country. Extracts were made from it in all the leading Whig papers in the United

States. He became so well known that wherever he went he was a kind of hero. He was gazed at and followed with curious eyes as a wonder. It must be kept in mind that Jonesboro was an interior town, in an interior section of the State, with no railroad, no water communications, and with only a tri-weekly stage coach. The arrival of a single stranger in the little town in those days would create such a sensation as nearly to suspend all business until his name and business were ascertained. In this village, and with this little paper, Mr. Brownlow became famous. There was not in the United States such another volcano as this paper became, constantly muttering, seething, and boiling. Woe to the man on whom the storm burst.

With all his patronage it was a hard matter to keep his little craft afloat. Several times Mr. Brownlow embarked in other enterprises to aid him in making a living, but always with disaster. Incompetent or dishonest associates or agents got the better of him every time. The truth is, he was too liberal, too unsuspecting, too negligent of details for a successful business man. He would become the surety of all who called on him, and then when pay day came around and the principal failed to pay, which often happened, he would bravely meet the debt himself, never shirking under any pretense whatever. He would pay security debts as well as his own as long as he had a dollar. With all their malice his malignant enemies never, during his long life, dared to charge him with personal dishonesty. They accused him of nearly everything except dishonesty, drunkenness, and licentiousness, but never of these offenses.

When Landon C. Haynes became an editor in the little town of Jonesboro, as before stated, a long and bitter editorial quarrel followed between him and Mr. Brownlow. Finally the latter drove him from the editorial chair, and he betook himself to the practice of law, where he became a rather successful lawyer.

In the spring of 1849 Brownlow determined to move his paper and family to Knoxville, which was a much larger place than Jonesboro. It was the commercial and political as well as the geographical center of East Tennessee as it is to-day. Scarcely had this been accomplished before he got into a long and bitter quarrel with the Knoxville *Register*, an old Whig paper, of good standing, whose history ran back to 1816. The *Register* had back of it four or five, or more, strong and wealthy stockholders. The controversy which followed was the most severe and desperate one Brownlow ever had. It became personal in the extreme. For years, day after day, these papers teemed with the bitterest denunciations. At one time it was determined, in his temporary absence in the country, to destroy Mr. Brownlow's paper by violence, but his friends rallied to its defense and the purpose was abandoned. After a long and sometimes apparently doubtful struggle, Mr. Brownlow triumphed. He succeeded in making his paper the organ of his party. Long before 1860 the men who had conducted this controversy with Brownlow had ceased to be Whigs and had gone over to the Democratic party. When the time for secession had come, they all naturally joined in that movement.

The men who were thus engaged in this controversy with Brownlow were men of wealth, talents, and high social position. One of them was John H. Crozier, who belonged to one of the oldest families of Knoxville. He was a lawyer by profession, a man of culture and wide intelligence. On the stump and at the bar he was a fluent and pointed speaker. At an early age he served as a member of the Legislature. In the canvasses of 1840, 1844, and 1848 he took an active part on the stump in behalf of the Whig party. In 1845 and 1847 he was elected a member of Congress, in which body he served with credit to himself and the district. He was a keen debater, an original thinker, and a strong, vigorous writer.

James and William Williams were two more of this combination arrayed against Mr. Brownlow. These men were educated, wealthy, and also belonged to an old family. The wealth they inherited was increased by shrewd business enterprises. They were both men of talents and possessed a high degree of intelligence. James Williams was especially noted for his ability. During the administration of Mr. Buchanan he was appointed and served as minister to Turkey.

The fourth person of the combination I have referred to was William G. Swan. He was perhaps the most talented and versatile, as he was certainly the boldest and most original thinker of the four. In point of ability he was no ordinary man. In 1851 he was elected Attorney General and Reporter of the State. Three or four years before the war he and John Mitchell, the celebrated "Irish Patriot," who had escaped from a confinement in the penal colony of Great Britain in Van Dieman's Land, started and edited a violent and extreme Southern paper in Knoxville, called *The Southern Citizen*, in which, among other things, they advocated the reopening of the African slave trade and a dissolution of the Union. About the year 1857 Mr. Swan was appointed by Governor Johnson Circuit Judge to fill a vacancy caused by the death of Judge James M. Welcker, which office he filled with ability and dignity. When the war came on he became in action what he had been in principle for a long time, an earnest secessionist. In 1861 he was elected to the Confederate Congress from the Knoxville district, defeating John Baxter, one of the most prominent Union leaders of a few months previous, and was re-elected in August, 1863.

These four men, forty years ago, were exceptional in ability. Their influence was great; their power immense. They wielded potent pens. Mr. Brownlow never had such a powerful combination of able and wealthy men arrayed against him. They were determined to destroy him. It was a merciless fight for political existence. In addition, Mr. Brownlow was sued for libel in the courts. He was also indicted in nearly every county in the judicial district for the alleged violation of an old forgotten and obsolete penal statute against advertising lottery schemes. With unshrinking courage he met all these attempts to destroy him, and bravely dared his enemies to do their worst. Nearly any other man in the United States would have been overwhelmed, crushed, and driven out of the country, for that finally became the object of these men. After a few years, however, the triumph of Mr. Brownlow became complete. He was not destroyed, but made stronger. His enemies were silenced and driven from the field while he remained victor. After vindicating the supremacy of his paper as the party organ of East Tennessee, he maintained this position in comparative peace up to the time of the breaking out of the Civil War. His paper daily grew in popular favor, and its circulation was greatly widened and increased. To meet the demands of the times he issued a tri-weekly as well as a weekly. At the commencement of the war its circulation had reached about 14,000 copies. This was enormous for a little interior town of about three thousand inhabitants. It went into every State and territory. Mr. Brownlow, for the first time in his life, now commenced making money. But the war soon put an end to this. In 1862 his press was confiscated by the Confederate authorities and sold.

It does not lie within the scope of this work to write biographies or enter into details, but merely to give sketches of noted individuals connected with the great loyal movement in East Tennessee in 1860-61. It is in this instance particularly my purpose to trace out the causes of the remarkable influence exercised by Mr. Brownlow on the people of East Tennessee in this great crisis, rather than give the details of his life.

Why did this man have and retain till his death such a hold on the hearts of the people? There must have been strong and sufficient reasons for this remarkable influence. Like Mr. Johnson he had no wealth, no powerful connections to build him up. Until 1862 or 1863, when he made some money by his latest book and by lecturing in Northern cities, it was almost literally true that he had accumulated nothing by his thirty years of incessant activity and toil. This influence, then, did not arise from extraneous circumstances, but was something personal to the man himself.

Perhaps no individual could be named in this country whose home character was so unlike that which he had among strangers. Seldom has any man lived who so constantly and so persistently presented to the world a false and distorted picture of himself, while the genuine picture was seen only by those who were near him. He seemed to delight in creating on the minds of strangers at a distance the most unfavorable impressions; in presenting a false and exaggerated, not to say a revolting, idea of himself. Those who did not know him, and judged him from his writings and speeches, would have supposed his heart was a boiling cauldron full of all evil passions—envy, hate, revenge, unforgiveness, and murderous intents. They could not have believed that the sunshine of peace and good will ever rested on his rugged and tempestuous brow, but that it was always covered with storms and dark clouds. When he wrote he dipped his pen in gall. He seemed to delight in a pandemonium of strife and storm and raging passion.

Yet, nothing could be more unlike than his apparent and his real nature. As a matter of fact, he was far from bitter and malignant. But few men had so much good will, such kindliness, such sympathy, such deep and universal charity. True, at a real or a fancied offense, he flared up in a tempest of wrathful indignation. He poured forth a flood of angry and terrible words. But that was the last of the matter unless the offense was repeated. He would laugh heartily, not in a mocking spirit, but in the utmost good nature over what he had said. By that time all anger had passed away and he was ready for peace. The offer of reconciliation was never declined by him. On accepting peace he neither asked nor granted terms. The quarrel was treated as a thing that had never existed; the reconciliation was sincere and complete; there was no looking backward. There was never a time in his life, in my opinion, when he would not have met the friendly approaches of his bitterest enemies half way; indeed, more than half way. His pride and haughty spirit would have kept him from taking the first step, but when taken by his enemy he would have met the offer in the most sincere and generous manner. Even his long and bitter quarrel with Andrew Johnson, the most malignant one of his life, which lasted more than twenty years, had nearly died out on his part long before 1861, so that the reconciliation of these two strong men, when it took place, was a mere matter of form, and without a word of explanation.

It often occurred to me, as it may have done to others who knew Mr. Brownlow thoroughly, that much of his fierceness and bitterness was assumed for effect. I could not credit the fact that a man who was so mild and gentle in private could be so terrible and so bitter as he appeared to be sometimes, even over a very moderate provocation. It gave him notoriety, made people talk about him, and caused his paper to be read. Besides, he enjoyed the excitement, the "hurly-burly of battle." I do not mean that he was not a sincere man, for he was in all things one of the sincerest, despising all deceitfulness and duplicity. Making allowance for the necessity laid on all party organs to support the principles of their party, it may be affirmed that he would advocate no measure which he did not believe to be right. Fortunately the harness of party is always adjustable, so as to fit nearly all persons. As we shall see hereafter, so great was Mr. Brownlow's devotion to what he thought right, that he had the courage more than once to separate for the time being from his party and stand for a while almost alone. In writing in the tumult and excitement of the moment he often used stronger language than he would have done in his calmer moments. He was hurried forward by the impetuosity of a mighty current of feeling and thought, which overleaped all due bounds and often carried him beyond the confines of cool reason. But he felt and believed all he said at the time. In all impassioned intellects, which act under the strong impulse of sincere conviction or of genius, there is a natural tendency to overcoloring and exaggeration. They see strongly, feel strongly, speak strongly. Mr. Brownlow was an excellent illustration of this truth. Under excitement his was a tempestuous, stormy nature, with powerful convictions.

Strangers, judging Mr. Brownlow by his writings, would most likely have supposed him to be cynical and disagreeable. Most erroneous impression. On the contrary he was warm-hearted, genial, and delightful. No stranger, perhaps, ever spent half an hour with him without an agreeable surprise, for instead of meeting a ferocious mastiff, as he perhaps expected, he met the kindest and the gentlest of men. It was a great mistake to suppose that he was an irritable and ill-natured man. As a general rule, in his daily intercourse with men, he was far beyond most men, mild, gentle, and good-natured. Under circumstances when most men would have given way to wrath, he was patient and forbearing. It was only when an insult was offered, or a wrong done him, that his temper flared up and the lightning flashed from his electric mind. In the family circle he was especially remarkable for his mildness and even temper, and it was the rarest thing for him to be out of humor. In fact, in amiability and patience he was in a high degree uncommon.

As a companion, rarely had he an equal. He abounded in, indeed overflowed with, humor, wit, anecdote, kindliness, and cheerfulness. Everybody delighted to be with him. Men naturally flocked around him. His personal magnetism was phenomenal. Without an effort, without desiring it, without thinking of it, without caring for it, he unconsciously stole away the hearts of men. His kindness to all around him, at all times, was perhaps his most striking characteristic, and he made no distinction between the high and the low, all alike being treated kindly. Literally it was almost an impossibility for him to say no to any request whatever, his heart responding affirmatively to every appeal for help or sympathy. During the greater part of his life he was kept in the depths of poverty by appeals for help and by his inability to say no, becoming security for all who called upon him. During all his life his house was open to all who chose to enter as abiding guests. It was the regular home of all the Methodist preachers and their families who happened to pass his way. In fact, it was a free tavern for all persons.

With few words and no ostentation, guests were made to feel perfectly at home. They came in when they pleased and departed when it suited them. Mrs. Brownlow, his faithful and noble wife, contributed by her never-failing kindness and gentleness to set all guests at ease the moment they entered the house. An earnest man and earnestly at work, Mr. Brownlow had no time for ceremonies. His manners, his tastes, his habits were all most simple. He was the least demonstrative of men— no gush of words, no compliments. Yet men saw in that plain man an original genius, a born leader and hero, and a true friend of humanity.

Another striking trait in the character of Mr. Brownlow was his generosity. Had he possessed large means, he would have been princely in liberality. He never turned away the poor empty-handed. His sympathy for the suffering was sincere and intense. One winter, in Knoxville, while a deep snow lay on the ground, there was suffering among the poor in his neighborhood. Learning this fact, he laid in a supply of food and went around and distributed it with his own hands. When the cholera visited this city in 1854, and almost decimated the population, instead of fleeing for safety, with a sublime and noble courage, he gave himself for nearly a month to the work of nursing and ministering to the sick and the dying and in burying the dead.

It is equally a mistake to suppose that Mr. Brownlow was revengeful or unforgiving. His malice, except under extraordinary wrong, lasted only during the heat of passion. It was as brief as it was violent. Hence it so often occurred in his life, that men whom he had abused with the utmost ferocity became his warmest friends. While it lasted his wrath was terrible, but he knew how to forgive. Mr. Brownlow was too magnanimous for anything mean or dishonorable toward even his worst enemies. Although stealthily waylaid and assailed by would-be assassins in the dark, or from behind, four or five different times, with deadly intent, and more than once with nearly fatal effect, he never attempted to punish the miserable cowards, much less retaliate on them.

Mr. Brownlow's whole life was spent in the earnest advocacy of education, development, and a higher civilization. He was an early and constant advocate of railroads and of every material improvement. While Andrew Johnson was opposing on the stump the construction of the railroad formerly known as the East Tennessee, Virginia, and Georgia road, he (Brownlow) was doing all he could to build this great artery in the heart of our section, which has proved to be, notwithstanding its illiberal and narrow policy, a source of wonderful blessing and prosperity. In him law and order, decency and morality, temperance and religion, found a stalwart defender. The Bible, the Sabbath, and the Sabbath-school, were earnestly upheld by him on all occasions. At no time did he, in any way, or by any word, pander to, or smile at, the sneering assaults made upon the Bible and on our holy religion, by pretended wise men in his day, and notably in later days, the poisonous influence of which is now pouring like a flood on this generation. On the contrary, he stood, as it were, with drawn sword, ready to defend these holy things against all comers. Until enfeebled by ill-health, he always attended church on the Sabbath day, either in town or the country, thus manifesting by his example as well as by his words his reverence for sacred things. In a word, on all moral questions, he was in harmony with the most advanced thought of the age, except on slavery. On this question the despotism of Southern sentiment held him as it did thousands of good men, in its iron fetters, until the Civil War came on.

Mr. Brownlow physically was a remarkable specimen of splendid manhood. In stature he was tall, erect, round, and symmetrical. He was full six feet high, and weighed about 175 pounds. In his prime, few men presented a more manly form. Robust and athletic, in perfect health, it naturally followed that his power of endurance was remarkable. Labor did not seem to exhaust him, and there was no limit to his energy. He was always active and at work. Whatever he undertook was done with rapidity. His frame was vital with energy and force, and there was not a sluggish faculty, member, or impulse in his whole being.

This country has produced few men so absolutely unique as Mr. Brownlow. He was like his fellow men in all respects; was in full harmony with them, and yet he stood out among them with a distinct individuality. He was original and still not odd. He was distinct, and yet not eccentric. He thought as other men, and acted, in most respects, as other men, but in all these manifestations there constantly flashed out that peculiar intensity which made him different from all other men. It was his individualism that distinguished him from all the world.

Mr. Brownlow was to his friends, and to the body of the people who came within his magic spell, irresistible. Men followed him as if impelled by a strange fascination.

The retentive power of Mr. Brownlow's mind was remarkable. It never seemed to lose anything. Whatever entered it was held by an iron grasp. This made him a fearful antagonist. He could at once recall all he had ever known in reference to the record and life of public men. If he became engaged in a controversy with any one of them, if there was a weak spot in that man's armor, either political or personal, an arrow was sure to reach the vulnerable point. He preserved carefully all letters received and all important documents. I have recently been furnished by his son, Colonel John B. Brownlow, with two letters written by me to him as early as 1847.

It was easy for friends to persuade Mr. Brownlow to do anything that did not violate his sense of right; to force him was impossible. A child could lead him; a giant could not drive him. When his mind was once made up, it was as immovable as the mountains. In decision of character he was phenomenal. Never debating long about anything, his mind acted quickly. Almost instantaneously he saw his way. While others were debating he had decided and was acting. At Barboursville, Ky., in November, 1863, during the siege of Knoxville by the Confederate forces under General Longstreet, a number of refugees, among them Baxter, Netherland, Fleming, myself, and others, were debating one morning whether they would remain in that little town, shut off from all communication with the country and await the result of the siege, or go on to Cincinnati, two hundred miles distant, where they could get the news. The council was undecided in opinion. Mr. Brownlow listened, but said not a word. Finally he arose and commenced packing his things. Some one asked him what he meant. Without stopping he replied, "I am going to start at once for Cincinnati." That broke up the conference. In half an hour all that disputing crowd, except one, perhaps, was on its way to Cincinnati, with Mr. Brownlow in the lead. More than once I have seen him in consultation with friends as to what should be written for his paper on some particular point. He would listen attentively for a while to all that was advanced, saying nothing himself. Finally he would hurriedly seize his pen, and commence writing, having decided the matter for himself.

Mr. Brownlow was not a great public speaker; and yet but few men could draw such crowds or so hold their undivided attention. In this respect, as in respect to nearly everything about this remarkable man, there was a magnetic power about him possessed by but few men. He was not eloquent, there was not a flower of rhetoric, not a single effort for mere effect in all his speeches. They were plain, strong, concise. Nothing could be more pointed, or more clear than his sentences, which were fairly heavy with thought, without a surplus word. He drove straight home to the center. His utterances were sharp, incisive, going to the very marrow of controversy. His voice was loud and could be heard at a great distance. He spoke with great deliberation and measured every word. While uttering his most terrible threats, he was as calm and composed outwardly as when sitting in his office talking to a friend. Indeed his absolute composure under the most exciting circumstances was one of his peculiarities. He never lost presence of mind nor self control. In 1852, I heard a so-called political discussion, but in fact a personal quarrel, between him and General Thomas D. Arnold, who was for a great many years well known in Tennessee as an anti-Jackson man and a Whig, and who for two terms had been a Member of Congress. Arnold had but few equals in wit, sarcasm, and personal vituperation. For nearly one hour he poured out a stream of abuse on Brownlow, in the bitterest and most taunting manner, with the most defiant spirit. During all this time Brownlow stood perfectly cool and collected, only occasionally smiling good naturedly at the worst parts of the speech. When the storm of words had spent its fury, then, that calm man proceeded in his rejoinder, in a deliberate manner, to make one of the most terrible diatribes ever uttered on the stump. Yet these two men were not badly matched.

With all his extravagance of utterance, even in the very midst of the vehemence and fury of passion, his mind was as cool and as deliberate as if addressing a Sabbath-school. There was no hurry, no flurry, no violence of manner. Each word, each sentence was weighed as carefully, apparently, as if he had been under the sanction of an oath. He was calm, collected, and deliberate even in his most bitter harangues. Never have I seen a mind so cool as his when under the influence of overpowering excitement. He stood as motionless as a statue when hurling against his enemies his most terrible denunciations. No provocation, no taunt, no jeer, could ever disturb or unsettle the perfect balance of his mind. There was no tremor on his lips, no quaver in the voice, no wild gesticulation. His voice, however, was full of terror, and sounded like the roar of an enraged lion.

There was never any confusion in the words and ideas of Mr. Brownlow—no halting, no hesitation. He knew what he wanted to say and he said it in the clearest and most concise manner. As the words dropped from his lips, they were ready for the press. So clearly did he see things, that his ideas at once drew around them the appropriate drapery of strong and vigorous speech. Before he lost his voice, in 1861-62, he spoke often, and always with marked effect. He was in fact a very powerful speaker.

Judging Mr. Brownlow by his photographs and pictures, which are generally correct likenesses, it would be supposed that he was a sour, stern man, yet nothing could be further from the fact. He was not stern; he was not sour. Good nature and kindly humor bubbled up from his heart as naturally as springs bubble up from the hillsides of his own loved East Tennessee. They were spontaneous and never ceasing. His humor was harmless and innocent. There was no sting, no poison in it. In his better days of health and robustness, his good natured humor was incessant. Sometimes it was grotesque; often it was a surprise, but always refreshing, cheerful, and kind. The following anecdote will illustrate how grotesque and unexpected his humor sometimes was.

One afternoon, in December, 1863, a number of gentlemen of whom I was one, were returning with him from Cincinnati, to their home at Knoxville, and were stopping for a night at a comfortable country inn near the foot of the "Big Hill," south of Richmond, Ky. The party had eaten their supper and had gone to their rooms to talk and smoke. Mr. Brownlow had undressed very early, as was his custom, and had gotten into bed. He closed his eyes and seemed to be asleep, but in fact was wide awake. He often did this when he did not wish to be bored with tiresome company. To his intimate friends this was the signal for fun and frolic and anecdote telling, which I have known to keep up until after midnight.

On this evening about the time he lay down a large Kentucky farmer of a genuine type, free and easy going, drove up to stay all night. He had just been to market and sold his surplus farm stock for a good sum in cash. Naturally he was feeling good. He had with him what no good Kentuckian ever travels without, a bottle of old Bourbon, which he had not neglected that raw evening. Soon after entering the inn he was told that the "celebrated Parson Brownlow" was in the house. He said he must see him. The fact that he had gone to bed did not stop him. On learning the room he occupied, he boldly entered and presented himself before Mr. Brownlow, lying in bed with his eyes closed. He said, "Is this Parson Brownlow?" The latter, opening his eyes, said that it was. The Kentuckian said: "Mr. Brownlow, I heard you were here and I just came in to see you. I have been a reader of your paper for many years." Here Mr. Brownlow in a deep, sepulchral tone, said solemnly and impressively, "And a good religious paper, too, you have been reading." The Kentuckian was confounded at this. He was too polite to deny it, and yet he did not quite like the idea of agreeing that Brownlow's paper was a "good religious" one. So, after hesitating a moment, he drawled out, "Y-e-s, it is a good religious paper, b-ut there are—for a religious paper—some *pretty rough places* in it, too." Mr. Brownlow continued immovable and imperturbable until after his visitor left, and then he broke out into a hearty laugh at the embarrassment and surprise of his new friend.

I have somewhere heard this anecdote, perhaps read it in some of Mr. Brownlow's early writings: When he was a young man he was fishing one Sunday on the banks of a river. A Methodist minister passed by and, reprimanding him severely, asked him what he was trying to catch. The reply was, "The Devil." "What kind of bait do you use?" said the preacher. "A Methodist minister," said Brownlow.

It can now be seen from a review of the foregoing characteristics why Mr. Brownlow's influence was so omnipotent with the great body of the people in East Tennessee at the breaking out of the war in 1861. I do not hesitate to affirm as my opinion, that in shaping and fixing the opinions of the Whigs at that time, in that never-to-be-forgotten contest, he exerted a deeper and wider influence in favor of the Union than any other man. This he did through his widely-circulated paper. The great body of the people loved him almost to idolatry. They believed in him, they had confidence in him.

CHAPTER II.

Fidelity to Friends—Newspaper Warfare with George D. Prentice—Attitude Toward Slavery—*Whig* of April 20, 1861—After Battle of Bull Run—Belief in Long Continuance of War—North Had No Conception of Spirit of War in South—North and South Not Alien Races—The Covenanter—The Merrimac—The Dutch, Irish, and German Contingent—Not Surprising Southern Soldiers Won First Victories—The Puritan—Small Farmer.

ONE of the striking features in the character of Mr. Brownlow was his fidelity to his friends, whom he never betrayed nor deserted. With all the tenacity of his strong will, with all the warmth of his big heart, he clung to those who had proved themselves true to him. He could not do too much for them. No sacrifice on his part was too great for them. To promote the political fortunes of John Bell he devoted the columns of his paper and his best talents for nearly twenty years, never wavering in his support until Mr. Bell, most reluctantly, I believe, joined the secession movement after the firing on Sumter. They parted in sadness, and not in anger. After that, if Mr. Brownlow ever said anything unkind of him, I have forgotten it. I witnessed their last interview, which took place in my house. It was sad, it was almost pitiable to see Mr. Bell in his fallen condition—so humble, so stricken with despair. Most plainly he saw and felt, as I believe, his fatal mistake. In a moment of weakness he had been caught in the toils of secession.

In working for friends Mr. Brownlow was noble, generous, and self-forgetful. There was no half-hearted devotion. There were two other personal and political friends in whose interest he never faltered—Meredith P. Gentry and Thomas A. R. Nelson. For the former he entertained an enthusiastic admiration; for the latter, profound respect and friendship.

No one who knew Mr. Brownlow ever questioned his high courage, both physical and moral, and it was too often tested for any doubt. In derision he was called the "fighting parson," an epithet calculated to produce an erroneous impression, for he was never but once the assailant. In all his rencontres, except as just stated, he fought in self-defense. He believed in this right, and was always prompt to use the means necessary for this purpose.

There was nothing that was mean or little about him. His was a big nature—all his instincts noble, his impulses generous, his purposes high, his thoughts open as day. No thin disguise, no deceitful veil concealed the real man. The world—all the world—knew his inmost mind. Candor, frankness, openness marked his whole career.

No one at this day will question the fact that he was a very remarkable man. In many respects he was the most singular, not to say striking, character of his generation. His intellect was unquestionably of a superior order. No one of mediocre intellect could have run his successful career. Successes like those achieved by him and Mr. Johnson must rest on inherent strength and power. Inferior men, by the aid of favoring circumstances, may blaze up for an hour. But here in these men, without wealth or education or adventitious aids, there was continuous, permanent success. Each step upward was so firmly planted as to permit other and higher steps. In the case of Mr. Brownlow these successes are all the more remarkable, because at no time did he rise by any base, or false, or flattering appeals to the prejudices or selfish passions of men.

The mind of Mr. Brownlow was singularly quick. He saw things at a glance, and with perfect clearness. There was no haze, no fog, no murkiness in his intellectual atmosphere. His ideas were as clear cut as gold coin fresh from the mint. His sentences were sharp, crisp, transparent. He aimed right at the mark. His thoughts, hurled by his vigorous intellect, went crashing through the center, like an arrow shot by the strong arms of a skillful bowman. In writing he dashed off his matter with the utmost rapidity. His ideas flowed into his mind in torrents, but there was no confusion, each thought coming in its natural sequence. What he wrote on the hot impulse was printed just as he wrote it. There was no correcting nor pruning. His intellect sifted out the dross as he went, leaving only the pure gold. Sometimes his language was rough, but it was always strong and ringing. His invective was terrible, falling on his victim with crushing, titanic force. In this respect he had but one equal in the country—the brilliant George D. Prentice of the Louisville *Journal*.*

Many a public man gained a notoriety from Mr. Brownlow's pen which he never could have won himself, and generally when he got through with a man in these controversies, that man was greatly injured in reputation.

Another instance of the power of Mr. Brownlow in controversy may be found in that of his last quarrel with Mr. Johnson, after the latter left the Presidency, of which an account is given in the latter part of this sketch.

Before the war, in common with nearly all Southern men, Brownlow was a firm believer in the institution of slavery, though not a slave owner. In 1858, in the city of Philadelphia, he had a joint debate lasting several days with the Rev. A. Pryne on this subject, in which he advocated the justice and morality of slavery as well as its economic advantages. At this day it is amazing to look back at the false and perverted ideas Southern men held at that time on this subject. It is to be observed, however, that they were brought up and educated from infancy in the belief that slavery was morally right.

---

*While Brownlow was Governor of Tennessee, in 1867, the most terrific newspaper warfare was carried on by these two men, in their respective papers, that ever occurred in this country. It arose in this way: Mr. George Baber, a young man on the newspaper staff of Mr. Prentice, wrote a short article, only a few inches in length, criticising the administration of Mr. Brownlow as Governor of Tennessee. Colonel John B. Brownlow, the eldest son of the Governor, then a young man also, seeing the article, wrote and published in an editorial a very bitter reply while his father was in Nashville. When the paper containing this reply reached Louisville Mr. Baber was overwhelmed at the difficulty he had unintentionally brought upon his principal. He took the article to Mr. Prentice in fear and trembling. When the latter read it, he only laughed good-humoredly and said he would answer it. At the same time he spoke of Mr. Brownlow in terms of friendship and admiration. He accordingly answered the article in that style peculiar to him when enraged. Then, on the other side, Mr. Brownlow took up the quarrel for himself. The controversy grew hotter and hotter, until nothing like it has perhaps ever been witnessed in the country. Prentice, after writing and reading to Mr. Baber one of his most brilliant articles, laughed most heartily at what he had said. He delighted in the noise and roar of battle. In this respect Mr. Brownlow was just like him. After writing his most furious articles against men, he would shake his head and laugh most heartily, as if he had perpetrated a good joke.

The above facts I recently learned from the lips of the two persons who involved their respective principals in the bitterest and most notable personal quarrel of that day. They were discussing that controversy in my presence in the city of Washington and laughing over the part that each had taken in it.

Therefore they never questioned the correctness of this belief. Indeed, but few men had the courage to do so. To have doubted would have fastened the brand of abolitionism on the doubter. No stigma was so odious and disgraceful as that of the abolitionist, and but few men had the courage to incur that certain and fearful odium. Mr. Brownlow thought on this subject in harmony with the almost universal belief among ministers as well as laymen in the South. The Reverend Drs. Palmer, Thornwell, Ross, Dabney, and others had defended slavery in the pulpit and the press, as Mr. Brownlow did, as a divine institution. However, when red-handed war, in the name and cause of slavery, clutched at the throat and aimed at the life of the nation, the latter, almost alone among all the prominent ministers of the South, broke to pieces his idol and turned away from it. With him the first, the highest, and the last duty was due not to slavery, but to his Government. His first allegiance and love were given to the Union, whether slavery should survive or whether it should perish.

Having supported John Bell for the Presidency in 1860 on the Constitutional (Union) platform, and being a Whig—indeed a Federalist—nothing was more natural than that Mr. Brownlow should have opposed secession after the election of Mr. Lincoln. In his paper of November 17, 1860, in an editorial he said:

"Let them (the Secessionists) know whenever they meet you that as law-abiding citizens, loyal to our blood-bought government, you will never consent to see our soil ravaged by the terrible strife which would result from secession, and on the very threshold proclaim your determination to oppose all the mad schemes of disunion and to stand by this Union of States. * * * Tell these secret emissaries and street talkers that you admit the value of *cotton* as an article of commerce, but remind them in the next breath that Kentucky and Missouri hemp, *as a necklace for* TRAITORS, is an article of still greater value for *home consumption.*"

In his issue of April 20, 1861, Mr. Brownlow said:

"The first shot fired by the rebels will unite the Northern States in the battle for the Union, and arm two hundred thousand men for the conflict."

Again in the same paper he said:

"We shall rejoice in the success of American arms over these seceding rebels as sincerely as we did in the triumph over the Spanish rebels on the bloody plains of Mexico."

On April 27, he said:

"Every paper in the fifteen slave States may declare for a Southern Confederacy, and charge the cause of this cruel and unnatural war on Lincoln; we shall deny the fact as long as we have our senses, and refuse to the day of our death to go into a Southern Confederacy, or to agree that honor, patriotism, or a love of country influenced the vile, hypocritical, corrupt, and insincere leaders who have plunged the Cotton States into this revolution."

I might quote extracts like the foregoing, almost enough to fill a large volume, showing the deep hatred of Mr. Brownlow for a Southern Confederacy.

Let me present some contrasts between the language and spirit of three noted men, written in July, 1861, after the great battle of Bull Run. The first is from the pen of the great War Secretary, Edwin M. Stanton, who had been Attorney General under Mr. Buchanan, but who was at this time a dissatisfied private citizen. It is hard to escape the suspicion of a personal pique on his part toward Mr. Lincoln because he was not retained by him in his Cabinet when Mr. Buchanan retired. In a letter addressed to Mr. Buchanan, lately President of the United States, dated July 26, 1861, Mr. Stanton said:*

"The dreadful disaster of Sunday can scarcely be mentioned. The imbecility of the Administration culminated in that catastrophe; an irretrievable misfortune and national disgrace, never to be forgotten, are to be added to the ruin of all peaceful pursuits and national bankruptcy as the result of Lincoln's 'running the machine.' * * * The capture of Washington seems now to be inevitable; during the whole of Monday and Tuesday it might have been taken without any resistance. The rout, overthrow, and utter demoralization of the whole army is complete. Even now I doubt whether any serious opposition to the entrance of the Confederate forces could be offered. While Lincoln, Scott, and the Cabinet are disputing as to who is to blame, the city is unguarded and the enemy is at hand."

This letter does Mr. Lincoln injustice. That there was weakness at that time in the prosecution of the war admits of no

---

*John Van Buren said that Mr. Buchanan sat in the White House like a bread-and-milk poultice drawing the rebellion to a head.

doubt. But Mr. Lincoln was doing all he could. He was inexperienced as his counselors all were. He had to trust the army officers, and a war of such immense proportions was new to them also. The army had to advance and offer battle before it was ready to satisfy the insane clamor of the North. No Copperhead would have sneered in that dark hour at Mr. Lincoln more savagely than Mr. Stanton did. It is not singular that it was addressed to James Buchanan.

The next is an extraordinary letter written by Horace Greeley, July 29, 1861, and addressed to Mr. Lincoln. Mr. Greeley, it must be kept in mind, was a Northern man and a Republican, who had done more, perhaps, than any one man in the United States, through his great paper, the New York *Tribune*, to embitter the two sections of the country. For weeks before the disastrous battle to which he refers, he had, day after day, urged an advance of the army at Washington. His battle cry had been, "On to Richmond." General Scott, then in command of the army, as well as Mr. Lincoln, knew the army was not ready to move, but an impatient public, incited and urged on by Mr. Greeley and others, clamored until it was deemed best to move, though unprepared. The result was the disaster at Bull Run, the first important battle of the war. Mr. Greeley's letter was as follows:

"This is my seventh sleepless night—yours, too, doubtless. * * * Can the rebels be beaten after all that has occurred, and in view of the actual state of feeling caused by our late awful disaster? If they can—and it is your business to ascertain and decide—write me that such is your judgment, so that I may know and do my duty. And if they *cannot* be beaten—if our recent disaster is fatal—do not fear to sacrifice yourself to your country. If the rebels are not to be beaten—if that is your judgment in view of all the light you can get—then every drop of blood hereafter shed in this quarrel will be wantonly, wickedly shed, and the guilt will rest hereafter on the soul of every promoter of the crime.

"If the Union is irrevocably gone, an armistice for thirty, sixty, ninety, one hundred and twenty days—better still, for a year—ought at once to be proposed, with a view to a peaceful adjustment. Then Congress should call a national convention to meet at the earliest possible day. * * * I do not consider myself at present a judge of anything but the public sentiment. That seems to me everywhere gathering and deepening against the prosecution of the war. The gloom in this city is funereal. * * * On every brow sits sullen, scorching, black despair. It would be easy to have Mr. Crittenden to move any proposition that ought to be adopted, or to have it come from any proper quarter. * * *"

Most wisely Mr. Lincoln never answered this remarkable letter. Now listen to the lion-hearted Brownlow, speaking from the heart of the Southern Confederacy—from a State in actual insurrection—surrounded by Confederate armies, and by men who sought his life. In his paper of July 13, 1861, he said, among other things:

"This great popular Union heart has thus far admirably withstood all such unfavorable influences, and is still stoutly braced for the conflict before it. The President calls for an army of 400,000 men, and for four hundred millions of dollars to put this war through and to crush out this wicked, treasonable, hell-born, and hell-bound rebellion. Congress will grant all these men and all this money, and we predict with perfect confidence that the Government forces will be victorious; that the Constitution and the laws will be upheld; that the wicked and corrupt men who inaugurated secession will be overthrown, and their names go down to posterity associated only with infamy."

Again in his paper of July 27, one day after Mr. Stanton's letter was written to Mr. Buchanan, and two days before that of Mr. Greeley, just quoted—all writing about the same question—he said:

"We publish the proceedings of a Peace Convention in West Tennessee, composed of delegates from counties voting in favor of the Union. The move is to memorialize the two governments to terminate the war. We believe it to be a wicked, unnatural and uncalled for war—that the South commenced it without sufficient cause—and that it ought never to have been commenced. But strange as it may seem to many of our readers, we are opposed to any sudden or abrupt termination of the war.

"We have been assured on all hands, by politicians, clergymen, and scores of the people that God is on the side of the Southern Confederacy, and that they are therefore bound to triumph. We are further assured by the press and the army officers that *one* Southern man can whip *five* Yankees. We do not believe either proposition, and never did, and therefore we favor prosecuting the war until we have these controverted questions settled. If God be on the side of the Confederate troops, we desire to go with them. And if one Southerner can whip five Yankees, we don't want to advocate a Union whose troops can't fight. These are questions which ought to be settled, and this can only be done by carrying on the war."

How artful is the above, and what a fine vein of sarcasm and irony runs through it!

On August 3, he said in an editorial:

"Our candid opinion is that the war will not terminate under three or four years. * * * The war was inaugurated in the South, and by the South, and the whole tone of the Southern people and press, and especially of the leading politicians, is favorable to a desperate and long-continued conflict. The tone of the administration at Washington, the spirit of Congress, and of the whole Northern people, is warlike, calling for a vindication of the Government and for its maintenance against a rebellion they believe was not called for. Denounced as vandal hordes and stigmatized as cowards, they are resolved upon vindicating their honor and giving the world the evidence of their courage. The capital of their government they are resolved on protecting, or dying within the sacred surroundings thereof."

It may be mentioned as a curious fact that the brilliant Greeley, in the latter part of 1862,* wrote to M. Mercier, the French Minister at Washington, suggesting that he should secure the mediation of the French Government between the contending belligerents in order to put an end to the war. So, too, he opened up negotiations for a cessation of the war with some irresponsible parties in Canada in 1864, and got himself into a rather ridiculous attitude. In fact, he gave Mr. Lincoln more trouble than an open enemy of the Government would have done. He was so vacillating, so unsteady, not to say so cranky, that he was constantly getting out of harmony with the ever-determined, level-headed, and unfaltering President. In 1862 he dismissed Charles A. Dana as managing editor of the New York *Tribune,* because Mr. Dana, as he states, was for vigorously prosecuting the war, while Mr. Greeley was for peace. His paper, from its vast influence with the great body of the Northern people, and from the well-known ability of Mr. Greeley, ought to have been the strongest support of Mr. Lincoln

---

*Nicolay and Hay, Vol. VI, p. 83.

in the prosecution of the war; but by reason of the vagaries of that erratic man it became sometimes an obstruction to the national cause.

It has never been clear to my mind whether the defeat of the Federal army at Bull Run was, in the end, a disaster to the North or a "blessing in disguise." Did it prolong the war? Was a disaster needed by the North to arouse it to a sense of the magnitude of its danger, and the stupendous task it had on hand? Would a Union victory have disheartened the South and broken its spirit? Would the Southern Confederacy have commenced falling to pieces after one signal defeat? I think I can safely say, emphatically no, as to the last two questions. That a defeat in the first great battle of the war would have disheartened to some extent the people of the South can be safely affirmed, but it would not have broken their spirit. They would have gathered up their strength for a new and mightier effort on some other field. They had staked all on the great issues of war, and their proud and determined spirit would never have yielded with one defeat, however disastrous. Never were men braver or more determined. They were animated by an intensity of feeling and an earnestness of purpose never surpassed in the annals of war. This feeling and purpose were shared by all classes, ages, and sexes. War—war until their independence should be won—became the sole purpose of the whole people. Nothing else was thought of, talked of, or dreamed of. Eternal war was to be waged until victory crowned their daring efforts. No sacrifice of life or of treasure was too costly in order to secure this great end. The spirit of this brave people was never broken. It finally yielded only to absolute exhaustion, when human endurance could bear no more, and when the power of effectual resistance had ceased. When Sheridan captured and burned the provision trains sent to supply the starving army at Appomattox, he conquered Lee. Despair then settled on the hearts of the starving men who had never known what fear was.

On the other hand, it cannot be denied that the Northern people were surprised and overwhelmed by their defeat at Bull Run. To use the language of Mr. Greeley, "there sat upon every brow, sullen, scorching, black despair." But they needed this defeat. Indeed they needed and got many Bull Runs before they realized the greatness of the contest in which they were engaged. Never were a people more greatly deluded in their opinions as to the war. Mr. Seward assured the Foreign Ambassadors that the uprising would be suppressed in ninety days. General Wool, when informed at Fortress Monroe of the fall of New Orleans, said that that would end the war.

The people of the North believed that the noise and wild cry for war in the South, with the boasted preparations, were mere braggadocio—the froth and foam of political excitement—which would soon evaporate and pass away. They had no conception of the delirious spirit of war which everywhere existed, impelling a whole people toward battlefields. They did not dream of their deep and determined purpose to achieve independence, or sacrifice all they had in the attempt. They did not know, or if they knew, they did not care for the fact that all business, all thought of business, was abandoned for the great purpose of war. Nor had they any idea of the vast resources of the South. They did not dream of the ingenuity and inventive genius which necessity would call forth, and did call forth, enabling the Southern people to supply the means and resources necessary for the equipment of armies, almost equal to those furnished by their own shops and factories, or purchased from abroad. They had no conception of the bravery and endurance which the well-reared and luxurious Southerner would manifest in sustaining a cause as dear to his heart as life itself. They had no conception either of the vast supplies of grain and provisions which Southern fields could furnish. They did not dream that the delicate sons of Southern planters, accustomed only to ease, luxury, and pleasure, would make as good soldiers as ever went into battle; that they could live for days at a time on half rations—composed of food such as would have created a mutiny in a Northern army; that they could endure hardships, fatigues, and privations such as were never surpassed. And back of all this the Northern people did not know, and could not realize the fact, that the women of the South, both young and old, high and low, were urging on their fathers and sons and brothers with an enthusiastic spirit scarcely ever known in history. The men who would not fight in such a glorious cause for the rights and the liberties of the South were denounced by them as cowards, recreants, and traitors, worthy only of infamy and dishonor. In fact, the earnest spirit of the people of the South in defense of their supposed rights was not understood by the North until the war was half over, and even then it was not wholly understood. Never were a people more earnest, more determined, and, for the most part, more honest in fighting, not only for their independence, but for their liberties likewise. The people of both sections sadly misunderstood each other. The North miscalculated, as we have pointed out, the spirit and the determination of the people of the South. The Southern people, on the contrary, greatly undervalued the courage of the Northern people. They believed honestly that Northern men would not fight. The boast and the claim were everywhere made that one Southern man could whip five Yankees.

Why the Southern people should have been so infatuated is incomprehensible. It would seem that history and a little reflection ought to have taught them better. The Northern and the Southern people were, for the larger part, of substantially the same blood and race. While far from being homogeneous in sentiment, opinion, and in customs, they were not so unlike as to make them two distinct peoples, as are the English and the French. There had been at all times, since the settlement of the colonies, a considerable intermingling of the people of the two sections. Northern people had come South, and Southern people had gone North, and especially into the Northwest. Ohio, Indiana, Illinois, and Iowa received a large percentage of their population from Virginia, Kentucky, and Tennessee. There were entire neighborhoods in Illinois composed of Tennesseans. Kansas was largely settled by people from Missouri, Kentucky, and Tennessee. The dominant race in Pennsylvania to-day, the Covenanters, commonly called the Scotch-Irish, and perhaps in New Jersey and Delaware also, as well as a large element in New York and Ohio, is the same race that is so large and influential in Virginia, Tennessee, Kentucky, North and South Carolina, and in Georgia, and indeed in all the Southern States. This race molded and fashioned the institutions of North Carolina, South Carolina, Tennessee, and Kentucky, and perhaps had the largest influence of any race in the same direction in Virginia. From the busy hives of those States, for more than fifty years, had poured toward the West a constant stream of Covenanter blood. The Puritan and the Covenanter, and to some extent the Cavalier, had met (in the West) on the same great theater of activity and enterprise, and had become a homogeneous people. The Dutch of New York and the Germans of Pennsylvania had, along with the Covenanters, found their way in considerable numbers into Virginia and Tennessee, while the Puritan had gone everywhere, and was to be found everywhere, at the opening of the late war.

Thus the people of the North and the South were largely of the same blood, except in New England, when our great Civil War broke out, and they were in no sense alien races. It is especially to be noted that the Covenanter—that hardy, tenacious, brave people, who never yielded, never turned back, but always went forward to the full accomplishment of its purpose— was scattered everywhere throughout the South, and through the North and the Northwest, and was to be found in every State and Territory, even in considerable numbers in New England. The whole history of that people—their deadly struggle for one hundred years with tyrants and priestly bigots in Scotland, their heroic sufferings in Ireland, and their splendid courage and noble patriotism in the Colonies in behalf of liberty— bore testimony to the fact that in whichever army they might be, whether in that of the North or that of the South, there would be unyielding courage and persistent fighting, and that the war would never cease until one side or the other was overcome by exhaustion.

Before the North, with almost humiliating subserviency, had ceased to dream of concessions and compromises, in 1861, there arose in the South, out of chaotic elements, a government working in harmonious order, strong and vigorous in its administration, and haughty, confident, and defiant in spirit. With almost incredible promptitude they organized, equipped, and put into the field large armies, led by able generals, and won great victories. For nearly four years they waged against nearly three times their numbers in population, an obstinate and unequal contest, becoming the wonder and the admiration of the civilized world. With scanty material they improvised warships which carried dismay into the navy of their great rival. The *Merrimac*, hurriedly constructed, swept everything before it and caused universal consternation up to the moment of the timely appearance of the *Monitor*, commanded by the daring Lieutenant John L. Worden, which, after perhaps the most remarkable fight recorded in naval warfare, put an end to this work of destruction. Confederate cruisers were put afloat, which threatened to drive from the high seas the commerce of the United States. No merchant ship was anywhere safe from the destructive energy and daring of such men as Captain Raphael Semmes. It was late in the war before the gallant Captain John A. Winslow, in his splendid ship, the *Kearsarge*, overtook the *Alabama* and challenged her to battle. After a splendid fight, in the presence of thousands of spectators who lined the French shore, the Confederate cruiser was sent to the bottom of the ocean.

A little recollection of history ought to have dispelled the idea that the Northern people would not fight. The racial elements of which this people was mostly composed were the Puritans, the Covenanters, the Dutch, the Germans, and the Irish. The Covenanters, as before stated, had long ago established their reputation for courage in their great contest with the crown of England, and with a Papal and Episcopal Prelacy in their struggle for religious freedom.

The Irish and the Germans were everywhere known to be brave. The Dutch were the descendants of the brave men who, under the lead of William the Silent, had made the grandest fight for freedom recorded in all history against the immense power of Phillip II of Spain, finally ending in the independence and the establishment of the Dutch Republic. The Puritans, too, had a history resplendent with deeds of noble courage. It was the untrained plowmen of New England, with a courage scarcely ever surpassed, who stood the first shock of the Revolution and made the names of Concord, Lexington, and Bunker Hill immortal.

It was the descendants of these several historic people, scattered from Maine to the Pacific Coast, which the Southern leaders challenged to battle. When the war opened they were engaged in the peaceful pursuits of life and wholly unused to war. Never, perhaps, were a people in feelings, thoughts, and habits less prepared for martial pursuits. A majority of them were small farmers engaged in tilling the soil. Others were tradesmen, mechanics, and laborers. But in them still lingered the spirit, though dormant for the time, of their ancestors.

It was no surprise that Southern soldiers won the first battles of the war. They possessed more dash, and were more impetuous than Northern men. In the sense of the word as used in the South, they had a keener sense of honor—more spirit, more chivalry. They were accustomed to fights and duels. An insult was sure to be followed by a blow, or must be avenged on the field of honor. The spirit of chivalry was a part of the life of the Southern gentlemen. The laws of honor were next in their hearts to their religion. To fail to resent an insult was a perpetual disgrace. They were ready for any danger, for the most daring enterprises. They sighed for glory in politics or in war. Such were the majority of the Southern people. They were brave, generous, and magnanimous. While fond of luxury and magnificence, these were as dross in comparison with honor and glory. They were intense in feeling, earnest in opinion, and prompt in action. Wealth and luxury were only stepping-stones on which to mount to power and position. They had a contempt for what Senator Hammond of South Carolina called the "mudsills"—the mechanics and laboring men—of the North. The Puritan was in the estimation of the South the synonym of abasement, selfishness, and hypocrisy. The shoemakers of Lynn and the cotton and wool spinners and weavers of Lowell were base churls, with no manhood, no spirit, no courage. I am happy to say that the South has no such feeling to-day.

The Puritan was supposed to be the type of the Northern people. He was the representative of perhaps the largest class. In temperament he was patient, tenacious, and resolute. In action he was persistent, never turning back, but always moving forward with steadiness of purpose toward the aim and object of life. With constant assiduity he pushed forward new enterprises, fostered education and science, and encouraged development and progress.

He settled the wilderness and embarked in commerce on the high seas among the nations, gathering treasure from every part of the globe. Wherever a dollar was to be made, there he was found receiving his full share. Like the ram seen in the vision, he pushed North and East, West and South. He was ready to argue and dispute. He demanded his own, even to the last iota. However humble his station, he gathered around himself all the comforts and conveniences of life. He read and thought and formed his own opinions. Books and newspapers and magazines were to be found in every home. He did not deem it necessary to fight at every insult. He was long suffering and forbearing, but no earthly power could make him yield to wrong or give up what he thought was right. Though he was smeared with dust and soot, he often possessed a cunning in logic and an extent of knowledge that would have surprised and confounded those who were disposed to sneer at him. Despised as he was by Southern men, he possessed an intelligence, a keen sense of right and wrong that made him tenacious in defense of whatever principles he had once espoused. When, therefore, he went to the battlefield he carried with him convictions so firmly rooted in his mind that he was ready to risk his life for them. No better material for soldiers could anywhere be found. He was guided by a sense of duty and fought for a purpose.

In estimating the qualities of Northern men for fighting the Southern people overlooked these elements in the character of the Puritans. They also overlooked the great class of small farmers who constituted the largest part of the Northern population. These were the men who constituted at least the larger part of all Northern armies. These were men for the most part who knew perfectly well the principles and issues involved in the war. When trained as soldiers, no men were braver or cooler in action. They were wanting in the impetuosity of Southern soldiers, but they had quite as much endurance, persistency, and determination. It has been said that an army when well trained is a machine. It is controlled by one man, guided by one mind, and moves as one man. The timid are inspired and carried along by the courage of the bravest. So, in battle, the same spirit runs along the whole line. It thus becomes a solid phalanx, a machine.

Judging by their past history, why should not the Puritan have fought as bravely as the Southerner? It was the ancestors of these men who wrested the crown from Charles I and sent him to the block. It was they who under the lead of Cromwell destroyed the monarchy of England and established the Commonwealth. It was the Puritan and the yeomanry of England who were fashioned by his genius and iron will into the most irresistible body of men seen since the time of the Roman Legions under Julius Cæsar. Before it the gentry and nobility of England under the fiery Rupert were scattered and almost annihilated on the field of Naseby. In nearly every conflict, in nearly every skirmish, the nobility and higher classes were overcome and signally routed by the psalm-singing Puritans. Naseby and Marston Moor are the lasting monuments of their bravery. Then, as at a later day, they were derided for their nasal drawling speech and wild fanaticism. They were sneered at as low-born churls, without spirit, without courage, and without manhood. But when the day of battle came a tremendous conviction of right and justice gave them a power and a might which nothing could withstand. These were the ancestors of the Massachusetts Puritans.

Come down to a later period; the Southern people should have remembered that the men opposed to them were capable of fighting by their conduct during the Mexican War. In the bloody battle of Buena Vista the soldiers of Illinois, under Hardin and Bissell, fought side by side with the soldiers of Arkansas under Yell; of Kentucky under Clay, McKee, and Marshall, and of Mississippi under Jefferson Davis. Nor has less honor been given to one than to the other. Hardin earned on that battlefield by the highest display of courage no less renown than Yell and McKee and Clay. He was equally lamented with them in his and their sad death on that bloody field of glory.

Such were some of the traits and characteristics of the two great belligerent forces which were arrayed against each other in the summer and fall of 1861. The South had been wrought up to a furious state of madness. The North was not yet in full earnest. It needed more defeats to arouse it from its sad delusions.

CHAPTER III.

Discontinued Publication of Paper, October 24, 1861—Flight of Union Men to Kentucky—Thornburg and Perez Dickinson Arrested—Brownlow Refuses to Take Oath—Abortive Attempt to Escape Into Kentucky — Bridge-burning, November 8, 1861 — Brownlow Escapes to Mountain—Crittenden Offers Passport After Letter from Benjamin—Brownlow Arrested—March 3, 1862, Permitted to Start for Nashville—Flag of Truce—Brownlow Meets Johnson at Capitol.

UNDER the gloomy conditions pointed out in the foregoing chapter, away down in the heart of the South, there was one man who realized the situation; who was not intimidated at the appalling dangers hanging over his country, and who still refused to bow his knee to Baal. This was W. G. Brownlow. In spite of the constant dangers which surrounded him, he continued to publish his paper until October 24, 1861. In no issue did it waver in his openly declared devotion to the Union. All men knew how he stood. In all the secession States his paper alone faltered not. All the other Union leaders and papers had long since gone over to the support of the Confederacy, or had silently disappeared. Let it be kept in mind, also, that the people of Tennessee had voted in June in favor of separation from the Federal Government; that every vestige of the authority of the United States had disappeared; that it was superseded by the insignia and the power of the Confederacy; that there was a Confederate army stationed at Knoxville, and that this point was Department Headquarters, with General Zollicoffer in command. Let it also be kept in mind that after the battle of Manassas the prospects of a restored Union, viewed from a Southern standpoint, were gloomy in the extreme. Mr. Nelson had been arrested and silenced. Mr. Johnson and Mr. Maynard and other prominent men were refugees in the North. The other leaders who had not fled, had become silent, forced to do so. Thousands of Union men who had nerved the heart and strengthened the arms of Mr. Brownlow and his associates while the fight was still going on, had fled, or were daily fleeing, for safety to Kentucky. Dr. J. W. Thornburgh had been arrested on a charge of treason, and taken to Nashville for imprisonment and trial. Mr. Perez Dickinson had also been arrested and other arrests were occurring daily. Universal gloom, fear, and despondency, like a dark pall, had settled on the hearts and minds of the Union people, and the light of hope was well nigh extinguished in all their hearts.

Yet amid all this darkness, Mr. Brownlow still pleaded for the Union, still kept the Stars and Stripes floating in defiance from his house. On October 12th, the following taunting article appeared in his paper:

"To Arms! To Arms! Ye Braves!"

"Come Tennesseeans! Ye who are the advocates of Southern Rights, for Separation and Disunion—ye who have lost your rights and feel willing to uphold the glorious flag of the South, in opposition to the Hessians arrayed under the despot, Lincoln, come to your country's rescue! Our gallant Governor, who led off in this State in the praiseworthy object of breaking up the old rickety Government in the hands of the Black Republicans, calls for 30,000 volunteers, in addition to the 55,000 already in the field. Shall we have them? If they do not volunteer, we shall have our State disgraced by *draft*, and then we must go under compulsion. Come, gentlemen! many of you have promised that 'when it becomes necessary,' you will turn out. That time has come and the *necessity* is upon us. Let us show our *faith* by our *works*. We have talked long and loud about fighting the Union shriekers and the vandal hordes under the Despot, Lincoln. Now we have an opening; some of us have even said we were willing for our sons to turn out and fight Union men. We have a chance at a terrible array of Unionists in Kentucky—let us volunteer, and General Sidney Johnston will either lead us on to victory, or something else. Come, ye braves, turn out and let the world see that you are in earnest in making war on the enemies of the South. Many of you have made big speeches in favor of the war. Not a few of you have attempted to sell the army supplies, and thousands of you are willing to stoop to fill the *offices* for the salaries they pay; and you have been so patriotic as to try to get your sons and other relatives into offices. Some of you have *hired yourselves as spies, under-strappers, and tools* in the glorious cause, at two to four dollars per day! Come, now, enter the ranks, as there is more honor in serving as a private. Come, gentlemen, *do* come, we insist, and enter the army as volunteers. You will feel bad, when *drafted*, and pointed out as one who had to be *driven* into the service of your country. Let these Union traitors submit to the draft, but let us who are true Southern men *volunteer*. Any of us are willing to be Judges, Attorneys, Clerks, Senators, Congressmen, and camp followers for *pay*, when out of danger, but who of us is willing to shoulder our knapsacks and muskets and meet the Hessians? Come, gentlemen, the eyes of the people are upon you and they want to see if you will pitch in. This is a good opening."

An article similar to the above was published by him in his paper of October 19th. There were so many prominent men in Knoxville who had urged on secession, but who failed to enter the army, to whom these taunting, bitter reproaches manifestly applied, that a cry of rage was at once raised against Brownlow. Believing that he was about to be arrested and indicted, he determined to do, what he had all along seen he would have to do, that is, suspend the publication of his paper. Accordingly on October 24, 1861, reinserting the two scathing articles referred to above, he bade farewell to his readers in a long editorial, a part of which is here given. Never at any period in his life did his iron will and heroic courage appear in grander outline. In danger of mobs, in danger of assassination, in danger of imprisonment, in the midst of all this peril, he still held his head aloft, as if defying the thunderbolt. He still continued to "cry aloud and spare not."

I know of nothing in the whole Civil War that equals his defiant words in the midst of these most appalling dangers. He said in his sad farewell issue:

"'This issue of the *Whig* must necessarily be the last for some time to come—I am unable to say how long. The Confederate authorities have determined upon my arrest, and I am to be indicted before the Grand Jury of the Confederate Court, which commenced its session in Nashville on Monday last. * * * I have the fact of my indictment and consequent arrest, for this week, from distinguished citizens, Legislators, and lawyers at Nashville of both parties. Gentlemen of high positions, and members of the Secession party, say that the indictment will be made, because of some 'treasonable articles' in late numbers of the *Whig*. * * *

"According to the usages of the Court, as heretofore established, I presume I could go free by taking the oath these authorities are administering to other Union men, but my settled purpose is not to do any such thing. I can doubtless be allowed my personal liberty by entering into bonds to keep the peace, and to demean myself properly towards the leaders of secession in Knoxville, who have been seeking to have me assassinated all summer and fall, as they desire me to do, for this is really the import of the thing, and one of the leading objects sought to be attained. Although I could give a bond for my good behavior, for one hundred thousand dollars, signed by fifty as good men as the country affords, I shall obstinately refuse to do even that, and if such a bond is drawn up and signed by others, I will render it null and void by refusing to sign it. In default of both, I expect to go to jail, and I am ready to start on one moment's notice. Not only so, but there I am prepared to lie, in solitary confinement, until I waste away because of imprisonment, or die from old age. Stimulated by a consciousness of innocent uprightness, I will submit to imprisonment for life, or die at the end of a rope, before I will make any humiliating concessions to any power on earth.

"I have committed no offense. I have not shouldered arms against the Confederate Government, nor the State, nor encouraged others to do so. I have discouraged rebellion, publicly and privately. I have not assumed a hostle attitude towards the civil or military authorities of this new Government. But I have committed grave, and I fear, unpardonable offenses. I have refused to make war on the Government of the United States; I have refused to publish to the world false and exaggerated accounts of the several engagements had between the contending armies; I have refused to write out and publish false accounts of the origin of this war, and of the breaking up of the best Government the world ever knew, and all this will I continue to do, if it cost me my life. Nay, when I agree to do such things, may a righteous God palsy my right arm and may the earth open and close in on me forever.

"I shall in no degree feel humbled by being cast into prison whenever it is the will of this august Government to put me there, but, on the contrary, I shall feel proud of my confinement. I shall go to jail, as John Rodgers went to the stake, for my PRINCIPLES. I shall go because I have failed to recognize the hand of God in the work of breaking up the American Government, and the inauguration of the most wicked, cruel, unnatural, and uncalled-for war ever recorded in history. I go because I have refused to laud to the skies the acts of tyranny, usurpation and oppression inflicted on the people of East Tennessee, because of their devotion to the Constitution and the laws of the Government, handed down to them by their Fathers, and the liberties secured to them by a war of seven long years of gloom, poverty, and trial. I repeat, I am proud of my position, and of my principles, and shall leave them to my children as a legacy far more valuable than a princely fortune, had I the latter to bestow.

"With me life has lost some of its energy—having passed six annual posts on the western slope of half a century—something of the fire of youth is exhausted, but I stand forth with the eloquence and energy of *right* to sustain and stimulate me in the maintenance of my principles.

"I will only say, in conclusion,—for I am not allowed the privilege to write,—that the people of this country have been unaccustomed to such wrongs, they can yet scarcely realize them. They are astounded for the time being with the quick succession of outrages that have come to them, and they stand horror-stricken, like men expecting ruin and annihilation. I may not live to see the day, but thousands of my readers will, when the people of this once prosperous country, will see that they are marching by 'double quick time' from freedom to bondage. They will then look these wanton outrages upon right and liberty full in the face, and my prediction is that they will 'stir the stones of Rome to rise and mutiny.' Wrongs less wanton and outrageous precipitated the French Revolution. Citizens cast into dungeons without charges of crime against them, and without the formalities of a trial by a jury; private property confiscated at the beck of those in power; the press humbled, muzzled, and suppressed, or prostituted to serve the ends of tyranny. The crimes of Louis XVI fell short of all this, and yet he lost his head. The people of this country, down-trodden and oppressed, still have the resolution of their illustrious forefathers who asserted their rights at Lexington and Bunker Hill."

It would be hard to find in all history a more defiant, a more lofty, or a more eloquent utterance than the foregoing.

Never in all his varied and stormy career did the soul of this man flash out with such sublime courage. Well and nobly did he say that he would leave his "principles" a legacy to his children, "far more valuable than a princely fortune."

Thus Mr. Brownlow, in the last number of his paper, proclaimed his love of the Union and his hatred of secession. With his last words, he hurled his haughty defiance at the Southern Confederacy. To add force and significance to his denunciation, and in bitter mockery and derision, he reproduced the two previous articles, which had given such deep offense, and had driven the insurgent leaders at whom they were aimed to the very verge of madness.

Long after Johnson, Maynard, and Carter were safe in the North; long after Nelson had yielded and urged others to yield; after Baxter had yielded and become a candidate for the Confederate Congress; after Trigg had gone North, and all others had become silent, and not a voice was heard in all the State or in the wide Confederacy, Mr. Brownlow was still heard defiantly pleading for the Union, and uttering the hope of disaster to the Confederate arms. At last, yielding to overwhelming necessity, he mournfully said that "one man alone could not fight the whole Southern Confederacy." Never did mortal make a more heroic fight. And so strong was he, so terrible to his enemies, that to the very last men were afraid to lay their hands on him.

Two or three nights after the last issuance of his paper, I bade a mournful farewell to him at his own house, and saw him ride off on horseback in the darkness, on his way to Kentucky, an exile and a wanderer. He had concluded that not only was his personal liberty in danger, but his life also. In truth his life was in peril every hour. It has always been amazing to me that he escaped unharmed.

Mr. Brownlow was accompanied on his proposed trip by John Williams, Andrew Knott, and by James H. Morris. The latter was subsequently killed as a Union soldier in the battle of Murfreesboro. His plan was to travel at night by unfrequented ways, and pass through some of the gaps in the mountains North of Knoxville, and thus escape into Kentucky, thence to the Federal lines at Camp Dick Robinson. But after making one night's journey, and going some distance into Anderson County, they had reliable information that the passes in the mountains were so carefully guarded by Confederate Cavalry, that it would be almost impossible to get through without arrest. So in view of this threatening danger, he and his party returned home. But few persons, perhaps not a half dozen outside of his own family, knew at the time, or perhaps ever knew, that he had been out of town.

But something had to be done. His enemies were determined on his destruction. Every hour he was in peril. No doubt he would have been killed before this time but for two things. First, he had influential friends among the Confederates who could be relied on to give him notice of danger. Second, his most inveterate enemies were afraid to allow him to be murdered, even if they had been disposed to get rid of him in that way. So great was his popularity with the Union men, that it was feared that his death by violence, would be followed by outbreaks and retaliation all over the country. And such no doubt would have been the case. Troublesome and dangerous as Mr. Brownlow was as an editor, there were few men who were so depraved or unwise as to wish him disposed of in a foul manner. The consequences were too serious for such a thought. Much as he was detested by many persons, no one of any standing or character in Knoxville would have countenanced any violence to his person, much less his assassination. But in times of revolution there are always desperate men thrown to the surface of society. His danger was from this source.

After the abortive attempt to escape into Kentucky and his return to his home, Mr. Brownlow determined to seek shelter in the recesses of the Smoky Mountains, which separate Tennessee from North Carolina. Accordingly on November 5, 1861, he again left home, and made his way to one of the secluded coves in these great mountains, where he knew he could find shelter and protection among the warm-hearted, loyal mountaineers. And so he did.

On the morning of November 9th, the country was startled by the news that the night before, armed men had attempted to burn all the important railroad bridges on the East Tennessee & Georgia, on the East Tennessee & Virginia, and on the Memphis & Charleston Railroads, between Bridgeport, Ala., and the Virginia line at Bristol. The two first named were in effect one line, 240 miles long, connecting Virginia with the South and the Southwest. The attempt to destroy the bridges on these roads was successful as to those over the Hiwassee, over Lick Creek, over the Watauga and as to two over Chickamauga creek on the Atlantic & Western road.*

The destruction of these bridges had the approval of Mr. Lincoln, General McClellan, and General George H. Thomas. The latter, with a few thousand men, had advanced as far as London, Ky., near the border of Tennessee, and intended at the critical moment to lead his army across the line, at Cumberland Gap, and break up all communications by this line between the Confederate armies in Virginia and the South and the Southwest. Men were already on their way to East Tennessee, or were selected in the vicinity of the different bridges, to execute the plan of burning the bridges on a certain designated night. When it was too late to change the time, or countermand the orders, General Sherman, for reasons explained elsewhere, ordered General Thomas to retrace his steps. Thus the contemplated advance into East Tennessee was abandoned. It was then too late to notify the men who had been selected to destroy the bridges.

As Mr. Brownlow was known to have been away from home at the time the bridges were burned, he was very naturally suspected of having some agency in or knowledge of the matter. The next day or night a squad of Confederate soldiers from Knoxville was sent out to hunt him up. But Mrs. Brownlow, his faithful wife, learning of this design, got two friends to carry the news to her husband that soldiers had been sent to arrest him. One of these was Mr. William Rule, then a young printer in Brownlow's office, afterwards a brave Captain in the Federal Army, and at this time (1899) Mayor of Knoxville, and for many years past the able editor of the Knoxville *Journal and Tribune*. These men crossed the Tennessee River in a canoe, after nightfall, slipped by the sentinels (for the town was then under martial law), procured horses on the other side from Mr. Caleb Baker, a wealthy farmer and an ardent Union man, and slipped in ahead of the squad of soldiers, and rode with all speed to the place where Mr. Brownlow was then concealed—a distance of forty-five or fifty miles. He had preached in Sevierville on the day preceding the night of the bridge burning, not knowing what was about to happen. On re-

---
*"See "East Tennessee and the Civil War," by the author, for an account of the bridge burnings, chap. XVII, p. 266.

ceiving notice of the new danger which beset him, he at once retreated some fifteen miles into the midst of the mountains, where for the time being he found shelter and security among the brave mountain people.

After remaining in the mountains about twenty days he quietly returned by night to within six miles of Knoxville, where he again concealed himself. While in the last retreat he received the following letter:

HEADQUARTERS,
KNOXVILLE, TENN., December 4, 1861.

W. G. BROWNLOW, ESQ.:

The Major General commanding directs me to say that upon calling at his headquarters within twenty-four hours you can get a passport to go into Kentucky, accompanied by a military escort, the route to be designated by General Crittenden.

I am, sir, very respectfully, your obedient servant,

A. S. CUNNINGHAM,
Acting Adjutant General.

This letter was caused by one from Hon. Judah P. Benjamin, Secretary of War at Richmond, addressed to General George B. Crittenden, who had succeeded General Zollicoffer in command at Knoxville. Mr. Benjamin's letter was procured by the representations, or through the influence of Mr. John Baxter, at that time in Richmond, who applied to the Secretary of War in behalf of Mr. Brownlow. In his letter, Mr. Benjamin said: "I cannot give him [Brownlow] a formal pass, though I would greatly prefer seeing him on the other side of our lines, as an *avowed enemy.* I wish, however, to say that I would be glad to learn that he has left Tennessee. * * *"

Within the twenty-four hours specified in the letter of General Crittenden, Mr. Brownlow reported in person to General Crittenden at his headquarters. A renewal of the promise was again made by him. December 7th was fixed as the day for starting, or two days afterward. Before the time arrived, Mr. Brownlow was arrested by the Confederate Marshal, on a warrant issued by Robert B. Reynolds, a Confederate Commissioner, sued out by J. C. Ramsey, Confederate States District Attorney, charging him with the crime of treason "in publishing a weekly and tri-weekly paper, known as Brownlow's Knoxville *Whig.*"

On being arrested Mr. Brownlow sent a note to General Crittenden, claiming his protection, on the ground that he had come in on his promise that he should be sent through the lines. This note was answered the next day, after Mr. Brownlow had spent one night in jail, by one "Harry I. Thornton, A. D. C.," saying: He [General Crittenden] does not consider that you are here upon his invitation in such manner as to claim his protection from an investigation by the civil authorities of the charges against you, which he clearly understood from yourself and your friends you would not seek to avoid."

Now, there was not one word in General Crittenden's letter of December 4th, about "an investigation by the civil authorities of charges" against him. It was a simple promise that he should "have a passport to go into Kentucky." The arrest and detention afterward for trial by the civil authorities were a gross violation of the plighted faith of General Crittenden. Gladly would I believe, as I do incline to believe, that he was at that time unfit for duty by reason of his habits, and therefore not fully responsible for this wrong. Whatever may have been the words used by Mr. Brownlow, the spirit of the whole negotiation was that by appearing at headquarters within a certain time he should have a passport and an escort to Kentucky. Upon that understanding he came in from his concealment, and surrendered himself to the military authorities.

Mr. Benjamin, the Confederate Secretary of War, seems to have been heartily ashamed of this whole transaction. In a letter dated December 22, 1861, addressed to J. C. Ramsey, in an effort to defend the honor of the Government, he said, among other things:

"If Brownlow had been in our hands, we might not have accepted his proposition, but deeming it better to have him as an open enemy on the other side of the lines, authority was given to General Crittenden *to assure him of protection across the border if he came into Knoxville.* * * *

"Better that any, the most dangerous enemy, however criminal, should escape, than that the honor and good faith of the Government be impugned or suspected * * * but everyone must see that Brownlow would be safe and at large, *if he had not supposed that his reliance on the promise made him would insure his safe departure from East Tennessee.*"

Whatever may be thought of the acts and words of Mr. Benjamin on other occasions, these words certainly reflect high credit on his sense of honor.

The day Mr. Brownlow was arrested, Mr. John Williams and I hunted up J. C. Ramsey, the Confederate States District Attorney, and offered to make a good bond in the sum of one hundred thousand dollars as security for Mr. Brownlow to keep him out of jail. Ramsey refused the bond, and Mr. Brownlow was at once sent to jail, where he remained from December 6th until the 30th. He was then released, to be immediately rearrested by an officer on a military charge. After this time, as he was very sick, he was permitted to remain in his own home under the guard of armed soldiers. His release from jail was due to the remonstrance and the noble instincts of Dr. Frank A. Ramsey, Medical Director of the Confederate Army at Knoxville—a big-hearted, good man. While he was in prison, I visited him once or oftener, and can bear witness to the horrible condition of the jail in which he was confined. It was filthy, and without a single feature to relieve it from the fitting application of the strongest epithets. It was crowded to suffocation, with not a single comfort. There a great number of the best men in East Tennessee were crowded together for no crimes except being Union men, or being suspected of having had some connection with or knowledge of the late bridge-burning. Well do I remember the Rev. Elijah Cate—tall and remarkable in appearance, with the weight of seventy years resting on him, his head white as snow—who, it was said, was put in prison for cheering the Stars and Stripes as they were borne by his house by some men on horseback.

Well might the faithful old servant of God burst forth into rapturous cheers, in that hour of darkness and despair, at the sight, once more, of the dear old flag of the Union, the emblem of freedom, now supplanted by a foreign banner. I can well imagine the good old man as he espied horsemen approaching along the banks of the French Broad, at early dawn, straining his aged eyes as he dimly caught a glimpse of an object not seen for many a long day, bursting out in joy, and exclaiming in his exaltation:

> "What is that which the breeze, o'er the towering steep,
> As it fitfully blows, now conceals, now discloses?
> Now it catches the gleam of the morning's first beam,
> In full glory reflected, now shines o'er the stream;
> 'Tis the star-spangled banner! O, long may it wave
> O'er the land of the free and the home of the brave!"

The very hills and trees might have clapped their hands for joy at this sight.

Mr. Brownlow was sick and naturally restless, like a caged lion in his confinement. He sighed for the freedom of speech, and for the freedom of an untrammeled press, in which to utter his burning thoughts. His great desire was to get North, where his untamed spirit could have that scope and vent for free speech, which he had exercised with such wonderful effect for thirty years in the mountains of East Tennessee. By his confinement in the crowded and loathsome prison, and his exposure in his wanderings, his wonderful constitution was broken down, his nervous system was destroyed and he became prematurely old and an invalid for the rest of his life. Fearing and believing that he was liable to be assassinated at any hour, and his friends sharing in this same fear and anxiety, in the month of February he determined to make one more effort to escape from his prison in his own house. Accordingly, through a friend a plan was matured for his escape to the Federal lines through the Cumberland Mountains. But in the meantime, on February 27th, Mr. Brownlow had appealed to Jefferson Davis for permission to be sent out of East Tennessee by way of Cumberland Gap or Nashville, as he had been assured he should be. On March 2d Mr. Benjamin granted this request and Major George H. Monsarret, a high-principled officer, commanding the post at Knoxville, was directed to have that order executed. Mr. Brownlow had been sick more than two months, but feeble as he was, he determined to start on March 3d. Accordingly on that day he left his home on the train for Nashville, escorted by Lieutenant John W. O'Brien, a cousin of Mrs. Brownlow, and accompanied by James P. Brownlow, his son, and by Samuel A. Rodgers, one of his truest and best friends. These men were all selected by Mr. Brownlow himself. Colonel Casey Young, for a number of years, since the war, a member of Congress from Memphis, a Colonel in the Confederate Army, did all that he could to facilitate the departure of Mr. Brownlow.

It is due to Mr. Benjamin to say that throughout this whole transaction, in reference to Mr. Brownlow, he seems to have acted with a regard for honor and humanity. And this is certainly true also in regard to the conduct of Colonel Robert

B. Vance and Major Monsarret, both of the Confederate Army.

At Loudon Mr. Brownlow was furnished ten armed men, as an escort, under the command of Captain Dill. At Athens some Confederate soldiers, on their return to the army from their homes, learning that Mr. Brownlow was on the west-bound train, made a rush for his car in a hostile spirit, but they were held at bay by the guard placed at each end of the car. At Wartrace, Middle Tennessee, they found General Hardee in command. He refused, on application, to grant a flag of truce, so as to permit the party to proceed. So, O'Brien and Rodgers were sent to Huntsville, Ala., to obtain the necessary authority from General Albert Sidney Johnston. That General issued the following order:

Headquarters Confederate District,
Huntsville, March 7, 1862.

Lieutenant O'Brien,
 Third Tennessee Regiment.

Sir: General A. S. Johnson, having just heard that you have brought W. G. Brownlow to Wartrace, as a prisoner, instructs you to return him to his home, or release him where he now is, as he may elect.

Respectfully,
W. W. Mackall.

Then General Crittenden was appealed to, and he granted the desired flag of truce. Finally, after a detention of ten days, the party was allowed to proceed, which it did in private conveyances. The day of their departure was a most anxious one for the little party, now consisting of Mr. Brownlow, and his son, James P. Brownlow, Mr. Samuel A. Rodgers, and Lieutenant O'Brien. It was known that John Morgan's command was ranging around through that part of the country, and Mr. Brownlow naturally feared to fall in with it. The party drove rapidly over a good road toward Nashville. At length it reached the Federal pickets. Mr. Brownlow sat in his carriage, still sick and feeble, and "wrinkled and drawn up." At the sight of the Federals, said Mr. Rodgers afterward, "he seemed to swell out and his wrinkles to disappear." He straightened up and became himself again. Jumping to the ground he exclaimed: "Glory to God in the highest, and on earth peace, good will toward all men, except a few hell-born and hell-bound rebels in Knoxville." Officers and soldiers, on hearing his name, gathered around him, and gave him a genuine soldiers' welcome—such a welcome as men seldom receive.

What must have been his feelings in that hour of his deliverance! After five months of wandering, concealment, imprisonment, suffering, and sickness; of uncertainty, danger, and sickening disappointment, but of courage and constancy never surpassed, he was at last under the protection of the banner of his idolatry. Never did an eagle released from its cage exult more in its liberty than did this now unfettered hero of freedom. Pausing but a short time, they were again soon on their way, driving rapidly toward Nashville. It was still daytime when they reached that place. Stopping at a hotel, Mr. Brownlow, with his usual promptitude, at once hurried off to the capitol to meet his friends.

In the capitol a scene was witnessed such as is seldom beheld by men. Andrew Johnson, now Military Governor of the State, and Mr. Brownlow had been the bitterest of enemies. For nearly twenty-five years they had not spoken to each other. They had said more bitter, even terrible, things against each other than any two men in the land. Now they stood together on the side of a common country. They met in the presence of a common peril and a threatened overwhelming national calamity. Civil war had driven both of them from their families and their homes. Both were exiles and wanderers. They knew not that they should ever be permitted to return to their homes. At a moment when the very existence of their government was in extreme peril, they were drawn toward each other by a bond of common sympathy, common danger, and a common love of country. When, therefore, these two strong, brave men met, forgetting their past quarrels and hatred, they rushed into each other's arms, and wept like women.*

---

*On his return from Nashville, Mr. (now Judge) Rodgers, who was then and afterward my law partner, and always my faithful and trusted friend, related this incident to me. He did not witness it himself, but heard it at the time in such a reliable way as to leave no doubt of its truthfulness. Too much credit can never be given to him for his faithfulness to Mr. Brownlow during all his trials. He exposed his own life to the greatest dangers and endured great hardships in serving his friend. Nature has given to the world few as fine men as Judge Samuel A. Rodgers.

CHAPTER IV.

In the North—Published Book, May, 1862—Mrs. Brownlow and Mrs. Maynard Sent Beyond the Lines—Brownlow and Family Return to Knoxville, October, 1863—January 9, 1865, Meeting in Nashville—State Constitution Amended—Elected Governor—Ku-Klux—Bond Issues—Reconstructive Measures—Review of Secession Movement.

AFTER spending a few days in Nashville Mr. Brownlow proceeded to Cincinnati, Chicago, Philadelphia, and other cities in the North, in each of which he delivered a lecture, giving an account of the condition of things in the South. In response to an almost universal demand for information in reference to the state of things in the insurrectionary States, and especially for an account of his own thrilling personal experiences in the Southern Confederacy, he began writing a book.

In May, 1862, two months after he left home, he had his book ready for the press. It was entitled "Sketches of the Rise, Progress, and Decline of Secession, with a Narrative of Personal Adventures Among the Rebels." The book contained 458 pages. The preparation of it shows the marvelous rapidity with which he worked. While he was writing it he was traveling from city to city, making speeches and being entertained, and was thus diverted from his work in every possible way. But he was at all times in life too earnest to lose much time in social entertainments. It is needless to say that wherever he went he was received with demonstrations of welcome and admiration such as are usually extended only to Presidents or to great victorious generals.

By the sale of his book and by his lectures, for the second time in life, Mr. Brownlow began to accumulate a little money; from this time until his retirement from the Senate of the United States, by the simplest habits and the strictest economy, he was able to lay by each year a little for old age. So it is pleasant to know that while at best he had only a very moderate competency his last days were not passed in pinching poverty. The smallness of the estate left by him, only a few thousands, was the best evidence of his honesty.

Of course, when Mr. Brownlow left for the North he left his

family behind, consisting of one son and five daughters, four of them of tender age. When accounts of the reception which he had received in the North, and of the sensation that his bitter speeches were creating were read in Tennessee, they provoked great indignation. Accordingly on April 21, 1862, the following order was issued:

HEADQUARTERS, DEPARTMENT OF EAST TENNESSEE,
OFFICE OF PROVOST MARSHAL,
April 21st, 1862.

MRS. W. G. BROWNLOW, Knoxville.

Madam: By Major General E. Kirby Smith I am directed most respectfully to inform you that you and your children are not held as hostages for the good behavior of your husband, as represented by him in a speech at Cincinnati recently, and that yourself and family will be *required* to pass beyond the Confederate States lines in thirty-six hours from this date.

Passports will be granted you from this office.

Very respectfully,
W. M. CHURCHWELL,
Colonel and Provost Marshal.

A similar notice was also served on Mrs. Maynard, wife of the Hon. Horace Maynard, and on her family; also on Mrs. Andrew Johnson and on Mrs. William B. Carter. At the request of Mrs. Brownlow the time of preparation for departure was extended three or four days. On the expiration of the time granted, Mrs. Brownlow and Mrs. Maynard, with their families, were placed in charge of Lieutenant Joseph H. Speed of the Confederate Army from Alabama, and sent North by way of Norfolk. Lieutenant Speed proved to be an honorable gentleman, and both families were always loud in praise of his kindness. He left nothing undone that he could do for their comfort.

Whatever may have been said for or against the practice of sending helpless families through the lines to their husbands or friends, it was certainly followed more or less by both governments. Where such persons were behaving themselves with propriety, it was certainly a cruel hardship to be sent away from their homes. No one at the time, or since, charged that the families who were removed in this instance were not conducting themselves with the utmost propriety. Both Mrs. Brownlow and Mrs. Maynard, as well as Mrs. Johnson, were exceptionally amiable and well behaved at all times and under all circumstances. In this case it was ungallant, for it was avowedly, at least in the case of Mrs. Brownlow, visiting the sins of the husband on innocent, helpless women.

In October, 1863, after the entrance of General Burnside with his army into Knoxville, Mr. Brownlow and his family again returned to their former home. Soon after his return he resumed the publication of his paper, which had been suspended for two years, his press having been confiscated.

In the early winter of 1864 Andrew Johnson, as Military Governor of Tennessee, with the approval of Mr. Lincoln, as elsewhere shown, took steps to place the State in practical relations with the Federal Government, preparatory to its resumption of its powers and rights as a loyal State. A meeting looking to this end was called to assemble in Nashville on January 9, 1865. In less than two days the work of amending the Constitution and providing for the re-establishment of the State Government had been accomplished. The haste of this proceeding was in all respects unworthy of the momentous occasion. But whether the work of the convention was wise or unwise the result, so far as Mr. Johnson was concerned, was what he desired. He went back to Washington with the honor of bringing back with him one of the States of the Union. In his inaugural address as Vice-President he boasted of this achievement.

Under the new order of things a Governor and a Legislature were to be elected in Tennessee. Mr. Johnson was out of the way. Who should the new Governor be? Should it be Mr. Nelson, Mr. Maynard, Mr. Baxter, or Mr. Netherland, or some less noted man? Nelson, Baxter, and Netherland had already shown such decided retrogressive tendencies that they were out of the question. Under these circumstances Mr. Brownlow was urged to become a candidate. After a little reflection he agreed to do so. I do not think he had ever thought of this office before. He was at that time editing his paper and discharging the duties of a respectable office in the Internal Revenue Department with a reasonable salary. As soon as his name was authoritatively given to the public, so popular was he that no other name was thereafter seriously considered. Having received the party nomination he was elected as a matter of course.

The administration of Governor Brownlow was stormy and tempestuous beyond anything in our political history. There was something in the man, but infinitely more in the times, that marked this as the *troubled* period in our civil history. Had the times been quiet, had those lately in insurrection and their new allies, who were recently recruited from the Union ranks under the guise of Conservatives, showed a more charitable spirit, his administration would have been as mild as that of those preceding the Civil War, for when not factiously opposed or assailed he was most conciliatory and peace-loving. On the contrary, he was opposed with ruthless vindictiveness, and all the worst elements of society, thrown upon the surface by a four years' war, arrayed themselves in opposition to his administration. Encouraged by the desertion of President Johnson, bands of desperate characters denominated "Ku-Klux" were organized in many counties in Middle and West Tennessee, who committed outrages on loyal men of the most startling and blood-curdling character. In the darkness of midnight they committed their terrible deeds.

Of all the men in the State Governor Brownlow was the last to think of tolerating such things. With his Cromwellian spirit and will he was the very man for this grave emergency. He accordingly dealt in no halfway measures. With the greatest promptitude, under the authority of an Act of the Legislature, he organized a part of the loyal militia of the State and sent them under determined officers, with what instructions I know not, into the counties where the Ku-Klux were committing their outrages. In a few weeks or months law and order were restored and loyal people were once more safe in their homes in the quiet hours of the night. The masked outlaws were taught that an iron hand held the reins of power in the State.

His enemies then made, and sometimes still make, a bitter outcry against Governor Brownlow and his militia. The only answer this deserves is to remind them that these secret outrages were the legitimate outgrowth of the war begun by them in Tennessee in 1861. When overpowered in the field, and they had given their parole of honor to behave themselves as good citizens, some of them, in violation of all law and all honor, manifested a spirit of insubordination in these secret midnight gatherings which no State could tolerate. By their conduct they placed themselves above and outside of regular government. The law could not reach them. It was a kind of insurrection conducted against the peace of the State. The perpetrators were masked and kept themselves concealed, and moved only at night and in large bodies. Before the light of day appeared they dispersed to their homes or secret hiding places after committing their terrible deeds. They were bound by dreadful oaths. No man dared to testify against them or inform on them, and even men who were suspected of an intention of doing so, or having done so, were cruelly treated. No jury could be found to punish them. Military force alone could reach the evil. This Governor Brownlow used. I do not stop to inquire whether or not the strict letter of the law was exceeded in its execution.* It is sufficient to know that the safety of the people demanded the most stringent and severe measures. *Salus populi, suprema est lex.* Nor have I inquired whether Governor Brownlow's acts in reference to these things were exactly regular. It is sufficient to know that these violators of law were defying all authority, and had inaugurated an insurrection too widespread and powerful to be put down by the civil authorities; that the means necessary to restore order and security were used, and that the troops were withdrawn as soon as organized opposition to law disappeared. It may be that these troops in some instances exceeded their authority and committed wrongs, and I expect they did. But this is an unfortunate incident of all wars.

Another charge often brought against the administration of Governor Brownlow and his party in Tennessee is that they overwhelmed the people of the State with a large bonded indebtedness. It is true that many bonds were issued under his administration, as many had been issued before, but consider the circumstances. In coming into power he found the railroads of the State worn out and in a state of dilapidation by reason of the heavy use they were exposed to during the four years of war. No repairs except those absolutely necessary had been made; many of the bridges had been burned; the rolling stock was mostly gone or worn out. The railroad companies were unable to put the roads in order; an appeal was therefore made to the Legislature by these roads for the loan of the credit of the State to aid in making repairs. The great interests of the State would suffer unless this were done. Therefore, as a matter of public policy and duty, many bonds were issued for that purpose—too many, I freely admit. The assistance thus rendered was deemed at the time to be an act of sound policy and a patriotic duty. In some cases the policy adopted was unwise. All parties at the time, however, seemed to acquiesce in it, if not to demand it. That some of these bonds were afterward dis-

---

*See Acts of Extra Session, 1868; Acts of September 10, 1868; small volume, p. 23. See Message.

honestly perverted from the uses contemplated by the Legislature, and used for private purposes, as they certainly were, proves only that some of the roads permitted these bonds to pass into the hands of dishonest agents. A large part, a majority, of them were issued to Democratic officers of roads. Besides all this, during the four years of war and for nearly two years afterward, the interest on our previous outstanding bonds, amounting to $5,169,750, had been accumulating. These bonds, beginning in 1835, had been issued to aid in the construction of railroads and turnpikes and for the erection of the State Capitol. The total indebtedness at this time was $25,277,406.66. To save the credit of the State this accumulated interest had to be provided by the issuance of new bonds. Repudiation had not yet been introduced into the State, or this interest and these bonds might have been settled at a cheaper rate.

It seems to be forgotten that it had been the policy of the State, sanctioned by its Constitution, long before the war, to encourage railroads and turnpikes by issuing its bonds or endorsing those of the companies thus engaged when a certain amount of work had been done. I have a statement from E. B. Craig, Treasurer, that the State loaned bonds to railroad companies prior to 1866 to the amount of $14,006,000, that the interest due on these bonds at that date was $3,769,507; that the State had endorsed "City of Memphis and Railroad Company's" bonds for $2,207,000, and that the accrued interest amounted in 1866 to $550,680, making principal and interest on the liabilities of the State on account of railroads $20,583,187.

The issuance of bonds after the war, and the necessity for their issuance, were the direct result of the war, begun in Tennessee in 1861 against the United States. Except for the desolations caused by the war, there would not have been the almost universal destruction of the property and resources of the State, and the necessity for issuing bonds.

I state frankly that the Legislature of 1865 and 1867 were wild and reckless in granting authority to issue bonds as above intimated. I go further and admit that, from the evidence brought out subsequently by investigating committees, there is almost conclusive proof of corruption on the part of some of the members of the Legislature in connection with that legislation, and in the use of the bonds after they were issued, by some of the persons in whose hands they fell.

Having admitted the errors or the crimes of the Union party, let us briefly show the condition of affairs previous to May 6, 1861.

That the administration of Brownlow was strong, vigorous, and without any halting feebleness, no one will deny. It has always been, and still is, the subject of the most malignant abuse on the part of his enemies. It lies not within the scope of this work to enter any detailed defense of the legislative and administrative measures of the reconstruction period in our State. These measures, whatever they were, were at the time supposed to be necessary to remedy the widespread destruction wrought by those who led the State into war. All of our material interests had been destroyed. The State had lost its personal property. The taxables had shrunk from $273,327,240 in 1860 to $214,446.24 in 1866. All business was suspended; all enterprises were ended. The State lay like a huge body in a condition of paralysis. All intellectual and moral development was arrested and turned back. Churches, colleges, and schoolhouses for the most part were deserted and closed, and many of them in ruins. Fences were gone. Farms were stripped of stock and of farm implements. The factories of the State were suspended and broken down. Railroads and bridges were all out of repair. Universal desolation prevailed. Evils, too, born of and fostered by war, had to be torn up by the roots. Widespread degeneracy prevailed in the country. A morbid desire to make fortunes—either honestly or dishonestly—seized the minds of many. Corruption abounded. Moral restraints were greatly weakened. Lawlessness was rampant. All these were the legitimate, the direct fruits of the war—a war inaugurated by the State before it was attacked or threatened.

If, therefore, the reconstructive measures in Tennessee were sometimes too severe, as I know they were, it was only the swift rebound from the opposite extreme. The bow had been bent too far. When unloosed its rebound was terrible in the other direction. It is always thus and always will be. Men maddened by the passions of Civil War, and smarting under manifold wrongs and persecutions, when restored to power, are apt and certain to go too far in avenging their wrongs. Moderation and forbearance on their part, from 1865 to 1867, would certainly have been the wiser policy. But the Union men of the State, when out of power, had not experienced from their enemies the exercise of these qualities, and were therefore in no humor to manifest a mercy which they had not received. But for the sake of the future peace of the people of the State, it is now manifest that a policy of reconciliation would have been better in the end. It must, however, be kept in mind that a defiance of lawful authority in a large district of the State, under Ku-Klux bands, was at this time dominant. This influenced and drove the authorities further and further from a policy of moderation. All this is a source of the profoundest regret.

I wish here to make several concessions in reference to the great questions of the Civil War not usually made, if ever before, by anyone writing from my viewpoint:

(1) The claim of State sovereignty, and of the right on the part of the States to secede or withdraw from the Union whenever in their judgment the compact should be violated, is as old as the government, and has in its support many eminent names and statesmen. At different periods of our existence certain classes of both sections, when thinking themselves aggrieved, threatened to exercise this right. The question never was settled by argument, nor general concurrence of opinion.

(2) It was unquestionably true that previous to the Civil War the Constitution, or compact of Union, had been violated by the Legislatures and the people of a number of Northern States, by the nullification and the open resistance to the execution of the Fugitive Slave law, which was passed in pursuance of the Constitution. But these acts were not the acts of Congress nor of the General Government, but wholly without the authority or sanction of either of them.

(3) The continued agitation of the slavery question, by Abolition societies and Abolition organs and speakers, the violence of their utterances, and the shameful imputations on the character of slave holders, were well calculated to produce the profound conviction in the South that there was no alternative but a resort to what they believed was their constitutional right of separation.

(4) Believing, as a majority of the Southern people did, that the States were sovereign and independent, having a right to

withdraw from the Union, and that their first allegiance and duty were due to their respective States, when secession took place, it was most natural and logical that they should honestly espouse the cause of the States with the conscientious conviction of patriotic duty.

No deduction can be drawn legitimately of the injustice of its cause by the failure of the Southern Confederacy; but from that fact may be urged with the stern certainty of logic the folly and unwisdom of secession. The conclusions of logic and the results of war are both confirmed by the most intelligent public opinion of the South, that the failure was not only a national blessing, but also a special blessing to the South. It is sufficient, it is enough, that a brave, proud people, while rejoicing in their grand record and celebrating their deeds of glory, acknowledge, perhaps with a tear, that the result was best. If the result was best, then it was a mistake in the beginning. If secession was a mistake, why not look with understanding upon those who opposed it.

There were peculiar reasons why Tennessee should not have taken the fatal step of seceding. Let it be remembered that war was inaugurated by the Legislature of the State long before there was a Federal soldier south of the Ohio River, by providing by a Legislative act for the organization of an army of 55,000 men, that in pursuance of that act as many soldiers as possible were at once put into the field, and that the number was subsequently increased to over 120,000; that a large sum of money, namely, five millions of dollars, was expended by the State for this purpose; that in the prosecution of the war nearly all the assets of the Bank of Tennessee, which held the school fund, were consumed in that way; that the Union Bank and the Planters' Bank, and nearly every other bank in the State, were ruined; that the school fund of the State was nearly all lost or expended in the war; that the railroads were run down and worn out; that the cattle, sheep, hogs, horses, mules, corn, hay, wheat, fences, timber, and nearly all other kinds of personal property were lost and destroyed; these things, in the aggregate, amounted to perhaps seventy-five or one hundred millions of dollars. All this is exclusive of the fifty, or perhaps one hundred, millions of dollars in slave property, lost in the State and lost by the war so unwisely inaugurated by the secession party. Besides all these losses, the people of the State are still bearing burdens of taxation caused by the war, and they will have to continue to do so for generations yet to come. There is annually paid out of the Treasury of the State about two hundred thousand dollars in the shape of pensions to maimed or disabled soldiers, most, if not all, of which, goes to those engaged in the insurrection. This I do not complain of. The people of the State who were so unwise as to rush into unnecessary war, ought to take care of the crippled soldiers and the widows of those who were killed in battle, or who died of disease in that war. This is right; this is just. But it is one of the direct burdens of this unwise war.

Concede that the great body of the people of Tennessee who went into the Civil War were honest in what they did; concede that they acted, as they thought, from the highest motives of self-interest and self-preservation; concede that, excepting a restricted number, they were governed by the purest love of country; concede that from their viewpoint they were noble patriots enlisted as they honestly thought in a noble cause; concede all these things, and most cheerfully I do concede them all,—and still the great fact remains in all its force, that the desolation and the vast destruction of property in the State would not have resulted but for the war. This conclusion cannot be distorted, cannot be concealed.

I admit that the Federal armies did their part of this work of destruction of property, but not the annihilation of the State banks and the waste of their assets, nor the loss of the school fund, nor the waste of the revenues of the State. But what caused these Federal Armies to come here? Mark the facts: there was not within the limits of the State of Tennessee, nor south of the Ohio River, on May 6, 1861, a single hostile Federal soldier, much less a hostile Federal Army. There was no threat from any quarter whatever of a hostile invasion of the State. All was peaceable within its borders, except the preparations being made by the Governor and the Legislature to make war on the United States. On that day an Act was passed by the Legislature, called a "Declaration of Independence and Ordinance dissolving the Federal Relations between the State of Tennessee and the United States of America." On the same day and as a part of the same Act, the "Constitution of the Provisional Government of the Confederate States of America" was adopted and ratified by the Legislature. On the same day Henry W. Hilliard, on the part of the Confederate States, and Gustavus A. Henry, A. W. O. Totten, and Washington Barrow, on the part of Tennessee, entered into and concluded a "Convention, Agreement, and Military League, between the high contracting parties, by which the whole military force, and military operations, offensive and defensive, of said State, in the impending conflict with the United States, shall (should) be under the chief control and direction of the President of the Confederate States." On May 7th, this Military League was ratified and confirmed by the Legislature. On the same day (the 7th) an Act was passed, authorizing and directing the Governor "to raise, organize, and equip a provisional force of volunteers for the defense of the State, to consist of 55,000 volunteers." This force was raised and put into the Confederate Army, as soon as it could be done.

It must be kept in mind that the people did not vote on the question of "Separation" or secession, until the 8th day of June following, so, more than a month before the Ordinance of Secession was ratified by the people of the State, on which, according to the secession theory, its validity depended, war had virtually been declared and commenced by the State against the United States. The Military League was not only a violation of the Constitution of the United States, but was in fact a "levying of war" against that Government.

And all this was done at a time when no hostile demonstration against the State had been made by the United States, and when none was threatened and none intended, unless the State should withdraw from the Union, or be guilty of some act of hostility. It must be remembered that in the proclamation of Mr. Lincoln, calling out 75,000 men to suppress the insurrection in the States named, of South Carolina, Georgia, Alabama, Florida, Mississippi, Louisiana, and Texas, the name of Tennessee does not appear. No threat was made against it. A most significant fact.

It thus appears that the Governor and the Legislature of the State, on the 6th day of May, without authority of the people thereof, but in violation of their will, as expressed in the February election, deliberately began war against the United States, by joining the Southern Confederacy, then at war with the former, and by raising armies for its use, and turning them over to the Confederate States. On the 27th day of April previously, Colonel Peter Turney's regiment of volunteers (the 1st Tennessee Infantry) embarked on a train for Virginia, having been accepted by the Confederate authorities and assigned to the Army of Virginia. Presumably all this was with the knowledge and consent of the Governor, and by his command. He must have issued Colonel Turney his commission. All this was done without provocation, or one justifiable reason, on the part of Tennessee. This was nearly entirely the work of one man, Isham G. Harris, then Governor of the State.

It will be noticed that the fact of secession was done by a *Legislative* Act, and passed by a body of men elected in August, 1859—twenty-one months previously. Admit the constitutional right of a State to secede from the Union, in as broad terms as possible, without cause or with cause, and still no lawyer will risk his reputation by insisting that this can be done by a legislative enactment. To withdraw from the Union, if the right exists at all, is an act of the highest sovereignty on the part of the people, as entering the Union was, and can be done only, even according to the theory of secession, by a Constitutional convention, the members of which have been duly elected thereto, and who for this purpose represent the collective sovereignty of the State. Who ever heard of a Legislature having the power to make constitutions or abrogate them; to make war; to enter into alliances; and to transfer the allegiance of the people, and the military resources of the State and its army to a foreign party, as this Legislature attempted to do in 1861! No, this was not legal, constitutional secession—if there can be such a thing—but revolution and force.

In review of these facts the election on June 9th to determine the question of the ratification or rejection of the Ordinance of Secession, was a mere idle form. The State, as we have seen, had seceded, or rather revolted, from the Union more than a month before this election, by its alliance, "offensive and defensive," with the Confederate States; by turning over to the latter its army; by the adoption of a Declaration of Independence and an Ordinance of Secession, and by sending troops to the seat of war. If the people had rejected the proposition to secede at the polls, it would have been all the same. That fatal measure was already practically accomplished. Who could have resisted it? What power could have stopped it with an ambitious Governor determined to push forward his revolutionary schemes backed by the army of the State and by the whole power of the Confederate States? The people would have been as powerless to resist it, as were the people of East Tennessee after the June election.

These acts and measures on the part of the Governor and the Legislature, were plain and palpable violations of the Constitution of the United States, and that of the State. The leading spirit who inspired all these measures is to-day the most honored citizen of the State. In 1861, in the plenitude of his power, the Governor formed alliances and made war as coolly as the Czar of Russia. He equipped and put into the field an army greater than was ever commanded by Washington, Jackson, or Scott. He played with war as with a toy. The people of the State were as children in his hands.

Let me say deliberately, but in the kindest spirit: the State should not have seceded; there was no necessity for it. There was not a single fact justifying it. It was a stupendous folly. It was productive of not a single benefit, but of untold and multiplied evils, which no man can number. By it every material interest of the State was laid low in ruin. Slavery, which seemed to have the first consideration in the minds of the Southern people, was forever destroyed. In vain President Lincoln, in his Inaugural Address, in the most assuring, the most supplicating words, begged the Southern States not to secede. He had frequently declared publicly, in the most solemn manner, that neither a President nor Congress had any power to interfere with slavery in the States where it then existed. He had declared also that the Fugitive Slave law was constitutional and must be enforced. The Republican party had elected him well knowing these opinions, and for the most part approving them. The Abolition party proper constituted but an insignificant part of the Northern people. Slavery was really in no danger, and would exist to-day, but for the transcendent madness and folly of its friends. Let it be kept in mind that all these illegal acts referred to were passed by a Legislature which had been elected in 1859, when no question of secession was before the voters of the State.

Let me cite the example of Kentucky—and I might mention Maryland and Missouri also—Kentucky did not secede from the Union, and therefore her people escaped all the ills and hardships of *reconstruction* and *disfranchisement*. Her school fund, her public revenues, and the assets of her banks, were not wasted in equipping armies and in a mad scheme of war. Her railroads, instead of being seized and sequestered as Confederate property, and used by the United States as such, grew rich by transporting government troops and supplies. At the end of the war they needed no aid from the State, in the form of bonds, to repair the waste of war. Out of respect for the declared "neutrality" of the State, not a Federal soldier was enlisted within her borders, nor did a Federal Army set foot on her soil, until after Confederate soldiers had seized and occupied Columbus, Bowling Green, and Cumberland Gap. As late as August, 1861, General L. H. Rousseau was enlisting his legion of Kentuckians for the Federal Army, in obedience to the will of the State, not in Kentucky, but on the other side of the Ohio, in the State of Indiana. Thus the neutrality of the State and the sentiments of her people were respected. Tennessee might have escaped all these evils also if she had listened to the voice of wisdom and moderation. The example of Kentucky is lasting proof of the supreme folly of Tennessee. She saved her revenues, saved her railroads, and made money out of them, and escaped reconstruction and disfranchisement. Will anyone to-day say that the policy of Kentucky was not wiser than that of Tennessee? If Kentucky were thus treated, can any one give reason why Tennessee would not have received the same treatment? Her sons—many of them—went South and fought for the Confederacy, as the sons of Maryland and Missouri did also, but as the State in its sovereign capacity did not secede from the Union, she was treated as a loyal State by the Government, as Maryland and Missouri were likewise. So Tennessee would have been treated.

On March 6, 1903, the Governor of Kentucky received from the United States, on account of money advanced for raising volunteers, and for interest on loans negotiated during the Civil War, the sum of $1,433,399—more than enough to pay off her public debt.

For the sake of argument, admit that Tennessee had the unquestioned constitutional right to secede from the Union. Will any candid man of this day point out a single benefit that she derived from the exercise of this right? Wherein was she benefited? Were her people made freer, happier, and better?

Have they larger liberties? Is the State more prosperous? Nearly all sensible men of this day admit that secession was a mistake, and rejoice that it failed.

Perhaps it was believed at first by those who were most active in the cause of secession in Tennessee that there would be no war: that the North would not fight; that it would meekly submit to a dismemberment of the Union. Let us charitably indulge this belief. All through the winter of 1860-61, until April, it did appear as if secession might be peaceably accomplished without war. The overwhelming sentiment of the North seemed to be against "coercion." Effort after effort was made in Congress and out of it, and by public meetings, by newspapers, by addresses to the public, in favor of a settlement of the questions in dispute—by a compromise of some kind, by concessions to the South—to save the nation from civil war. Mr. Lincoln earnestly deprecated war. Up to the fatal shot fired at Fort Sumter, he had not mustered a man for the defenses of the Union. The Southern Confederacy was in full existence with an army, and with all its departments in full operation. It was a government. And for anything that can be seen now, or that could be seen then, it might have gone on in its career unmolested until it had established its independence, by the silent acquiescence of the old government. But the new government, confident in its strength, becoming impatient at the delay of Tennessee, Virginia, and North Carolina, and possibly at the hesitation of Kentucky, Missouri, and Maryland, and hoping by "striking a blow" to rouse a wild passion for war, and thus to draw those States to its side, without any military necessity, struck that blow in Charleston, and immediately kindled the flame of war from the center to the uttermost boundaries of our country. Contrary to what was anticipated, there was a united North and a divided South.

There were many able and far-sighted men in the State in 1861 who deplored the secession of Tennessee as an act of folly and of inconsiderate haste. There were such men as John Bell, Justice John M. Catron, Ex-Governor William B. Campbell, Return J. Meigs, John Trimble, William H. Polk, Dr. W. P. Jones, Bailie Peyton, Emerson Etheridge, Alvin Hawkins, Andrew Johnson, T. A. R. Nelson, James W. Deadrick, N. G. Taylor, John Netherland, Samuel Milligan, W. G. Brownlow, Horace Maynard, John Baxter, and Connally F. Trigg. Surely these men were the equals in judgment, intellect, and patriotism of any similar number in the State.

The reasons influencing their minds were many, and they were of the most momentous gravity. In the very threshold they saw the danger to the existence of the institution of slavery itself—the very cause of the war. It was hazarding its existence upon the chances of battle, with three slave States, in their sovereign capacity, and with a very considerable part of the population of three others, in sympathy with the Union. The amazing folly of abandoning the guarantees of the Constitution for the protection of slavery, and appealing to the sword, in the face of nearly three fighting men against one, and with immensely superior resources for war, thus giving the Abolitionists and a part of the Free-soilers an opportunity and a pretext they had long desired of destroying that institution, is almost inconceivable in its folly. The South, in a spirit of chivalry, in effect said to the North: "The Constitution protects slavery wherever it now exists, and you dare not touch it. But we will tear to pieces that instrument and abandon our advantages under it, by seceding from the Union, and we challenge you to settle the moral question by a contest of arms."

These eminent men, as many others did in the South, warned the Southern people of the danger of secession, but in the whirlwind and delirium of popular excitement, their voices and admonitions were not heeded.

These losses which I have enumerated in the foregoing pages will be repaired by the flight of years, except the sufferings, the tears of anguish, and the fearful loss of life among noble Tennesseeans. But there are some great, but partial compensations:

(1) The doctrine of State sovereignty—the right of a State to secede at will from the Union—though still prevailing as a theory of the Constitution, was greatly weakened by the results of the war, and is not likely to be resorted to as a practical remedy for grievances by any of the States for generations to come, if ever again.

(2) The idea of national sovereignty as contradistinguished from State sovereignty and State independence, was immensely strengthened by the result of the late war. The idea of a Union "one and indivisible" has taken hold of the popular

mind and heart, and nothing but a great and terrible war to divide it—could have accomplished this.

(3) The sectional question of slavery, being eliminated forever from the forum of agitation, there is no human probability of any question ever arising that will draw one-third or one-half of the co-terminus States of any section unitedly into the act of revolting against the government.

There is compensation, too, in the reflection that the national government came out of the war with a prestige, with a halo of glory, it never had before, arising out of the splendid feats of arms performed on a hundred battlefields by the gallant sons both of the North and of the South. Then the almost marvelous power of recuperation shown by both sections—especially in the South, which was left in almost hopeless ruin and desolation—is well calculated to exalt our pride. The nation was left by the war with a debt of twenty-seven hundred millions of dollars to be provided, and yet that debt has been reduced eighteen hundred millions, and our government's bonds are floated at a lower rate of interest than any in the world. The whole country—the South, after a period of readjustment, as well as the North—sprang forward on a career of prosperity and development such as has never been surpassed, if ever equaled, in the history of human affairs.

CHAPTER V.

Brownlow Re-elected, 1867—Emerson Etheridge—Isham G. Harris—Brownlow Elected to United States Senate, October, 1867—Johnson Arraigns Brownlow—The Reply—Author's Personal Relations with Brownlow.

IN 1867 Governor Brownlow was a candidate for re-election, receiving the party nomination without opposition. During his first term bitter opposition to him had sprung up among certain men who had formerly been Union sympathizers. The leader in this movement was the somewhat celebrated Emerson Etheridge, for several terms a distinguished Whig member of Congress. He was put forward as a candidate for Governor against Mr. Brownlow, backed and supported by such men as T. A. R. Nelson, John Baxter, John Netherland, J. M. Fleming, John Williams, and certain prominent men in Middle and West Tennessee. Mr. Etheridge took the stump and made a very bitter and a very powerful canvass. The administration of Governor Brownlow and his party was arraigned as only Mr. Etheridge could have done it. He was the most brilliant and the most versatile man at that time in the State. With no early advantages and no education, except that acquired at old-fashioned country schools, he had become one of the most accurate and polished speakers in the State. His mind was stored with a vast fund of useful as well as polite knowledge. He was a constant reader, and his memory was something wonderful. It is said that years afterward he could still call by memory the roll of the House of Representatives of which he was clerk in 1861. His reading embraced a wide range of topics. Long ago he returned from his political wanderings of 1867, and his brief alliance with the secession party to the faith of the old Whig party, of which he had been so bright an ornament. He deserted his new spouse, for which he had but little love, with the words of the nuptial ceremony still sounding in his ears. Unquestionably he was one of the strongest characters that had appeared in Tennessee for many years. As a public man he possessed certain peculiarities, not in the least affecting his moral standing, that were always a drawback to him. In this category may be placed his frank, outspoken independence and his eccentricities. His honesty, both as a public and a private citizen, has always been conceded. His private life was spotless. As a conversationalist, in his prime, he was unusual. In Washington or wherever he might be he always had a crowd around him, listening to his brilliant conversation. Next after Haskell and Gentry he was the brightest man in the State. His mind was not massive like John Baxter's, but it was quick and electrical.*

Mr. Etheridge pressed his canvass in 1867 with great power and bitterness, only to be disastrously beaten. Governor Brownlow was unable to take the stump on account of the failure of his voice, but he was triumphantly re-elected, running ahead of his party. His second term, like the first, was stormy and full of exciting incidents. During this term the Ku-Klux were again at their nefarious work, but the strong arm and will of the Governor triumphed and violence was everywhere suppressed.

The weakest points in Mr. Brownlow's character were his absolute trust in the good faith of his friends, and the readiness with which he became reconciled to his enemies. The first exposed him in public life to the wiles of false and corrupt men as it did General Grant also. The second exposed him to the charge of inconsistency and insincerity. These charges were not in fact just. The first was the result of too much faith in the honesty of men and his inability to say no. The second arose from a grand spirit of magnanimity. He was so generous, so trustful, so forgiving that he took all men to be what they professed to be.

His treatment, while Governor, of Isham G. Harris after the war is a good illustration of his magnanimity. Harris, it will be remembered, was Governor of Tennessee in 1861. It was almost exclusively through his influence and exertions that Tennessee was finally induced to secede after one signal failure. His courage, ability, and iron will accomplished this result in the face of a Union majority in the previous February election of 64,000 votes. Harris was very bitter toward Union men. He did everything that could be done, whether legal or illegal, for the cause of secession. No man in the South was more active, or more bitter, or more successful in the cause of disunion. He had boldly inaugurated secession in defiance of the popular will as expressed at the ballot box by entering into a "military

---

*He died in 1902.

league" with the Southern Confederacy before the people of the State voted for secession. He had organized an army and made war on the United States by sending troops to Virginia weeks before the vote in favor of separation. From that time until the day of his precipitate flight from the State, after the fall of Fort Donelson, in February, 1862, he had carried things with an imperial will. Yet there was something manly and noble in his manner of doing things. No man was so cordially hated by Union men. When the State Government was reorganized the Legislature directed the Governor to offer a reward of five thousand dollars for his apprehension.

On the downfall of the Confederacy Harris, with a number of other violent Confederates, went to Cordova, Mexico, where they proposed to establish a colony from the Southern States and engage in the business of raising coffee. William M. Gwin, an ex-Senator from California, was one of these voluntary exiles. Maximilian created Gwin Duke of Sonora. The overthrow of Maximilian made it necessary for Harris and Gwin and their followers to get out of Mexico as they had gotten out of the United States. The fate of the unfortunate Maximilian was a warning to them that revolutionists in Mexico who fail, especially foreigners who attempt to overturn the government, were not regarded as heroes and objects of popular idolatry as in the United States. Harris was not anxious to die in Mexico, as he had not been in the United States, so he again began his wanderings. This time he went to Liverpool, where he became a commission merchant. He was an exile, while his family and friends were in the United States. It is impossible to realize how anxious one thus situated would be to return to his home and his kindred, and yet who dared not do so. So Harris became restless and sick at heart. Greatly as he hated the United States, he burned with desire to return to it. But appalling difficulties were in the way. His old and bitter enemy, Andrew Johnson, by a strange fortune, was President. To apply to him for pardon was revolting to his proud spirit. He would starve first, would remain an exile forever before humbling himself before that man he hated above all others. And Brownlow, the terrible Brownlow, was Governor of Tennessee, that great State which he had plunged by his iron will into secession. But he would trust Brownlow while he would not Johnson. Brownlow was tender-hearted, and if he gave his word of promise, that promise would be sacredly kept like an oath. Humiliating as it was to appeal to his enemies for clemency, and revolting as it was to live in a government controlled by hated Yankees, yet he determined to submit to both. Accordingly, he wrote to his late associate in the work of secession, ex-Governor Neill S. Brown, to sound Brownlow and to intercede for him. Governor Brown went with the letter to Brownlow and frankly stated that he came to appeal for clemency on behalf of the man who had done more to take Tennessee out of the Union than any other person, and therefore had done more damage to the State. That man now desired to return to his home, to become a peaceable citizen, to resume the practice of law and to try to support his family. Under this appeal all the long-cherished prejudices of Governor Brownlow at once gave way. The immense loss the State had sustained by reason of Harris' conduct—the overwhelming ruin and universal desolation he had brought to the people of the State—were all forgotten by that great, forgiving heart at the recital of the sufferings of the exile and the poverty of his family. A pledge of protection and immunity was generously and unconditionally given. Governor Brownlow at once sent a message to the Legislature, asking it to withdraw the offer of a reward for the arrest of Harris, which was accordingly done on November 11, 1867.*

As soon as the mail could carry the news to Liverpool Harris set sail for the United States. On his arrival in New York, without meeting anyone who knew him, he hurried on to Nashville and stopped with a friend at a private house. The next morning, being the Sabbath, at an early hour, before it was known he was in the city, Harris and ex-Governor Brown presented themselves before Governor Brownlow. When the latter saw them approaching, with extended arms he advanced to meet Harris, saying: "While the lamp holds out to burn, the vilest sinner may return." Harris and Brown both laughed feebly at this pleasantry, but it was plain that the former did not enjoy it. The case of Harris was then discussed. He was apprehensive that he would be arrested the moment he reached his home in Paris. Governor Brownlow assured him of his protection,

---

*It is a curious fact that the Act of the Legislature repealing the law offering a reward for Harris, winds up with a brand on him: "that the Governor is hereby instructed to revoke his proclamation offering a reward for the apprehension of said Isham G. Harris, *the traitor.*"

and directed him to telegraph him if he should be arrested, and he would become his bail.*

The following extract is taken from a letter in the Atlanta *Constitution* of 1886, inspired, if not written, by the Hon. W. C. Whitthorne, the intimate friend of Harris, and no doubt written at his (Harris') suggestion. This gives a little different version of this affair:

"With this (a reward of $5000) hanging over him, when the rebellion collapsed, Harris made haste for Mexico, and upon the failure of the French Empire sailed for Europe. Meantime his family was without means of comfortable support. Governor Brownlow, softening much toward Harris, and becoming convinced in his own mind that in some of his former charges and denunciations he had done Governor Harris injustice, sent for one of the receivers whom he had appointed to take charge of a State railroad, and told him to appoint quietly a relative (a son) of Governor Harris to a position which would enable him to support the family. This was done.

"When Harris returned from Europe he went directly to Nashville and called on the Governor, by whom he was received with unexpected cordiality. Harris explained that he had come to surrender himself, preferring that to a summary arrest. Brownlow insisted that no trouble would then come from the old proclamation of reward for his capture. Harris insisted that as the United States marshal had a warrant for his arrest he would prefer to have it settled before he should go home. When he met his family he desired, if possible, it should be in peace. The Governor told him to go home at once, and he would arrange the matter with the marshal. This he did by becoming bondsman for Harris' appearance when wanted.

"The night of Harris' arrival at home one of the Unionists of the place telegraphed the Governor that Harris had returned and suggested prompt and quiet measures for his arrest. Governor Brownlow replied that he was fully informed of Harris' movements, and that he was on a bond for his appearance.

"In the change of time and politics, Harris, upon whose head a price had been put by Brownlow for treason, came to represent his State in the Senate. * * * The moment it came within

---

*This is the statement of this transaction given by Governor Brownlow in his lifetime, as well as by Ex-Governor Neill S. Brown, who negotiated for the return of Harris.

his power to do so he used his influence to keep a relative of his old antagonist, but later friend, in place. * * *"

Thus the leader of secession in Tennessee, the brains and the will power of his party, and one of the last men in the South to give up the struggle, returned peaceably to his home to resume his ordinary duties without arrest and without punishment. And yet such men complain of the cruel treatment they received at the hands of the Government after the war!

Governor Harris returned to his home, in Paris, Tenn., and resumed his old profession—the practice of law. In 1877 he was elected to the United States Senate, which position he still holds. He is serving his third term in the Senate. Notwithstanding his advanced age he is still the leader of his party in the State. There has been a singular inconsistency in his character as a public man since he became Senator. At home, in Tennessee, he is regarded as bitter and extreme in his opinions. He always takes the side of extreme Bourbonism in his speeches. Evidently he fully understands how to cater to the rabid tastes of his followers. In the Senate, on the contrary, he seldom makes speeches, and when he does they are nearly entirely free from narrow partisanism and sectional bitterness. At Washington he is regarded as a very broad and liberal-minded statesman, who has lifted himself above the narrowness of Southern politicians. Like wine, he is supposed to have grown milder with age. At home he is known to be what he was in 1861.

I record with pleasure, however, that wherever he may be he is always bold, open, and manly. No concealment nor deception marks his course. Among his fellow Senators he is held in high esteem and respect. His ability is conceded on all sides. Indeed, he is regarded as the ablest man in his party in the Senate from the South.*

During the first term of the administration of Governor Brownlow the Thirteenth and Fourteenth Amendments to the Constitution of the United States were ratified by the Legislature of the State on his recommendation. During their consideration President Johnson used all his influence and the promise of offices to defeat their ratification.

---

*Since the above was written Senator Harris departed this life in 1897. With faults he combined many noble traits. He was frank, independent, and straightforward. He was always honest, both as a man and a politician. There was no indirectness in him. His fidelity to his friends and his faithfulness to his promises were remarkable.

In October, 1867, Governor Brownlow was elected by the Legislature to a seat in the United States Senate. His majority was twenty-five over all competitors. If he had announced himself before members became committed to other candidates, his election would have been almost unanimous. His competitors were the Hon. Horace Maynard, Andrew J. Fletcher, Colonel William B. Stokes, and General Joseph A. Cooper. Mr. Maynard, on learning that Mr. Brownlow was a candidate, wisely withdrew from the race.

Mr. Brownlow remained in the discharge of his duties as Governor until the latter part of February, 1869. On March 4, the very day Mr. Johnson retired from the Presidency, and that on which General Grant became President, he took his seat as Senator, the successor of the Hon. David T. Patterson, the son-in-law of Mr. Johnson. Thus Mr. Johnson and Judge Patterson, who were placed in power by the opponents of the Democratic party, having gone over to that party, were sent into retirement by public sentiment at the same time. On the same day they were succeeded in their respective offices by unflinching patriots, Grant and Brownlow. The credentials of Governor Brownlow as Senator were presented to the Senate by the great war Governor of Indiana, Oliver P. Morton.

While the race for Senator was pending Mr. Brownlow asked his son what people were saying about his candidacy. His son replied that some of his opponents said it was an outrage for him to seek the Senatorial term of six years when he was about to step into eternity. "They say," Brownlow replied, "I am going to die, do they? Well," said he with a smile, "I expect to live the term out, but, if I don't, the Senate chamber is not a bad place from which to depart for Heaven." Six years and four months after taking his seat as Senator a friend called to see him one morning in his home, in Knoxville, and finding him writing asked him what he was doing. He replied: "I am dictating an obituary notice of the death of Andrew Johnson. When I was elected to the Senate it was objected to me that I would not live out my term, and here I am, with a good appetite and a clear conscience, writing the obituary of my successor."

While Senator he was punctual in his attendance and faithful in the discharge of all his duties, though an invalid. While co-operating in all party questions with the Republicans, he at the same time preserved the right of individual judgment. General

Grant as President had no firmer, truer friend, and yet on at least two important occasions, and perhaps oftener, he voted against the recommendations of the Executive. He yielded no blind subserviency to the President, though he greatly admired him. He regarded him as the best and truest man in the Republican party. Mr. Brownlow delivered no oral speeches. His voice was gone, and his nervous prostration was such that he had to recline on a couch all his time when not in the Senate chamber. Whatever he wished to say, therefore, was invariably written out and read by the Clerk. His speeches were always clear, pointed, and strong. There was no such thing as misunderstanding his crisp and ringing utterances. It was a pathetic sight to witness this noble old Roman, reclining day by day in his invalid chair, watching with intense interest the proceedings of the Senate, his mind all alive as in the days of his wonderful physical vigor. His body was enfeebled, but not his intellect. The latter still glowed with all the fire and energy of 1861, when his pen electrified the hearts of loyal East Tennesseeans. And ill fared the man, even in his enfeebled old age, whose temerity roused the old lion.

During his term of six years it can be safely affirmed that Senator Brownlow did nothing to lower the dignity of his high office, nothing unworthy of the great State he had the honor to represent. Never were her people represented with more faithfulness, or with more dignity. When he left the Senate he left it with the respect and confidence of all his fellow Senators. He left the office, too, as he had entered it—poor. No charges of ill-gotten wealth ever blurred his name. Even in Tennessee, with all the abuse that has been heaped upon his administration, no charge of venality or personal corruption has ever been laid at his door. No one has ever dared to say that he had ever been personally corrupt. With all the investigating committees raised by the Democrats, after they came into power in 1870, no spot nor stain was ever found in his record. Whatever may have been the case with the crowd of worthless and corrupt men who at the close of the war came to the surface and naturally gathered around those in power for the sake of plunder, as they did around both Brownlow and Grant, in none of the nefarious operations of these men was he a participant. Like Grant, too, his readiness to oblige, his devotion to his friends, and his too ready credulity, exposed him to the wiles of such men, of bad men, not in the least suspecting their purpose. This was the weakness of Governor Brownlow. No danger, no threat of an enemy, could move him, but it was hard, almost impossible for him to say no to a friend.

It is a singular circumstance that Mr. Johnson should have been the successor of Mr. Brownlow in the Senate as the latter had been his successor as Governor. Mr. Johnson was elected Senator in 1875, and took his seat on March 4 in an extraordinary session of the Senate. But for this extra session of the Senate he would never have entered on his duties as Senator under his election in 1875, for he died on the 31st day of the following July.

As it was, he was there long enough to revive his old quarrel with General Grant and Mr. Brownlow. It would seem that an ex-President of the United States, who had been restored to the Senate after two desperate contests, would have been content to wear his fresh honors with peaceable dignity. But not so with this ex-President. The dark, deep, tempestuous passions pent up in his bosom for long years must find an outlet. On the first opportunity he poured forth the hot lava of his heart on his great enemy, General Grant, and on his old rival, Brownlow. The former, from his height of exaltation and with the unaffected dignity which marks the superior mind, treated the assault with silence, more withering than the bitterest words. But the latter, from his sick couch, gathered up his remaining strength for his last struggle with his old enemy.

Johnson, in his blind rage, was floundering about to find something to say against the invalid who lately occupied the seat now held by himself. This invalid, who had held for six years a seat in the Senate with so much senatorial dignity, had gone home, as it was generally supposed, to die, carrying with him the respect and sympathy of a majority of his countrymen. Johnson, without the slightest ground, went out of his way to arraign Brownlow as the "refractory Governor" of Tennessee for his course while the Fourteenth Amendment was pending before the Legislature. He accused him of having tried "to control the Legislature." Mr. Brownlow, in his answer, shows what everybody at the time knew to be so, that he and the great body of both houses of the Legislature were in perfect accord as to the Fourteenth Amendment. He also shows that a few "refractory" members, through the influence of Mr. Johnson as

President, had absented themselves from the Legislative hall, though present in the House, in order to prevent a quorum. He says on this point:

"Recurring to President Johnson's attempt to influence the action of the Legislature on the proposed Fourteenth Amendment, I will say that several days before the meeting of the Legislature Johnson ascertained that a majority of the body would vote for the Amendment. To carry out his lawless purpose to defeat the amendment, his emissaries came from Washington to Tennessee and wrote from the Capitol to their friends in this State that 'the President desired that the Legislature be broken up rather than the amendment be ratified.' It was understood at Nashville that members who would 'bolt' and aid in the revolutionary scheme conceived and inaugurated by President Johnson to defeat the amendment would be rewarded by Federal appointments.

"And it is a singular coincidence that many of the seditionists were subsequently rewarded by the President with Federal appointments. Letters from the bosom friends of the President at Washington came to members of the Legislature, and those supposed to have influence with them, as thickly as autumn leaves in a brisk gale, advising the breaking up of the Legislature in order to defeat the amendment. One of the bolters received a letter from the Hon. Edmund Cooper, President Johnson's private secretary, 'advising him to absent himself from his seat in the Legislature that the amendment to the Constitution might be defeated at all hazards.'

"The Nashville *Press and Times* of July 18, 1866, contained this extract from the Cincinnati *Gazette's* Washington correspondent: 'Last night Mr. Cooper (the President's private secretary) declared to a company of gentlemen that if the President could possibly prevent the assembling of a quorum of the Tennessee Legislature he would surely do it.'"

Again Mr. Brownlow says: "The whole question in controversy in Tennessee was whether in palpable violation of the Constitution of the State, a small minority of the Legislature, acting under the advice of Andrew Johnson, as President of the United States, should, by lawless revolutionary means, block legislation and break up the Legislature of the State. This was the sole question as the record shows. The statements of Senator Johnson to the contrary are what you Northern people term 'misrepresenting the truth of history,' but what we in Tennessee call 'unmitigated lying.'

"As Governor of the State, and contrary to the wishes of Andrew Johnson, I convened the Legislature in extraordinary session for the purpose of submitting to it the ratification or rejection of the Fourteenth Article of Amendment to the Constitution, which had only recently been passed by Congress. * * * But Andrew Johnson, as President, determined to interfere in the administration of the government of the State, and did interfere in as flagrant a manner as President Grant is even charged with doing by the Democratic press of to-day or by this same Andrew Johnson. He had the effrontery to endeavor to browbeat and bully me and the loyal majority of the Legislature associated with me into acquiescence in that miserable political abortion, known as 'My policy.' * * *

"The sequel, however, proved that he was 'barking up the wrong tree,' and when he issued orders to me he was not dealing with Perry of South Carolina nor one of the Provisional Governors of the Cotton States, who held his commission and felt that they owed their position to him. I was nominated and elected by the loyal people of the State, and in defiance of the known opposition of Andrew Johnson. In a convention of five hundred and thirty or forty delegates I was nominated by acclamation, and that, too, after Andrew Johnson had been laboring for weeks to prevent it. * * * Johnson opposed me because he desired to hold at the same time the offices of Vice-President and Governor of Tennessee. From his previous knowledge of my character he apprehended difficulty in running the State government of Tennessee while I held the office of Governor. * * *"

Finally, Mr. Brownlow, after a long and calm but searching review of the question at issue between him and Mr. Johnson, says:

"Andrew Johnson and myself made war on each other about thirty-eight years ago, and have kept it up without intermission ever since, save during a brief period when he 'threw up the sponge' and made overtures for peace. Now that he has renewed the war in the Senate, I say to him:

". . . Lay on, Macduff,
And damn'd be him who first cries, Hold, enough!"

The refutation of the charges and insinuations of Mr. Johnson was conclusive and overwhelming. The tone of the reply was in the main mild and dignified. It presented Mr. Johnson's overweening disposition to interfere with and control all legislation in Congress, as well as in the late insurgent States, to suit his "policy" in so clear a light that it must have been exceedingly mortifying to him. This triumphant reply, coming on the heels of the almost universal cry of indignation against him for his indecent attack on President Grant, must have had a most depressing effect on his proud spirit. When his death occurred three months afterward I was disposed to believe that Mr. Brownlow's letter helped to hasten his end. General Grant remarked afterward that he did not see "how anything more pointed and vigorous could be written" than this letter of Mr. Brownlow. This was the last fight of these two men. In three months Mr. Johnson passed away, "his last battle fought, his last victory won." Two years later Mr. Brownlow also silently passed away, amid the tears of a loyal people, grateful to his memory for his faithfulness when Mr. Johnson deserted them. On April 29, 1877, in the seventy-second year of his age, William Gannaway Brownlow departed this life, in his home in Knoxville, sincerely mourned as but few men have ever been.

At the risk of being charged with indelicacy I venture to speak of my own personal relations with Mr. Brownlow, as they throw much light on his character. Our acquaintanceship commenced in 1839 or 1840, while I was yet a boy. We lived in adjoining counties. From the first our relations were cordial. From 1844 up to the time of his death we were on the most intimate and confidential terms. There was never a break in this friendship. Twice during this time, namely, in the Presidential race of 1852, when he supported Mr. Webster, and again in the Gubernatorial canvass of 1869, when he supported Governor Senter, we differed widely as to men and supported different candidates, but this wrought no change in our personal relations. In 1844, just after I left college, we published a joint list of appointments for public speaking, and were together in the counties of Sullivan, Carter, Greene, and Cocke, making speeches for Mr. Clay. Traveling together, on horseback, as we did in those days, and speaking together, we naturally became intimate.

Four years after this, in 1848, I removed away from my old

home in Greeneville to Knoxville, a larger and far more important town. In 1849 Mr. Brownlow visited Knoxville and held a consultation as to the advisability of his removing with his paper to this larger town. He decided to make a change of residence, and he at once put his purpose in execution. From that time forward his paper had a larger field for circulation and wider influence. It became a real power in the State.

After an experience of over fifty-five years with men, I can safely affirm that he was one of the truest and most unselfish of men in his friendship I ever knew. Daily and hourly he manifested his beneficence to those around him. I venture to say that he did more kindness to those with whom he came in contact than any man who ever lived in the State. No wonder he had a hold on the affections of the people who knew him, such as no other man I have ever met. He was a popular idol. On the other hand, his independence, his positive, brave, outspoken words of censure or condemnation made for him the bitterest enemies any man ever had. Yet many of these became in after life his truest friends. He bore no malice and was always ready for reconciliation. These reconciliations were always as simple and as natural as those of children. There was not a word of explanation—no ceremony, no apologies—but simply cordial speaking and acting as old friends.

A man who could excite in the hearts and minds of men the tenderest emotions of friendship, and for forty years retain this feeling by personal magnetism and noble acts alone, surely could not have been a bad man. Bad men do not attract, but repel.

When I was a young man Mr. Brownlow rendered me a favor, not of a pecuniary character, which was in part the foundation of whatever good fortune afterward attended me. For this I was always profoundly grateful. In after life the memory of this act always kept alive my faithfulness and devotion to him. He constantly rendered me acts of kindness all through life. And I, in return for all this, was constant in my efforts to serve him. I have the consciousness of having been faithful and of some service to him. Some extracts from a letter written to me, three years before his death, show how magnanimous he was and how appreciative of any acts of kindness on the part of others. I quote from it for the further purpose of showing his estimate of General Grant:

UNITED STATES SENATE CHAMBER,
WASHINGTON, February 23, 1874.
DEAR JUDGE:
I have to acknowledge the receipt of your kind letter of a few days since in reply to my own informing you that you had been appointed by the President a Visitor to West Point.

I totally disagree with you in one position taken in your letter, viz., that I have done *more* for you than you for me. True, as you state, I have been your friend from boyhood, but you have been my friend from your boyhood, and I feel that you have done me as many kindnesses and been of as much service to me as I have done or been to you. Be this as it may, neither you nor I will ever stop, when either is called on by the other, to make a calculation as to who was ahead. The difference between you and others with whom I have been intimately associated consists simply in this—you have a more grateful appreciation of kindnesses done you than most men.

There are no emoluments in the appointment which the President has given you, but I have been gratified at it, because it will enable you to become personally acquainted with Grant under favorable auspices. . . . And after you have become acquainted with him, if you make a favorable impression on him, as I doubt not you will do, you will be enabled to exercise influence with him whether you shall be a member of Congress while his term lasts or not. There are many men not in Congress who have as much influence, if not more influence, with him than anybody in Congress. This fact is, among other things, why I like Grant. If a man has his friendship or esteem, he is not afraid to give him his support, whether he is supported by a member of Congress or not.

I have given the President an earnest and honest, but not obsequious support, and he understands this perfectly. I have reason to believe that he has the most kindly feelings for me. I was for the confirmation of Williams [for one of the Judges of the Supreme Court], and believed then and now that the press of the country did Williams and Grant injustice in that matter. I was warmly opposed to the confirmation of Caleb Cushing [for the same position], and regarded the President as having made a grave mistake in appointing him. But, with all his faults, Grant is the best man in our party, and I hope he will be re-elected. He has more *heart* than any leader we have, and I admire his steadfast devotion to his friends.

You must come on to the West Point examination. I want you to meet the President, because I want him to esteem you as I do. It is but a year until I shall have forever bidden farewell to public life. When I retire I mean to retire in earnest. Advancing age and bad health admonish me that my course is rapidly drawing to a close. I shall not on that account, however, cease to feel an interest in a few tried and long-trusted friends like yourself.

I hope to see you in Congress or Judge of the U. S. District Court of Tennessee. . . .

Your friend,
W. G. BROWNLOW.

This was the Brownlow, the author I knew—full of kindliness, gentleness, frankness, and gratitude. And this was as he manifested himself in daily life to all his friends.

One word in reference to my going to Congress. I can truthfully say that I did not desire the position. More than once the position was within my easy grasp. For many reasons I did not wish it. And now in my old age I look back with satisfaction that during all that time I was able to resist the sometimes most flattering prospects held out to me by my friends to seek Congressional honors. Nor did I ever seek the position of a United States District judgeship. Public offices have never had any special attractions for me. The attractions of home far outweighed them with me.

CHAPTER VI.

Brownlow's Popularity—An Editor Rather than a Party Politician—Remarkable Individuality—Compliment from Knoxville *Register*--Press Tributes to Governor Brownlow—Memory—Place in History.

MR. BROWNLOW's modesty, perhaps I should say his self-abnegation, was equaled only by his boldness. There was in him no egotism, no boasting, no self-glorification. Flattery fell on him as water on a rock. He must have been well advanced in life, and long after his name had filled the land before he became conscious of his superior powers. When an election for Governor was to take place in 1865 he had apparently never thought of the office until he was urged to become a candidate. Again, in 1867, when a Senator was to be elected he did not seek the position, nor apparently think of it, until he was again pressed to become a candidate. In the meantime four candidates were seeking the office, among them Mr. Maynard, who had received many pledges of support. The Legislature at that time was composed almost exclusively of loyal old Whigs. With them he was the most popular man in the State. For them he had been making sacrifices all his life—time, money, and editorial labors—but seeking nothing for himself until pressed to do so. Unlike certain editors of this day, he did not expect to be liberally paid for praise and puffs. The columns of his paper, as well as his editorial labors, were given almost gratuitously to his party. He wrote from honest convictions alone. No hope of reward ever induced him to advocate men or measures he did not approve. During his long editorial life he was conspicuously consistent in the advocacy of principles. He was a Whig in every fiber, and never departed from that faith. If his party put up for office objectional men, as it did at times, he refused to support them, but remained true to his party. On account of these things he never lost prestige with it.

He was totally unfamiliar with party machinery and party tricks. With dauntless courage and unparalleled independence he pursued the open highway of right. He walked in no devious byways. His was a plain, manly fight, made in the open day, in the sight of all mankind. No one ever doubted where he stood, or on what side. His frank, brave, clarion-like words always proclaimed his position. In truth he was the most independent man of his time. He was apparently rageful and fierce, ravenous as a lion for prey. But in private life he was the gentlest, tenderest, most childlike of men. Said a stranger once on being introduced to him: "Mr. Brownlow, I have known you a long time by character." "Which character," replied Brownlow, "have you gotten hold of? for I have two characters, one given me by my friends, the other by my enemies."

He possessed a remarkable individuality. He was not like anyone else, nor was anyone like him. He stood like an object against the sky, clear and distinct in outline. While he thus stood alone, he was in sympathy, feeling, and action in perfect harmony with all around him. He was always in touch with the people—never apart from them. Yet he never flattered them; never pandered to their prejudices or their base passions. He stood ready to reprove them when they were wrong. His word was law, and yet there was no dictation. He simply told his party what he thought and intended doing.

His convictions were earnest and sincere; his feelings deep and intense. In the language applied to another: "His feelings, acute and earnest, had given all their warmth to his principles, and what he once believed his duty commanded he pursued with the devout self-dedication of a religious obligation. To this temper, which by some secret of its constitution has a spell to sway the minds of mankind, there was added a captivating personality."

An Ohio gentleman who located in East Tennessee after the war, who had been a Union soldier, and then like so many Northern men, turned to be a most bitter Democrat, some years ago asked a prominent gentleman who had been a friend of the South during the Civil War what kind of a man Brownlow was. He replied: "He was a man who never turned his back on a friend or an enemy."

The remarks of Macaulay on Sir James MacKintosh are not inapplicable to Mr. Brownlow:

"He had a quick eye for the redeeming parts of character, and a large toleration for the infirmities of men exposed to strong temptations. But this lenity did not arise from ignorance or neglect of moral distinctions. On every occasion he showed himself firm where principles were in question, but full of charity towards individuals."

One of the highest compliments ever paid to the ability of Mr. Brownlow was contained in the Knoxville *Register*, a secession sheet, in February, 1862, written by some bitter enemy who was protesting against his release from custody and against his being allowed to go North. The writer said:

"We do not desire to be understood as attaching an undue importance to the discharge of Brownlow from the custody of the Confederate authorities. The writer of this has known this individual for years. He is, in few words, a diplomat of the first water. Brownlow rarely undertakes anything unless he sees his way entirely through the millstone. He covers over his really profound knowledge of human nature with an appearance of eccentricity and extravagance. If any of our readers indulge the idea that Brownlow is not 'smart' in the full acceptation of the term, they should abolish the delusion at once and forever. Crafty, cunning, generous to his particular friends, benevolent and charitable to their faults, ungrateful and implacable to his enemies, we cannot refrain from saying that he is the best judge of human nature within the bounds of the Southern Confederacy.

"In procuring from the Confederate authorities a safe conduct to a point within the Hessian lines, he has exhibited the most consummate will. * * * Brownlow was triumphant and Benjamin outwitted. In fact, we do not know whether to laugh or get mad with the manner in which Brownlow has wound the Confederate Government around his thumb. * * *

"Brownlow! God forbid that we should unnecessarily magnify the importance of his name, but there are facts connected with the character of the man which a just and discriminating public would condemn if we did not give them due notice.

"In brief, Brownlow has preached at every church and schoolhouse, made stump speeches at every crossroad, and knows every man, woman, and child, and their fathers and grandfathers before them, in East Tennessee. As a Methodist circuit rider, a political stump speaker, a temperance orator, and the editor of a newspaper, he has been equally successful in our division of the State."

The following tribute to the memory of Governor Brownlow appeared after his death in the Austin *Statesman*, edited by a life-long Democrat, Colonel L. J. DuPre, who was formerly a citizen of Tennessee and an officer in the Confederate Army, stationed at Knoxville part of the time during the war, and who was a large-minded, generous man:

" * * * Whatever may be said of William G. Brownlow, as he was in the pulpit, in the sanctum, or as a politician, his personal honesty was never questioned, his boundless generosity never doubted, and in private life his truthfulness was never suspected. He was personally the most generous of men and most devoted and tenacious in his attachments, and the very poor in East Tennessee never knew such a friend. When Knoxville was once ravaged by cholera there was no hut of poverty and wretchedness that did not have its pale watcher by the bedside of the plague-stricken in the person of the violent, fighting parson. When Brownlow's *Whig* was the most successful newspaper in money-making in the South, the editor and proprietor who railed out so bitterly against his partisan enemies, gave money to the poor and helpless until he was himself almost impoverished. Bitterly as he was denounced and fiercely as he was hated as a party leader, it was never safe where Brownlow, the man and private citizen, was personally known to denounce his name or deeds. His friends were not exclusively of his own church or party, and Brownlow's grave will be bedewed with tears by the whole population of Knoxville. His widow is as gentle and amiable and practical as the inflammable parson was full of enthusiasm and violent as a preacher, editor, and party leader. In fact, Brownlow never came before the footlights save as a tragedian. Behind the scenes the very Brownlow himself was as kindly and generous and gentle as became the husband of such a wife. Now that he is dead the public will learn for the first time, long as Brownlow has been conspicuous, that there were two Brownlows as different from each other as light from darkness. The press and people of East Tennessee will now tell how very little they knew of the private citizen, the friend and philanthropist, who only knew the preacher, the fiery editor, and furious party-leader. Brownlow, when in good health, was an admirable story-teller. As a fireside colloquist he was simply peerless. Here was ever illustrated all that was admirable in his many-sided character. He knew personally all the party-leaders of his time. He was an acute listener and observer, and his sketches of great men were inimitable. As a Methodist, as an editor, as a stump speaker, he was irresistible in the midst of his adherents of mountains and valleys, and when we remember that he was a Whig and Andrew Johnson, his neighbor at Greeneville, a Democrat, both omnipotent, each in his own party, it is not amazing that these two led after them into Unionism the great body of the people of the mountainous districts of three coterminous States."

I add two other extracts, one from the Memphis *Avalanche*, and the other from the Memphis *Ledger*, both Democratic papers.

From the Memphis *Avalanche*—"'Parson' Brownlow belonged to that class of 'good haters' so dear to Dr. Johnson. Yet a more tender, kinder heart never beat beneath the bodice of a woman. His hates were public. They grew out of political or religious controversies. To his friends and neighbors in private life his heart went out in kind acts and deeds. His charities were numberless and unostentatious. The heart of the fearless, fiery politician who in excitement hurled the thunderbolts of burning invective at his antagonists, and was even willing in his zeal to lay aside his religious creed and enforce argument with something stronger than words, could bleed in the presence of a child's grief. By the people with whom most of his life was spent he was much beloved as a neighbor and a friend. Nothing in his stormy career served to alienate him from their affections. They overlooked and forgave the faults springing from his impetuous nature, for they knew something of the heart that beat within."

From the Memphis *Ledger*—"He was true to his friends and relentless toward his enemies. He could express more vituperativeness and scorching hate than any half a dozen men that ever appeared in American politics. His style has been imitated, but never successfully copied, by men of less native intellect and courage. His private life was an utter contradiction of the nature he exhibited in public. Socially, he was genial and sympathetic, in his family almost idolized, and among his immediate neighbors, especially the poor, he was held in the highest esteem. The man was a strange compound, and there are no more like him. The style of journalism by which he brought himself into notice and became so terrible to his enemies happily passed away before its author, and is no longer tolerated by an intelligent public. Whatever his faults and the warp of his nature, he was honest, fearless and consistent in his way."

Finally, my remarks made at a public memorial meeting, held in Knoxville immediately after Mr. Brownlow's death, are given:

"Mr. President: In rising to second the resolutions just read, I avail myself of the opportunity to pay a slight tribute to the memory of an old friend. I have known Governor Brownlow well and intimately for many years, and I can truthfully say he was a *remarkable* man. With no adventitious aids, with no great fortune, he won honor and achieved greatness, and filled the land with his fame. To-day his name is known and his memory honored in every hamlet, village, and city of the land.

"Of all the public men whom I have known he stood the nearest to and was most in sympathy with the great body of the people, and this was the secret of his wonderful power and influence. He swayed the public mind, where he was well known, with a magnetic power such as no other man could exert. He was the sincere and unpretending friend of the people. All were treated alike, all with kindness, whether rich or poor. No man was ever refused a favor by him. He was the most generous man I ever knew. His 'hand was open as day to melting charity.' Though the idol of the people and a great popular leader, he was no demagogue. He did not win popularity by flattering the people, but rather by his deep sympathy with them and by a manly defense of their rights. He feared not, when it was right, to censure them, or to oppose their will or defy their wrath. He was utterly fearless. Thirty years ago, when Federalism was exceedingly odious, he gloried everywhere in being a Federalist of the school of Alexander Hamilton. His undaunted courage, both physical and moral, has won the admiration of the world. By his bold and fearless words in his speeches and writings he has often presented himself to the public in an untrue light, as implacable, bitter, and unforgiving. He was the very contrary. To his enemies, while the battle lasted, he was fierce and terrible as the Nemean lion; to his friends and his family he was gentle and playful as the lamb. He was full of sympathy, full of kindness, full of forgiveness, full of the most childlike tenderness and sweetness.

"The last of three remarkable men who lived in adjoining counties—Johnson, Nelson, and Brownlow—has passed away. Johnson, strong, self-reliant, aggressive, and invincible, fought his way to the highest seat of honor; Nelson, the noble and the true, full of courage, full of a fiery, lofty eloquence, the Chevalier

Bayard of the South, without fear and without reproach; and Brownlow, with keen intellect, noble devotion to right, personal magnetism, determined will, and an audacity in courage never surpassed.

"All these remarkable men have passed away, leaving only their names and deeds and memory behind. Yesterday they were with us; we heard their mighty voices; to-day they are silent in the stillness of death.

"In the presence of the mighty dead all passion should be hushed into silence. Anciently, among the old Greeks, no mortal body was supposed to be able to cross the river Styx into the shadowy land beyond; so, here, hatred, malice, and envy should not pass the threshold of the chamber of death.

"Mr. President, our friend fell not until his mission was fulfilled. In his life, as well as in his death, he was like the lofty oak of his native mountains—tough, compact, unyielding in fiber; casting its roots deep into the earth and lifting its spreading branches high into the sky; the gentle breeze moved not its giant form; it falls not until in the fullness of time the axe is laid to its roots, or until upheaved by the earthquake, or swept by the fury of the tornado."

All things considered, Mr. Brownlow should, and I believe will, stand out in history as the most conspicuous of all the Union leaders of the South. No comparison can be justly drawn between him and the Union leaders of Kentucky and Missouri. These States were never out of the Union. Their loyal people were at all times under the protection of national authority, and the national army. There was, therefore, no strain at any time on the loyalty of the Union leaders of these States. If any of them ever grew weak it was not caused by danger, or pressure, or despair, but resulted from waning patriotism.

How different the case with Mr. Brownlow. For more than four months before his paper was suspended, the last vestige and sign of the authority of the United States had disappeared in Tennessee. Yet, during all this time, with unparalleled audacity, he openly and defiantly denounced the Confederate Government as a dreadful despotism. He boldly proclaimed that he would be rejoiced at all its defeats and at its overthrow. Finally, in hourly danger of his life, he became a wanderer in the depths of the mountains. At last lured by a false promise of protection he returned to his home and was arrested and thrown into a filthy prison, where he was kept nearly a month. When, to save his life, he was released from prison he was kept under military guard in his own house more than two months longer. Long before this every prominent Union leader except himself had disappeared, or become silent, or joined the enemy. No other Union leader in all the secession States had since May, 1861, dared to raise a feeble voice publicly in behalf of the Union. And yet during all this time the voice of this brave man was still heard cheering on the loyal and the true, and proudly defying and insulting those making war on the Government. Where was there a parallel to his case?

ANDREW JOHNSON.

CHAPTER I.

Early Youth—Apprenticeship in Greenville, S. C.—Removal to Greeneville, Tenn, Where Tailor Shop Still Stands—Elected to Legislature, 1835—Defeated, 1837—Again Elected, 1839.

ANDREW JOHNSON was born, as is well known, near Raleigh, N. C., in 1808. His parents were poor and very humble. In Raleigh he was bound at the age of ten as an apprentice to learn the trade of a tailor, and worked at his trade for two years at Laurens Court House, S. C.* It is reasonably certain that he worked for a while also in Greenville, S. C. In 1826 he determined to move to the West, and accordingly started on his journey. One Saturday afternoon in the beautiful month of May, a little one-horse wagon, primitive in construction, drawn by a poor and blind horse, was driven into the outskirts of the village of Greeneville, Tenn., where the exhausted horse was halted. In this low flat ground there rises an excellent spring, then open to public use, but long afterward purchased by the boy who drove the wagon. Over the spring there now droops a large willow tree, planted by him when a sprig, taken, it is said, from the celebrated willow over the grave of Napoleon, in St. Helena. The last residence of this adventurous boy stands on a lot that embraces this spring, now owned and occupied by the Hon. Andrew J. Patterson, his grandson. In the wagon, or accompanying it, were Mrs. Mary McDonough Dougherty, the mother of Andrew Johnson, and Turner Dougherty, her second husband, and Andrew himself, eighteen years of age. They had crossed the mountains into East Ten-

---

*Mr. Johnson was bound out to a man of the name of J. J. Selby. Selby was a hard and cruel master, according to the statement of W. W. Jordon, a neighbor of Mr. Johnson in Greeneville, Tenn., to whom the latter detailed all the facts of his early life. He ran away, when he was about seventeen, because of ill-treatment, after giving Selby a good whipping. This is the account given by Mr. Jordon, derived from Mr. Johnson and recently published by the daughter of Jordon, Blanche Gray Jordon.

nessee from North Carolina by the road leading to Jonesboro, the same road, it is believed, by which Andrew Jackson had entered the State about forty years previously. These two men, remarkable in more senses than one, traveled the same road in their poverty and obscurity until they both reached the object of their aspirations. Both were young, both were filled with irrepressible ambition. Jackson came as a lawyer, Johnson came as a journeyman tailor. Jackson came as a knight, finely mounted, leading a racer, with a brace of pistols in his holsters; and several hundred dollars in gold. Johnson came in a cart driving one poor horse.

Soon after the arrival of the little party, Andrew, with a quick elastic step, went into the village in search of old Joseph Brown,* from whom he wished to purchase corn fodder. Mr. Brown was soon found, for at that day it was an easy matter to find any of the citizens of the little town, so few were they. William R. Brown, a son of Joseph, a mere lad, was sent with Johnson to Brown's farm a mile away, to procure the fodder.

The next morning the peaceful stillness of a Sabbath in a Presbyterian Scotch-Irish village reigned over Greeneville. Scarcely a sound was heard save the singing of birds in the neighboring groves, and the noise of the water falling from the race-head of a little mill that stood at the foot of a great hill south of the town—for though the mill rested on the Sabbath day, the water flowed on unceasingly. The scene was full of beauty and loveliness. The atmosphere was laden with the perfume of honeysuckles and wild roses. From the neat gardens cultivated flowers shed their fragrance on the soft air. Greeneville, at all times lovely, was never more so than on that bright May morning, as it lay in solemn stillness flooded with light, nestling serenely among its green hills. From the tops of these hills, which so charmingly encircle the town, was seen off a few miles southward the great Smoky Mountains, more than six

---

*The said Joseph Brown was formerly a Scotch-Irish school teacher and a Justice of the Peace. He was a worthy man and the patriarch of Greeneville. Away back, in the dim past, I had the advantage of his learning, as well as of his ferrule, when in the due course of his alternations from schoolhouse to schoolhouse, then so common, his school fell within my reach.

"A man severe he was, and stern to view;
I knew him well, and every truant knew;
Well had the boding tremblers learned to trace
The day's disasters in his morning face."

thousand feet in height, stretching away forty or fifty miles southward and eastward in surpassing grandeur. The mountains, their lofty summits and wide and graceful sweep of outline lifted up sharply against the deep blue sky, presented a view of restful majesty rarely to be found.

On this Sabbath day, young Andrew Johnson again went up into the village. Whether, as he walked along the main street with quick determined steps, indicative of the powerful will within, he dreamed of the future—of schemes of ambition—no one can ever tell. Naturally he directed his steps to the post-office. The office was in the storehouse of William Dixon, a wealthy as well as a worthy Covenanter from Ireland. He had been postmaster for a long time, and was so to remain until his death nearly twenty years afterward. Andrew took a seat in the store, and either asked for, or someone handed him, a newspaper, and he began to read. Little did the villagers who stood around dream that in that boy there was a man of destiny.

John A. Brown, elder brother of William R. Brown, the lad who had gone for the fodder the day before, was a clerk in the store. Seeing Johnson was a stranger, perhaps attracted by his appearance, he entered into conversation with him. He learned where the lad was from; that he had merely stopped over to rest, that he was on his way to the West. He also learned that Johnson was a tailor by trade. Thereupon Brown urged the young man to settle in Greeneville, telling him the only tailor there, a Mr. Maloney, was getting old and was not able to do much work. As a further inducement for him to remain he proposed to Johnson to let him make for himself at once a suit of broadcloth.

These and perhaps other considerations had the effect of changing the mind of Johnson. So, the next morning he came to the store, got the material for the suit and made it up. Johnson's first suit as a tailor, in Tennessee, was made for John A. Brown, and his location in the State was largely, if not entirely, due to the fact that he got that job. How trifling are the circumstances which often shape our ends,

"Rough hew them as we may."

How far his destiny might have been changed had he gone further West, no one can tell. I believe he would have risen into prominence, no matter where he might have gone, provided the population (where he settled) had been such as to afford a field, as Greene County did, for his peculiar talents. But no other part of the country, except East Tennessee, would have given him his ladder to the presidency, in 1861-5.*

Mr. Johnson was married in Greeneville, Tenn., in 1826, to Eliza McCardle. Her father was a Scotchman and a shoemaker. I believe Mrs. Johnson was as well educated as the facilities in Greeneville permitted at that day,—they were not remarkable. According to the universal testimony of those who knew her, she was a worthy woman, of an extremely retiring disposition. Although I lived near by in the small village, until I was twenty-eight years of age, I have no recollection of ever seeing her. After the death of Mrs. Johnson's father, her mother married a silversmith named Moses Whitesides.

The facts I have given, on the authority of William R. Brown, derived from his brother John, and from the family, as to the ability of Mr. Johnson to read when he first reached Tennessee, before he had ever seen his future wife, effectually dispose of the story, so often and so pathetically told by his enthusiastic admirers, that he was taught to read by his wife after they were married. Those who knew the activity of his mind, his eager desire for knowledge, his industry and his intense ambition, would, independently of these positive facts, be slow to believe that a young man of his capacity and application, reared in a place like Raleigh, where there were good schools, could reach the age of eighteen without learning to read. To say the least of it, it looks like a sensational story, intended to add éclat to a half romantic life, crowned even without this incident with marvelous success. I might add that the story is inherently improbable.

There are other facts, however, which tend to show the falsity of this story. While Johnson was an apprentice in Raleigh, a man of leisure and of wealth, named Hill, used to go among the workingmen in that city, reading to them ex-

---

*The foregoing facts as to Johnson I obtained in 1891 from the lips of William R. Brown, the younger brother of John A. Brown and the son-in-law of Johnson, he having married Mrs. Mary Stover. No one stands higher for integrity and veracity than he. In reply to a direct question Brown told me emphatically that it was not true that Mrs. Johnson had taught her husband to read; that such was not the understanding in the family.

tracts from the speeches of great orators out of the "United States Speaker." Johnson heard him read from this book, and afterwards went to Mr. Hill to borrow the book, saying that having heard him read from it he had been stimulated to learn to read. Thereupon Hill told him that if he could prove that he could read, he would give him the book. Johnson took the book, read from it, and Hill made him a present of it.*

There is still one more fact bearing on this point. When Johnson worked in Greenville, S. C., before he removed to Tennessee, he became acquainted with a young lawyer there, named Benjamin F. Perry. Perry used to lend books to him. When Johnson was President he appointed this same Benjamin F. Perry Provisional Governor of South Carolina, and it was he who told about lending him books. No doubt the kindness of Perry was recalled long afterward, and had weight in securing his appointment as Governor. The Hon. Kenneth Rayner, formerly a member of Congress from North Carolina, in his anonymous life of Johnson, says, that the latter could read before he left his native State. No doubt he got this fact from Johnson himself.

About 1831 or 1832 I first began to hear of Andrew Johnson. He had become a prominent tailor and was considered a very stylish one. At that time he was training himself to think and speak in the town debating society, in which he early became a leader. He read everything he could find, often having an open book before him on his bench while he worked. But in a small out-of-the-way village there were but few books at that day. Hence the range of his reading was then, and afterward, narrow. Throughout his life his quotations and references to history and mythology were nearly always the same. Fond as he was of making a show of extensive reading, by the use of quotations, he had no general storehouse to

---

*These facts I obtained from a gentleman to whom they were told by one who was at the time of Mr. Johnson's death perhaps his most intimate friend. I refer to Hon. Joseph S. Fowler, who was formerly a United States Senator from Tennessee. Fowler once saw this book in Johnson's library. Mr. Johnson once told the same tale to W. W. Jordon, his neighbor, according to a recently published statement, though that statement makes Johnson learn his letters and to read with the aid of a friend from that book. Johnson told Jordon that he still owned the book. The Rev. J. S. Jones has recently published the life of Andrew Johnson under advice of Mrs. Patterson, and he states that Johnson learned to read in North Carolina.

draw from, and in consequence had to use the same ones over and over again. To one who heard him often they became very trite and commonplace.

In all of Johnson's speeches, there is no evidence that he was familiar with the masters of English literature, such as Shakespeare and Milton, whose works are storehouses of beauty, genius, and thought. His reading was confined almost exclusively to political and party questions. In no sense was he a man of general intelligence. How could he have been? He neither had leisure nor books. Greeneville contained only a few hundred people. Its society was excellent. There was some wealth and a reasonable percentage of culture. It was on a par with its neighbors. There was not, however, in the village a single man of wide intelligence, who could become an example to young Johnson. Good books were rare and perhaps there were not one hundred standard works of literature in the town. I doubt if there was a private library, outside of one or two law offices, of two hundred volumes. There was not a public library in the town. It is true that there was an excellent library of six thousand volumes at Greeneville College, three miles south of the town, but Mr. Johnson had no time to go such a distance for books, even could he have obtained permission to use them. Being poor, and having to work unceasingly to support his family, to buy books was beyond his power. He had no spare money. There were no book-stores. Books, if purchased, must be ordered from Philadelphia or New York. So, Mr. Johnson was certainly excusable in his early career, for not knowing more of books. In his later years, after he became a public man, when he had money, opportunity, and leisure, he made a mistake in not seeking more liberal culture, by means of an acquaintance with the great authors of the world.

These were not all of his early disadvantages. There were in those days no popular lectures, no magazines, certainly none for remote Greeneville. There was not a newspaper in his county, none in the State that contained much information. There were no great daily papers, such as we all have now, of from twelve to forty pages, full of valuable matter. The tranquillity of the village was seldom disturbed even by a menagerie, the delight of villagers and rural people. Once, and once only, a wax-work show representing Napoleon and other celebrities exhibited there, then passed on like a vision, never to return. How often I have sighed for the return of that exhibition, more marvelous to my boyhood mind than all the wonders of the greatest World's Fair. The average preachers of that day were not educators, but were generally as barren as Sahara. True, there were a few great preachers in East Tennessee, such as Frederick A. Ross, James Gallaher, Dr. Isaac Anderson, and the celebrated David Nelson, but Johnson seldom went to church, and was not fond of Doctors of Divinity.

In spite of adverse surroundings, Johnson grew in mental activity and culture. Surely it was hard to make bricks without straw. He literally snatched information from every passing event. Questioning everything, he would know the reason of every fact. With a mind burning with the fires of internal heat, arguing and disputing with everyone and about everything, no proposition was accepted on faith. He sifted and tested everything in the crucible of his own mind. The process of analyzing, eliminating, and combining was always going on. He was naturally and inherently disputatious, cautious, and pugnacious, and opposition was his delight. Those who entered his shop were drawn into argument. From the bright young men of the college near by, whose tailor he was, by questions and argument he extracted many a useful fact. By them, too, no doubt, his young ambition was stimulated and set aflame.

In 1835, at the age of twenty-seven, Johnson's political career began. He became a candidate for the lower house of the Legislature for the district composed of the counties of Greene and Washington. His competitor was Matthew Stevenson, a worthy citizen, of moral worth and high social standing, who had been the year before a prominent member of the convention called to revise the Constitution of the State. From the first it was manifest, to the surprise of everyone, that Stevenson was no match in debate for his young antagonist. Johnson hacked and arraigned Stevenson until his friends pitied him. From the first, Johnson manifested that adroitness, ability, and aggressiveness in debate, as well as a disposition to pander to the prejudice of the people, which distinguished him so highly through all his subsequent career. He was almost brutal in his assaults.

All the kindly amenities of high debate between gentlemen were wanting. When people heard him speak, they could scarcely credit their own senses, so much ability did he display. They exclaimed: "Is not this the poor young tailor?"

The canvass resulted as might have been expected between two such unequally constituted men—Johnson was elected by a small plurality. The vote was counted at a point on the border line of the two counties, he being present to witness the count. The next day a number of persons, among them myself, then a mere boy, rode out two or three miles to meet the young conqueror returning home, in triumph, after his first victory. He was calm, cold, unmoved at the demonstration. As I look back now, it seems that he said by his conduct, "This is only what I deserve and shall expect in the future." It may be safely assumed from the above that I started in life an enthusiastic admirer of Andrew Johnson.

Upon entering the Legislature, Johnson made himself notorious by opposing a motion to invite the ministers of the Gospel of the city to open the daily sessions with prayer.

It was during this Legislature that a charter incorporating the Hiwassee Railroad Company in East Tennessee, and perhaps granting it State aid also, was presented for passage. Johnson did all he could in opposition to it. This was perhaps the first railroad charter granted in the State, and the Hiwassee Railroad, as it was then called, was the first one put under construction.

It is curious what absurd and ridiculous ideas men of the best sense and intelligence, at that day, entertained concerning railroads. Had I not heard with my own ears, I should hardly credit what I am about to state. In one of Johnson's canvasses for the Legislature—I am not certain as to the year—I heard him make a speech, in which he argued at length that railroad charters were unconstitutional because they created monopolies and perpetuities. But this was not so alarming and dangerous, in his view, as the dire consequences which would result from these roads. He insisted that they would be a fearful curse to the country, because they would stop the travel along our public highways, on horseback, in carriages and with wagons, and thus destroy the wayside taverns. Quite as great an evil would be the fact that they would throw out of employment the many six-horse teams then engaged in East Tennessee, in hauling our surplus produce to distant markets, and in bringing back to our merchants the groceries and merchandise needed by the people. I never have known Johnson to plead more earnestly for the rights of the people than he did on these subjects.*

It is perhaps not the duty of the humble biographer to decide the desirability of wayside taverns and six-horse teams on one side, and railroads on the other!

As to the higher objection to railroads, urged by Johnson with great earnestness, that they were unconstitutional because they were monopolies and perpetuities, all honest men should bow with respect before the conscientious convictions of the "Defender of the Constitution," as he was sometimes called!

To be serious: whether Johnson's opposition to railroads was the result of want of information, or because he thought he could make votes by it, is hard to tell. Possibly both causes had influence. Here is a dilemma. To conclude that he was conscientiously opposed to railroads reflects on his intelligence. On the contrary, to assume that he was simply trying to catch votes by his opposition, casts a reflection on his honesty, and that I refrain from doing.

But he was correct in his prophetic vision! The good old wayside inns are gone! If there was ever perfect luxury on earth, an old-fashioned country tavern like that of James Bell at Campbell's Station, or that of Mr. Lackey further on, constituted that luxury in all its perfection, to the tired, hungry traveler, after a long day's ride on horseback.†

---

*In olden times, before railroads, goods were hauled by great six-horse teams from Baltimore and from Philadelphia to East Tennessee, and sometimes even to Nashville.

†Captain James Bell kept one of those ideal wayside inns at Campbell Station, fifteen miles west of Knoxville, on the old main stage road leading to Nashville. He was a bustling, accommodating, delightful landlord who anticipated every want of the traveler. He was fond of relating reminiscences of distinguished men who had enjoyed the comfort of his house. A short time before his death, a few years ago, he told me the following incident in reference to Andrew Jackson which has never been reported correctly. Jackson always stopped with him in going to and returning from Washington. On one occasion, while President, on his way to the Hermitage, he stopped in Knoxville for the night and sent a message to notify Captain Bell that he would be at his house the next morning with his retinue for breakfast. It happened that Governor John Branch of North Carolina (I think it was he), on his way home from the West, had stopped there also. General Jackson and he were bitter enemies. An old, unsettled difficulty existed between them growing out of the quarrel and disruption of General Jackson's Cabinet, of which Governor Branch was a retiring member, about the celebrated Mrs. General John H. Eaton. Branch was plucky and determined, and when General Jackson drove up to the hotel, to his amazement he saw

The opposition of Johnson to the first railroad in East Tennessee proved a very serious matter to him. He evidently miscalculated its effect on his popularity.

There was in the Legislature of 1835 with Mr. Johnson a young man from Washington County—Brookins Campbell. Educated, amiable in disposition, honorable in deportment, possessed of fair talents, his friends claimed for him exceptional ability, and regarded him with high hopes. In the Legislature he had voted for the railroad measures which Johnson had opposed. On his return home, a few of the friends of internal improvements in Greene County,—which county Campbell did not represent,—headed by Dr. Alexander Williams, determined to manifest their approval of his course on this question, by asking him to partake of a public dinner in Greeneville, the home of Johnson. The demonstration was also intended as a rebuke to Johnson for his course. Mr. Campbell accepted and attended. He was complimented and toasted, and of course made a speech justifying his vote. I was present, though only a mere boy. I cannot say that I had any decided opinions on the question at issue one way or the other. But I wanted to attend a banquet, which word had to my inexperienced mind a magic sound.

After the banqueting was over, I met Mr. Johnson on the street, where he talked to me quite a while. Looking back at it now, his talk to me, a lad of fifteen, seems singular. He was somewhat under the influence of liquor and in a towering rage. Dr. Williams, Campbell, and his other enemies, came in for a due share of his compliments. On account of my age, he seemed not to regard my presence at the banquet as offensive, and treated me as one of tender years.

---

his enemy sitting on the porch. He realized at a glance that there was danger of a personal difficulty. Captain Bell was at the carriage the moment it arrived to welcome the great Chief. Jackson took in the situation as quick as thought. Without alighting, he explained to his host the danger of a difficulty, apologized for the trouble he had given, asked to be excused, and drove on some nine miles to Captain William Lackey's for his breakfast.

This illustrates what was well known to many persons in Tennessee, that while General Jackson was a man of unquestioned courage, he showed discretion as well as valor where the former was demanded.

This incident very recently, and long after the above was written, has been published in a book entitled "Lost Stitches in Tennessee History," but many of the facts are misstated, according to the statement made to me by Captain Bell.

NOTABLE MEN OF TENNESSEE 367

The result was, as intended, that when the next canvass came around, in 1837, Campbell was put forward by the friends of railroads as a candidate in opposition to Johnson, to represent Greene and Washington Counties. The race was hot and bitter on the part of Johnson, but dignified, manly, and earnest on the part of Campbell. Johnson proved, as ought to have been foreseen, more than a match for his opponent on the stump. In this canvass he gave evidence of that talent for playing on the popular prejudices and the passions of men which afterward made him so noted. Campbell had voted in the Legislature for a bill to employ a geologist, to investigate and report upon the mineral and agricultural resources of the State. Under this law, Dr. Girard Troost, one of the most learned scientists of the day, was employed at a small salary. Johnson assailed this law and arraigned Campbell for voting for it with all the arguments and ridicule he possessed. He held up to the scorn and amusement of the people Dr. Troost's travels about the State, peering about for snails, snakes, shells, rocks, and fossils. Here again the people were about to lose their liberties. Extravagance was creeping into high places. Under the lashing ridicule poured upon the head of Campbell, for this and other sins, he appeared a veritable culprit. But notwithstanding, he was popular, especially in Washington (his own) County, and was elected by a small plurality.

Andrew Johnson was relegated to private life, going back to his tailor's bench in no pleasant temper. It gave him, however, two more years for study and preparation for his subsequent remarkable career. Those who may have supposed his political future was ended by this defeat knew nothing of the force of the dormant fires burning within his breast. There never was a time, and there never would have come a time, had he lived years longer and achieved even more distinguished honors, when that restless spirit would have been quiet and satisfied.

In 1835 Johnson was known as a Whig, and in a legislative caucus helped to nominate Judge Hugh Lawson White, of Tennessee, as a candidate for the presidency in opposition to Martin Van Buren. Judge White did not perhaps at that time call himself a Whig, but he was supported by Whigs and by many voters not in that party, in opposition to Jackson and Van Buren. From that time till 1839 Johnson's politics was unknown or not clearly defined. The Whigs thought he was still of their faith, but not of a pronounced type. He was certainly not an open Democrat. Many bitter sayings of his against the Democratic party used to be repeated, and are remembered even to this day.

In 1839 Campbell was a candidate for re-election, as a Democrat. Johnson arranged with the Whigs of Washington County, as it was alleged at the time, to run as a Whig in opposition to Campbell, provided the Whigs would put out no other candidate. Soon after this arrangement was made, Robert Sevier, a pronounced Whig, announced himself as a candidate. This disturbed the plans of the Whigs, as well as those of Mr. Johnson. In order to defeat Campbell, which was then the ruling passion of this ambitious man, it would not do for two Whigs to oppose him. So he took a new tack. In a speech at Jacob Broyles' in Greene County he declared himself a follower of John C. Calhoun in politics; in other words, a Calhoun State's Rights Democrat. But by January, 1840, having defeated Campbell, he seemed to tire of his loneliness as the almost solitary follower in the State of South Carolina's favorite statesman. So he now joined the regular Jacksonian Democracy, and supported Van Buren for the presidency.*

Early in his political career Johnson found in the labor of the convicts in our penitentiary a fruitful field for the display of his peculiar genius. There were perhaps only two or three hundred convicts in the penitentiary when his keen intellect first detected the danger lurking therein to the free labor of the State. He at once sounded the alarm to his unsuspecting countrymen, and pointed out the danger of this competition. His cry of warning was sounded in all his speeches. This evil must be extinguished! The danger of the people from competition of convict with free labor, arising from these two or three hundred convicts shut up within stone walls, was scarcely less than that threatened by the destruction of taverns, wagon traffic, and by the building of railroads. All were, in the estimation of Mr. Johnson, evils of gigantic proportions, and must, like the infant Hercules, be strangled in their beginnings.

---

*Campbell, who was a quiet, excellent man, lived a retired life, overshadowed by his great rival, until about the year 1855, when he was elected to Congress, but died before the expiration of his term.

CHAPTER II.

Democracy of Greene County—Johnson Elector for State at Large on Van Buren Ticket, 1840—Elected State Senator, 1841—Elected to Congress, 1843—Represented First District for Ten Years—Introduced Homestead Bill During Second Term—Elected Governor of Tennessee, 1853.

THE Democracy of Greene County in the olden times deserves special notice, because it was the genuine article and had the true trade mark. There was no such thing as counterfeiting it. It deserves mention for the further reason that upon it, as a foundation, Mr. Johnson builded his political fortunes. To the Democrats of that county, as he always told them, he owed all he was. He took them as babes, and first by milk, and afterward by strong meats, nurtured them into the stalwarts they became. He made of them a muscular race of men. He knew how to build men as well as how to clothe them. No granite foundation was surer or firmer. There was an exact fitness between him and these people. They were solid, compact, petrified. In vain opposition orators launched facts and arguments against the incrustation of prejudice which enveloped these Greene County Democrats. The impact rang like an anvil stricken by a hammer, but it made no impression. He led them whithersoever he would. He knew their names and they knew his voice. A stranger they would not follow. With an almost religious faith these men had always believed in Andrew Jackson, and they feared when Jackson departed, all would be over with this government, and that there would be left no one fit to rule. When Johnson appeared they were consoled with the hope that he might save the country. Long before any others, the Democracy of Greene County saw in Johnson a successor to Jackson. They always expected his coming "to the Presidency." It was a thing in their estimation that must happen.

While Johnson became a type of those who were to follow, he had a prototype in one John Balch, a man who was in his meridian when Johnson came on the public stage. The former was a son of the noted Presbyterian divine, Hezekiah Balch, the founder of Greeneville College. Hezekiah Balch was a ripe scholar, an original thinker, and elegant gentleman, and was, withal, noble and brave. The son, by some freak of nature, was rough, wild, dissipated, and cared for neither God nor man. Ambitious and aspiring, he possessed ability sufficient to become a leader of the ignorant. Wholly without the restraint of moral discipline, or fear of public sentiment, there was nothing John Balch was not ready for in politics, and he was, moreover, emboldened by his successes.

A few years later there appeared another man, Jacob Bewley, of even more talent and shrewdness. Bewley was rather a phenomenal man, possessing great natural ability, and being endowed with cunning in a high degree. He always preferred shadowy ways, and could tread the most devious paths. In person he was large, his head immense, his voice low and sweet, and his conversation charming, abounding in wit, humor, and pathetic incident. Altogether he was perhaps a little too "childlike and bland." He had always not only smiles but a copious supply of tears ready for use.

Balch was educated; Bewley was not. These two men were always candidates for the Legislature against each other, and each was several times elected. Their discussions were pitched on a plane of vulgarity seldom surpassed. Balch was the bolder, Bewley the more artful of the two. There was indeed no limit to Bewley's subtle ways.*

Bewley was not a bad man in the larger sense of the term. He was a good neighbor and citizen. These things I have referred to were simply the innocent divertisements of politics— the means of winning votes. The times were very primitive—a period of Arcadian simplicity. Customs have changed vastly since those days, when the result of an election depended on the

---

*In one of their canvasses Balch repeatedly charged Bewley with having voted in the Legislature for some measure that was very unpopular, and read from the Journal to prove it. Bewley became very sore under it. Watching his opportunity, he slipped the book out of Balch's saddle-pockets, tore out the leaf containing the vote, and replaced the book. At the next speaking Balch made his usual charge, which Bewley solemnly denied, daring him to prove it. Balch reached for his Journal, turned to the page, but was confounded to find that the proof was gone. Bewley, exultant, and with tears in his eyes, called on the people to witness how his competitor had slandered an innocent man. Balch charged in vain that Bewley had torn a leaf from the Journal.

number of votes cast for the respective candidates. That was supposed in that rude age to be democratic-republican government. How benighted! Cimmerian darkness! Now what is called "the machine" manufactures as well as counts votes. It possesses the quality of throwing out the "tares" which the enemy may have sown, or of transmuting them into pure wheat. Further, it can duplicate the wheat, or multiply it to meet every demand. A singular peculiarity about this "machine" is, that, with almost human sensitiveness, it shrinks from public gaze. A single prying eye deranges the machinery. It loves shady retreats as do poets and lovers, and its most effective work is done in the darkness with no eye to see save that of the machine boss. Only two are needed to run it; indeed one skillful man is sufficient. It can be seen at a glance what a great invention the "machine" is. No need of a candidate's making speeches or spending money, if he will only grease the machine and set it running right. For more than fifteen years Balch and Bewley were the ruling spirits in the elections of Greene County. By these men was the Democracy of that county molded and prepared for the coming and long reign of Andrew Johnson, a greater man than either. When parties divided in 1835, Bewley became a Whig, Balch remaining always a genuine Democrat.

Another man, John McGaughey, sometimes figured in these contests, but, in contrast with Balch and Bewley, McGaughey was tall, grave, and dignified, and was possessed of fair ability and high integrity, considering the hazy political atmosphere of the time.

Amid such surroundings Andrew Johnson first opened his eyes on the political world. It is no great wonder that he sought to climb by the ladder he had seen Balch and Bewley successfully ascending. We are all more or less influenced by environment. How much the natural bent of Johnson's mind had to be twisted to make it conform to existing conditions need not trouble the historian, for if any such twisting, if any moral struggle ever took place, no one knew it. Judging him by the subsequent acts and words, he met the very conditions that suited his nature. He found the Greene County Democrats in a plastic, indeed in almost a chaotic state. They had one fixed belief only—an immutable faith in Andrew Jackson. Beyond this their sober minds had never learned to stray. Johnson seized on this fact to weld them into a compact mass.

In the winter or spring of 1840 Johnson, having concluded that his chances of promotion were best in the Democratic party, called that party together in mass meeting in Greeneville. The time had come for him to proclaim himself and his mission. Henceforth he was to be a prophet unto this people. He sent out runners to let them know that he had a message to deliver. On the appointed day all the strongholds of Democracy sent forth their men. There was scarcely an able-bodied man left at home. They came on horseback, on foot, in wagons. They came with no music, with no banners, but silently, in the strength and simple power of an irresistible outpouring. A rude platform, made of goods boxes, posted against the court house, served as a rostrum. Between ten and eleven o'clock Johnson appeared on the scene, with weighty thought depicted on his brow. George W. Foute, Clerk of the County Court, came forward with the resolutions prepared under the immediate direction of Mr. Johnson. Foute was a clever fellow, had a clear, sonorous voice, and was an admirable reader. He always read the resolutions. These were an epitome of the speech which was to follow, for Johnson never allowed but one speech on such occasions, and that was his own.

The resolutions recited the controversy which had taken place between the two antagonistic forms of government that divided our fathers in framing the Federal Constitution. They gave the views of Hamilton in favor of a strong centralized government; and held him up as the father of Federalism, and Jefferson as the father of the Democratic party. They assailed John Adams and the Alien and Sedition Laws; praised the resolutions of '98 and '99; charged bargain, intrigue, corruption on Henry Clay. They portrayed General Jackson as the second Saviour of his country, especially eulogizing him for strangling the Bank of the United States, the great greedy monster that was about to destroy the liberties of the people; and finally, these resolutions never failed to arraign the Whig party as the successor of the old Federal party, which had hung out blue lights to the enemy, and had worn black cockades in the war of 1812, and had tried to paralyze the war by the Hartford Convention.

Mr. Johnson's speech followed in the same line. He spoke usually from two to three hours. He commenced in a low, soft tone, and grew louder as he warmed up. After an hour or so, his voice rang out on the air in loud, not unmusical tones, heard distinctly a great distance, and seemed particularly adapted to the open air. There was no hurried utterance, yet no hesitation, no dragging, no effort after words. The speech went right on, the exact language coming to his lips to express the idea in his mind. Altogether, on such occasions, he was forcible and powerful, without being eloquent. He held his crowd spellbound. There was always in his speeches more or less wit, humor, and anecdote, which relieved them from tedium and heaviness.

On Mr. Johnson's great days Richard M. Woods, for many years high Sheriff of Greene County, and at one time United States marshal, was always present to preserve order, and to give the sign by nods and smiles when to shout or when to laugh. A good man he was, brave and upright. He had been Captain under General Jackson in 1812. In many respects he was like the old Chief, being a natural leader of men, and was a venerable patriarch in the ranks of Democracy.

As Mr. Johnson grew warm and hurled the terrible thunder of his wrath against the old Federalists, the shouts sent up by the Democracy could be heard far and wide among the surrounding hills. As he pictured the old Federal party in fearful colors, and pathetically entreated the people to stand firm upon the Constitution, his hearers would huddle closer together, as if for mutual protection, and plant their feet more firmly upon the ground. When he informed them, as he never perhaps once in his life failed to do, that "eternal vigilance was the price of liberty," and that "power was always stealing from the many to give to the few," they would furtively glance around to see if anyone was trying to steal from them!

After traversing the whole wide field of politics, Mr. Johnson wound up by the use of a figure drawn from the road, exhorting the party in an impassioned appeal to stand together "hand in hand, shoulder to shoulder, foot to foot, and to make a long pull, a strong pull, and a pull altogether." This delicate allusion to the honored custom among the wagoners of that day of doubling teams, and assisting one another out of mudholes by all lending a helping hand in pushing and pulling, seemed to set the old wagoners wild with delight. The crowd became tumultuous. Its hurrahs were like the sound of many waters. The din and uproar became almost infernal.

But, after all, these things were, as someone has said of Wagner's music, "not so bad as they sounded."

It was usually nearly night when the crowd dispersed. In their boundless enthusiasm they tarried late. Many of those present lived fifteen or twenty miles away, or even farther. For such a long journey, a supply of strength was laid in at the saloons. When night overtook them on their homeward way, in the bewildered condition of their intellects, they recalled dim images of "blue lights and black cockades," and in every dark wood they feared to see these monsters, whatever they were, confront them!

While the resolutions of this first meeting were not patented, or secured by copyright, they were kept and preserved for the next meeting. These meetings were held biennially. Substantially the same resolutions were always brought out and used. Why not? They were constructed by the best workmen and out of the best material. As they dealt with no living issue, it was never necessary to alter them. They also formed the text for Johnson's speech and as that was always in those days in substance the same, it was manifestly best that the resolutions should assume and hold a permanent form also. This had one great advantage—they became, like a sun dial, a regulator from year to year. By them the Democracy of that county could always find out where it stood, "where it was at." Otherwise there was danger of straying and getting lost.

The picture I have given of the Jacksonian Democracy of Greene County as it was in olden times was more or less true of the party in all upper East Tennessee at that period.

I have never quite understood how these Democrats managed to change front so suddenly in December, 1860. In October Johnson told them that Breckinridge, Davis, & Co., were right, that Lincoln and Seward were traitors, trying to overthrow the Constitution. In a little over one month later, he told them that Breckinridge and Davis were traitors, and that Lincoln and Seward were patriots. He had swung clear around the circle. When his followers saw what he had done, they quickly and obediently did the same. It was truly touching to see the devotion of the "old guard" to their leader. I shall not inquire too closely into this change on his part, or on theirs, because it brought over to the Union side as thoroughly a disciplined set of veteran soldiers as ever went into battle. Nor can I exactly account for the fact that the long-trained band of Whigs of Greene County, who had always been Union men, turned and fled to the other side when they saw Johnson and his old followers approaching as friends. Perhaps they feared the gift-bearing Greeks: *"Timeo Danaos et dona ferentes."* To use Mr. Johnson's favorite figure, when these scarred Democratic veterans looked across the "circle" and saw their old Whig enemies standing on the Democratic camping ground, directly facing them, it must have been a curious, as well as a puzzling reflection to Johnson's followers to know how the Whigs got there. Some of these Democrats no doubt, were perplexed as much as Landon C. Haynes' cowboy, who, when lost in the depths of the forest, exclaimed: "Good Lord! on which side of the creek am I?" But it mattered not if the new situation was not clear to the bewildered intellects of these staunch Johnson worshippers; they followed the star of Cæsar, and that was enough!

In 1840 Andrew Johnson occupied a high position in the Democratic party of the State. He had ceased to be a Calhoun Democrat, and had identified himself with the Democracy of Tennessee. He had by this time become well known throughout the State, having served two terms in the Legislature, and when the party, in the winter of 1840, selected electors for the State at large on the Van Buren ticket, he was made one of them. This selection was a notable one and very honorable to him. He was only thirty-two years of age, and had been in public life but five years; indeed, only three, for from 1837 to 1839 he was retired, having failed in an election. In the State at that period the Democratic party had such great men as Felix Grundy, James K. Polk, Aaron V. Brown, Cave Johnson, A. O. P. Nicholson, Andrew Ewing, and others, nearly all of whom were then, or afterward, Senators in Congress or Governors of the State. Yet over the heads of these men Johnson was selected to bear the Democratic banner in the bitter contest of 1840.

The electors for the State at large on the Whig side were Ephraim H. Foster and Spencer Jarnagin. Foster had lately been a United States Senator. The Democratic Legislature had instructed him and his colleague, the venerable Judge Hugh L. White, to vote for the subtreasury bill in Congress, and to support all the leading measures of Van Buren's administration.

They declined to obey instructions, resigned, and came home, to appeal to the people. Judge White died soon afterward. Early in the spring of 1840, Foster entered upon the most memorable and brilliant canvass ever conducted in the State. He was a splendid speaker, commanding in appearance, magnetic and captivating in address, a veritable knight in honor and courage. The political conditions of the spring of 1840 were all favorable to such a canvass as Foster inaugurated. He was bitter in denunciation, fiery and eloquent in his appeals. Wherever he went he aroused a resistless enthusiasm never witnessed before nor since in this State. He swept through the counties on the high tide of popular excitement, with the *éclat* of a conqueror. Literally thousands upon thousands followed him. His speeches, while perhaps equaled occasionally by others, —though unquestionably of a very high order,—were so exactly in harmony with the spirit of the times and the temper of the people, that they produced by far the greatest effect ever produced by any public speaker in the State.

Foster's associate on the electoral ticket, Spencer Jarnagin, was his intellectual superior, but greatly his inferior as a speaker and a leader. I doubt if the State has ever produced the intellectual superior of Jarnagin. He deserved to be ranked below only such men as Webster. But he had no ambition, no high purpose, no great driving, moral force. He reached the United States Senate, but achieved no lasting fame.

Johnson, in this canvass, undertook to follow Foster and Jarnagin in their triumphal march. The latter would not divide time with him. Johnson, therefore, did what was under the circumstances the wisest thing—he followed on, and drew off all the hearers he could from Foster and Jarnagin. His speeches, though not wanting in a certain Johnsonian ability, were tame in comparison with the stirring battle cry of Foster. I heard the latter often during this canvass. Johnson certainly never appeared to a more sorry disadvantage, than when thus trailing after the magnificent Foster, to whom the shouting thousands were doing homage. But no small obstacle could daunt Johnson's courage, nor prevent him from going forward in his destined career. Long afterward, in 1861, I saw him, apparently the very impersonation of noble patriotism, followed by nearly as large crowds—crowds of determined Union men—as followed Foster in 1840.

In 1841 Johnson was elected a State Senator. In 1843 he was first elected a member of Congress. In 1845 he was again elected. It was during his second term that he introduced his "Homestead Bill," which proposed to give to every head of a family, out of the public domains, a homestead of one hundred and sixty acres, provided he would settle on it. Session after session Johnson continued to introduce this measure. Finally in 1862 the Bill, or a somewhat similar one, was taken up, passed, and became a law. A vast majority of the people of the United States ridiculed this measure at first. I regarded it as an act of pure demagogism. It was believed that the motive which actuated Johnson was to gain popularity rather than a sincere sympathy with the people. But the measure has proved to be in some respects a most beneficent law. Under it the distant territories have been settled by an industrious and hardy class, who are adding greatly to the annual wealth of the nation. It has given homes to hundreds of thousands of people, who otherwise would be homeless. It has, also, to some extent, arrested the policy that was becoming dangerous of bestowing vast subsidies on grasping railroad corporations. This at one time threatened to absorb all our public domain, and has absorbed a large part of it. Johnson was unquestionably the author of the Homestead policy, or, more correctly, the author of the first bill introduced in Congress, giving to each actual settler a homestead. The credit of the passage of the measure is sometimes given, and in a certain sense correctly, to Galusha A. Grow, of Pennsylvania. But Johnson had been advocating and introducing homestead bills long before Grow entered Congress. Johnson introduced the first bill on the subject in 1846. He continued to press the matter on the attention of the House as long as he remained a member of that body. Mr. Grow did not enter Congress until 1851. The Republican party finally adopted the measure as a part of their platform, and it was passed mainly by Republican votes. The only members of the House from Tennessee, besides Johnson, who ever voted for this measure were George W. Jones and Mr. Clements. To John Quincy Adams belongs the credit of first advocating the policy of giving our public lands to actual settlers. Johnson probably caught the idea from him.

When Johnson became a candidate for Congress the district had recently been changed, so as to make it Democratic, by about fifteen hundred majority. For ten years he continued to represent the first district, being elected by about fifteen hundred majority each time except in 1847, when his majority dropped down to 314. In 1851 Johnson was opposed by Landon C. Haynes, a leading Democrat, who was his bitter enemy, and had long desired to have his seat in Congress. Haynes was a lawyer, a fluent, ready speaker, and regarded as a man of great eloquence. His voice was excellent, and he graced his speeches with wit and humor. Altogether he was a very taking popular orator, but glittering rather than solid. The campaign was intensely bitter and personal, the rival candidates accusing each other of every dishonorable act they had ever committed, or had been charged with committing. For six hours each day they bandied epithets and exchanged accusations, any one of which, if true, was sufficient to render the culprit unfit to represent an honest people in Congress. Let it be kept in mind that this canvass was conducted between two of the leading Democrats of the State. Johnson had already served eight years in Congress. Haynes had been in the Legislature several times, and had been a Speaker of the lower house. He was regarded by some of his too partial friends as a greater man than Johnson. When Tennessee left the Union in 1861, he was honored by an election as a Senator to the Confederate Congress.

The result of the canvass was just as I would have expected. The superior ability, courage, and tact of Johnson triumphed. Although Haynes was the better speaker, he lacked the force, the steady courage of Johnson, and the latter constantly got the advantage of his eloquent competitor. In truth, eloquence never availed much against the irresistible logic of facts always so dexterously used by this artful man. No rhetoric, no amount of word painting could withstand the trenchant blows he struck. Neither Haynes, nor Gustavus A. Henry, the most effective speaker in the State, could counteract the impression produced by the array of facts used by Johnson. With these there was always served a sufficient amount of demagogism to give them an exceedingly agreeable flavor. It was no surprise, therefore, that Johnson was elected, he receiving the larger part of the Whig votes of the district.

In 1853 Andrew Johnson was nominated by his party for Governor. He earnestly sought the nomination. Outside of

East Tennessee neither the leaders nor the mass of the party favored his nomination. In the middle part of the State, where a majority of the party resided, delegates were appointed to the nominating convention favorable to the Hon. Andrew Ewing of Nashville. Ewing was an eminent lawyer, a man of the purest and the most exalted character. He had represented the Nashville district in Congress while it was Whig in politics, and was very popular, being a member of an old aristocratic family.*

Johnson's nomination came about in this wise. Ewing, sometime in the past, had carelessly assented to an opinion expressed by a third party that Johnson ought to be nominated for Governor, as a rebuke to the Whigs for gerrymandering his district. It was a mere thoughtless expression, by which he had no intention of committing himself to Johnson. This casual remark was communicated to Johnson, who artfully chose to treat it as a pledge in his favor. Ewing had no recollection of ever making such a pledge. When the convention assembled, Johnson, by letter or verbal message, said to Ewing, "I place my interests in your hands." Ewing arose in the convention, when it was on the point of nominating him, and having read Johnson's letter, withdrew from the contest, saying that a sense of delicacy forbade his being any longer a candidate, and advising his friends to support Johnson. Thereupon the latter was nominated. Yet in 1857, Johnson aided in electing Nicholson Senator over Ewing.

The leaders throughout the State, with rare exceptions, then and ever afterward, were opposed to Johnson. They had also been opposed to him in his race for Congress. They despised his methods and hated him. He had, however, a solid support among the common people, and with this backing he easily secured the submission of the leaders. He had a way of either winning over the latter, or intimidating them into silence. The little ones he won by coaxing and flattery; the powerful, he secured as masters in those days secured obedience from their slaves. Many a proud slaveholder in Tennessee had to submit to Johnson's castigation. His defeat at any time would have delighted them, but they did not dare move a little finger against him.

When Democrats crossed the path of his advancement, John-

*The celebrated Henry Watterson married the daughter of Andrew Ewing.

son was as ready to fight them as he was the Whigs He bristled all over with fight. His life had been a desperate struggle, first with poverty, afterward with political and personal foes. All along the line of his public career lay the bodies of his slain enemies. Party, to him, as to most politicians, was valuable only because it enabled him to mount upon the shoulders of his followers and thus rise to power. What a mass of corruption party sometimes makes men carry! The boasted love of the people, with most politicians, is an empty pretense for the sake of authority, and "hath this extent, no more." The people often rejoice under the load they bear, supposing they are bearing aloft a divinity, when in fact they are carrying only an "Old Man of the Sea," whom they cannot shake off.

Johnson's Whig competitor for Governor was Gustavus A. Henry. He was decidedly the most delightful orator as well as one of the most elegant men in the State. At mass meetings, where oratory was needed, he was always the hero of the day. Frank and manly, in person he was grand, in countenance fascinating, in manner electrical, with a voice of surpassing melody.

But when it came to logic, facts, and hard licks, in daily debates, with his adroit competitor, Henry's best friends could hardly say he was Johnson's full match. The result was, Johnson was elected by a majority of 2250 votes. From that time until the breaking out of the Civil War, Henry was never prominent in the politics of the State. When the war came on, he was elected a Senator to the Confederate Congress. The incident that occurred in this canvass for Governor worth mentioning, was a good-humored passage between the two candidates, in their speeches at Knoxville. Johnson in his closing rejoinder said: "They call my competitor 'The Eagle Orator.' The eagle is a bird of prey. Where is his prey? I see no blood on his beak, I do not feel his talons in my flesh." "No," said Henry, as quick as thought, "the eagle is a royal bird, and never preys on carrion."

William B. Campbell was the retiring Governor. For some cause he had not been a candidate for re-election. He was an honorable gentleman, and possessed great personal popularity. As a Colonel of the 1st Tennessee Regiment in the Mexican War, he had won distinction as a gallant officer and soldier. No man in the State stood better with the people. When the day for inauguration of the new Governor arrived, Governor Campbell, with true courtesy, called at Johnson's hotel, and informed him that he was ready with the carriage to escort him to the inaugural ceremonies. Mr. Johnson replied, as was correctly reported, that he did not want a carriage, that he was going to walk with the people. And walk he did! What was the astonishment of the stately Campbell, who so highly respected the dignity of the office he was about to relinquish!

But, confounded as Campbell must have been at the unexampled precedent set by the new Governor, this was as nothing in comparison with what his feelings must have been when he heard from the lips of the new dignitary what is known as the "converging lines," or "Jacob's Ladder" Inaugural Address. Such a document it is impossible to find among grave State papers anywhere on this continent during our entire history. Johnson in this drew a picture of a new Commonwealth, under the reign of Democracy, or a Theocracy, for it is impossible to tell which he meant. The lines are so drawn as to leave a confused impression of what was intended. The idea appears to have been to draw an analogy between the Christian Religion and the "Democracy" of Tennessee, of which Mr. Johnson was the type as well as the exemplification. Imagine the extreme absurdity of comparing any political party to the Christian religion! If any less prominent person had written this address, he would have been set down as a crank. It was in fact a ridiculous production, mere idle vaporing. It might well be consigned to that vast receptacle of nonsense, of light and airy nothings, described by Milton

> "As a limbo large and broad, since called
> The Paradise of Fools."

Among other things Johnson said that Democracy and Religion are "moving along converging lines toward each other." This was doubtless new to some good people present who had fears that Democracy was going in an opposite direction! "When," said he, "Democracy and Religion shall meet and unite, the Milennial morning will dawn." No doubt of that! But when shall that come to pass? He also said that "Democracy and the Divinity in Man," are the same. This may be so, but the old Whigs of that day, in their blindness, certainly had a different opinion of this "Divinity." If the "Democracy of Tennessee" was its highest manifestation, these Whigs, foolish people! would have preferred some other "divinity."

More than two thousand years ago Plato wrote a treatise on a "Republic" conceived in his own great mind. In the fifteenth century, Sir Thomas More wrote a book entitled "Utopia" or "An Ideal Republic." Recently Edward Bellamy has written his celebrated "Looking Backward," which presents a new plan for a Republic. All these ideal forms of Government were located on this earth. Johnson, on the contrary, locates the place of the reign of Democracy somewhere in the dizzy heights of the infinite above, with no way of getting there except by Jacob's ladder. But he assuringly told the young men that they could find a position somewhere between the lower and upper extremes of the ladder, commensurate, at least, with their virtues and merit, if not equal to their ambition.

I doubt if Mr. Johnson could ever have gotten many to locate in this empyreal commonwealth. Jacob's ladder sets up very straight and high. Few dare try to climb it. It is hard to go upward. But turn the ladder the other way, and how easy and natural to go downward!

This enchanting vision, seen by the prophetic mind of Mr. Johnson of this "Milennial Morning," of the reign of Democracy and the "Divinity of Man," and an ideal republic in the celestial regions, was received by that hard and perverse generation only with laughter and ridicule. It only proved how far his thoughts outran his times, and adds another example to the many previous ones that a prophet is not without honor, save in his own country!

Even Nineveh, that great and wicked city, believed Jonah, and repented at his preaching, but Tennessee refused to believe the words of her great prophet!

CHAPTER III.

Succeeded Himself as Governor, 1855—Campaign with Gentry—Arraignment of "Know-Nothing Party."

THE canvass of 1855, in the political world, was one of intense interest and expectation. A new party, calling itself the American, but popularly styled the "Know-Nothing Party," had mysteriously appeared, secretly manifesting a strength in certain quarters that threatened the very existence of old political organizations. No one knew where this movement would end, nor what would be the extent of its destructive work. At first many aspiring persons of both the old political parties, who wished to be on the strong side, hastened to make sure of their footing by joining it. Its first impulse forward gave promise of universal victory. The old politicians were in absolute dismay.

Unfortunately for the American party an election for Governor was to take place in Virginia in the spring of that year. The celebrated Henry A. Wise was the Democratic candidate for that position. He was too daring to be intimidated by any danger, however great. With all his energy and spirit he took the field, and assailed the new party with an audacity and a bitterness which he only could command. After one of the most intensely acrimonious contests ever known, Wise was elected, and Know-Nothingism destroyed in that State.

A general election was to take place in Tennessee in the following August. Mr. Johnson was the Democratic candidate to succeed himself as Governor. Meredith P. Gentry was nominated by the American and Whig parties as his competitor. Gentry had been for a long time prior to 1853 a distinguished member of Congress. As he was known to be brave and brilliant, extraordinary things were expected of him, and it was believed that Johnson would be no match for him on the stump. Gentry was regarded indeed as one of the first orators of the time, even in that striking period of fine orators. John Quincy Adams, the sage and statesman, had pronounced him the best orator in Congress. He had come upon the stage of public life before the decadence in statesmanship began in Tennessee, while great men still held public sway. Jackson continued powerful, if not dominant. The profound Hugh Lawson White still held his honored seat in the Senate of the United States. The accomplished and sweet tongued Felix Grundy, Mr. Clay's only rival in their young days, had not yet passed the meridian of his splendid career. Polk had gained a national reputation as a debater in Congress, and as Speaker of the House. The gifted John Bell, while still young, had won renown as a thinker, and as the able Speaker of the House gave sure promise of that high ability afterward conspicuously manifested. The chivalrous Ephraim H. Foster had secured the second time a seat in the United States Senate by his masterly canvass of 1840, when he traversed the State from end to end, drawing crowds literally of thousands and tens of thousands, arousing a storm of wild enthusiasm never witnessed in this State either before or since. The intellectual giant, Spencer Jarnagin, who afterward drew, as a lawyer and a statesman, the highest compliments for ability from Mr. Webster and Judge Story, in that same canvass, also obtained a seat in the Senate as the colleague of Mr. Foster. The knightly Bailie Peyton was in his prime, having long since achieved national reputation as a member of Congress. Cave Johnson and Aaron V. Brown, each of whom served in Congress for many years, and each of whom became a Cabinet officer, and one the Governor of the State, were both distinguished for their talents. James C. Jones, the farmer, had suddenly appeared and astonished men by his dashing oratory and unequaled powers as a popular speaker, which enabled him in two successive canvasses for Governor to triumph signally over the adroit debater, James K. Polk. About this time Emerson Etheridge came upon the public stage as one of the first debaters of the State, and though young, gave promise of that marked power which he afterward successfully sustained for nearly fifty years. Suddenly, too, William T. Haskell, while scarcely twenty-one years of age, began to dazzle men by the most extraordinary display of brilliant rhetoric ever heard in the State, and perhaps ever heard anywhere in this country, except from Patrick Henry and S. S. Prentiss. Besides these distinguished men, there were also Andrew Johnson, A. O. P. Nicholson, Milton Brown, Edwin Ewing, Gustavus A. Henry, Andrew Ewing, Robert L. Caruthers, William T. Senter, Thomas A. R. Nelson, John Netherland, Landon C. Haynes, and John H.

Crozier, all men of ability. Certainly this is a long list of remarkable men, all in active life at one time, and all in one State. None of these, however, surpassed Gentry in power as an orator. His oratory consisted in the condensation of noble thought, presented in the boldest, most striking language, and in an irresistible manner. Evidently Tennessee has sadly degenerated since the bright epoch of 1840.

In 1855 Mr. Johnson was regarded as the strongest man on the stump in his own party, in the State. Expectation, therefore, stood on tip-toe in anticipation of the meeting of the two candidates for Governor.

The first discussion was to take place at Murfreesboro, Rutherford County, thirty miles East of Nashville, in the very center of the rich lands of Middle Tennessee. This was a Whig County by a few hundred majority. Its people were wealthy and intelligent. On the day fixed for the opening of the canvass the leading politicians and citizens of Nashville and of all the adjoining towns and counties flocked to Murfreesboro to hear the opening discussion. Men were already greatly excited. In no canvass, previous to the war, was there ever manifested so much bitter personal ill-will as in that of 1855. Many men came to the speaking on that day armed, expecting there would be a difficulty. Johnson knew the feverish excitement which prevailed, knew also that the new party was compact, and confident in its strength. A timid man would have been cautious in his attacks, but he adopted no such policy. Imitating the example of Henry A. Wise, he assailed Know-Nothingism with an audacity unknown before even to himself. Men were confounded at his boldness. He arraigned the party for its signs, its grips, and passwords, its oaths and secret conclaves, its midnight gatherings, its narrowness, littleness, and proscriptiveness. He charged that the members were sworn to tell a lie when they first entered the order. He exclaimed with all his bitterness: "Show me a Know-Nothing, and I will show you a loathsome reptile on whose neck every honest man should put his feet." He finally charged that they were "no better than John A. Murrell's clan of outlaws."*

---

*John A. Murrell had been the leader of a band of murderers and robbers twenty or thirty years before that time, operating in the western part of this State and in Mississippi and Arkansas, and had been sent to the penitentiary for his many offenses. His trial and the history of his life were the great sensations of that day. He is still regarded as a sort of Robin Hood.

Under his terrible denunciations the audience had become pale with rage and as still as death, waiting to see what next would happen. At these last words, many voices burst out: "It's a lie, it's a lie." Instantly the cocking of pistols was heard on every side, followed by ominous silence. Men ceased to breathe. Their hearts stopped beating. In this terrible suspense all became motionless. Johnson stood for a short time unmoved, gazing around on the fearful scene he had evoked, and then deliberately resumed his speech. All danger was now gone. At the critical moment the slightest belligerent demonstration—the movement of a finger even—would have produced a scene of blood and death. Brave and determined men were there. Fortunately no one was over hasty. All felt the danger, and its very imminence averted the calamity.

After Johnson had finished his tirade against the Know-Nothings, Gentry arose to reply. It was expected that a new scene of excitement would follow. The friends of Gentry expected him to denounce in direct terms the charges and insinuations of Johnson as falsehoods. Yet these men should have known better. He did no such thing. In a lofty manner he proceeded to defend the principles of the American Party, and to repel the base charges brought against it. His speech was dignified, eloquent, abounding in withering sarcasm, but in not a single word or sentence did he forget his own high sense of self-respect. It was observed that he had not avowed himself a member of the new party, and his defense of it was not as earnest as had been expected.

The result, therefore, of this first debate was unfavorable to Gentry. His friends went away disappointed and discouraged. They never quite recovered from this feeling. It was believed at the time that if he had boldly identified himself with the new order, had repelled in the strongest language and with an indignant spirit the venomous attacks of Johnson, he would have been triumphantly elected. With Johnson's fearful arraignment of the secret order and oath-bound party, and the apparently half-hearted defense made of it by Gentry, its friends became despondent and timid all over the State. On the other hand, Johnson's daring assaults had filled his friends with the highest courage and enthusiasm. Nor was this all. At the first appearance of the order, many Democrats had hastened to join it, some because they approved of its principles, and some because they thought it would become the highway to power. But when Andrew Johnson began thundering his terrible denunciations against it, calling on all honest men to come out of the midnight dens of this wicked party, Democrats all over the State commenced hurriedly tumbling out of the order, so great was their haste to escape odium.

Gentry's course was never fully understood by his party. It is to me no mystery. He was no coward, either physically or morally. He could dare as much as any man. Indeed, in the courage and manly frankness with which he gave utterance to his opinions, he was more like Mr. Clay than any public man of his time. His thoughts were as open as day. His conduct on the stump with Johnson to some appeared cowardly, but it was far from it. He suffered his opponent to abuse his party in the most insulting manner. This had the appearance and certainly the effect of bullying on Johnson's part. Gentry's friends went away from every discussion, notwithstanding his splendid speeches, with a feeling of defeat in their hearts. His conduct was the result of his civility and sense of honor, and no earthly consideration could have induced him to depart from the principles of honorable debate.

An incident at Clinton, East Tennessee, will illustrate. When the candidates reached that place, having been over the middle and the western parts of the State, an informal meeting of Gentry's friends was held at which it was determined to send a committee to him, to urge on him a more vigorous and personal canvass. This committee was composed of two of his warmest friends, William G. Brownlow and myself. They represented to him that the people of East Tennessee were accustomed to hot discussions, that they expected them, and that it would be well to lay aside his dignity, and to treat Johnson as he was in the daily habit of being treated by him.

Mr. Gentry straightened himself up in his loftiest attitude, assuming that majestic air and dignity natural to him and stopped the committee saying: "I know what you mean, gentlemen; you want me to commence by denouncing Johnson as a scoundrel, and growing stronger in denunciation until I reach the grand climax. Let me say that I think I know how to act as a gentleman, and what the rules of honorable debate among gentlemen require. I cannot degrade my manhood, even if my competitor does do so; no, not even to secure my election. If you wish me to get down to the level of my competitor, I beg you to hunt another to take my place, and let me retire at least with my own self-respect and with unsullied honor."

Here that part of the conference came suddenly to an end.

The discussion at Clinton passed off without any unusual incident. Johnson continued to arraign the American party with bitterness and terrible power. Gentry, on the other hand, defended the party against these assaults with more spirit than he had done at Murfreesboro. His speech was a splendid specimen of argument and genuine eloquence. It required all his self-control, when answering the points of his competitor, to suppress his swelling indignation. More than once he seemed on the point of throwing away his courtesy and hurling the thunderbolts of his wrath on Johnson's head. As it was, within the limits of honorable debate, his speech bristled with keen sarcasm, biting wit, and scarcely concealed contempt. Yet, so artful and powerful had Johnson's speech been, that the friends of Gentry were far from being jubilant, rather the contrary.

The next day the debate at Jacksboro was more spirited. Johnson introduced into the discussion his celebrated "white basis" proposition, offered in the Legislature in 1842. This was that "the basis to be observed in laying off the State into Congressional Districts shall" (should) "be the voting population, without regard to the three-fifths of the negro population." Thus he proposed to disregard the very letter of the Constitution of the United States, which he as a member of the Legislature had taken an oath to support. His object was to strengthen himself as the white man's friend in the mountain counties, where nine-tenths of the voters were non-slaveholders. The introduction of that question was out of place. He was in a county and a region where there were few slaves, and he hoped to make a few votes by this appeal to the prejudices of the ignorant non-slaveholders. He always knew how to introduce principles and opinions suited to the locality where he was to speak. He had denied, as had his organ and friends, in the cotten region of the State, where there were a great many slaves, that this "white basis" resolution was an issue in the canvass. When he reached this region, he brought it up, as he said it "involved a great principle, one which concerned the rights and interests of the masses." Gentry's answer to Johnson on this question was masterly and withering.

Johnson and Gentry traversed the counties on the North side of the State to the Virginia line, then turned westward along the Southern border. When they reached Knoxville Mr. Gentry was ill. He and his competitor on this account made an agreement that the canvass should close so far as speaking was concerned. As it was near election day, it was thought to be very generous on Johnson's part to give up speaking. They agreed that Johnson. in his own person, and Gentry, through a friend, should explain to the large crowd present the reasons for failing to speak at so important a place as Knoxville. I was requested by Mr. Gentry to represent him, and to present to the people his deep regret at being unable to make any more speeches. This I did in a little speech not exceeding three minutes. We supposed Johnson would not much exceed my time. This was the spirit of the agreement. Instead, he made almost a regular speech. He spoke from fifteen to twenty-five minutes upon matters manifestly covered by his agreement. I was indignant, but nothing could be done to stop him. Nor was this all, for he went on to the remaining appointments in Blount, Monroe, and other counties, where he gathered his friends around him in public rooms and said in substance: "I am not allowed by agreement with my competitor to make a speech. If I were allowed to do so, I would say 'So and so,'" going over the grounds of discussion betwen him and his competitor. Thus he talked to the crowd gathered to hear him until it was time to take his departure for another county. Each day he made many speeches on the issues of the canvass. He had gained credit for great magnanimity in giving up his appointments. That fact became widely known, while his subsequent conduct, after he left Knoxville, was only heard of by a few. The *National Intelligencer* came out with a most complimentary editorial, praising him for generosity toward his ailing competitor. Ignorant of what Johnson was doing, Mr. Gentry had gone on to his home in Middle Tennessee, resting on the agreement made.

This canvass terminated with the re-election of Johnson. His majority was 2020. Looking back at it now, the result is not surprising. Gentry was known to be a Know-Nothing. At first he could not avow the fact, but after the obligation of secrecy was removed he did so. In the meantime the secrecy feature of the order had done him and his cause incalculable harm. There is in the minds of a majority of men a widespread and deepseated prejudice against secret, oath-bound organizations. It was especially so at that time, and Johnson, by his furious and vindictive denunciations intensified this feeling. Every Catholic in the State, as well as some foreign-born citizens not Catholics, voted against Gentry. These, with those who could not support a secret organization, must have amounted to at least three thousand votes, possibly to a considerably larger number.

I doubt whether Meredith P. Gentry ever sympathized with the American Party. His was one of those big, open, generous natures that had no love for narrowness nor proscription.

CHAPTER IV.

Elected to United States Senate, 1857—In 1860 the Democratic Delegates from Tennessee to Charleston Instructed to Vote for Johnson for President—December 18, 19, Speech in United States Senate in Opposition to Secession—Spring of 1861, Canvass with Nelson to Save the State—Hindman's Proposition to Arrest Johnson at Rodgersville Thwarted by John R. Branner, President of Railroad—Made Brigadier General by Mr. Lincoln and Appointed Military Governor of Tennessee on Fall of Fort Donelson, February, 1862.

In 1857, after the expiration of his second term as Governor, Mr. Johnson secured his long-coveted prize—a seat in the United States Senate. Many of the leaders of his party were opposed to his election. But how could they prevent it? He was the idol of the Democratic masses, on them he securely leaned. He trusted them. In return they honored him. On all occasions he spoke with contempt of the aristocratic leaders, rejoicing at every opportunity of humiliating them. Sometimes he even denounced certain of them by name. He intimidated those who did not voluntarily follow him. Of all the men in his party in the State, he was the boldest toward his opponents, as well as intellectually the most dominant and masterful. Isham G. Harris, his equal in courage and nearly so in brains, and with very much greater promptitude in acting, had not yet stamped his strong character upon the minds of the people of the State. In robust strength Johnson stood alone in his party. His reign at this time was absolute.

Each new success of Johnson was a surprise to all who knew him, a bitter disappointment to his enemies in his own party. Men were slow to give him credit for the ability which all now must admit he possessed. They could not realize that the poor tailor of a few years before, living in an obscure village, had, unaided by wealth or kindred, not only triumphed over the most brilliant men in the Whig party, but had also made the proud and high-born leaders of the Democratic party bow their unwilling necks, on which he planted his imperial feet in his tireless effort for higher power. At each ascending step he grew more and more haughty. In battle he asked for no quarter; in victory he gave none. At each new elevation he threw down on his enemies haughty looks of defiance and scorn, and triumphantly shook his fresh laurels in their faces. All that his enemies whom he had overthrown in his own party could do, was to cry: "Tailor!" "Plebeian!" "Lowborn!" and other like endearing epithets.*

But these successes were no surprise to Johnson himself. They were just what he had planned, worked for, and dreamed of, what he thought he deserved. He was not excessively vain and inflated, but he felt within himself great powers, which gave him confidence and a steady equipoise. With calm repose and undaunted courage he felt equal to any enterprise, however perilous, or to any position, however exalted. He never feared defeat.

In 1860 the Democratic Party of Tennessee, in Convention assembled, recommended to the national Democratic party the name of Mr. Johnson for the Presidency. The delegates chosen to the Charleston Convention (April 23, 1860) were instructed to vote for him. When Mr. Breckinridge was nominated for this position at Baltimore by the ultra-Southern wing of the party, Johnson after much hesitation and long incubation, gave him his support. This may seem surprising to some, but it should not seem so. Johnson was an extreme Democrat. All his fortunes and hopes were tied up with that party. Nine-tenths of his friends in Tennessee also supported Breckinridge. He had to keep in line with them, for in three years his term in the Senate would expire. Of course, he wished a re-election. But with all his shrewdness he could not foresee the suddenness and the violence of the storm that was about to burst upon the country. No one could anticipate the fearful upturning and uprooting of the very foundations of political parties. Soon after the election Johnson awoke to find, with astonishment, everything drifting away from the old landmarks. It was too late to follow in the direction of secession if he had been inclined to do so. Other men, even more daring, had taken the lead. In revolutions he who is the quickest to act gets

---

*The next day after the election in 1872, in which he, Maynard, and General Frank Cheatham, a gallant Confederate officer, were candidates for Congress for the State at large, Mr. Maynard being elected, he (Johnson) said with clenched teeth, in a bitter, sibilant voice and with a dreadful oath, he had accomplished by his race all he expected—he had "reduced the rebel brigadiers to the ranks."

the lead, the undecided being left behind, and Johnson belonged to the latter class. Besides, he was no favorite of the revolutionists. They questioned his faithfulness to the institutions of the South. He had offered his "white basis" resolution in the Legislature, had defended it in his canvass with Gentry when he reached the white population of East Tennessee. He was not slow to see these things.

Johnson was never a disunionist. He hated the Southern leaders; at least there was no sympathy between him and them. They looked down on him. When he supported Breckinridge for the presidency, he did so because he was supporting a Democrat with whose views his own more nearly coincided than with those of either of the other candidates.* As a party man he should have supported Breckinridge. I believe it may be said that this support was entirely independent of the question of secession. It was suspicious at the time, but in view of his subsequent heroic and unparalleled defense of the Union it proved nothing. His own fortunes were bound up with those of the Democratic party. So far as his ascendency in Tennessee was concerned, it could do him no good for Mr. Bell and his Union followers to succeed in the State. He could gain nothing at their hands. But later on, when Mr. Bell had carried the State, and he saw his own party tending toward secession, and realized that he had probably lost control of it, he naturally looked around for new alliances.

With keen sagacity he believed the government would triumph if a conflict of arms should be madly precipitated. In calculating changes he saw that in that event those involved in secession would be ruined. If he cast his fortunes with the Union, he trusted in his popularity to remain supreme in Tennessee. In the North, after his noble stand, he would become a popular idol. So, in six weeks, after making violent Breckinridge speeches, he became the foremost champion of the North. No one was so full of zeal, nor burned with such intense devotion to the Union.

In the early part of November, 1860, Mr. Johnson left his home in Greeneville for Washington, to take his seat in the Senate. If he informed anyone before his departure of his change of views in reference to party allegiance, I have never

---

*Bell and Lincoln.

heard of the fact. Perhaps his mind had not yet arrived at a decision, for he was proverbially slow in forming, or at least in announcing, opinions on new questions. He knew at the time he cast his vote for Breckenridge the determination of the Southern leaders in a part of the cotton States to attempt to withdraw their States from the Union, in the event of the election of a sectional president, for the purpose of these men had been openly proclaimed all over these States. William L. Yancey, the boldest and perhaps the most brilliant of these leaders, had been advocating secession for years. As far back as 1856 the Hon. Preston S. Brooks of South Carolina, at a public dinner given in his honor, by the people of that State, proclaimed that "the Constitution of the United States should be torn to fragments, and a Southern Constitution formed in which every State should be a slave State." It was said ten thousand persons were present at the time and approved this address. Senator Butler and Senator Toombs were both present, and made speeches endorsing the declaration of Mr. Brooks.

The intention to dissolve the Union was not openly proclaimed in Tennessee, Kentucky, Virginia, and Maryland, and perhaps not in North Carolina, but all intelligent men knew the fact notwithstanding. Of all the Southern States, possibly excepting Maryland and Missouri, Tennessee seemed to a reflecting mind the least likely to become false to the national Government. Jackson, though dead, was still the inspiration and the idol of the Democratic party. His intense love and warm devotion to the Union filled the hearts of his disciples with a like devotion. His many remarkable sayings in its behalf were treasured up in their memories as sacred words. The idolized leader of the Whig party in Tennessee had been Henry Clay, and his burning words of love for the Union glowed in every Whig heart. Thus there was in both parties in Tennessee an inherited sentiment of loyalty to the Union almost as intense as the love for the religion of their fathers. So strong was this sentiment that to propose to dissolve it was deemed almost sacrilegious. Prior to 1860 any public man in the State bold enough to propose a dissolution of the Government would have been consigned to a position of infamy and execration. The canvass of that year, and the triumph of a sectional party, wrought to some extent a change in public sentiment, but it was far from being a revolution. In November, 1860, the only prominent man in the State having much influence in favor of a dissolution was Isham G. Harris, then Governor. When therefore, Johnson made his celebrated speech on the 18th and 19th of December, 1860, in opposition to secession, he had abundant reason for believing he had his State behind him. No doubt he confidently trusted in his power and ability to guide it in its course.

Mr. Johnson's speech on that occasion produced on the public mind a profound impression. It electrified the North; it startled and stunned the South. In one section it was hailed with unbounded joy; in the other it was received with bitter curses and execrations. Ex-Senator Thomas L. Clingman, of North Carolina, in his "Recollections," says no speech ever made produced such an effect. That is probably true. No speaker ever had a greater opportunity. And yet, judged by the higher standards, it was not a great speech. Its wonderful effect was due to its earnestness, its boldness, and its unexpectedness. No one, either North or South, so far as I know, anticipated such a speech. No one expected Mr. Johnson to denounce with bitter and defiant tones his six weeks' erstwhile associates. It was therefore a startling surprise. Already the first trembling of the throes of civil war was felt. While Mr. Johnson was still speaking, South Carolina was rudely severing the bonds of Union. Four or five other States were preparing to follow her example. Civil war was seen in the near distance. The North was petrified with amazement, if not with fear. No one could forecast the future nor see the end. A whole nation stood breathless in expectancy. Amid such conditions, Mr. Johnson arose in the Senate. The occasion was profoundly impressive. The opportunity was the greatest in history—greater than that of Hampden and Pym in the British Parliament, greater than that of Mirabeau in the Constituent Assembly of France, greater than that of Patrick Henry in the House of Burgesses in Virginia, greater than that of Mr. Webster when he made his wonderful speech—the greatest of his life and perhaps the greatest of his age—in the Senate in reply to Mr. Hayne. Mr. Webster could see only the beneficence of the Union and the glory of its flag, but he could not see except in prophetic vision the destruction of the one and the Stars disappearing from the other. But even while Mr.

Johnson spoke he could feel the earth rocked under his very feet by the storm of dissolution. A nation of forty millions hung in the balance vibrating between union and dissolution, between hope and fear.

This speech, as an argument, as a warning, an inspiration, was a striking one. It flashed as a powerful light on the darkness and gloom of the hour. It was the first message of courage to the almost despairing North. No other Union man, North or South in Congress, had the boldness at that time to make such a speech.

As the good it accomplished for the country was immense—incalculable—it would be ungracious to search too closely for the motives that inspired it. It is reasonably certain that Mr. Johnson felt confident Tennessee would not become disloyal. He did not believe the common people of the State, with whom lay his strength, could be drawn into a scheme to destroy the Government. But few people believed at that time that such a thing could happen. If, however, Tennessee should swing away from the Union and join a Southern Confederacy, his chances for advancement would be better in the North than in the South. His aim was the presidency of his country, whatever that country might be. That had been for years his ambition. That very year he had been a candidate for that office before the Charleston Convention. By remaining true to the Union, and bitterly denouncing secession, while other Southern Senators proved faithless, he would make himself so conspicuously prominent in the North as to be in a direct line to the Presidency. I am far from assuming or supposing Mr. Johnson's heart did not concur in what he did. I have no evidence to warrant such a conclusion. But he was human; he was a politician. If duty and the convictions of his mind coincided with his aspirations and his chance of promotion, there should be no surprise that he chose the course that met both conditions. On the whole I am satisfied he was animated by patriotic motives.

After the delivery of the speech, Johnson at once became the most popular man in the North, excepting Lincoln. No other Senator had dared to make such a speech, so bold, so unequivocal, so direct in denunciation. No other Union Senator's speech could have produced such widespread and intense effect. The same speech, in substance, if made by Mr. Seward, or Mr. Sumner, elegant, polished, and gilded with beautiful phrases and flowing rhetoric, as it would have been, would have fallen almost unheeded on the ears of the country. It was the quarter from whence it came, the person, the opportune moment chosen that surprised and enkindled the country as never before.

It was perhaps well for the fame of Johnson that he did not attempt to repeat this speech during that session of Congress. He did, however, make spirited replies on several occasions to criticisms, and to taunts aimed at him by the friends of disunion. He was their special target during all the weeks of that short session. Some of the Southern Senators had already withdrawn; others remained, but they were aggressive and defiant. Wigfall of Texas had taunted the friends of the Government with the declaration that the Union was no more—was dissolved —dead; and he added that it was only a question whether there should be a decent funeral or an Irish wake.

I take some extracts from a writer descriptive of a remarkable occurrence.*

"The time was the night of March 3, 1861, the very last day of the thirty-sixth Congress—the eve of the inauguration of Lincoln and Hamlin.

"He [Johnson] was the chief actor in an episode in the Senate of the United States, the most remarkable and the most intensely dramatic which ever occurred in that famous deliberative body. It was the only occasion ever known when the spectators in the galleries of the senate stood upon their seats, swung their hats in the air and gave three cheers for a speaker, and that, too, in spite of the pounding of the presiding officer, and the stern order to clear the galleries and arrest the offenders."

Johnson had replied to some strictures made by "Old Joe Lane," of Oregon, and the latter came upon the floor with a long manuscript speech, which he read, and when Johnson attempted to answer, he was so continuously interrupted that it was apparent the majority did not intend he should have an opportunity to reply. Stephen A. Douglas, late candidate for the presidency, interfered in the name of fair play, and the Tennesseean was allowed to proceed.

Johnson talked of treason and alluded to the touchiness of the Southern leaders on that subject. He asked why it was not a legitimate subject of discussion on the floor. He read

---

*"Observer" in the Knoxville *Journal and Tribune.*

the definition of the crime as laid down in the Constitution, and intimated that the fathers of the country had not been so squeamish about defining it.

"Show me the man," he said, "who has been engaged in these conspiracies, who has fired upon our flag, who has given instructions to take our forts and custom houses, our arsenals and dockyards, and I will show you a traitor."

Here Johnson was interrupted by applause, and the presiding officer threatened to have the galleries cleared.

"If the individuals are pointed out to me who are engaged in nightly conspiracies, in secret conclaves, in issuing orders directing the capture of our forts and the taking of our custom houses, I will show who the traitors are; and doing that, the persons pointed out, coming within the purview and scope of the Constitution, were I president of the United States I would do as Thomas Jefferson did in 1806 with Aaron Burr. I would have them arrested, and if convicted within the scope and meaning of the Constitution, by the Eternal God! I would execute them!"

It is difficult to catch the spirit of the scene. A spectator swung his hat and yelled to the presiding officer, "Arrest and be damned!"

Johnson, continuing, alluded to the bullying and truculent attitude of his assailants—Lane himself had the reputation of a fighter, he had gone to Mexico as a common soldier and returned a general, and it was common taunt of the so-called fire-eaters that Northern men would not fight, and of course a Southern "mudsill" with Northern principles was beneath contempt—and said:

"These two eyes of mine never looked upon anything in the shape of mortal men that this heart feared."

"Throughout the delivery of the speech the occupants of the galleries themselves had tried to restrain their emotions, and when it was concluded, there was only a buzzing. After a second, Mr. Johnson waved his hand and said: 'Mr. President, I have done.' Then Hon. J. B. Grinel, afterward a member of the House from Iowa, stood up in his seat, swung his hat in the air, and called for three cheers for Andy Johnson and the Union, and then there occurred a scene, the like of which was never known in the Senate before nor since."

On the adjournment of Congress, after some delay, Johnson

returned to his home in Tennessee, to throw the weight of his talents and influence in behalf of the Union in the contest then fiercely raging in that State. The attempt made by Governor Harris, in February, 1861, to carry the State out of the Union had been defeated by a popular majority of 25,000 votes. He was now making a second effort. He had called the Legislature together to assemble in extra session on the 25th of April, to consider for the second time the question of the secession of the State.

April 12, 1861, there flashed along the wires the news that the Confederate batteries in Charleston had opened fire on Fort Sumter. A few hours later it was heralded over the world that the fort had fallen, that the national flag lay low in the dust. The whole country was frenzied with excitement. Never in our history had there been such universal outburst of feeling and passion as now prevailed. Almost in an hour sixty thousand men, in an unreasoning madness and infatuation, deserted the Union ranks in Tennessee, and went over to the new Confederacy. Nearly every Union leader in Middle and West Tennessee had either preceded or followed the masses in their sudden change. The cry, "To arms!" was heard all over the land. Soon armed squadrons were seen moving to the front.

In April Johnson entered the canvass with more than his usual courage and ability in an effort to save the State. At first he made speeches by himself. Later he and the Hon. Thomas A. R. Nelson, a member of the Lower House, united, and filled a long list of joint appointments. This was a happy arrangement. No man in East Tennessee commanded the confidence of the Whigs in so high a degree as Nelson, and no man the Democrats to the extent of Johnson. Both were powerful on the stump; both were earnest and determined, and both were absolutely fearless. The crowds which attended their meetings and followed them from day to day numbered thousands. They spoke in nearly every county in East Tennessee, and in some counties more than once. Mr. Nelson was exact in his statement of facts, and scrupulously careful, not to suppress or distort anything. He was also bold beyond nearly any man of his day in denouncing what he believed to be wrong. His speeches in this canvass were fair, high-toned, able, argumentative, but at the same time scathing against secession. They were also full of fire and stirring eloquence.

Johnson was always at his best before large popular assemblies. In this canvass he was less bitter than ever before. The supreme peril of the country and the awful momentousness of the hour lifted him to broader, more generous views. He pleaded for his distracted country with a passionate earnestness that moved men's hearts as he had never moved them before. It is doubtful whether in all the land such impressive and powerful speeches were made for the Union as were made by these two men. Mr. Johnson did not go beyond the limits of East Tennessee. He gave to me as a reason why he did not go to Middle Tennessee that the people there would not allow him to speak.* That was probably true.

The influence exerted by these men on the general result was beyond doubt marked. In the previous February election, with the same question in substance (but not in form) before the people, the majority for the Union was 25,532. In June the majority dropped down to 19,141—a falling off of 6391 votes —notwithstanding their presence. Mr. Johnson from his peculiar position was able to exert a larger influence than any other Union leader.

The remarkable change wrought in the Democratic party was mainly, indeed almost entirely, the work of Andrew Johnson. Of the prominent Democratic leaders in East Tennessee, he alone stood for the Union. There were a few local leaders of influence in their immediate region, but not many, who united with him. The others all promptly followed the logical teachings of the party in the canvass of 1860. The 12,890 Democrats who thus came out of the Breckinridge party and followed Johnson over to the support of the Union cause were composed almost entirely of the mass of the people. Nothing in the whole history of Andrew Johnson shows so strikingly as this canvass the dominating power he held over the minds of his party in the section where he lived. Perhaps no such example of devotion and confidence can be found in our political annals.†

---

*He urged me to go to Middle Tennessee to make speeches, saying the people there would not listen to him, but he thought they would to me.

†The vote in Greene County, the home of Johnson, was a remarkable illustration of this influence. In the Presidential election Mr. Breckinridge's plurality over Mr. Bell was 1006 votes, Mr. Douglas only receiving 35 votes. In the following June the Union majority was 1947, notwithstanding several hundred Bell Whigs went over to secession in this election.

The transfer of allegiance of a majority of the Democrats from the party of their love (a party they had been taught to believe was of almost immaculate purity) to a union with the Whigs whom they hated, and infinitely worse to a union with Freesoilers and Abolitionists, whom they both feared and abhorred, was one of transcendent ascendency. The number thus influenced would doubtless have been much larger could Mr. Johnson have been heard in the canvass of January and February as he was heard four months later. Many, it is true, had read his speech in the Senate of the 18th and 19th of December, but in few men was the difference so marked as in this case between the effect produced by the reading of his speeches, and by hearing him deliver them before a popular assembly. It was as the difference between reading a piece of music by note, and hearing that rendered by a great master. The magnetic voice, the action, the earnestness, the fire, the subtle contagion of sympathy and enthusiasm passing from speaker to hearer, sway assemblies and make the triumphs of oratory. How often are we disappointed when reading with cold criticism speeches pronounced great by those who heard them!

While the canvass was in progress Johnson was the object of the most violent hatred on the part of the secessionists. His name was everywhere received with execration. This was manifested toward him in a much more intense degree than against Nelson and the other Union leaders. He was regarded as a traitor to his party. It was no surprise that the leaders of the old Whig party were supporters of the Union cause. That had been their creed for thirty years, their rallying cry in 1860. But Johnson belonged to an opposite school of politics, whose theories and teachings ended logically in the right of secession. This school had openly inculcated the summer before, in a large part of the South, the duty of secession in a contingency which had now arisen. There had been no condemnation nor dissent from these views, but if newspaper reports were trustworthy, he had once or twice uttered sentiments which could only be construed as an acquiescence in the policy of the leaders. Now, when he denounced these leaders for doing what he must have known they contemplated, and which by co-operation he had encouraged them to do, he invoked on himself a depth and intensity of hate inconceivable in its ferocity. On the railroads he was in deadly peril of life. From three or four points he was warned not to attend his appointments, not to attempt to speak. He refrained from going to Middle Tennessee, because of the ill-feeling there against him. Yet for six weeks, heedless of the dangers which daily encompassed him, he bravely went forward in the mission of helping to save the Union. It can be safely affirmed that at no time, either in peace or in war, has any man displayed cooler or higher courage than he during the dark days of April, May, and June, 1861. At no time in his life did he seem so earnest, so brave, so fair, so persuasive, so elevated, and so powerful as when pleading for the Union.

Two or three weeks before the close of this canvass, Thomas C. Hindman of Arkansas, who was born in Knox County, fifteen miles from Knoxville, near the birthplace of Admiral Farragut, was in the above-named city, with a regiment of soldiers, on his way to Virginia. He was the guest of the Hon. Landon C. Haynes, Senator-elect to the Confederate Congress. During the evening nearly all the leading secessionists of the city called on him. Naturally Johnson became the subject of conversation. Hindman thought it a great outrage that Johnson should be allowed to go over the country making Union speeches, though the State had not yet voted in favor of secession. Johnson and Nelson were to speak the next day at Rogersville, sixty-five or seventy miles East of Knoxville. Hindman proposed to take a train and a company of soldiers the next morning and go to that place and arrest Johnson and probably Nelson also. All those present, excepting two, approved of Hindman's proposition. Mr. Haynes, while not expressly approving or dissenting, said that the arrest of Johnson would not stop the trouble, that there were other men of influence besides him who would still lead the people if he were silenced.

At this conference there was present a man who had been a personal and political friend of Johnson from boyhood. Though a warm friend of Southern independence, he disapproved of his arrest. He therefore informed John H. Branner, president of the railroad which Hindman must use in order to reach Rogersville, of the latter's purpose. Branner was also a friend of the South, but he feared the Union men would be indignant with him for furnishing an extra train to be used in arresting one of their favorite leaders, and in revenge would destroy railroad property. To avoid a direct refusal to Hindman's demand, he sent every engine he had out on the road. The next morning Hindman appeared and demanded a train. Mr. Branner was bland, polite, wished to accommodate General Hindman and help the Southern cause by every means within his power, but he was very sorry that every engine he had in the world was out on duty, and none of them would be in before that evening. He regretted so much that General Hindman had not asked for the train earlier!

It thus came about that no attempt was made to arrest Johnson. Those who knew the reckless courage of General Hindman can easily conceive that if he had gotten to Rogersville, Johnson would have been either arrested or killed. It is morally certain that Johnson and Nelson would not have tamely submitted to an arrest, surrounded as they were by friends.*

A few days after the close of the canvass, and the return of Johnson to his home in Greeneville, doubtless realizing that Tennessee was not a safe place for him after its alliance with the Southern Confederacy, he wisely determined to leave for the North. Selecting three trusty friends to accompany him beyond the State line, he, with his little party, left his home for the North, in open daylight, about the 14th of June, by way of Cumberland Gap and Cincinnati, traveling overland. The distance to Cumberland Gap, which is a common point on the lines separating Virginia, Kentucky, and Tennessee, was about sixty miles. At Bean Station Johnson struck the public highway used since the day of Daniel Boone, who passed through that celebrated Gap on his way to Kentucky in 1760 or 1761.

At Bean Station James Lafferty, well known at that day as a noisy Democratic politician, who had been a militia General on the staff of Governor Trousdale, indignant that such a traitor as he esteemed Johnson to be, should escape, called on the people assembled there to aid him in arresting the fugitive. But not a man responded to his call. Johnson quietly passed on, crossing Clinch Mountain, reached Cumberland Mountain,

---

*The facts in reference to the conference at Mr. Haynes' house, with the names of the persons present, and of the design of General Hindman to arrest Johnson and probably Nelson, have been in my possession for many years. They were communicated to a friend of his (who communicated them to me) by the late Thomas J. Powell, of Washington, D. C., a cousin of the wife of Senator Haynes. He was present at the conference and was then a citizen of Knoxville.

and passing through Cumberland Gap, came into the State of Kentucky in the forenoon of the third day. In Kentucky he was in no danger, therefore after passing some distance from the State line his friends returned to their homes, while Johnson continued on through Kentucky to Cincinnati, and thence to Washington.

This whole trip was in keeping with Johnson's character for courage and deliberateness. He started and traveled in the open day, except the night of the third day, a part of the way along the most public highways in the country. He was in no danger from the rural population along his route. His danger was that he would be met or overtaken by Confederate cavalry and arrested. There were a number of regiments of soldiers in East Tennessee at that time, and some companies, if not regiments of cavalry. It must have been known by the Confederate authorities in Knoxville that Johnson was on his way to Cumberland Gap, for Greeneville was in telegraphic and railroad communication with the former place. It is a matter of surprise that he was not intercepted at Bean Station or Tazewell, as he might have been, unless it was the policy of the Confederate authorities to get him out of the State.

On the fall of Fort Donelson, February, 1862, and the occupation of Nashville by the army of General Buell, Johnson was made a Brigadier General by President Lincoln, and appointed Military Governor of Tennessee. This office he held until he became Vice-President, March 4, 1865, a period of three years. The administration of Johnson as Military Governor was characterized by vigor, not to say extreme rigor, as will appear in the next chapter.

When Mr. Johnson left his home in Greeneville, Tenn., June, 1861, he became an exile not to return for nearly eight years. Remarkable as was the career of Andrew Johnson, brave and unconquerable as he was, sometimes standing out alone in defiance of the public opinion of his day, yet it would be difficult for the most gifted writer to make of him a popular hero, with qualities to catch the fancy and kindle the imagination. He was so practical, so rugged, so belligerent, so real and unideal, that there was nothing in him or about him to influence the imagination. And, yet, indeed, in reference to him, truth was stranger than fiction. How extraordinary his triumphs of perseverance and ambition over poverty and obscurity, over enmities and opposition! What strange vicissitudes of fortune! How marvelous his destiny! Leaving as an exile in 1861, fleeing from home, danger, the wrath of a hostile government, amid the din and noise of war, with two governments in existence, yet returning to that home eight years afterward, crowned with the honor of having been the President of a re-united country!

CHAPTER V.

Policy as Military Governor—April 12, 1864, Knoxville-Greeneville Convention Convened for Third Time—Majority Report Aimed at Johnson—"Convention" at Nashville, January, 1865—Noted Oath for Regulation of Election of Electors—McClellan Electors Ask Lincoln to Revoke the Oath—Lincoln Declined—Johnson Takes Oath as Vice-President March 4, 1865—Remarkable Utterances—Johnson's Change of Views After Lincoln's Death—Mr. Blaine's Views of President Johnson's Reconstruction Measures—Mr. Seward's Relations with the President.

JOHNSON's power as Military Governor was unlimited. The right of pulling down and setting up was exercised by him unsparingly. The condition of things then existing in the State demanded a brave heart and an iron will. On the fall of Nashville and Memphis, in the winter and spring of 1862, the disloyal parts of the State fell under the jurisdiction of the Military Governor. To preserve order and prevent conspiracies against the Government of the United States required all the alertness and vigor of the now imperial ruler. It has never been doubted that his administration was free from weakness. The most ultra-Unionists could hardly have desired the exercise of more vigor than was at all times manifested by him. He imprisoned whomsoever he would. He levied at his will heavy assessments of money on the wealthy secessionists of Middle Tennessee.

The object of these levies was to aid in supporting the families of persons who had been influenced to join the secession movement by the advice and the example of these leading men. Many of these poor men had gone South with the Confederate army, leaving their families destitute. Some had been killed in battle or had died of disease. This money was to be used, and so far as I ever heard, was used, for the relief of these needy persons. There may have been a stronger motive than mere sympathy that prompted the collection of this money. Governor Johnson had proclaimed everywhere that treason must be made odious, and to this end that the rich, intelligent "conscious rebels" must be punished and stripped of their wealth and power. These assessments, imposed under the plea of charity for the needy, were the first step in the direction of the fulfillment of his favorite policy of punishment, disgrace, and impoverishment. His mailed hand was laid on gently at first. If anyone refused to pay the sums demanded, the remedy was easily found in the fertile brain of a person exercising absolute authority, with a military force and willing instruments behind him to enforce his orders. Those failing to comply with the orders were sent to prison until solitude and reflection gave them clearer light.

On April 12, 1864, the celebrated Knoxville-Greeneville Convention of 1861, convened for the third time, on the call of its President, the Hon. T. A. R. Nelson. This time it met in Knoxville. Soon it was found that there was a wide diversity of opinion in the Convention, which broke out into an angry debate on the first opportunity. Some of this feeling was personal, and some of it was due to political differences which had sprung up within the last three years. Some of it was referable to the opposition which had grown up in regard to the conduct and policy of Andrew Johnson, Military Governor of Tennessee. Very soon these conflicting opinions became crystallized into the form of resolutions, which precipitated a two or three days' debate. Passion ran exceedingly high. The old leaders in the Greeneville Convention, such as Nelson, Baxter, Carter, Spears, Heiskell and Fleming, found themselves confronted by a new set of men who to a large extent belonged to the army, and who had imbibed by suffering and persecution, feelings quite unlike those of the men who had neither suffered nor entered the army.

Finally, on the fourth day of the Convention, without any vote on either side on the resolutions which had been offered, on motion of Samuel Milligan, that body voted to adjourn *sine die*. And thus ended that famous Convention of 1864, which had done so much to encourage and inspire the Union men of East Tennessee with hope and confidence. A very large part of the fight in the Convention, on the part of the friends of the majority report, was aimed at Mr. Johnson. He was finally invited by the Convention to attend and address that body, and he did so in a very bitter spirit, indulging in a personal quarrel with Mr. Carter.

In a day or two after the adjournment of this Convention a mass meeting of citizens was held in Knoxville. There was a large crowd of people, citizens and soldiers, present. It was known that Governor Johnson would address the meeting, and people were anxious to hear him. The minds of many people were in a state of uncertainty in view of the rapidly changing condition of public affairs. This was especially so as to the policy of emancipation, inaugurated a few months before that time by Mr. Lincoln. There were other matters also relating to the policy of the administration of Mr. Lincoln and the prosecution of the war, that were creating more or less discontent among persons well recognized as Union men. It was well known that such prominent men as Nelson, Baxter and Carter condemned the emancipation policy of Mr. Lincoln, and held extremely conservative views on all questions concerning the future policy of the Government in its treatment of those in arms against it. It was therefore most natural that the people should have been extremely solicitous to hear the views of Governor Johnson, who was justly regarded as the highest exponent in the State of the policy of Mr. Lincoln, in reference to the questions which divided the public mind.

The mass meeting was gotten up on the suggestion and for the benefit of Governor Johnson. Of course he was the chief speaker. It may be of interest to many persons to know how meetings of this kind were generally managed by old politicians. The resolutions were dictated by Mr. Johnson himself, and written by his private secretary, William A. Browning. They were then taken to William G. Brownlow, and he was requested to read and offer them as his own. He approved them and was willing to offer them as his own, but owing to the partial loss of his voice, he could not read them, and suggested that I should be requested to read them. When this was communicated to Governor Johnson, he said it was a good suggestion, that the gentlemen named were both old-line Whigs, and in that way he would secure their influence with that party, which constituted a majority of the loyal people. Accordingly he sent a messenger to me requesting me to read his resolutions, which I agreed to do, reserving the right to make an explanation when doing so. When the meeting was called to order, I was called on, as if I had never heard of them before, to read some resolutions which Mr. Brownlow wished to offer. This I did, and then explained that I did not agree with the plan suggested for the reorganization of our State Government.

NOTABLE MEN OF TENNESSEE   409

When Mr. Johnson arose to speak, he said, as if he had known nothing that was to take place, that he had listened with great interest to the resolutions offered by his friend, Mr. Brownlow, and he took great pleasure in saying they met his hearty approval. No doubt the resolution which declared that the meeting had "full confidence in the integrity and patriotism of Andrew Johnson, Military Governor of the State," did meet with his hearty approval and gave him great pleasure!

Governor Johnson's speech, which followed, was a very able, as well as a very bitter one. Here, he proclaimed as he had done before his celebrated creed, that "treason must be made odious, and traitors be punished and impoverished."

One of the duties prescribed in the commission of Mr. Johnson was to aid the people in re-establishing a State Government, loyal to the Government of the United States. Accordingly on January 8, 1865, there was held in Nashville what was styled a "Convention" of the loyal people of Tennessee. It was convoked by five men who called themselves the "Executive Committee of Tennessee." By whom or by what body of men they were appointed an executive committee does not appear. But is was at that time a well-known fact that this call for a Convention was inspired and directed by Andrew Johnson. It was a misnomer, however, in the graver sense of the word, to designate this meeting as a Convention. It was simply a mass meeting. The call said: "If you cannot meet in your counties, come upon your own personal responsibility." Every man therefore attended who wished to do so. A part of the State was still held by the Confederates, and a representation from all of it was not possible.

Notwithstanding the irregular character of this meeting, it at once proceeded, under the advice and direction of Mr. Johnson, to the work of revising the Constitution. Its first act was the abolition of slavery in the State by an amendment to the Constitution. This was done with as much gravity as if it had been a regular convention of delegates chosen by the people, while in fact not one of the persons present at this meeting, so far as I ever heard, had been either elected or appointed by any constituent.

It is freely admitted that at that time there was no constitutional mode open to the people by which the State could be restored to its proper relations with the national Government.

The secession of the State had broken down and destroyed all the modes known to the Constitution for its revision. Any mode adopted under the circumstances would have been irregular and justifiable only by public necessity—*Salus populi, suprema est lex*. There was no Legislature in existence to call a convention or propose amendments, its term having expired. But there were two methods of proceeding open to the Governor, either one of which would have been better than the plan adopted.

One was an election of a new Legislature; the other, the election of delegates to a Constitutional Convention. Under his commission, as Military Governor, Mr. Johnson was clothed with "authority to exercise such powers as may be [were] necessary and proper to enable the loyal people of Tennessee to present such a republican form of State Government as will entitle the State to the guarantee of the United States therefor." No specific method of doing this was pointed out. But it was no doubt expected that some mode recognized in the constitutional history of the country for organizing States, would be adopted. Independent of this authority, either of the modes indicated above, while not regular, would have been a dignified and impressive resumption of the powers of government on the part of the people, and would have carried with it at all times very much more weight than the plan adopted. The ordinary machinery for accomplishing this purpose had been annihilated by the secession of the State. The military government then existing was merely the creature of war, and could not last. The loyal people had a right in some way to restore the government and resume its functions. But how? Under the clause of the Constitution making it the duty of Congress "to guarantee to each State a republican form of government" had Congress the power to treat them as if in a territorial condition, and by an enabling act authorize them to form a new Constitution? Be that as it may, this had not been done, and certainly there was some mode of reorganizing the State, and the nearest approach to regularity was the best.

The plan adopted to get the State back into "practical relations" with the general Government, was the most irregular that could have been chosen. Yet, when the amendments proposed by this mass meeting were afterward ratified by a majority of the qualified voters, taking part in the election, they became binding on all the people of the State. If the Military Governor, instead of calling a mass meeting, had ordered an election of delegates to a convention in a regular way, and if the body thus selected had proceeded in a dignified and deliberate manner to revise the Constitution, certainly the instrument thus promulgated would have carried with it very much more weight than did the crude and hasty one sent forth by this meeting. There had been ample time for doing this. The instrument adopted was always a source of discontent to many of the loyal people of the State. A number of the persons present, notably Judge John C. Gaut, R. R. Butler, and L. C. Houk, protested against the action of the convention. The majority of the loyal people had no notice nor suspicion that this body of men would proceed to revise the Constitution. Many of them were indignant at its action. To it may be traced many of the errors afterward committed by the Legislature, and much of the subsequent discontent of the people. That Mr. Johnson was responsible for all this no one could doubt. He had been elected Vice-President, and his term as Military Governor was to end on or before March 3d. His ambition was to carry to Washington his own State, as a reconstructed member of the Union, and present it as a rich jewel to the nation. It would give him new prestige and *éclat*. Hence his sudden haste just at the close of his service as Military Governor. At Knoxville, in April, 1864, in the resolutions prepared by himself, he had declared for a "Constitutional Convention to be chosen by the loyal people of the State." Again, these resolutions spoke of the "election of delegates to the Convention," etc. Spring and summer and fall passed and no convention was called. Finally, in December a meeting was called by five men, as we have seen, and not by the Governor, which was to assemble on the 19th of the month. No notice was given in the call that the work of revising the Constitution would be undertaken by that body. With his usual procrastination Mr. Johnson had allowed the period between April and January to pass without any action, and now there was not sufficient time before he must leave for Washington for the accomplishment of this work in a deliberate manner.

Even Governor Harris, when he sought to carry the State out of the Union, observed the forms of law in his first attempt, by calling the Legislature together to act on his propositions. He did not submit them to a mass meeting of self-appointed delegates. And why was there this long delay in calling a regular convention, as Mr. Johnson had virtually promised to do? Was it because he did not want to vacate his office and his power before March 3d, when he would step into a higher position? As soon as the State should be reorganized and recognized by Congress, the office of Military Governor would be at an end. In the meantime the people of the State were kept under military rule and one man's power, from September, 1863, when General Burnside relieved East Tennessee, until March, 1865, with all the courts closed. The work of reorganizing the State and of revising the Constitution might have been and should have been accomplished in a regular, decent way one year, and possibly two, earlier than it was, and the State admitted back into the Union. The last of the Confederate armies was driven out of Middle and West Tennessee in the summer of 1863, and out of the greater part of East Tennessee in September of the same year.

After the so-called convention of January 9, 1865, Governor Johnson issued his proclamation ordering elections to be held throughout the State, to fill the various offices then vacant. He seems to have had great faith in the efficacy of oaths. In this proclamation all voters were required to take the following oath:

"I solemnly swear that I will henceforth support the Constitution of the United States and defend it against the assaults of all its enemies; that I will hereafter be, and conduct myself as a true and faithful citizen of the United States, freely and voluntarily claiming to be subject to all the duties and obligations, and entitled to all the rights and privileges of such citizenship; that I ardently desire the suppression of the present insurrection and rebellion against the Government of the United States, the success of its armies and the defeat of all who oppose them; and that the Constitution of the United States and all laws and proclamations made in pursuance thereof may be speedily and permanently established and enforced over all the people, States, and territories thereof; and further, that I will hereafter aid and assist all loyal people in the accomplishment of these results."

Mr. Jefferson Davis, in his book "The Rise and Fall of the

Confederate Government,"* thus speaks of Mr. Johnson's administration as Military Governor of Tennessee:

"The administration was conducted according to the will and pleasure of the Governor, which was the supreme law. Public officers were required to take an oath of allegiance to the United States Government, and upon refusal were expelled from office. Newspaper offices were closed and the publication suppressed. Subsequently the offices were closed out under the provisions of the confiscation act. All persons using 'treasonable and seditious' language were arrested and required to take the oath of allegiance to the Government of the United States, and give bonds for the future, or to go into exile. Clergymen upon their refusal to take the oath, were confined in the prisons, until they could be sent away. School teachers and editors, and finally large numbers of private citizens, were arrested and held until they took the oath. * * *"

In his proclamation ordering the election above referred to, Governor Johnson says:

"It is not expected that the enemies of the United States will propose to vote, nor is it intended that they be permitted to vote, or hold office."

The most noted oath ever devised by the Military Governor was the one he required for the regulation of the election of electors for President and Vice-President in 1864. It will be remembered that his name was on the ticket with Mr. Lincoln as the nominee of his party for Vice-President. It will also be remembered that the Democratic party, in its convention at Chicago, which nominated General George B. McClellan for the presidency against Mr. Lincoln, declared in its platform that the war for the suppression of the insurrection was "a failure." It further declared in "favor of cessation of hostilities, or an armistice with the view of treating for peace." The McClellan party put out a full electoral ticket in Tennessee, with the names of persons who had formerly been highly honored in the State. To meet this new phase in politics our Military Governor was equal to the emergency. He not only required all voters to swear they "ardently desired the suppression of the rebellion," and "rejoiced over the defeat of the rebel armies," but also that they were opposed (quoting the words of the Chicago platform)

*Vol. I, Chap. XXVII., p. 285.

to any "cessation of hostilities, or an armistice, with a view to treating for peace."

This proclamation and oath created a great sensation at the time. An address, signed by the McClellan electors, was drawn up, and sent to Mr. Lincoln, asking him to revoke the oath. A delegation, headed by a distinguished soldier and statesman, went to Washington to see Mr. Lincoln, but the latter declined to interfere. How could anyone vote sincerely believing in that platform? He was required to take an oath repudiating the very platform upon which he and his party stood.

The public addresses made by Governor Johnson, from time to time, during the last few months of his administration as Military Governor of Tennessee, are remarkable specimens of oratory. Perhaps no prominent public man in this country has ever so astonished the world as he did by his public speeches from 1864 to 1867.

But by far the most remarkable utterance ever made by Mr. Johnson was his address, made just before taking the oath of office as Vice-President, March 4, 1865. I copy the following account of this speech from the Knoxville *Whig*, as it appeared in the New York papers in 1865:

"Mr. Johnson, before taking the oath of office, made a short speech, which, as in the case of Mr. Hamlin, was nearly inaudible owing to the want of order which prevailed among the women in the galleries. 'By the choice of the people,' he said, 'he had been made presiding officer of this body, and in presenting himself here in obedience to the behests of the Constitution of the United States, it would, perhaps, not be out of place to remark just here what a striking thing the Constitution was. It was the Constitution of the people of the country, and under it here to-day, before the American Senate, he felt that he was a man and an American citizen. He was a proud illustration of the fact that, under the Constitution, a man could rise from the ranks to occupy the second place in the gift of the American people and of the American Government. Those of us who labored our whole lives for the establishment of a free government know how to cherish its great blessings. He would say to Senators and others before him—to the Supreme Court which sits before him—that they all get their power from the people of this country.' Turning toward Mr. Chase, Mr. Johnson said: 'And your exaltation and position depend upon the people.'

Then, turning toward the Cabinet, he said: 'And I will say to you, Mr. Secretary Seward, and to you, Mr. Secretary Stanton, and to you, Mr. Secretary [to a gentleman near by, *sotto voce*, Who is Secretary of the Navy? The person addressed replied in a whisper, Mr. Welles] and to you Mr. Secretary Welles, I would say you all derive your power from the people.' Mr. Johnson then remarked that the great element of vitality in this government was its nearness and proximity to the people. He wanted to say to all who heard him, in the face of the American people, that all power was derived from the people. He would say, in the hearing of the foreign ministers, for he was going to tell the truth here to-day, that he was a plebeian,—he thanked God for it. It was the popular heart of this nation that was beating to sustain Cabinet officials and the President of the United States. It was a strange occasion that called a plebeian like him to tell such things as these. Mr. Johnson adverted to affairs in Tennessee and the abolition of slavery there. He thanked God Tennessee was a State in the Union and had never been out of it. The State Government had been discontinued for a time—there had been an interregnum, a hiatus—but she had never been out of the Union. He stood here to-day as her representative. On this day she would elect a Governor and a Legislature, and she would very soon send Senators and members to Congress."

Not long after the death of Mr. Lincoln, it was observable that the views and feelings of Mr. Johnson were undergoing a change in reference to those lately in insurrection. At first this change was hailed with delight by the great body of loyal people, for they had feared he would be too bloody and unrelenting in his policy.

The magnanimous Grant thus speaks of his apprehensions as to the future policy of Mr. Johnson after the assassination of Mr. Lincoln, and he reflects, in what he says, the feelings and opinions of a large majority of the Northern people at that time:

"It would be impossible for me to describe the feeling that overcame me at the news of these assassinations [Mr. Lincoln's and Mr. Seward's, as reported], more especially the assassination of the President. I knew his goodness of heart, his generosity, his yielding disposition, his desire to have everybody happy, and above all his desire to see all the people of the United States enter again upon the full privileges of citizenship with equality among all. I knew also the feeling that Mr. Johnson had expressed in speeches and conversation against the Southern people, and I feared that his course toward them would be such as to repel, and make them unwilling citizens, and if they became such they would remain so for a long while. I felt that reconstruction had been set back no telling how far."*

Again General Grant said:

"Mr. Johnson's course toward the South did engender bitterness of feeling. His denunciations of treason and his ever ready remark: 'Treason is a crime and must be made odious,' was repeated to all those men of the South who came to him to get some assurance of safety, so that they might go to work at something with the feeling that what they obtained would be secured to them. He uttered his denunciations with great vehemence, and as they were accompanied with no assurances of safety, many Southerners were driven to a point almost beyond endurance. * * *

"The Southerners who read the denunciations of themselves and their people [by the President who was supposed to represent the feelings of those over whom he presided] must have supposed that he uttered the sentiments of the Northern people; whereas, as a matter of fact, but for the assassination of Mr. Lincoln, I believe the great majority of the Northern people, and the soldiers unanimously, would have been in favor of a speedy reconstruction, on terms that would be least humiliating to the people who had rebelled against the Government. They believed, I have no doubt, as I did, that besides being the mildest, it was also the wisest policy."

But soon they saw with amazement that the man who had been the most extreme of all our public men in his demand for punishment was becoming the most lenient, and making himself the champion of those lately in arms.

Not more remarkable was his change in December, 1860, from the extreme wing of Southern agitators to the support of the Republican party, than the reversal of feeling and opinion on his part in reference to those lately hostile to the Government, which occurred not long after he became President. This was the more surprising in each case because he was not a vacillating

---

*Grant's Memoirs, Vol. II, pp. 508-9.

man. On the contrary, he was noted for the dogged tenacity with which he clung to his opinions. He was not only firm, but obstinate. But while he was both firm and obstinate he was also calculating. He was wise in forecasting coming events. It is hard to escape the conclusion that both these changes were the result of a deliberate reckoning of chances. He supported Breckinridge, not because he cared for slavery, nor was in favor of secession, but because in so doing he was in line with his party, whose assistance in Tennessee he would need and must have, when the time for his re-election to the Senate should come around. When he saw that the leaders of the cotton States were going to establish a new government, he thought no doubt he could keep Tennessee out of the Southern movement, and could thus cement his power more firmly than before. But few men in Tennessee believed or dreamed in 1860 that Jackson's State and home would ever raise a parricidal hand against the Union. The thought was insulting to the memory of its great and idolized defender. It would be strange indeed if Mr. Johnson did not share in this almost universal belief. He expected to be able to crush any effort in that direction. For a number of years previously he had been supreme in the councils of his party in the State. He made and unmade public men at his will.

But if he failed to hold Tennessee in the national column, his chances for advancement, from his point of view, would be better in the North than in the South. He knew that he had always been suspected and to some extent despised by the extreme Southern leaders. In birth, education, and social position, he was never regarded by them as their equal, and he felt it keenly. In a new confederacy he knew, as well as they, there would be no honors for him. He had never been an ultra-slavery propagandist. Mr. Johnson was too shrewd and sagacious not to see the immense probability of the triumph of the Government in the approaching conflict. With his boundless ambition, it was natural for him to count the effect of such a struggle upon his own fortunes. Patriotism united with interest and judgment in finally fixing his position. His chances for political advancement, therefore, were better in the North than in the South, especially if he could hold and carry Tennessee with him. With his own State in his hands, preserved from secession with his might and power, he would stand before the North as the greatest Southern champion of the Union. He would be next in esteem to Mr. Lincoln. Then the presidency! Why not succeed Mr. Lincoln? Who could tell what might happen? This bright vision was an enchanting one. And how mysteriously and with what marvelous exactness this most improbable of things came to pass!

And the other change, from the most malignant hatred, to the tenderest love for those lately in arms, how came it about? Over and over again Mr. Johnson had proclaimed in his addresses in Tennessee, while Military Governor, that "treason must be made odious and rebels be punished and impoverished." He said this in Knoxville, as we have seen, in April, 1864. In Nashville he had prominent leaders arrested and thrown into prison because they were disloyal. He levied heavy contributions on their property. He went to Washington breathing out threats against them. In learning of the surrender of General Lee, he earnestly protested to Mr. Lincoln against the indulgent terms which General Grant had accorded the vanquished army. He believed that the whole army should have been held as prisoners of war, and General Lee kept in confinement. He insisted that Lee should be tried for treason, and but for the decided protest of General Grant, he would have been arrested and put up on trial.

A few days after Mr. Johnson became President, he said in an address: "The people must understand that treason is the blackest of crimes and will surely be punished. * * * Let it be engraven on every mind that treason is a crime and shall suffer its penalty." On one occasion, he exclaimed: "The halter for intelligent, influential traitors!" Before he became President, he declared that "traitors should be arrested, tried, convicted, and hanged." Even blunt, honest, old Ben Wade, who was regarded as one of the bitterest men in the North, was startled at the vindictive spirit displayed by Mr. Johnson toward the secessionists.

And yet, in a few brief weeks, Mr. Johnson issued his proclamation of Amnesty and Pardon, granting a pardon to all who had been in the secession movement, upon the simple condition of taking a prescribed oath, certain classes being excepted from the benefits of the proclamation. I do not say that this was wrong, but that it was wise and just, for pardon and amnesty had to come sooner or later, if we were to become again a reunited people.

I hesitate to affirm positively that Mr. Johnson deliberately betrayed the North. When he succeeded to the Presidency he assumed grave and high duties toward the whole country. He was lifted up into a higher, a broader field, not only of patriotism, but of feeling also. His horizon was greatly enlarged. He became, as it were, the father of the people of all sections. The bitter partisan was, or should have been, merged in the noble patriot. The highest good of all should have been, and possibly was, at first, his aim. The desire of leaving a good name behind, of securing the love of his countrymen as a just ruler, would naturally prompt a magnanimous man to a course far above that of the mere designing politician. Possibly these were in part the reasons which at first influenced Mr. Johnson. If so, they were noble and honorable. But this revolution of feeling was so sudden and remarkable that men wondered at it, as well they might. Many began to criticise it; some openly and severely to condemn it. His motives were questioned. He, in turn, became enraged at this opposition, and turned upon his critics with bitter denunciations.

It is possible that another motive may have influenced Mr. Johnson quite as much as that suggested. Mr. Blaine says that the reconstruction measures of Mr. Johnson originated in the mind of Mr. Seward, and that they were on his part intended as measures of love and reconciliation. That may be, and doubtless is, true. But it seemed strange that Mr. Johnson, one of the least loving of men, should so suddenly become an apostle of love. Of all his qualities this was supposed to be the least prominent. Other feelings than that of love were known usually to dominate him.

No sooner had the amnesty proclamation been published, than applications for special pardons began to come in to the President. Immediately he commenced pardoning the same classes which he had excluded from the benefit of the general amnesty. All were restored upon precisely the same terms. Was this done to bind to him the leading men of the South by the strongest tie known to honorable men—that of gratitude—a class whose crimes were too dark, as he pretended, to be embraced in the general amnesty? He had distinguished the leaders by excluding them from the general amnesty, and a second time distinguished them by special pardons, thus doubly separating them from the common people.

Mr. Seward may have flattered himself that he had obtained his chief's approval of his plan of love and reconciliation for the Southern States; but Mr. Johnson, if true to the history of his past life, looked away beyond the things, to their effect on his own political fortunes. Doubtless he was willing for Mr. Seward to indulge in such pleasing fancies. As for himself, he was a practical statesman, and accustomed to consider alone those things which tended to strengthen and consolidate his own power. He was subtle in policy and far reaching in forethought. Schemes of philanthropy could not fascinate his cool head. It was electoral votes he desired. These the Southern States would have, and they must be secured. At the same time, it was a pleasant reflection to him, no doubt, that by a humane policy he might also win the good opinion and respect of a class of persons among whom he was born and had lived, and who had always looked down upon him.

A magnanimous mind, touched by the misfortunes of a brave people, whose misguided judgment and ambition had led them into an act of supreme folly, might have been influenced by sympathy alone to overlook their acts in their day of extreme desolation, and restore them to full political brotherhood as citizens. But Johnson had never been distinguished for magnanimity nor mercy. But what he would not do from magnanimity nor mercy, he would do from self-interest.

I have elsewhere said Johnson was bitter and unforgiving, but that he was also calculating. A presidential election was ahead, no matter if it was three years off. What more natural than that the Southern people should vote for the man who had broken the shackles of their bondage and restored them to power?

By means of his immense patronage he might be able to detach from the Republican party in the North enough votes, when united with the Democratic votes, to carry the old Democratic States. Thus he would be elected President by the people. What matter if Sumner, Wade, Stevens, and Biddings did howl and rage, provided the people were for him? He could hardly hope to keep on good terms with the strong, proud, arrogant radical leaders. They would not yield a particle, neither would he. Since his unfortunate appearance and address at his inauguration, they, as well as many others in the North, were already alienated to some extent, and he could not depend on them to support him. He must, therefore, look elsewhere.

It was evidently the expectation of Mr. Johnson, in his sudden change of position, to draw away a large following from the Republican party, and to divide it. He counted on the powerful influence of Mr. Seward with the party. He also counted on the influence of Seward's old political partner, Thurlow Weed. Now that the Union was saved, many of the War Democrats, perhaps nearly all, who had attached themselves to the Republican party, to save the Government, would come back to the Democratic fold, from natural instinct. With a division in the Republican party, the return of many or all of the War Democrats, and the support of the disloyal element in the North, the prospect looked bright for carrying many of the Northern States for Mr. Johnson in the next presidential election. Unquestionably the Presidency was his object. With the aid of the Southern States, which would be readmitted into the Union under his policy, and which would support him from motives of gratitude, combined with those he would carry in the North, the way to his election would be clear. Perhaps in the beginning he did not mean to go as far as he finally went; perhaps he did not contemplate an irrevocable separation from the Republican party, and certainly he did not foresee the almost united opposition of the party to his policy. But opposition, as it always had, drove him forward in a headlong course of fury and desperation until he lost all sense of consistency.

Not less remarkable was the madness of the Southern people, guided by his infatuated advice. They could have been, and would have been, almost certainly, restored to all their rights, with a few exceptions, in the year 1866, on taking a simple oath, if they had adopted the fourteenth Amendment to the Constitution. But they indignantly rejected it. Congress was then driven, most reluctantly and contrary to its first purpose, to enter upon and adopt the series of harsh measures as means of national repose and future security, known as the Reconstruction Acts, which, unforeseen by Congress, resulted so disastrously to the people of the South. Under negro, and carpet-bag rule, grievous wrongs were suffered by the South, which were attributed to the hate of the Republican party, when, in fact, they were the result of the folly of their adviser, Andrew Johnson, and of their own lack of knowledge.

No such changes as Mr. Johnson's,—so radical and thorough, from a state of intense implacableness to one of effusive consideration,—can be found recorded in history. Love and forgiveness were not qualities of his heart. Some other powerful motive must be found sufficient to neutralize his recent terrible hatred of the Southern leaders, to effect this revolution in feeling. This was ambition, the ambition to triumph over all opposition, to put his feet on the necks of his enemies, to be elected President by the vote of the people. This overrode, and, at times, quieted all other passions, even hate and revenge.

CHAPTER VI.

Bitter Quarrel Between President and Congress—Impeachment of Johnson—Failure of Southern States to Ratify "Fourteenth Amendment"—Contest Between Mr. Johnson and Republican Party—Attitude of Prominent Republicans Toward Negro Suffrage — Reconstruction — Negro Rule—Fifteenth Amendment—Civil Rights Bill—Johnson's Opposition to Fourteenth Amendment.

Soon after the issuance of the amnesty proclamation there sprang up an angry quarrel between Mr. Johnson and Congress. The breach between them each day became wider. As the quarrel grew in intensity, Johnson drifted farther and farther away from the Republican party. Finally he became completely identified in sympathy, as well as in principle, with those lately hostile to the Government. It was hardly to be expected that the determined men who were leaders of the Republican party, in Congress, flushed with their recent victory in the State elections, and sustained by nearly three-fourths of a majorty in both branches of Congress, would quietly submit to the domineering will of the President. Johnson, on the other hand, with a supreme confidence in his own power, went forward in the policy which he had proposed, not shrinking from this deadly contest. Congress with unwavering firmness, swiftly passed measure after measure designed for the security and protection of the National Union. Johnson, again and again, resorted to his constitutional right of vetoing these measures. Scarcely were his veto messages read in Congress before the measures were triumphantly passed by Constitutional majorities over his vetoes. The President became more and more favorable to the late enemies of the Government. He encouraged them in every conceivable way by words and by speeches to persist in their course.

This embittered quarrel between the President and Congress went on for about two years, until at last the House of Representatives, driven to desperation by the repeated acts of the President intended to defeat the nation's will, preferred articles of impeachment against him. Never before in the history of our Government had there been an attempt to im-

423

peach a President. After a protracted trial before the Senate, sitting as the highest judicial body in the land, Mr. Johnson only escaped conviction by the narrow margin of one vote.

The strength of the impeachment of Johnson rested upon the charge that he had violated the Tenure of Office Act, by an attempt to remove Mr. Stanton from the office of the Secretaryship of War. Stanton had been appointed to that office by Mr. Lincoln, and held over under Johnson without reappointment. A quarrel had arisen between these two functionaries as to the plan to be pursued in reconstructing the late seceding States, Stanton taking sides with Congress. Johnson wished to get rid of him, because he was an obstruction in the way of the execution of his plans, hence the attempt to remove him.

Whatever may be thought of the conduct of Mr. Johnson prior to his trial, it is the better judgment of the world to-day that the impeachment proceeding was an unfortunate mistake. As a precedent, the conviction of a President of the United States, without the clearest proof of the commission of high crimes and misdemeanors, might prove to be at some future time most mischievous; besides, it was never clear that Mr. Johnson was guilty of an impeachable crime. As remarked recently by an eminent Republican lawyer:* "The executive office was on trial" in this impeachment, and it was fortunate for the country that Mr. Johnson was acquitted. Mr. Blaine says, in regard to his trial: "No impartial reader can examine the record of the pleadings and arguments of the managers who appeared on behalf of the House, without feeling that the President was impeached for one series of misdemeanors and tried for another series."

I am not criticising Mr. Johnson for his plan of reconstructing the late secession States, nor for his sympathy with the Southern people. His plan may have been the best that could have been devised. I believe firmly that his policy would have proved such if the Southern people had accepted it in a fraternal spirit, and at the same time had ratified the Fourteenth Amendment to the Constitution. If these two things had been done cheerfully and in good faith, there can scarcely exist a doubt that in twenty months after the surrender of General Lee, the Southern States would all have been restored to their old places in the Union.

*Joseph H. Choate.

Of course, the result would have been that the control of the late secession States would at once have passed into the hands of those lately in arms against the Government. That mattered not, for such happened in the end anyway, and was right, with proper guarantees and conditions and was inevitable sooner or later under any plan of reconstruction. All can now see that it was best that it should happen quickly. The colored people have finally fallen under the political power of the whites in every insurrectionary State, and they so remain, notwithstanding the Fifteenth Amendment and the Civil Rights Bill. That, too, was inevitable. Ignorant colored men, however superior in numbers, are no match for the intelligent, masterful white race. If the whites of these States had retained the control of their own internal affairs, after the close of the war, the condition of the colored people would have been made at least as tolerable as it became after the return of the whites to power, and almost certainly much more so. The whites were, at that time, more kindly disposed towards their late slaves than they became later after they witnessed the corrupt, and sometimes insolent, rule of the latter, while they, and their adventurous associates, the carpet-baggers, were in the ascendency. The slave owners felt no resentment toward their late slaves until they saw the latter exalted over themselves. But their indignation was naturally aroused when they beheld those who were lately obedient to their every command, and whom they still regarded as their rightful property, and knew to be vastly their inferiors, exercising high rights denied to themselves, and holding honorable offices from which they were debarred. In addition to this, when they saw their late slaves used as the blind instruments of corrupt men, a feeling of intense indignation sprang up in their minds against those slaves, for whom they once entertained only feelings of kindness.

The quarrel between Johnson and Congress was a national calamity. The Provisional Governments in several of the late insurrectionary States, established under the Acts of Congress, with the evils that followed, and the sea of hate and malignant passion which swelled up, waiting for the day of vengence, would never have had an existence but for that quarrel. Except for it, too, the movement to impeach Mr. Johnson, which still further intensified this ill-feeling, would not have been made. Above all, and far beyond all, it postponed indefinitely the day of genuine reconciliation, and left on the minds of the Southern people an almost unalterable conviction that they had been harshly treated by the National Government. It was most natural that the people of the South, urged on by the President of the United States, with a few Republicans and the whole Democratic party, of the North, should have felt as they had felt in the days of their ascendency before the War, strong, proud, and independent.

In the early part of 1867, it became manifest to Congress that the ten Secession States would not ratify the Fourteenth Amendment. It became equally evident that the colored people would not have the right of the elective franchise conferred on them, and yet these States intended to claim the right of counting them in apportioning members of Congress and Presidential electors. The adoption of this amendment would have forced them either to confer upon the colored people the right of voting, or to submit to a diminished representation. They sought to avoid both of these alternatives. This was probably one of the paramount obstacles in the way of ratification. They were unwilling to give up any of their power, and persistently refused either to do so or to enfranchise the negro.

Here then was presented the anomaly of States lately in insurrection against the Government, by their conduct, if not their words, claiming in the national Legislature and in the electoral colleges a larger representation than was allowed to an equal number of white men in the loyal States. It would seem that no one could have been found so unreasonable as to entertain such an idea as that above indicated.

How wisely, or how unwisely, Congress dealt with this question of reconstruction, has been and will continue to be a source of controversy. It was, however, an unspeakable misfortune, which can never be sufficiently deplored, that it was necessary to deal with it at all. Out of it sprang, directly or indirectly, nearly all of the evils which the Southern people were afterward called on to endure.

Maddened by the obstructive policy of Mr. Johnson, as well as by the defiant attitude of the ten insurrectionary States, Congress came together in December, 1866, in a mood very different from that which animated it a year before. Without much delay or faltering there followed during the next fifteen months four Acts which formed the Congressional plan of reconstruction. Under and by virtue of these Acts, the governments organized under the proclamation of Mr. Johnson were swept out of existence, and the ten States were put under military rule, until new governments could be constructed according to the terms of the Acts. As rapidly as could be the States were reorganized, and passed into the hands of loyal men, the colored men being the decided majority in every State. This domination of a small minority of white men, with a large majority of colored men, continued until the ever swelling tide of popular indignation on the part of those who had been deprived of political rights rose so high, that it became resistless, and finally swept away forever what was known as "Carpet-Bag Government."

It does not lie within the scope of this work to enter into a discussion of the working of these governments, nor the practices which prevailed under them. Much less shall I undertake to defend them. It is sufficient to say, after making due allowance for exaggeration, that if one tithe of what has been said of these governments is true, they deserved demolition. It was these, with the antecedent and subsequent events accompanying them, that more than all things else, much more even than war itself, left a hatred in the minds and hearts of a majority of the Southern people which time alone can remove. This part of our national history is a sad one to contemplate. There can be but few genuine friends of our country who would not wish that the reconstruction measures had never been enacted; that the necessity for these acts had never arisen. But for them the great uprising in the South in behalf of its constitutional rights, suddenly precipitating a whole nation into the most stupendous civil war recorded in the annals of time, might have passed into history as simply an outburst of passion on the part of an impulsive people, and the deeds of marvelous gallantry could have been claimed as a common inheritance of glory, by every citizen within the broad limits of both North and South, and the war would have left behind it the impression of merely a brilliant military pageant, with scarcely a trace of bitterness remaining. Great deeds on the battlefield, whether at Gettysburg, or at Chancellorsville, or Chickamauga, and great Generals, whether Grant or Lee, Sherman or Johnston, Sheridan or Jackson, would have been proudly pointed to by all then as to-day, as American Generals and American deeds. Peace and fraternal love might soon have come to the hearts and homes of every good and patriotic citizen of the land. How splendid such an immediate ending of this deplorable contest! This happy era was dawning on the country in 1865, when Mr. Johnson commenced reviving the dissensions between the two sections. By his perverseness, and his arrogant defiance of those who had elevated him to power, on one side, and by the delusive hope of easier terms and entire deliverance excited by him on the other, he drove the two sections further and further apart, both at last maddened to the very verge of frenzy. Then followed that long and bitter contest between Mr. Johnson and the Republican party. For over three years this new contest raged nearly as furiously as did the question of independence during the Civil War.

Finally Congress came to the conclusion that there was still one more measure necessary for the security of the country, and especially for the safety of the colored people. This was the Fifteenth Amendment to the Constitution. It is a singular fact that, at the close of the war, and for a good while afterward, none of our public men or at least but a few of them, thought of conferring the right of suffrage indiscriminately on this race. In 1864 Mr. Lincoln, in a letter to Governor Hahn of Louisiana, cautiously and hesitatingly said: "I barely suggest for your private consideration whether some of the colored people may not be let in [as voters], as for instance the very intelligent, and especially those who have fought gallantly in our ranks. They would probably help in some trying time in the future to keep the jewel of Liberty in the family." Johnson, in some of his letters to his provisional Governors, in 1865, suggested that the elective franchise might be extended to all persons of color "who can read the Constitution of the United States and write their names, also to those who owned estates of not less than two hundred and fifty dollars, and pay taxes thereon." In 1864 Congress had passed an Act declaring the terms on which the insurrectionary States might be admitted to representation in Congress. One of these was that "involuntary servitude shall be forever prohibited," but there was no provision that the right of suffrage, either partial or universal, should be conferred on the freedmen. The late Vice-President Wilson of Massachusetts, about that time, said "men might differ about the power or expediency of giving the right of suffrage to the negro." While the Fourteenth Amendment was in consideration in the Senate, Mr. Henderson proposed in the Senate an amendment to it which in effect provided for negro suffrage in all the States, but it received only ten votes. This was in the spring of 1866. In this same year Governor Morton, the leader of the Republican party, in a message to the Legislature of Indiana, strongly opposed negro suffrage. General Jacob D. Cox, one of the best and coolest-headed men in the Republican party, as a candidate for Governor of Ohio, in 1866, took open and decided ground against conferring this right.

Mr. Blaine says on this point: "The truth was that the Republicans of the North, constituting, as was shown by the elections of 1865, a majority in every State, were deeply concerned as to the fate and future of the colored population of the South. Only a minority of Republicans were ready to demand suffrage for those who had been recently emancipated, and who, from the ignorance peculiar to servitude, were presumably unfit to be entrusted with the elective franchise. * * * The great mass of the Republicans stopped short of the demand for the conferment of suffrage on the negro. That privilege was indeed still denied him in a majority of the loyal States, and it seemed illogical and unwarrantable to expect a more advanced philanthrophy, a higher sense of justice from the South than had been attained by the North."*

In the great debate on reconstruction in the House of Representatives, which commenced in December, 1865—the longest in its history—Thaddeus Stevens, the brilliant leader of the House, in opening the discussion did not insist on negro suffrage. "Mr. Stevens' obvious theory at that time," says Mr. Blaine, "was not to touch the question of suffrage by national interposition, but to reach it more effectively perhaps by excluding the entire colored population from the basis of Congressional representation until, by the action of the Southern States themselves, the elective franchise should be conceded to the colored population."†

A few days after this speech of Stevens, Mr. Spalding, who represented one of the districts of the Western Reserve of Ohio

*Blaine, Volume II., p. 92.
†Id., p. 129.

—the most radical district in the United States—laid down five fundamental propositions as conditions to be observed in reconstructing insurrectionary States, and it is significant that colored suffrage was not among them. Ignatius Donnelly, a radical Republican, in an able speech in the House, left it clear that there was no disposition at that period among Republicans to confer on the negro the right to vote.

Mr. Fessenden, one of the most radical Republicans, discussing the Freedman's Bureau Bill, said:

"I take it that no one contends—I think the Honorable Senator from Massachusetts himself [Sumner] who is the great champion of universal suffrage, would hardly contend—that now, at this time, the whole of the population of the recent slave States is fit to be admitted to the exercise of the right of suffrage. I presume that no man who looks at the question dispassionately and calmly could contend that the mass of those who were recently slaves (undoubtly there may be exceptions) and who have been kept in ignorance all their lives, oppressed and more or less forbidden to acquire information, are fitted at this stage to exercise the right of suffrage, or could be trusted to do it unless under such good advice as those better informed might be prepared to give them."

In the House, when the reconstruction measures came up for consideration, "there was some apprehension in the minds of members on both sides that the broad character of the bill might include the right to suffrage, but to prevent that result Mr. Wilson moved to add a new section declaring that nothing in this Act shall be so construed as to affect the laws of any State concerning the right of suffrage. * * * The amendment was *unanimously* agreed to, not one voice on either side of the House being raised against it."

As we have seen, the Fourteenth Amendment, which made the colored people citizens of the United States, did not confer the right of suffrage. It did provide, however, that they should not be counted in the apportionment of representatives in Congress, and in choosing electors for President and Vice-President, unless the right of suffrage was conferred. If they were counted without the conferring of this right, the South would gain thirty-five or forty more representatives in Congress over those accorded to an equal number of population in the Northern States. It was hoped that the people of the States recently in insurrection would see the justice of this proposition, and either confer on the colored people the right to vote, or adopt the Fourteenth Amendment, and submit to a diminished representation. There was no disposition on the part of Congress to force colored suffrage on the Southern people. They were left entirely free to adopt the amendment or not.

Slowly the Republican party and the public sentiment of the North had advanced from universal emancipation, by the Thirteenth Amendment (passed January, 1865) to the conferment of citizenship by the Fourteenth Amendment (passed June, 1866) and from that to impartial suffrage in the enfranchisement of the colored race, by the Fifteenth Amendment, passed on February 26, 1869. It took a little more than four years to reach the last important step, from January, 1865, to February, 1869. These are important facts; they conclusively prove that reconstruction, as finally adopted, and the Fifteenth Amendment were afterthoughts, the result of hostile developments in the South. The persistent efforts of President Johnson from May, 1865, to the close of his term, to thwart the action and will of the people, and the rejection of the Fourteenth Amendment and other evidences of hostility on the part of the Southern people, gradually forced Congress from one measure of public security to another, not dreamed of in 1865. In the same way the public sentiment in the North advanced toward the final consummation reached in 1869, just in proportion to the efforts made by Johnson to defeat the work of reconstruction. If the people lately in insurrection had accepted the results of the war in good faith, as they evidently did until Mr. Johnson became their leader and champion, and inspired them with the hope of regaining by the ballot what they had lost by the sword; if they had manifested a disposition as individuals in their legislative capacity, to treat the freedman with fairness; if they had remembered that they had risked all on the wager of battle and lost—that they were hopelessly defeated; if they had relied on the clemency and magnanimity of their recent enemies in the war, as evident by the terms of surrender so generously accorded by General Grant to General Lee and his brave army, most of the measures of reconstruction, as well as the Fifteenth Amendment in all human probability, never would have been passed.

The wisdom of the reconstruction measures is not here asserted. As to them, there were grave reasons of doubt, and they proved in the end to be most unwise and full of evil. It was a misfortune that the right of suffrage was conferred on a race nine-tenths of whom were then and still are wholly unprepared for the exercise of this priceless privilege of a free citizen. And as long as a large part of them regard their votes as valuable simply as so much merchandise, to be sold to the highest bidder, they will be an unsafe depository of this sacred right.

That President Johnson, when he issued his proclamation of amnesty and pardon, influenced, as Mr. Blaine says, by the arguments and seductive eloquence of Mr. Seward, his brilliant Secretary of State, should have desired the restoration of peace and good feeling between the people of the two sections of the Union, is very probable. If he did not, we must reckon him as one of the worst men who ever lived. Judging him by his acts and professions, he appeared to be controlled at this particular time by the noblest impulses and the most enlightened principles of statesmanship. If so, in this he had caught the spirit and reflected the feeling of a vast majority of the loyal people of the North. In the boundlessness of their joy over their unparalleled triumph with almost one voice they demanded peace, reconciliation, and a restored Union.

The pleasing hope was confidently entertained—how was it possible to entertain any other?—that the Southern people, so distinguished for magnanimity, would receive the generous terms offered them in the same spirit which inspired their proffer on the part of the North. It was believed that the return of peace would bring with it national repose and good will.

As to what was the wisest and best mode of reconstructing the States lately in insurrection, has never been settled by a general consensus of opinion. Mr. Johnson held to the opinion that the acts of secession were null and void, and therefore that these States had never been out of the Union; in this was implied a denial of the right to secede. Mr. Lincoln, the clearest-headed statesman of his day, thought this question not a "practically material one," but merely a "pernicious abstraction." He said: "We all agreed that the seceded States, so called, are out of their practical relations with the Union, and that the sole object of the Government is to get them back into their practical relation. I believe it is easier to do this without deciding or even considering whether these States have ever been out of the Union. The States finding themselves once more at home, it would seem immaterial to me to inquire whether they had ever been abroad."

Whether these States had been out of the Union or not, it was certain that their relations with it had been disturbed and suspended. Some act, either executive or legislative, was necessary to restore these relations. Having thrown off their allegiance to the Government, and having been reduced to submission by force of arms, they were not by that fact, *ipso facto*, restored to their old places as members of the Union. They now occupied a position somewhat analogous to that of territories. Possibly it required an Act of Congress in order to be restored as States. Congress took this view of the question. Mr. Lincoln and Mr. Johnson held the opposite opinion.

But besides this question, as to which Congress or the Executive should initiate and direct the proceedings preliminary to the reconstruction of the seceding States, there were other grave and perplexing questions to be solved. What were the terms upon which they should be so rehabilitated? Clearly the Government had the right to prescribe such terms as would guarantee to the people of those States a republican form of government, and protect them against invasion and domestic violence, and to adopt such measures as would tend to prevent a recurrence of secession.

Then who should participate in this work of reorganizing civil governments? Should those lately in arms perform this work, or aid in it; or should the whites who had been loyal alone perform it; or should the colored people be in part entrusted with this duty?

Johnson probably adopted the only alternative practicable under the cimcumstances. He conferred this right, first, on the loyal whites, secondly, on the secessionists on the single condition of their taking the oath of loyalty and fidelity to the Government. It is a well-known fact that Congress denied the right of the Executive to carry on alone the work of reconstruction. That was the beginning of the quarrel between Mr. Johnson and that body. Mr. Lincoln, however, had exercised the same power in reorganizing the State of Tennessee, and had previously reorganized Louisiana and Arkansas in the same way.

On September 19, 1863, after the occupation of East Tennessee by General Burnside, as we have seen, Mr. Lincoln had given authority to Mr. Johnson, as Military Governor of Tennessee, "to exercise such powers as may be necessary and proper to enable the loyal people of Tennessee to present such a republican form of Government as will entitle the State to the guarantee of the United States therefor." Under this authority, by the advice and under the direction of Mr. Johnson, Tennessee was reorganized in January, 1865, and July 10, 1866, restored as one of the States of the Union.

When "telegraphic intelligence" of the action of the Tennessee Legislature, ratifying the Fourteenth Amendment, reached the Capitol, without waiting for official information of the fact, a joint resolution was at once introduced in the House, providing for the readmission of the State into the Union, with the right of representation in Congress, the preamble reciting in effect that the State "had in good faith ratified the Fourteenth Amendment." This resolution under the previous question was pushed rapidly through Congress, the House adopting it by a vote of 125 ayes to 12 nays. Six days after the ratification, Tennessee had her senators and representatives seated in Congress. So it is believed that it would have been with the other States if they had not rejected the terms of readmission so generously offered them.

Here was a precedent, almost as strong as law, for the readmission of all the other secession States, on the single condition of the ratification of the Fourteenth Amendment.

It can scarcely be credited that a people so lately overwhelmed in war and encompassed by many and great disasters, could have being guilty of the amazing folly of rejecting such mild terms of restoration to political rights.

At the close of the war, while there were some in the triumphant party, like Johnson, General Butler, Thaddeus Stevens, and Wade, who clamored for blood, the majority of the war party in the North, in the exuberance of joy at a restored Union and the return of peace, was ready to forgive and to spare those lately in hostility. Had Mr. Lincoln lived, his whole life is proof that his magnanimous heart would have been dedicated to the task of reconciliation, and that the last term of his administration would have been given to the work of peace, as the first had been to the work of war. After the death of the martyred President, the generous Grant stood as a wall of protection between the terrible ferocity of Johnson and those lately in arms. When trouble again arose, in 1866, in a letter to General Richard Taylor, the brother-in-law of Jefferson Davis, in the most tender terms Grant advised and appealed to the Southern people to adopt the Fourteenth Amendment, and to accept the situation in good faith on their own account.

Mr. Johnson, by his conversations and speeches "perverted the inclinations and intentions of the South, and by reflex action those of the North." He converted feelings of reconciliation on both sides into hatred and distrust.

It was subsequently clearly proved by telegraphic dispatches brought to light that Johnson used all his influence to prevent the Southern States from ratifying the Fourteenth Amendment.

Governor Parsons of Alabama telegraphed him that the Fourteenth Amendment might be reconsidered by the Legislature, if an enabling Act could be passed by Congress for the admission of the State to representation, to whom he replied: "What possible good can be obtained by reconsidering the Constitutional Amendment? I know of none in the present condition of affairs. * * *"

Drunk with the vast power he exercised, made giddy by the incense of flattery offered him by a mighty crowd of suppliants for favors and pardons, maddened by the terrible rebuke he had received in the election of 1866, and by the opposition of Congress, Johnson went forward in his course of defiance to the expressed will of the people and the policy of Congress. His stubbornness is without a parallel in our political annals. His influence exerted in favor of the Amendment, instead of against it, it is believed, would have secured its adoption in every one of the ten States which rejected it. Their Senators and Representatives would in all probability have been permitted to resume their seats in the national Legislature very soon afterward.

What untold evils Mr. Johnson inflicted on the country, and especially on the unhappy South, need not be, and indeed cannot be, set forth in all their fearful reality.

His conduct is amazing when it is considered that the readmission of insurrectionary States into the Union, even with the adoption of the Fourteenth Amendment, would have been the triumph *of his own* plan of reconstruction, inaugurated by him in July, 1865. Congress might have proclaimed ever so earnestly that the work of reconstructing the seceding States must originate with it, and be conducted under its authority, and yet, if in fact the reconstruction had been accomplished by the authority of the President alone, and not under an Act of Congress, the work would have been that of the President and not that of Congress. This was precisely the condition of the question when the Legislature of the several seceding States were considering the Fourteenth Amendment. These Legislatures owed their existence to and derived their power, primarily alone, from the President, and not from Congress. If the States had at that time, by the ratification of the Amendment, come back into the Union, they would have come through the door opened to them by him.

To comprehend the full force of this position it must be kept in mind that the Congressional measure of reconstruction was not enacted into a law until March 2, 1867, nearly twenty-one months after Mr. Johnson had inaugurated his plan. If the States had been readmitted as contemplated by Mr. Johnson, the Congressional plan would never have had an existence; there would have been no necessity for it.

Mr. Johnson's masterful spirit could brook no opposition. It kindled his uncontrollable ambition, and drove him forward in a course of headlong fury. Naturally he considered his plan of reconstruction the best. He may have thought the Fourteenth Amendment unjust; he overlooked the fact that if that were rejected, greater evils might follow, as they did follow.

Admitting that he was honest in his change of views; that Mr. Seward had converted him; that his heart had undergone a remarkable change—a change from a state of the most virulent hate to one of love and sympathy—why, then, did he, as a practical statesman, as a man of common sense, exasperate and provoke to utter madness the overwhelming majority in Congress and in the North by opposing with a violence inconceivable in one of his exalted position the adoption of the Fourteenth Amendment? Why did he not advise the South, if he was sincerely its friend, as General Grant did, that that measure was the best then attainable, and that if rejected, there was danger that it would be followed by much harder terms. His position demanded, on his part, the utmost calmness and impartiality, the highest justice and equipoise, as a mediator between the two sections. A truly great man, one who rose to the height and breadth of the momentous occasion like the great Washington, would have acted the part of an impartial and a loving father of the people of both sections. In 1860-61, he had been pre-eminent in strengthening the national cause; in 1865-69 he was pre-eminent in perpetuating national discord.

That the Southern people resisted the governments subsequently imposed upon them by military force, was only the impulse of brave freemen. In a brief period they overthrew these governments, and once more regained their independence, but they took this independence not only with the Fourteenth Amendment, but with the Fifteenth Amendment as well. Thus their last state was worse than the first could possibly have been under the Fourteenth Amendment. At the end of many years of desolation the Southern States were, in respect to their independence, only where they would have been at the end of one year under this Amendment. But in other respects what a loser? Who can estimate their losses? The calamities of reconstruction and negro rule, the Fifteenth Amendment and negro suffrage, the Civil Rights Bill and the postponement of the day of reconciliation—these were some of the evils of the rejection of the first term offered the South. What did the South gain—what good did she accomplish—by the rejection? Rather, what multiplied evils did she not suffer as the direct proof of her unwisdom?

And as it was, the magnitude of the misfortune, growing out of the failure on the part of the secession States to return to their true relations with the Union by accepting the Fourteenth Amendment, and the subsequent enforcement of the Congressional plan of reconstruction, by military, negro, and carpet-bag rule, can never be estimated.

None of the parties to the schemes of reconstruction—neither Mr. Johnson, nor the people of the lately seceding States, nor the Republican Congress—saw the calamitous consequences of their equally unwise acts. If they had done so, we must believe their humanity would have shrunk back aghast at the sight. Neither party accomplished, except in a small degree, what it sought. All were in the end deluded, frenzied with bitterness and rage. Mr. Johnson retired from his office a disappointed man, the most unpopular President we ever had, possibly excepting

John Tyler. The Southern people, after years of suffering and disfranchisement, came out of the great tragedy of reconstruction, broken in all things except in spirit. The Republican party, so strong and haughty in 1865-1867, emerged from this contest in 1872-73 with its prestige dimmed, its power threatened, with scarcely courage to defend the reconstruction measures from that day to this. The Government, too, when, in 1876, the Southern people rose up in arms and overthrew the negro and carpet-bag rule, looked on in cold indifference, either impotent to prevent the wreck, or unwilling to risk anything for such governments.

It is hard to conceive the motive of the opposition of Mr. Johnson to the Fourteenth Amendment. Following the precedent set in the case of Tennessee, its ratification by the seceded States would have secured, it is confidently believed, their restoration to the Union, the very consummation he was so loudly and earnestly demanding. Further and more important, as it required two-thirds of each House of Congress to propose Amendments to the Constitution, the Fifteenth Amendment, conferring the ballot on colored men, could not have passed the Senate after the return of Southern Senators without their votes, therefore never would have become a part of our Constitution. Even if it had passed, it could not have received the assent of three-fourths of the States, and thus the evil would have been escaped.

How grandly Mr. Johnson might appear in history to-day: the "Author of Reconstruction; the Restorer of Concord." These might have been his proud titles to glory. If he had thrown the weight of his immense influence in the South, as President, on the side of reconciliation and submission, he might have accomplished this work of restoration without a jar. When he opposed the ratification of the Amendment, and induced in part at least the secession States to reject it, he defeated his own plan of reconstruction, and threw away a chance for fame rarely falling to the lot of men. He missed an opportunity such as does not occur to rulers once in a century. The path of duty and the path of permanent fame ran parallel to each other, but unfortunately he missed them both. Johnson might have had all the glory of this great work, and gone down in history throughout all coming time as a benefactor of his country, worthy to be named with Washington and Lincoln.

CHAPTER VII.

Johnson Defeated for United States Senate by Henry Cooper, 1869—Defeated for Lower House of Congress by James White, 1870—Defeated for Congress from State at Large by Horace Maynard, 1872—January, 1875, elected to United States Senate—Assails President Grant in the Extraordinary Session Convened March 4—Johnson's Views as to Payment of National Bonds—Bonds Issued by Tennessee.

SCARCELY had Mr. Johnson left the Presidency before he began looking for another office. The first one of sufficient dignity for his ambition presented itself in 1869. The term of Hon. Joseph S. Fowler as a United States Senator was soon to expire. He became a candidate for re-election. Notwithstanding Mr. Fowler's vote had saved President Johnson from conviction on the impeachment trial, the latter did not hesitate to become a candidate against him. T. A. R. Nelson was urged to become a candidate, and it was believed that he could have been elected had he yielded to the request of his friends. But he had expressed to Mr. Johnson a wish that he (Johnson) might me elected, and with that high sense of honor which distinguished him, he refused to allow his name to be used. The contest was very exciting and bitter. The Democrats were in the majority in the Legislature, but were divided, while the Republicans held the balance of power. Finally, Henry Cooper, a Democrat, was nominated in a caucus as the straight Democratic candidate. Mr. Cooper was not prominent in his party, but favorable circumstances and negative rather than positive qualities gave him the possibilities of success. His brother, Edmund Cooper, at one time the Private Secretary of Mr. Johnson while he was President, and an intimate friend, was a member of the Legislature. He had been voting for Johnson and was his special champion. On the nomination of his brother, however, he deserted Johnson and voted for the former. The result was Johnson was defeated by four votes. The Senator-elect was an upright man and had a fair reputation for talents, but never became distinguished as a Senator. Johnson was very indignant against Edmund Cooper, and never forgave him. He denounced him in the bitterest words for his desertion.

Mr. Johnson's next effort was to be elected to the Lower House of Congress in 1870, from his old district, but he was defeated in the nominating Convention by James White. Two years later he was a candidate for Congress from the State at large. The ultra wing of the Democratic party nominated General B. F. Cheatham, a brave and gallant Confederate General. The Republicans nominated Hon. Horace Maynard. The three candidates canvassed the entire State together. With a divided Democratic party, the contest resulted in the election of Maynard, and thus Johnson was a third time defeated in his insatiable ambition for power and office.

His next effort was to secure the Senatorship in 1875. In order to succeed he canvassed in advance certain parts of the State. The contest was exciting and extremely acrimonious. Most of the old Bourbon Democratic leaders, whom he had pardoned a few years before, fought him with the most stubborn determination. Ex-Governor John C. Brown and General William B. Bate were both candidates against him. Both of these had been distinguished Generals. Their friends pressed their claims, not because of their superior ability over Johnson, but because of their military services to the Southern Confederacy. They were both men of ability. Prominent men all over the State flocked to Nashville, to take part either for or in opposition to Mr. Johnson. No such excitement in a Senatorial contest ever occurred in the State. It was a desperate effort not only to defeat but to destroy Mr. Johnson. On the other hand, he fought his enemies with all his iron will and marvelous courage. Every influential man in the State who was opposed to him was brought to Nashville to aid in his overthrow. Some of these, after their arrival, he captured by subtle diplomacy, of which he was a master when he chose to condescend from his proud imperiousness to its use. The bitterest opposition came from the Democratic party.

Among others who came to Nashville to work against Johnson was the celebrated General Nathan B. Forrest. Johnson called on him, and referred in pleasant terms to their ante-bellum friendship, and to the warm support he used to receive from Forrest. He then referred to his present contest for Senator, and said in substance: "General John C. Brown and General W. B. Bate are put forward against me on the *pretended* ground that the State owes them honors because they were leaders of their people in war. Now, if there were any sincerity in the reasons assigned, instead of hostility to me, I could respect the motives of my opponents. Our people have always shown their appreciation of distinguished military services. Witness the election of Washington, Jackson, Harrison, Taylor, and thousands of others, to positions of honor. But these politicians who oppose me are not sincere in their professions of gratitude for military service. If they were, they would support you, General Forrest, for Senator, or they would have elected you Governor before this time. You were a General in fact, as well as in name. Your brilliant, daring feats as a soldier have given you a world-wide fame, and are the admiration of even your late enemies. But who are Brown and Bate?" said he (applying a terrible denunciatory epithet), "only one-horse Generals. Never should my enemies speak of gratitude for military service while these little generals are preferred to you."*

The result of this interview was, that Forrest took the next train for his home in Memphis.† He could not work for Johnson, for he was committed the other way, but he would not work against him. Never did the invincible will and wonderful power of Mr. Johnson to control men appear to more conspicuous advantage than during this memorable contest. All

---

*Mr. Johnson did General Bate great injustice by these criticisms. He was, in fact, a brave and splendid officer. I believe General Brown was also. General Bate was one of the purest and noblest men of the age. Later, he was twice elected Governor and three times elected to the Senate, and was distinguished in that body by lofty and honorable deportment.

†General Forrest was one of nature's great soldiers. Without education of any kind, either military or otherwise, he became unquestionably one of the great cavalry leaders of the war. I am far from endorsing some things he did as a general and some things in him as a man. But military genius shone conspicuously in him during all his career. Both Generals Grant and Sherman, and also Lord Wolseley, Commander-in-Chief of the British Army, complimented him. Grant in his Memoirs said, "Forrest was probably the ablest cavalry officer of the South." The Earl of Chatham said in Parliament, after the battle of Plassey, of Robert Clive: "He was a heaven-born general, who, without military education or training, surpassed all the generals of his time." Lord Mahon, in his "History of England," says of General Burgoyne that he was such an elegant scholar and writer that it was a delight to the scholars of England to read his official reports of his *defeats*, but the people greatly preferred the reports of victory by the Duke of Marlborough in bad English. Doubtless Forrest could not write elegant English, but his reports of victories were always eagerly read.

the opposition to him in the State, which had been gathering for forty years, was concentrated in an unrelenting, determined effort to overthrow him. Bold, defiant, and unshaken, he withstood the merciless assaults of his enemies, and finally triumphed. It was the proudest hour of his life. Music, fireworks, and public demonstrations of the most exciting character, turned the night that followed his election into one of exultation. Seldom, if ever, had Johnson seemed greater than at this moment of victory over the strongest and the most malignant opposition.

But I am sorry to record that this splendid victory was marred by a broken pledge on Johnson's part. The small band of Republicans in the Legislature held the balance of power in the joint convention. They for the most part were scattering their votes. They could elect Johnson whenever they chose to do so, but they were afraid that if he were in the Senate, he would revive his personal quarrel with President Grant. Mr. Johnson, learning of this apprehension, had an interview with one of the leading Republicans, and perhaps with others, in which he pledged himself, if elected, not to revive this quarrel, nor to make any personal war on Grant. On this pledge the gentleman referred to, and others also, agreed to support Johnson. The balloting at the next meeting of the joint convention went on as usual. Finally Johnson lacked but one vote of an election. The tally was kept by this man as well as by others. At the critical moment, but before the result of the ballot was announced, in the midst of a breathless silence, this Republican arose and changed his vote from the person for whom he had just voted, to Andrew Johnson. A wild shout instantly arose; Johnson was elected. All knew it. The result was known long before the presiding officer announced it. This was the crowning triumph of Johnson's political career.

This election took place in January, 1875. Ordinarily Johnson would not have taken his seat in the Senate until the following December. But President Grant convened the Senate in extraordinary session on March 4th to act on a treaty which his administration had made with King Kalakaua of the Sandwich Islands. Usually, too, treaties are considered by the Senate in secret session, but in this case that body voted to consider the treaty with open doors. Except for this extra

session Mr. Johnson would have never taken his seat, for he died the following July. It was during this session of the Senate that he violated his pledge given before his election, as above stated. In the course of his speech he assailed the character of President Grant in the most violent manner. Deep indignation was excited throughout the land. But the public did not know of the broken pledge behind this act of bad taste. Terrible indeed must have been his vindictiveness to induce him to violate a promise, without which he never would have been elected to the Senate. Personally, the author knows nothing of this pledge. He only gives the statement of the man to whom it was made, and of others, often and notoriously repeated in this State immediately after and since that Senatorial election.*
He would most gladly believe that there was some misunderstanding, some misconception of what Mr. Johnson said and promised. In another place I have given him credit for truthfulness throughout his life, both as a public man and as a private citizen. And I here repeat that this was his general character.

Johnson presented peculiarities in his mental qualities, sometimes apparent contradictions. He was totally unlike any other public man of his day. He seemed to have many vagaries, but when these are closely examined by those who knew him well, it will be found that they were not such in fact. His mind was clear, strong, and well-balanced. His common sense was remarkable. In all things he was eminently practical. He had no fancy, no imagination. The cause that induced him to utter absurdities was in his moral nature and not in his intellectual.

The measures about which Mr. Johnson was the wildest were in reference to the payment of our National and State debts. The first impression created by these, would be that his ideas on these subjects were the result of a disordered mind. This was far from true. On the contrary, they were in fact a part of his lifelong tactics to obtain and retain popularity and power. His ideas were also somewhat tinged and influenced by those agragrian feelings which lay at the bottom of his heart and in which he always indulged. Throughout his life, he had two principles of action which he constantly followed as a means of attaining political ascendency. These were the flattery of the people; secondly, the inculcation of the idea of a natural

---

*The Hon. Henry R. Gibson, ex-member of Congress.

and irreconcilable antagonism between capital and labor, wealth and poverty. These two ideas seem to have been the basis of his political creed. He never could get away from them, nor above them. They appear more or less distinctly in all his speeches.

Let us first notice his views as to the payment of our national bonds. These bonds were issued at a dark hour during the Civil War, to raise money to equip and pay our armies for fighting for the preservation of the government, and to prevent national bankruptcy. They were taken, at first, by bankers, capitalists, artisans, farmers, and widows—by every class of people in fact—in a burst of patriotic enthusiasm, not knowing whether they would ever get a dollar for them or not. The Union was preserved, the country saved, and the bonds became valuable. Had the Union failed, they would probably have become almost as worthless as our Continental money became after the Revolution. Mr. Johnson in his annual message to Congress, of December, 1868, among other things said:

"A system that produces such results is justly regarded as favoring the few at the expense of the many, and has led to the further inquiry whether our bondholders, in view of the large profits they have enjoyed, would themselves be averse to a settlement of our indebtedness upon a plan which would yield them a fair remuneration, and at the same time be just to the nation. Our national credit should be sacredly observed, but in making provision for our creditors, we should not forget what is due to the masses of the people. It may be assumed that the holders of our securities have already received upon their bonds a larger amount than their original investment, measured by a gold standard. Upon this statement of the facts it would seem but just and equitable that the six per cent. interest now paid by the government should be applied to the reduction of the principal in semi-annual installments, which in sixteen years and eight months would liquidate the entire national debt.

"Six per cent. in gold would at present rates be equal to nine per cent. in currency, and equivalent to the payment of the debt one and a half times in a fraction less than seventeen years. This, in connection with all the other advantages derived from their investment, would afford to the public creditors a fair and liberal compensation for the use of their capital, and with this they should be satisfied. The lessons of the past admonish the lender that it is not well to be over anxious in exacting from the borrower rigid compliance with the letter of the bond."*

In the last sentence of the last paragraph he throws out a vague warning to the bondholders that worse harm may befall them if they declined to accede to his generous plan of repudiation. This was no intellectual vagary. It must be attributed to the causes stated above. It was an attempt to raise a great national issue between bondholders and nonbondholders, and thus to secure for himself the support of the latter class, known to be a majority of the people. As these bonds were nearly all held in the North, it was intended to array still further the Southern people against that section and to ingratiate himself more firmly in their affections.

A singular report was circulated about the time this remarkable message was sent to Congress, which if true, shows the wise forethought of Mr. Johnson as a practical financier. He had in the bank of Jay Cooke & Co. about $69,000 of these detested United States bonds. These he prudently, as he thought, converted into cash; cash did not run out of date. When that great banking house failed this money was on deposit with it. But he subsequently managed to recover it all.

Most of the bonds he proposed to repudiate had changed hands since they were issued, the subsequent holders paying full value for them and generally a heavy premium. Millions of dollars worth of them were held by widows, orphans, guardians, trustees, and by mechanics and farmers. All classes held them, many of them putting their all into them, on the solemn pledge of the Government that they would be paid. And yet here was a deliberate proposition made in a message to Congress to rob the people of their hard-earned savings, and when the bonds had run seventeen years to wipe them out of existence. This proposition exceeds in audacity anything to be found in all our history. Hundreds of millions of bonds were owned by people abroad, who had bought them at a full price on the faith of the Government.

Let it be kept in mind that these were not the wild, incoherent ideas of a visionary man. Johnson was not such. He did not

---

*Cong. Globe, part 3, appendix, 1868-9, pp. 2 and 3.

intellectually belong to the class of men who believe in follies. Why, then, did he utter such startling doctrines? One motive sprang from his undying hatred of the rich, or as he styled them, the aristocracy of the country. The other motive was his insatiable desire for popularity and power.

Let it be remembered that these sentiments did not emanate from an obscure source. They came from a man who had been Governor of his State, both Civil and Military, Senator in Congress, Vice-President of the United States at its greatest epoch, and at that very time was the Chief Executive of the nation. He had seen the outburst of patriotism with which all classes of loyal people had responded to the earnest call of the Government for help, and had poured out their hoarded gold to pay for these bonds, in order to save the Government. He knew, too, that if it had been written on the face of the bonds, as a part of the contract, that sixteen years and eight months' interest was to satisfy and extinguish the principal of the bonds, not a dollar's worth could have been sold. Patriotic men might have given money to the Government lavishly, and thousands would have done so freely, but they would not have invested a dollar in a mockery of a security.

At the time this astounding doctrine was put forth in the message of President Johnson, the country had become so accustomed to surprising things from him, that it excited less indignation than its startling character warranted. Besides this, the country was still in the throes of that angry contest over questions of reconstruction which Mr. Johnson had provoked, and therefore it did not heed a proposition so unlikely to become a serious one in the national councils. Otherwise he would have been buried beneath a tidal wave of indignation.

This proposition was most unjust. It was in effect saying to every woman and child in the land, to every guardian of minors, to every executor and administrator holding bonds for the benefit of women and children, to all charitable and educational institutions, to every farmer, mechanic, and laborer, to all, high or low, rich or poor, who had loaned their earnings to the Government in its hour of need, and had taken its bonds as security: "You must surrender your bonds at the end of sixteen years and eight months, without receiving the principal."

What would Mr. Johnson have thought if he had loaned money to a man, payable at the end of sixteen years and eight months—the interest of which had been regularly paid—if the maker, when he demanded payment, had said: "Sir, your debt is paid. Have I not paid the interest regularly, and does not that equal the debt and discharge it?"*

In reference to the bonds issued by Tennessee, Johnson was the first man in the State to suggest and advocate their repudiation. After his retirement from the Presidency in 1869 he became a candidate, as we have seen, for a seat in the United States Senate. To secure his election he made speeches in several of the largest towns, and among others at Columbia. In his speech at that place, he took ground in favor of repudiating all bonds, State and national, after the interest paid on them equaled the sum received for said bonds, by the State or nation. He said no generation had a moral or legal right to entail a debt on a succeeding generation, and that was what a bonded debt did. This generation had no right to issue bonds to be paid by the next.

Hon. John H. Savage, a former member of Congress, went to Columbia to answer Mr. Johnson, but the latter refused to divide time with him. But Savage spoke by himself, and denounced Johnson as a repudiator, seeking to bring dishonor on Tennessee's fair name.

In a discussion in Lebanon, Tenn., October 9, 1874, between Johnson and the same Savage, Johnson was reported by a correspondent of the Louisville *Courier-Journal* as saying:

"No nation has ever been burdened with a permanent public debt and remained free. Sooner than leave our posterity to become a race of serfs under an immense debt, I would throw off every dollar of it. Our people cannot much longer bear

---

*Mr. Johnson seems to have borrowed this idea from Mr. Jefferson. In a letter to James Madison (Vol. III, p. 27, of Jefferson's writings) he affirmed, as Johnson did in Tennessee, that one generation of men had no right to contract debts which another must pay, and consequently that the validity of an obligation of that sort is to be ascertained by reference to bills (tables) of mortality in order to see if a majority of the contracting generation has died off and the obligation to pay has been extinguished. This period seems to have been fixed at nineteen years. Jefferson also maintained that "every law and even Constitution naturally expires at the end of this term (nineteen years)." Tucker's Life of Jeffeson, Vol. I, p. 291. "Observations on Thomas Jefferson," by Henry Lee, p. 79 and note.

these burdens. They cry for relief, and must have it, and we must get clear of at least a portion of our public debt. If refusing to pay a portion of a debt is repudiation, then the country is full of repudiators."

In a speech at Murfreesboro, Tenn., he said that there was not as much as $500,000 of our State (Tennessee) debt that was constitutional and binding on the people. This declaration was amazing in view of the fact that a considerable part of the bonds, constituting the State debt, were issued during his administration, as Governor, were signed by him, and their issuance approved by him.

In October, 1874, Johnson made a speech in Chattanooga, which was repeated in Nashville a few days later, in which he argued that the people of the State were not bound in morals to pay more than one-half of a State debt. This speech was reported in the Memphis *Avalanche*.

While he was a candidate for Congress he made a speech in Memphis, in 1872, the burden of which was that the war had transferred the value of the slaves of the South to the bondholders of the North. He inveighed bitterly against these "bloated bondholders" who were "sitting behind great stacks of bonds," making their living by "clipping coupons," while the people of the South were slaves for all coming time, being forced to contribute their labor to the payment of the enormous public debt.

Thus Johnson went over the State, in 1869, 1872, and in 1874, sapping and undermining the credit of the State. His utterances were not hasty, but deliberate and well matured. He never delivered an opinion on grave questions of public policy without the most careful consideration. He conned over every sentiment he was to utter in a public speech for weeks beforehand. No man could have weighed the effect that each word and sentence was to have on the public mind more carefully.

At first Johnson had but few followers in his crusade against the public credit of the State. But soon he made converts. The argument was used by many that, as most of our bonds were held by people in the North, and as the North had set our slaves free, it would only be an act of even-handed justice to repudiate these bonds. Men of prominence took this position on the stump. John H. Savage set out by denouncing Johnson, as we have seen, and finally after the death of the latter, became the leader of the repudiationists, advocating the payment of 33 1-3 cents on the dollar, and that "not of right, but of grace." He insisted that the North had taken from the South, in the one item of slaves alone, two thousand millions of dollars, and for that reason, if I catch his meaning in his carefully prepared pamphlet on the State debt, the people of the State were not bound to pay the bonds. The argument is false in logic, as well as in morals. Because I am robbed, does that justify me in robbing the next man I meet? As a matter of fact, eight-tenths perhaps of these bonds were legally issued and honestly applied to the purpose for which they were intended.*

When the question of repudiation first came prominently before the people of Tennessee, Senator Isham G. Harris was an earnest advocate of the State credit. He wrote a long letter, which was published, upholding with his usual ability the honor and good faith of the State. But after a while, observing the trend of Democratic opinion, and that it was impossible to breast the storm of State repudiation Johnson had raised, but now borne onward by Marks, Savage, and Wilson, Harris marched under the banner of his party, and for the first time in his life marched behind and not at the head of the column. These men had taken up the banner which had fallen at the death of Johnson.

Repudiation, or more correctly, the scaling of the public debt in Tennessee, was at last accomplished. And let it be remembered that it was mostly the work of Democracy. A few brave men in that party earnestly strove to avert the stigma, but in vain. Hon. John V. Wright, the regular Democratic candidate for Governor, made a splendid and gallant fight for the honor of the State. At no time since the war have such thrillingly eloquent appeals to the honor and justice of the people been heard as fell from his lips. It was like the old-time oratory of Gentry and Haskell. Ex-Governor James D. Porter, a noble Roman, also stood firm to the end. Ex-Senator James E. Bailey also fought gallantly to save the credit of the State. After the death

---

*Colonel Savage, I am glad to say, still lives (June, 1901) in a vigorous old age, an honest, outspoken man, never concealing any opinion from the world.

of Andrew Johnson, the ablest advocate of repudiation, or scaling the debt in the State was Samuel F. Wilson, the candidate of that wing of the party for Governor, and at present an able and most worthy member of the Chancery Court of Appeals. The State not only scaled the bonds one-half, but it reduced the interest which they bore to three per cent.—double repudiation.

CHAPTER VIII.

My Early Impressions of Andrew Johnson—Compared with Other Public Men of His Time—Some of His Peculiar Traits and Characteristics—Intimate Friends and Their Influence—Mr. Johnson in the Senate, 1860—Personal Character and Habits—Critical Attitude of Contemporaries—Celebrated Speech in Knoxville April, 1861.

To describe Mr. Johnson as he really was about 1832 or 1833, when I first became old enough to know him, is no easy matter, though few men of this day so impressed themselves upon my young mind. From the beginning he was no ordinary man. At his first appearance in public life, his speeches were strong and sensational. His facts were presented in a bold and vigorous manner. There was in them that salt of bitterness, that impressive personality, which characterized him in so marked a degree in after life. Even then he gained victories over every antagonist. His delivery, if not elegant, was at least easy, natural, and pleasing. His flow of language was wonderful considering he was uneducated and inexperienced as a speaker. There was nothing violent or spasmodic in his manner. His voice was good and pleasant. In the course of time it became one of great compass and power.

Mr. Johnson was about 5 feet 10 inches in height, and weighed near 175 pounds. His limbs were strong and muscular, his movements active, indicating superior physical strength. His power of endurance was exceptionally great. His shoulders were large, his head massive, round and broad, his neck short and stout. His forehead was not exceptionally high, but very wide and perpendicular. Above his eyes, at the point where the phrenologists locate the reasoning faculties (causality) were two remarkable bumps or protuberances swelling out from his brow. His complexion was dark, his eyes black and piercing; his countenance, when in repose, gloomy; when lighted up by a smile, it became attractive. In ordinary conversation his voice was low and soft. His action, while not stately, was easy and rather graceful. In appearance he was far from being rustic. On the whole, nature stamped him as a remarkable man.

Johnson seldom came upon the streets of the village. When he did, it was with a quick, elastic step, giving evidence of the energetic and restless spirit within.

While following his trade, he did most of his work himself. He was a fashionable and a good tailor. From my earliest recollection his shop was the same one which is now, or was until recently, shown to strangers. On the signboard there were the words:

A. JOHNSON, TAILOR

While at work Mr. Johnson discussed with those who came in such questions as were agitating his own mind. He delighted in argument and controversy. Naturally he was belligerent and pugnacious. Besides, he was cautious and suspicious. Everything that did not originate with him was viewed with distrust. No man's opinions were adopted by him on faith. Everything was sifted in his own analytical mind. He was more or less envious of those above him. There was a deep-seated, burning hatred of all men who stood in his way. The passion of his life was the desire of power. It was a consuming one. Nothing, not even its highest fulfillment, could satisfy it.

Ordinarily he did not seem excessively vain, and yet he clung with extreme tenacity to his own opinions. For forty years no man in his own party, in Greene County, dared to oppose or question his plans or policy. He was an absolute autocrat in this respect.

When engaged in a canvass, Johnson could be seen frequently on the streets. He generally gathered a little crowd around him and talked as if making a speech. He was always a hero in the estimation of his friends. In his intercourse with the body of the people there was at all times more or less reserve in the expression of opinions. The Democratic masses followed him blindly and enthusiastically, with the homage always paid by inferiors to superior talents.

Andrew Johnson was an extraordinary man. He had no early advantages, nor did the little village in which he settled afford him any. There was not even a literary society from which he could gather or imbibe information. It sheltered no specially eminent men to imitate as models. Yet alone, unaided, he developed in mental power until his fame filled the land. He came on the stage when Tennessee was full of distinguished men, and at every step he had to encounter these. He met envy on one side, political opposition on the other. And yet this man, this poor obscure tailor, was at the age of twenty-nine known throughout the State. At thirty-two he was on the stump as elector for the State at large, meeting in debate the brilliant men of the Whig party. Bravely and ably he performed this task during the stormy days of the canvass of 1840. Never in the history of the country did so much talent appear as at this time. Clay, Webster, Choate, S. S. Prentiss, Corwin, W. C. Preston, Grundy, Crittenden, Tom Marshall, and many other orators, only a little less distinguished, rose above the horizon in splendor. In all the encounters of this canvass, Johnson sustained himself as an adroit debater and skillful speaker. Indeed, it was one of his peculiarities that he was always equal to any demands on his powers. He never made an absolute failure. Put him against an inferior and he would triumph; put him against a superior and he would acquit himself with credit.

Mr. Johnson was not brilliant and sparkling, but he was original and entertaining. His intellect was solid and strong. He was an investigator, a thinker, and the reason for all things must appear. With slow mental processes, he weighed and compared everything, omitting no element of consideration. His mind, too astute to be deceived, when it once rested in its conclusions, could not be shaken. Having no reverence for the prestige of distinguished names, upon all subjects he thought for himself. He was an iconoclast of the most pronounced type, pulling down and breaking to pieces as suited his own haughty will.

Johnson deserves to be ranked high among the intellectual men of the country. Not in the first class with Hamilton, Webster, Clay, Calhoun, and Lincoln; but not greatly below, if below at all, the first men in the second class of his day, such as Conkling, Douglas, Fessenden, Bell, Blaine, Seward, Chase, and Henry Winter Davis.

Suppose Mr. Johnson had passed through college, had had access all his life to libraries, magazines, and newspapers, with ample leisure to read, with no compulsion for grinding, everyday toil, is it not probable he would have become, with his studious habits and unconquerable ambition, a very different man, possibly a far greater one? A bright young fellow passing through such a training would know more books—more facts of history at twenty-seven, the age at which Johnson entered upon his public career, than he had acquired after a life of wonderful activity. Johnson's first twenty-seven years were spent in unremitting manual labor and were largely lost. He acquired no reserve equipment of learning for the future. Let us suppose the brightest of the prominent men I have named, in the second class, had been in his situation at the age of twenty-seven, would that one have produced on his country a more lasting impression than Johnson did? Johnson's natural ability—his capacity to think, to investigate, to originate—was of a high order. Few men have had so much native intellect. Besides, he had industrious habits and was thirsting for knowledge.

The marked deficiencies of Mr. Johnson were language and information—elegant language, exact and precise, in which to present his ideas, and wide range of knowledge for argument and reflection, for adornment and illustration. He was sadly lacking in discipline of mind—the ability to discriminate, to compare, to analyze,—which early and continuous education give. He was without the graceful expression, nice taste, acquired by association from infancy with scholarly people. He had ideas, but no vehicle for making them effective. No one, however superior his natural mechanical talents, could construct a delicate watch without the necessary training and tools. Give him these, and how easy the task and how perfect the accomplishment! In an unusual degree Mr. Johnson was without the discipline, the material necesssary for high intellectual achievement. That he accomplished what he did, that he was able to rise to such eminence, under such unfavorable conditions, among competitors of such conspicuous talents, is indeed cause of profound amazement. He was far above Charles Sumner, and could never have resembled him.

It is a fact—but by no means a remarkable one—that few uneducated men rise to greatness. It should rather excite surprise that any at all do. General Jackson and Mr. Lincoln are the most notable examples in our history of greatness achieved with deficient early education. They were, however, exceptional in natural ability, as they were in all respects. They were the favored sons of Heaven. But they were not entirely without education. Jackson early had the advantages of association with able lawyers, and of refined society, while Lincoln was from boyhood a diligent student, educating himself. Both were admitted when young to the bar—the best school for mental discipline furnished by the age, outside of the university.

Nothing quickens the mind like close conflict with an astute lawyer, in the discussion of profound legal questions. The highest faculties of the intellect are called forth and sharpened by opposition, as steel sharpens steel. No fancy, no declamation, no loose use of words avails, but exactness, concentration, and logic are demanded. Johnson missed the advantage of these intellectual encounters and the daily association with members of the bar. Instead he had the drudgery of earning a living in a calling giving no leisure. He was not only the sole President, but the only great man in our country who never attended school a day in his life.

Mr. Johnson has never received the credit for ability he deserves. There are several obvious reasons why he has always been underrated.

He would have ranked higher had it not been for his habit of pandering to the passions of the people. This lowered him in the opinion of all the better educated classes of all parties. Grant that he was the friend of the masses; that did not make it necessary for him to foster hatred between the poor and the rich. That was no reason for arraying one class against another. Mr. Lincoln always proved himself, by his acts, very much more than by his professions, a friend of the people. In this respect, however, Mr. Johnson only did what many prominent politicians of both the leading parties are doing to day.*

Johnson lost much by lack of the amenities of life. He was sadly wanting in sympathy and in kindliness of manner. The refined and cultivated he apparently disliked. These reminded him of his own deficiencies, and in the depths of his heart he detested them. In fact, he hated everything superior to himself. He was conscious of the gulf which separated him from the more refined class of society. On all occasions his speeches tended to divide society, to array the poor and ignorant against the wealthy and intelligent. He was a natural leveler. All his theories and appeals were based on the supposed gullibility of the masses. He never appealed to the broad, enlightened in-

---

*He seems to have been the pioneer "insurgent."

telligence of the world. Any public man who excites the contempt or the derision of his fellowmen is sure to be undervalued.

That Mr. Johnson was naturally cynical and morose was only too evident from his gloomy countenance. This feeling, no doubt, was increased by his poverty. He plainly saw the advantage that wealth and culture gave. That thought filled his ambitious soul with rage. He disliked the possessor of these things. This natural tendency was increased by a difficulty with one of his rich neighbors, which probably gave more or less coloring to Johnson's feeling throughout his whole life.

After Mr. Johnson became President, he improved in outward manner, and became much more agreeable. When he chose he could be delightful, but it was hard to undo the habits of forty years. It was impossible to change his own disposition. There was little that was gentle about him. Towards his enemies he was implacable and unforgiving. He had few intimates.

In the solitariness of his own thoughts he seemed to revel, his mind was active, and forever revolving something new. For society or idle pleasures he had no taste, and in the common everyday affairs he took no interest. One absorbing passion consumed his life. His caution was excessive. When a new political question arose, or one of grave expediency, he would deliberate long and anxiously over it. The difficulty would not be, as to its justice, but as to its party effect, or perhaps, as to its effect upon his own personal fortunes. He would discuss the question with friends, would state hypothetical cases, and argue them; he would invite criticism and then he would answer it. He would thus call out all the arguments for or against a measure.

He was in a high degree unsociable, preferring solitude. Occasionally he wanted, indeed seemed to require, a friend, a solitary person. But it was a hearer he needed; someone to listen while he discanted on some new idea. It was not personal, but mental sociability he desired; food for the mind, not for the heart.

There were two apparent exceptions to the statement that he had no intimate friends. He did have two. These were Samuel Milligan and John Jones, both of his county. The former was a lawyer of Greeneville, and became, in 1865, one of the Supreme Judges of Tennessee, and afterward a member of the Court of Claims at Washington.

Judge Milligan was a college graduate. In his mental operations he was slow, cautious, and logical. Give him time and he was sure to reach a correct conclusion. He was remarkably free from prejudice and passion, and honest above all men I ever knew. At an early day Johnson took him into his confidence, and no safer, truer, or more worthy confidant could have been found.

John Jones was also college-bred, and had studied law, but never followed it as a profession. In dress, habits, and appearance he was the most rural of men. He was almost an anchorite. While he was a farmer, he cared little about farming, or anything else except reading and thinking. His mind was clear, penetrating, and original—indeed, intellectually he was remarkable. Withal he was perfectly honest and candid. This was the man Johnson needed, and he early made him his friend and adviser. When any new question arose, demanding thought and thorough investigation, he would send to the country for Jones, and take him to his house, where the latter would stay for days in consultation with Johnson. Hence Johnson was enabled to appear on the stump, in all his canvasses, thoroughly prepared at every point both for attack and defense.

The world will never know, can never know, how much the political fortunes of Mr. Johnson were helped and shaped by the advice of these two men. Hardly anything shows his sound judgment more clearly than the fact that he kept near him two such strong, honest advisers. The three had served in the Legislature together in 1841 and became friends for life. Jones was not a social companion of Mr. Johnson; he was a helper and counselor. Milligan was more than this; he was an intimate friend.

Mr. Johnson was always true to his trusted friends. He held fast to those once admitted to his confidence. His devotion to Judge Milligan and the honors he bestowed on him prove the truth of this. Other examples might be given to the same effect. Indeed, individually he was not false in dealing with men. The virtue of candor he possessed in a much higher degree than most public men. There was no deceit in him. It was always well known what he thought of those around him. If he was an enemy, he was too independent and too bitter to conceal the fact. I am not aware of a single instance in which he promised a favor, which he failed to bestow. True, whenever it would promote his personal ambition, he did not hesitate to set aside a debt of gratitude or to bury the deepest hatreds, and become reconciled to his worst enemy. Still he was not, as a rule, either a false, a deceitful, or an untruthful man. Excepting the case of the unfortunate question of veracity between him and General Grant, and the instance already referred to in another chapter, I have no recollection of his veracity ever being seriously called in question.

Johnson was not a great, nor a polished orator, yet he was effective and powerful on the stump, and an able and adroit debater. In a long series of debates I am not sure that he ever met his match. Certainly Gustavus A. Henry was not his equal, and, on the whole, he had the advantage over Mr. Gentry.

There was in some respects a striking similarity between Johnson and Stephen A. Douglas. Both were strong on the stump, both were bold and aggressive, both were more or less unscrupulous about the means used to accomplish their ends, and both pandered to the prejudices of the people. Johnson's strength was on the stump, and not in the Senate. He was always interesting on this stage. Men listened to him because he talked about himself and talked about others. This might not please some, but it did please the majority. He made himself felt by his boldness and sometimes by his offensiveness. He had the faculty of impressing his facts on the minds of his hearers as few could do. This arose in part from the earnestness of his manner, the novelty of his matter, and the pungency of his words. Take Gustavus Henry for a comparison. After his discussion with Johnson, men went away remembering him as a handsome, graceful orator, and but little else. As to Johnson, they recalled and could repeat his facts, his arguments, his striking points, and his terrible denunciations. No public speaker in the State has ever left his ideas so deeply impressed on the public mind. Whether men approved or condemned his views, they were certain to remember them.

Johnson had great faith in the efficacy of popular speaking. Indeed, in his earlier days, this was the only direct mode of reaching a rural population, newspapers, which nowadays go everywhere, not circulating much among them. Johnson had accomplished everything by speaking. He could not write. No one cared to read his speeches. But people would listen to the delivery of his bitter harangues. These were plentifully seasoned with salt, vinegar, and red pepper, and served steaming hot. They had a decidedly pungent taste that most men liked.

In his younger days, when Johnson wished to impress a new idea on the people, on an appointed day, he would call the people together, and would deliver to them one of his long harangues. When Military Governor of Tennessee, and afterward when he became Vice-President he wished to deliver a pronunciamento against his fellow citizens in arms against the government, he would be opportunely serenaded (of course he did not himself arrange it beforehand) and would then give relief to his burdened mind. When he wished to arouse the people to the dangerous designs of Congress, he chartered a train and traveled over the country making speeches at every station from New York to St. Louis, and as Petroleum V. Nasby said, "distributing to the people copies of the Constitution."* He

---

*Nasby says that this journey was undertaken by Mr. Johnson "to arouse the people to the sense of danger of concentrating power in the hands of Congress, instead of diffusing it throughout the hands of one man." Nasby's book, entitled "Swinging Around the Circle," giving an account of this journey, is the most humorous book of that day. I copy from the Chicago *Inter-Ocean* an account of the incidents connected with one of the receptions, probably that at Cleveland, Ohio, during this celebrated trip:

"There is nothing in history that corresponds to that wonderful swing of President Johnson from Washington to Chicago by way of Robin Hood's barn. Mr. Johnson planned the trip with infinite cunning. He prided himself on being a commoner, and he believed that he understood the people, and that if he could meet them face to face he would convince them that the President was right and Congress was wrong. To get the love of the people he carried with him General Grant, Admiral Farragut, Secretaries Seward, Welles, and Randall, General Custer, and other men well known to the people. He reasoned that, accompanied by the popular idols of the day, he would be sure of enthusiastic reception everywhere. That was all he asked. Give him a big crowd and he was confident that he could win them over.

"The President started from Washington with a chip on his shoulder. The very first crowd he met knocked it off without ceremony. It soon became clear that the people were in a resentful mood, and after two or three clashes some of Mr. Johnson's best friends recommended a change of programme. Many believed that the President, seeing the mood of the people, would yield, but they didn't know the man. I had seen him face all sorts of crowds while he was Military Governor of Tennessee; I had heard him scold the leading citizens of Nashville as he would a lot of school children; had seen him, when a mob threatened his life, stride out into the street and march the full length of the city at the head of a procession carrying the Stars and Stripes, and I knew he would relish keenly a scrap with those who defied him.

"At one point a crowd of fifty thousand people had gathered, mainly

preached a crusade against Congress, as Peter the Hermit, many centuries before, preached a crusade against the Mohammedans of the Holy Land; with this difference, however: Peter set all Christendom ablaze with martial ardor; Johnson set all this country aroar with laughter.

In the Senate Johnson was far from being great. His speeches were not remarkable for logic, statesmanship, or learning. They often abounded in personalities and in unworthy appeals to prejudice. There were no splendid passages that will live in political history, to be quoted by coming generations. Indeed, narrowness and partisanship completely obscured all breadth and elevation of view. The only possible exception to this statement was his speeches in East Tennessee, in the spring of 1861, when the dangers which confronted the country seemed to give him a dignity, a fervor of eloquence, an intensity of patriotism unknown in him previously.

---

to see Grant, Farragut, and Seward. There was tremendous enthusiasm over the party, and the President was elated. But when he rose to speak the crowd hooted and hissed and set up a great shout for Grant. The people had seen through the President's scheme and were turning the tables on him by using Grant and Farragut to humiliate and punish him. The President saw the strategy of the move and he was as furious as he was helpless. In every interval of quiet he would attempt to speak, but every word he uttered would be lost in the thunder of the shouts for Grant. It was a painful spectacle and everybody was embarrassed. The crowd would not listen to the chairman or any other local celebrity.

"General Custer, then at the height of his popularity, stepped forward, in his dramatic, imperious way, believing that he could quiet the tumult. The crowd was friendly, but it howled him down, and the dashing cavalryman took his seat, with the remark that he would like to clear the grounds with a brigade of calvary. Johnson, looking down on the tumult, saw smiling, contemptuous faces, but no hatred. He turned to Grant, who had retired to the rear of the platform, and said petulantly: 'General, you will have to speak to them.' General Grant said decisively: 'I will not.' Then the President said more graciously: 'Won't you show yourself, General?' Grant stepped forward, and after a round of cheers the people were as quiet as a church in prayer time. Waiting an instant, Grant raised his hand, made a gesture toward Johnson, and said clearly: 'The President of the United States.'

"The incident was a simple one, but it spoke volumes. Grant's face was full of indignation and reproach, and the crowd, accepting his rebuke, listened to the President for an hour. And the President did not spare the people. He scolded them to his heart's content, replied to all their taunts, talked back to every man that opened his mouth, and seemed to enjoy the performance as a warhorse would a battle. The people took the scolding in good part and realized that they had come in contact with a new sort of President. They heard him in respectful silence, but they disapproved of him, as the President knew when the votes were counted at the election that fall."

It is true that his 18th and 19th of December speech, in the Senate of 1860, produced perhaps the most profound impression of any speech ever made in the country, but that was not because of its eloquence but because of its startling unexpectedness, its daring positions, its noble patriotism, and the breathless anxiety with which the North was listening—waiting, indeed —for a word of hope from the South. It was the spirit of the speech, the golden opportunity seized and well used, and not the words, that gave permanence to that effort. It inspired the bewildered, despairing North with new hope. It was a vivid light suddenly flashed upon the profoundest darkness.

In canvassing with competitors, Johnson went just as far in personal remarks as it was safe to go. He studied the dispositon of his adversary, and ascertained how much personal indignity he would endure. In his debate there was seldom any exhibition of manly courtesy. A kind act or word on his part toward an opposing party was almost unknown. He seemed to be too bitter ever to feel the elevation that inspires noble sentiments.* Another peculiarity of his was that in any given case no man could count on what he would do, except that he was sure to do something unexpected, and very likely something disagreeable.

Johnson never went into society in his own town. Before he became President he lived in his own home in almost exclusive retirement, never attending social gatherings. He had one somewhat remarkable habit, considering his desire for popularity, his constant custom of pandering to the prejudices of the people, and that was he always dressed well. He wore the finest material, and when he appeared was always faultlessly neat. I never saw him shabbily attired. He thought correctly, that to secure the respect of the people and have them look up to him as superior to themselves, he must make the most of his personal appearance. There is very much more in this than demagogues often think. People are never flattered by having a favorite appear before them in mean garb.

---

*The following incident will illustrate what I have been saying: When he and Gustavus A. Henry, who was the very soul of courtesy, were canvassing for Governor in 1853, soon after the canvass opened Johnson asked a friend if Henry would fight. The reply was that Mr. Henry was very amiable and peaceable, and would avoid a personal difficulty unless the insults were very gross and offensive. "Then," said Johnson, "I will give him hell to-day."

It does not lie within the scope of this sketch to speak of Mr. Johnson's family. I venture, however, to go out of the way to pay my profound respects to the worth of his daughter, the late Mrs. Patterson. The people of this land, long since, with one voice, pronounced their verdict in favor of her modest but conspicuous merit and womanly virtues.

Johnson left at his death a fair estate. It may be safely affirmed that it was honestly acquired. Although he filled many public trusts, and had many opportunities to make money, the suspicion of dishonesty in reference to public funds never attached to his name. While he was the Civil Governor of the State, every department of the public service was carefully watched and guarded. There was no speculation, no dishonesty, no public scandals during his administration. While he was Military Governor of Tennessee he had a large amount of public money in his hands, but all was honestly accounted for, so far as is known. Indeed, in the use of public money, as well as in the use of his own he was careful and economical. He had the reputation of being close and parsimonious. He cannot be blamed for this. He started out very poor. All he made was earned slowly and by incessant toil. In order to become comfortable, he had to deny himself many things. He daily felt the hardships of poverty. Within him was the consciousness of strength and power. Around him he saw men far his inferiors, surrounded with the luxuries of life, while he was compelled to toil in poverty. Under circumstances like these, he strove to rise by the most rigid economy. He was right. In after years, when he had become independent in money matters, whether he too closely adhered to his early habits, it is not for me to say. These are matters upon which, within certain reasonable limitations, each person must judge for himself, and from such judgment there is no appeal.

The estate left by Johnson, of from one hundred to one hundred and fifty thousand dollars, was a very pretty sum in a little interior village. Had he been a corrupt man, his estate might have been easily swollen to a million. The self-denial and privations of early life certainly justly entitled him to comfort and independence in old age. I know to some extent with what extreme carefulness and self-denial his fortune was built up to moderate proportions.

Of the personal character and habits of Andrew Johnson,

already much has been given, but something yet remains to be said. I doubt if his true character will ever be known by the public as it was by those immediately around him. He was so extreme in his views and utterances, and so angular in outline, that it is difficult to describe him as he was. It is hard for those who knew his fierce nature and indomitable will to treat of his virtues and failings with the calm judgment necessary for a just and clear appreciation of the man. By his wonderful personality he stamped himself indelibly on the public mind, and became a part of the history as well as the rightful property of the country. His character, therefore, is open to public criticism. It will be observed that I have in this sketch carefully avoided the sanctity of the domestic circle, and dealing with facts too sacred for the public eye; these do not concern my narrative.

While in many respects Mr. Johnson can be held up as a model for the young men of the country, in others, he cannot be. All men must pay homage to the indomitable will, energy, and courage which enabled him to overcome the most adverse conditions in life, and to rise by his own strength to the most exalted positions of honor. I bow with profound admiration to the statesman or the soldier who successfully cuts his way through obstacles that appall ordinary men, and firmly plants his feet on the highest round of power. Such was the career of Mr. Johnson. While he thus rose and conquered all opposition and filled the land with his name and fame, he was at all times for himself. Personal ambition controlled his life. In the earlier part of his career, if not in the latter part, he strove to rise by working on the baser passions of men, sowing broadcast the seeds of hate and bitterness between classes. An appeal to prejudice was his most effective argument. While able, he was narrow and harsh. In his life as a private citizen he manifested much of that same supreme regard for self only that he did as a public man. If he ever took any active interest in the welfare of the community in which he lived, and which honored him for forty years; if he ever proposed, advocated, or helped any measures tending toward the amelioration of society or the public around him—anything for the promotion of education, art, science, temperance, morality, manufactures, or general progress—anything for the benefit of the toiling masses, for the unfortunate and the helpless, tending to lift them up and make them better and happier, I have never heard of it.

What constitutes a good citizen? It certainly is not one whose life is entirely selfish. A man may be moral in conduct, and honest in his dealings, and yet live so entirely for himself, and so little for others, that he may be no blessing, but the contrary, to the community. Rather is he a good citizen whose life and example are such that they do something, however humble his sphere, toward increasing the happiness of mankind, and in promoting the welfare of his fellow citizens. He whose acts are just, whose conduct is kind and helpful, who is an inspiration to others to do better, that man is a good citizen. These are not the criteria by which men are usually judged, but they ought to be the test of good citizenship.

Consider, for a moment, the contrast between Jefferson and Johnson. Jefferson, for twenty years after his retirement, spent his leisure in trying to ameliorate the condition of the people of his State. He gave his profound intellect to the task of general education, as well as to that of building up the great University of Virginia,—an imperishable monument of his far-seeing vision. He did all he could to improve the condition of the farming classes. Like Mr. Webster, at a later day, he thought it not beneath his greatness to work on the problem of improving farm implements. Each of these distinguished men invented a new turning plow.*

Johnson, on the contrary, spent his last years hunting office, quarreling with his enemies, and trying to punish them for some long-gone-by wrong. The evening of his life was, as its morning and its noon had been, stormy and tempestuous. There was no mellow sunset gilding the horizon with its soft light.

As said once before, Johnson had few of the gentle amenities of life. It was possibly unfortunate that he had no love for society. Until he became President he avoided its attractions

---

*One of the attractive curiosities of the late World's Fair at Chicago was the turning plow invented by Mr. Webster. It was an immense concern of great length and size, and looked as if it must have required at least four oxen to use it. The moldboard was made of beaten iron in several pieces, put together with rivets and held by strong iron bars. It was at best an awkward, clumsy concern in comparison with the light steel plows introduced within the last fifteen years. Still, it was an improvement on the old wooden moldboard which I can recollect and which was in use when I was a boy. Mr. Jefferson's plow I did not see.

entirely. In outward conduct he was apparently cold and disdainful. He denounced aristocrats, yet imitated them, and if not one at heart himself, he had all their worst ways. His life was exclusive. He stirred up the bad passions of the lower classes. Men who had large property, though earned by honest toil, if they belonged to the opposite party, were denounced as the enemies of the people. He flattered the people—many of them ignorant and degraded—with the most fulsome words.

More bitter, and perhaps mean, things were said about Johnson in his day than about any other public man in the United States. I give a few of these. Thus:

Senator Thomas L. Clingham of North Carolina, who served in the Senate with Johnson, says in his "Recollections," "The driving force of his mind was selfishness, envy, and malice."

The distinguished Democratic orator, Landon C. Haynes, in 1851, the competitor of Johnson for Congress, on his return from Nashville while the latter was Governor was asked how he (the Governor) was getting along. "Oh, finely," was the reply; "he is boarding with a butcher and skinning (cattle) for his board."

In 1855, soon after the defeat of Meredith P. Gentry by Johnson for Governor, the former, with some friends, among them W. G. Brownlow, was in a private room in the City Hotel of Nashville. Gentry was under the influence of liquor, and was criticising Johnson as only he could do. Brownlow checked him and said that instead of cursing Johnson, he was commanded to pray for his salvation. Gentry replied to this in an impassioned burst of scorn: "What! pray for the salvation of Andrew Johnson! Why! to save him would exhaust the plan of Salvation, and where would the rest of us be!"

Johnson's life was full of stormy passions. It had no rest, and but little sunshine in it. He was strong and self-willed; had excessive confidence in his own power, was obstinate and dogmatic, and had little respect for the opinion of others.

Mr. Seward may have flattered himself, while in his cabinet, that he was influencing him, and shaping his (Johnson's) policy. Never was there a greater mistake. That strong man was master. He was doubtless deferential toward Mr. Seward, but it was in order to use him. Seward with all his ability was in Johnson's hands only as clay in the hands of the potter. And yet with all his imperiousness Johnson, when he desired, could be gracious and winning.

It should have been a foregone conclusion, on the death of Mr. Lincoln, that Johnson and such men as Wade, Fessenden, Chandler, Morton, Stevens, Henry Winter Davis, Conkling, and the other Republican leaders would quarrel. It ought to have been known also that unless he should be allowed his own way, absolutely and entirely, in the reconstruction of the secession States, he would defy Congress. But somehow these things were not realized. Standing out as the only Senator from the seceding States who remained true to the old flag,

"Among the faithless, faithful only he,"

he had made himself so singularly conspicuous that it threw almost a luminous circle around him. His courage, too, had been heroic. He had been an exile from his family and from his home town. His speeches exceeded in patriotic fervor and in bitter denunciation of secession those of any other public man. From these causes his name was gilded with a dazzling luster.

When, therefore, in the spring of 1864, the national Convention came to select an associate for Lincoln on the presidential ticket, and when it was known by that body, as it was, that Lincoln desired Johnson selected for that place, it is not surprising that he should have been nominated.*

Mr. Johnson's life was one intense, unceasing, desperate, upward struggle. Never was a human breast fired by a more restless, inextinguishable love of power. His ambition was boundless. To it he sacrificed everything—society, pleasure, and ease. None of these had allurements sufficient to draw him from his purpose. The hope of power was the all-controlling object of life. In all the wide universe he worshiped no deity but that of ambition—the ambition to rise, to become great, to have his name sounded abroad, and to bestride the world.

Johnson was a man of the coolest and most unquestioned

---

*Messrs. Nicolay and Hay deny in their "Life of Lincoln" that the latter wished Johnson nominated or used any influence to that end. But the weight of the testimony which had been brought to light since this book appeared tends to the conclusion that he did use his influence in favor of the nomination of Johnson. Mr. Lincoln desired him on the ticket as a representative of the War Democrats.

courage. When he was assailed on account of his loyalty by a mob of ruffians, in Lynchburg, Va., on his way home from Washington, in the spring of 1861, and one of them attempted to pull his nose, he drew his revolver, and kept the whole pack at bay.

When he made his great speech in Knoxville, in April, 1861, I had been in the habit of hearing him speak for well-nigh thirty years.* I had never seen him so cool, so determined, so eloquent and so impressive in bearing, as on that day. For once, at least, he seemed to have the full stature and the lofty thoughts of a statesman. Whatever his motive may have been, in espousing the cause of the Union, there was certainly that day the appearance on his part of absolute sincerity. As he appeared before that large assemblage of earnest, expectant listeners, and appealed with burning words for the preservation of the Union, my heart—all hearts—turned toward him as never before. It seemed as if his lips had been touched by a live coal off the very altar of patriotism. But one such opportunity occurs to a public man in a lifetime. Deeply conscious of the awfulness of the crisis, with thick clouds around him, he arose to the full height of the great occasion. A disinterested love of country seemed to glow in his heart, flame out in his countenance, and burn on his tongue. As with outstretched arms and melting voice he stood that day pleading so persuasively, so kindly, so powerfully for his distracted country, he rose to the very heights of splendid eloquence, and called to mind the fiery spirit and noble thoughts of Demosthenes before the Athenian people.

---

*Johnson's last canvass for legislature occurred in 1835.

www.ingramcontent.com/pod-product-compliance
Lightning Source LLC
Chambersburg PA
CBHW072128220426
43664CB00013B/2176